The British, The Bandits and The Bordermen

The British, The Bandits and The Bordermen

From the Diaries and Articles of

K.F. Rustamji

Edited by

P.V. Rajgopal

First published 2009, reprinted in December, 2009

ISBN 978-81-8328-135-5

Published by
Wisdom Tree,
4779/23, Ansari Road,
Darya Ganj, New Delhi-2
Ph.: 23247966/67/68
wisdomtreebooks@gmail.com

Printed in India at Print Perfect

To
The men and officers of
Madhya Pradesh Police and
Border Security Force
under my command,
who laid down their lives
in the discharge of their duties.

Absurd may be the tale I tell
Ill-suited to the marching times,
I loved the lips from which it fell
So let it stand among my rhymes.

Toru Dutt
(1856 – 1877)

The first two lines of the above poem were found scribbled at several places in Rustamji's diaries and notes.

Contents

Acknowledgements *ix*
Introduction *xiii*
My Diaries *xxi*

PART I 1916 – 1938

Chapter 1 My Family 3
Chapter 2 School and College 11

PART II 1938 – 1947

Chapter 3 Training Period 23
Chapter 4 Pakistan Takes Shape 47
Chapter 5 Quit India Disturbances 61
Chapter 6 Effects of War and Famine 75
Chapter 7 Independence and Partition 91
Chapter 8 Analysis of British Rule in India 101

PART III 1947 – 1958

Chapter 9 Integration of Princely States 115
Chapter 10 Hyderabad Police Action 123
Chapter 11 Six Years with Nehru 143

PART IV 1958 – 1965

Chapter 12 The Bandits 157
Chapter 13 Vinoba Bhave's Mission 195
Chapter 14 Communal Riots 207
Chapter 15 Chinese Aggression 219
Chapter 16 Nehru's Death 229

PART V 1965 – 1976

Chapter 17 Start of the BSF 243
Chapter 18 Indo-Pak War 257
Chapter 19 Internal Security Duties 273
Chapter 20 Attempt to Hijack Rajiv Gandhi's Plane 287
Chapter 21 Liberation of Bangladesh 291
Chapter 22 War on the Western Front 331

PART VI 1976 – 2003

Chapter 23 National Police Commission 341
Chapter 24 I Started the PIL 347
Chapter 25 Honours and Old Age 353
Chapter 26 The Imperishable Me 359
Epilogue *369*
Appendix I 373
Appendix II 375
Index 376

Acknowledgements

When I took up the editing of more than 10,000 pages of the writings of K.F. Rustamji to bring out this book, I had retired from service. That is a stage in a civil servant's life when he has to be on his own. To the few who have helped me, I would like to acknowledge my deep debt of gratitude. I would like to particularly thank:

- The officers and staff of the Nehru Memorial Museum and Library, more particularly the staff of the Manuscript Section who have been exceptionally helpful to me.
- Cyrus K. Rustamji, without whose help and encouragement at every ste p, I would not have been able to bring out this book, and Kerman Rustamji for writing the Epilogue.
- Dr A.K. Saxena, professor of management at the National Police Academy, Hyderabad, who has been helping me in this project since 1999, when I was Director of that Academy.
- Ashwini Kumar, former DG BSF, who went out of his way to help me in writing some chapters on the BSF.
- Golok Majumdar, retired DGP of West Bengal and former IG BSF whom I interviewed four times — each interview lasting several hours. If it were not for these interviews, the Bangladesh story would have remained unknown to non-Bengalis and the role of the BSF would not have been highlighted.
- Late Swami Sadasivananda, (known by the name of Brig B.C. Pande in the BSF) who helped me with some portions on the

liberation war of Bangladesh and his family members for giving me some of his personal papers after his death in May 2007.

- T.A. Chari, R.S. Mooshahary and A.K. Mitra, former chiefs of the BSF, for their cooperation at various stages.
- Dr Bhashyam Kasturi, for all the help he rendered, including going through the manuscript in the initial stages.
- R.P. Modi, former IGP of Madhya Pradesh who gave me vivid pictures of the encounters he had with the dacoit gangs led by Gabbar Singh, Lakhan Singh and Putli Bai.
- Vijai Shukul, retired Additional DGP Madhya Pradesh, for clarifying some facts about the history of Madhya Pradesh Police and giving me photographs from his collection.
- S. Ramakrishnan and R.K. Johri, Additonal DGs of police of West Bengal, who readily helped me whenever I approached them.
- Narayan B. Menon, formerly of KPMG, and son of M. Balakrishna Menon, an IP officer of 1938 batch, for going through the manuscript from cover to cover and giving me very valuable suggestions.
- P.V. Narasiah, my brother who went through the manuscript and P.V. Balakrishna, my advocate nephew, who helped me with some points pertaining to legal matters.
- P. Rammanohar who helped me with the chapter on Hyderabad Police Action.
- Rajiv, my son, a constant source of help at every step, who kept encouraging me throughout the three years I was involved with the project.
- Monali, my daughter-in-law, a voracious reader herself, who went through the manuscript with a fine comb and gave me excellent suggestions to make it more readable.
- Aditya Manas and Sunny Kalaga, who helped me with the typing of the manuscript and Farid Bazmi, librarian, Police Headquarters, Bhopal for giving me Rustamji's articles published in Madhya Pradesh Police journals.
- The publisher, Wisdom Tree and to some others who did not want to be named.

I often pride myself on one thing, and that is that whatever events occurs in India, somehow or other get me involved in it.

"I often pride myself on one thing and that is that whatever event occurs in India, somehow or (the) other gets me involved in it."

(Entry in Rustamji's diary on 8 April 1958). When Rustamji was a Deputy Director in the Intelligence Bureau (IB), he was asked to enquire into the scam relating to the nationalisation (in 1956) of 243 insurance companies to form the Life Insurance Corporation of India (LIC). On the basis of his report, 172 cases were registered. The Central Bureau of Investigation (CBI) had not come into existence till then. The IB was looking into such matters.

Introduction

Khusro Faramurz Rustamji is accepted as a colossus in the police fraternity. He is the only police officer, so far, to have been awarded the Padma Vibhushan, India's second highest civilian honour. During his long and illustrious career, he was witness to many historical developments in pre and post-Independent India. This book, which is based on his diaries and articles, presents a first person account, not so much about this police icon himself, as about some of those tumultuous developments of our history as seen and experienced and recorded by him.

Rather than presenting a ringside view of history, the book is more in the nature of an account of a man who was inside the ring itself, as it were, and wrote about the 'bout' immediately thereafter. Several decades later, Rustamji analysed the events he witnessed, in great detail in his numerous articles. I have harmoniously coalesced both the accounts to present an eyewitness narration of the factual details and an assessment of their historical significance made by him from the safe distance of time and experience, supplemented by extensive reading.

This book is based on more than 3,500 pages of his diaries, written on a regular basis from November 1938 to December 1970, on foolscap size paper, as well as his notes and articles, which run into about 7,000 pages of printed and typed material. I depended more on the diaries as they were recorded a day or two after the event, and reflect more accurately the factual content as well the mood of the times.

The various posts occupied by Rustamji helped in his involvement with several epoch making events. During the British days, there were some administrative services known as the Secretary of State services. The Indian Civil Service (ICS) and the Indian Police (IP) were two key services among them. Rustamji joined the IP in 1938, and served under the British during the twilight of the Raj for nine years.

Soon after Independence, in December 1947, he was involved with the integration of the princely States of Chhattisgarh. A few months later, he took part in the Hyderabad Police Action (HPA), which was ordered by the Government of India in 1948 as the then ruler of the princely State of Hyderabad, the Nizam, was planning to declare independence from India. Subsequently, as Deputy Inspector General (DIG) of police in that State, he dealt with the first communist insurgency, forerunner of the present day Maoist activity.

He was selected to be the Chief Security Officer to Prime Minister Nehru in 1952. For six years he functioned as Nehru's shadow, during the period when Nehru was most active building up India as one country, laying the foundation of its economic development and also promoting the newly independent country's standing in the comity of nations. Rustamji became the Inspector General of Police (IGP) of Madhya Pradesh Police in 1958 and had to deal with the infamous dacoits in the northern areas of the State.

In 1965, at the age of forty-nine, he was selected to raise the Border Security Force (BSF) and the young force played a stellar role in the liberation of Bangladesh and the Indo-Pak War of December 1971.

After retirement from the BSF in 1974, Rustamji's services were retained as Special Secretary in the Ministry of Home Affairs. It was on the basis of the "Rustamji Commitee Report" submitted by him in July 1975 that the Indian Coast Guard, an organisation that polices the long Indian coast during peace time, was set up in February 1977. He was also instrumental in setting up the National Police Commission in 1977 and was made a member of that Commission, which recommended far-reaching police reforms.

Interestingly, it was an ex-policeman's concern for civil liberties which resulted in the filing of India's first Public Interest

Litigation (PIL) in February 1979. It was Rustamji's two articles in a national daily on the under-trials of Bihar that became the subject of the PIL, which in due course gave rise to the phenomenon of judicial activism.

I came in contact with Rustamji in 1998, when I was Director of the National Police Academy (NPA) in Hyderabad. I asked him why he had never thought of writing his autobiography despite an illustrious career and his acknowledged gift of writing. He replied with a counter question, "Who's going to read it?" I asked him if he would permit me to write his biography. He readily agreed and told me that he would place all his diaries and articles at my disposal.

I interviewed Rustamji thrice and at the close of the third interview, he placed three conditions. The first was that his biography should be based solely on his writings. He told me, "You shall not ask anybody about me in order to write my biography." The second was that it should be in chronological order. And the condition, which he uttered in a grave voice was, "Donate the profits of the book to the Police Welfare Fund of the NPA." I agreed to all his three rather restrictive conditions. Finally, when I was leaving, he relented slightly and said, "Now that I have given my writings to you, I lose all rights over them. It is up to you, what you make of them and how you use them."

Taking advantage of his carte blanche statement and keeping in mind his own doubts whether many people would be interested in reading about his life, in 2005 I brought out the first volume entitled, *I Was Nehru's Shadow*, which covered the period when he was Chief Security Officer to India's first Prime Minister. The book was an instant success. It was widely reviewed and it also figured on the best-sellers' list thrice. It went in for a reprint within two months of its launch.

Buoyed by its success, I have brought out this second volume. Strictly speaking, this book cannot be categorised as a biography. I felt it would not be proper on my part to base a book 'solely on his writings', as stipulated by him, and claim to have written his biography. It has been formatted to take the shape of an 'autobiographical narrative'— a first person account of Rustamji's life, his experiences and his views.

I have selected extracts from his diaries (which he often referred to as his journal) and his articles and placed them in a chronological order to serve as a history of India's political developments from about 1924 or so. In his diaries of the pre-Independence period, Rustamji captures the picture of the countryside in abject poverty but submitting itself, with ominous silence, to the will of God and the foreign ruler. The village life with its poverty, disease and backwardness has been chronicled in lucid detail; so has the neglect of the welfare of the people over centuries by decadent feudal chiefs and to some extent, British rulers. He has described how the freedom movement awakened India from centuries of slumber.

A watershed in the awakening of the masses, according to him, was the 1937 elections, when candidates for the provincial assemblies reached out to the villagers promising them a way out of their miseries, if elected. He paints a delightful picture of voters going to the polling booths during the elections to the local bodies in 1938, paying obeisance to the ballot boxes and casting their votes, with reverence, for Mahatma Gandhi — the Congress party candidate. The young Rustamji felt that bringing about a realisation among the masses that they also count in the scheme of things was the greatest achievement of the Congress party.

Rustamji considers the Civil Disobedience Movement of August 1942, later given the name Quit India Movement by journalists and historians, as the agitation which made the British finally come to the conclusion that the time had come for them to leave India. His interpretation of the success of the Quit India Movement is different from that of later day Marxist historians, who, due to their own ideological compulsions, have toned down its effect on the imperial rulers. The disturbances during the movement have been enumerated in great detail in his diaries because he was involved in quelling them, and also analysed in his writings in subsequent years. The main thrust of his argument has been that the movement made the British realise that the entire country was behind one leader — Mahatma Gandhi, who had, in the words of Jawaharlal Nehru, cast a "hypnotic spell" over the masses and had an "amazing power to inspire and enthuse a whole people." Secondly, an even more ominous development was that the movement had stirred the masses in the interior areas as well.

British intelligence, with its superb capacity for analysis and forecasts, and think-tanks in Britain must have prepared an assessment of the likely scenario that would emerge once the Congress leaders, who were all imprisoned in August 1942, would be released in 1945 and the unrest would spread to the non-urban areas. They therefore started the process of drawing lines on the map partitioning the country a few years before Justice Radcliffe formalised it in 1947. Their policy from then on was 'divide and quit.' This fact has been established by well researched books that have come out in recent times.

Despite all the good that the British did for the country, which Rustamji eulogises in his writings, they also made many wrong moves in India and other parts of Asia, keeping in mind their own strategic concerns. These have given rise to problems which several countries are facing even to this day.

After Independence, Rustamji was fortunate enough to be posted in places where he again witnessed history on the march. However, his diaries do not reflect in detail his immense contribution to transforming the Madhya Pradesh Police from a medieval force to a modern one during the seven years he was IGP of the state. His diaries are full of the accounts of the action against the dacoits, which is only one aspect of the myriad problems faced by him in the new state — though a major one and an absorbing one, too.

I was up against a similar problem writing about the nine years he was Director General (DG) BSF. The diaries for the period 1965 to 1970 are mostly devoted to the internal security duties done by the BSF and the political situation prevailing in different parts of the country in those years. It is probably his humility that prevented him from writing about his own achievements for the BSF in the initial years of raising the organisation. His diaries for the period from January 1971 to December 1976 are not available. My enquiries revealed that he had kept an account of the events leading up to the Indo-Pak War of 1971, but it appears, he eliminated them due to the sensitive nature of the entries.

I trust readers who have served, or are serving in these organisations would appreciate the fact that I have not taken upon myself to write the history of the Madhya Pradesh Police or the BSF. I have limited myself to some historical events of those years, which have been mentioned in his diaries and articles and which have an interest for the general reader.

While going through one of his articles written in 1997, I found that he was pained at the distorted version and false claims made by a very senior army officer regarding the Bangladesh operations. Commenting on that officer's claims, Rustamji had written, "I wonder how an author could cheat so brazenly." These are strong words, unusual for Rustamji. This remark made me feel that before the achievements of the BSF in general and Rustamji, in particular, are lost I should, in this volume, record them for posterity by interviewing some of the main players from among the BSF officers who took part in the Indo-Pak conflict of 1971 and who are now in their eighties and nineties, and incorporate their inputs in as much detail as possible.

I have taken care to ensure that I do not divulge any classified information due to the latest government instructions on the subject. I have mentioned only those details which have been mentioned earlier by Rustamji or officers of the BSF or other services in their writings or their TV or press interviews.

Condensing nearly 10,000 pages of his writings into a small volume was a difficult task. It was, however, a pleasure going through his writings. There is hardly any correction in his handwritten diaries, which are peppered with poetic quotations and also give an idea of his vast knowledge, his wide range of reading and his uncanny Nostradamus-like ability to read the future course of events. I have tried to retain the flavour of the original papers by quoting him almost verbatim, even to the extent of spelling the names of places as he had done in his diaries. At several places in his diaries, Rustamji had expressed his desire that they should be edited and made available for reading. I feel grateful to him for entrusting me with that honour.

People with whom I had spoken to about Rustamji have referred to him as a great nationalist, a wonderful human being, an artist, a great visionary, a strategist par excellence, a person with secular credentials, a man with a disdain for trifles, and above all, an inspiring leader who became a legend in his lifetime.

I can justifiably claim to have come to know the man much better than many who were closely associated with him. He has admitted in his diaries, "I had no friends so I poured out all the joys and sorrows of my heart into my journal." He has referred to his journal as his "truest friend" and "spokesman of my heart." After going through his journal and other writings very minutely, I have come to the conclusion that he was an introvert, who was highly sensitive and was easily hurt by criticism. His greatest qualities were his humility, his honesty and his belief in doing a 'good deed' to the needy, and uttering a 'good word' to his team members and his juniors. He repeatedly vowed never to think ill of anyone or comment upon him in his diaries and stuck to it. Good deeds, good thoughts and good words are the three basic tenets of Zoroastrian religion and he practised them despite the fact he professed to be an agnostic and never went to a temple or an agiary (Parsee fire temple). Above all, what impressed me personally was his courage of conviction. He was never afraid of expressing his opinion and standing alone when it came to taking a decision which was in the interest of the country and the less privileged people.

I would therefore sum up the man and his achievements in the lines that I have come across in Sri Aurobindo's monumental epic *Savitri*:

> *As a star, uncompanioned, moves in heaven*
> *Unastonished by the immensities of Space,*
> *Travelling infinity by its own light,*
> *The great are strongest when they stand alone.*

P.V. Rajgopal
May 2009

"My fondest hope is that it will be edited by Naju, or Kerman, or Rusi Lalkaka, or by all of them together — and I know that with them it will be safe. They know me and I know they will endeavour to make these notes like me. That is all that I ask.

I did not know that there would be a CYRUS."

(Diary entry of 8 March 1957. Cyrus, his son, was born in November 1962). Several times Rustamji expressed the hope that his diaries or journal, as he sometimes called it, would be edited and published. Why he did not do it himself remains unexplained.

My Diaries

The writing bug has always been in me. In fact, I wrote my first book in 1928 when I was a twelve-year-old boy. We had gone to Bombay (now known as Mumbai) for the *navjot* ceremony (a Zoroastrian ritual) of my cousin Firoze and there along with another boy, Hoshang, I wrote a small novel.

When I joined the IP in March 1938, I was transported into a different world. I knew I was living in stirring times and had the good fortune of meeting interesting people and witnessing historical developments. I therefore started making a record in the form of a journal from the first day in Police Station Garhakota in Saugor (now spelt as Sagar) district, where I was posted in November 1938 for six months, to learn the work of a Station House Officer (SHO).

I began in order to keep myself busy and learn to be observant. In a way it has helped me to understand myself, to find my personal identity and to chart my course of action. I have been driven by a compulsion to know myself. I continued with the journal for all the thirty-six years of my service in the police. After retirement, I started writing what I called a 'Tour Diary' and later took to writing articles for newspapers and magazines, though I did not give up scribbling a few lines in my journal whenever I felt like confiding my thoughts to someone.

I had no friends so I poured out all the joys and sorrows of my heart into my journal, which, in all the years, had become for me more than a friend. It was closest thing in my life. The journal became the spokesman of my heart, the purifier of my thoughts and the source of my strength.

My diary is different because it is not entirely a personal record. It is a record of many things that I have seen or heard. And along with it there are a few pages which are not based on personal experience, but an analysis of the contemporary scene.

In my diary I kept on trying to predict what would happen, although it had no importance even for me, except that it gave me a certain satisfaction perhaps when I went through it in later years. That is the trouble with a diarist. He knows the present and is worried because he does not know the future. His readers, however, will wonder why he blindly peered so much into the future and looked so little at the present.

I have written this diary without a thought of it ever becoming public. I have, therefore, written without reserve. I have hesitated to modify even when I found I was wrong. Or rather, I have not cared to modify, because what I have written is past, even forgotten. This is one of the greatest mistakes that a diarist can make — the defect of judging events and persons on the spur of the moment.

It is in the very nature of a diarist to be superficial. He watches people and events, and writes down what passes through his mind. The diarist's mind is like a cine camera that takes impressions of the scene before it. It does not correct; it should not even speculate. It records the first impressions of the moment, and these can be important.

The reader must take the diary for what it is — the sunlight and shadow on one's mind. There is only one condition that must be fulfilled — the diarist must write the truth. He must truthfully record what he feels, what he thinks, what he saw or heard. The real test of the diarist is truth.

And if it is a good diary it will reflect the doubts and changes in the diarist's mind. It will have contradictions, contrary impressions, inconsistencies, superficial judgements and wrong angles — but it will still be the truth.

I never showed the diary to anyone — not even my wife. The only person who had seen some pages is Prakash Tandon (the first Indian Chairman of Hindustan Lever). He gave me some suggestions

for writing the journal when I first showed it to him in Aurangabad in 1948. He again spent a day with me in Bhopal in May 1962. I showed him another part of my journal. Since then he had published a book. His advice was:
"You've got to make up your mind about what you are writing for. Are you writing for publication, or merely for yourself? You have to make up your mind."
"I don't know what I am writing for. I am writing apparently without any plan, without any objective."

He looked disappointed. "If you don't make up your mind to put it into shape, you may just leave it as it is."

I didn't say it, but I thought, 'That would be the best. Leave it there as it is, the childish jokes, the school boy humour, the cynicism, the defeatism of middle age. Leave it as it is — the egoism, the subjectivity, the vulgarity, the mistakes in grammar, the clichés, the wounded feelings, the stupidity of writing a diary. Leave it as it is, and one day perhaps I will have the supreme courage to publish it as it is, or to put it all in a heap and set it ablaze. But in the end, I must admit, it is perhaps this journal that has made me what I turned out to be.'

In conclusion, I would like to say that I have written these notes without a single word of criticism or advice. I am blissfully ignorant of what anyone reading them would find in them or whether he would appreciate them. I only know I wrote because I had an urge in me to write. I have written them because I have enjoyed working on them as if it were a mission of my life. But I cannot conceal a writer's pride in them.

My fondest hope is that my diaries will be edited and years hence, when people read them, I hope they will feel for a few minutes the pulse of the times in which I lived, the breath of the men who mattered in my life, and perhaps my age.[1]

K.F. Rustamji

---

[1]Rustamji very often made comments about his diaries. The above is a compilation of his comments over the years.

Photograph of Rustamji as a five-year-old boy taken in Bikaner in 1921. With him is his cousin Perin.

"My father, Faramurz and his two brothers lost their father at an early age. He died in the great plague of Bombay at the end of the nineteenth century...... the eldest brother, Jamshed, rose to be the *Dewan* (Prime Minister) of Jaora (now in Madhya Pradesh) and the youngest Cawashaw became the Finance Minister, Bikaner State (in Rajasthan)."

(Photo courtesy Cyrus Rustamji)

Group photograph of the Rustamji family taken in 1937.

Standing (L to R): Rustam (brother), Dorab Lalkaka (Nargis' husband), Khursheed (sister), Khusro (self), Goolcheher (sister), Faramroze Billimoria (Zarina's husband) and Jal Patel (Roshan's husband).
Sitting (L to R): Parin (Rustam's wife), Nargis (sister), Banoobai (mother), Faramurz (father), Zarina (sister) and Roshan (sister).
Bottom row: Baji Billimoria, Coomi Vatcha (cousin), Homai Billimoria, Shireen Lalkaka and Rusi Lalkaka.

Group photograph of police officers of Saugor district taken in March 1938. The SP of the district, R.H.A. Burrell is seated sixth from the left. On his left are Rustamji and B.M. Shukul, Deputy Superintendent of Police.

The ceremonial dress of police officers in most states in those days consisted of tunic, cross belt, pith hat/turban and riding boots.

(Photo courtesy Vijai Shukul, Retired Addl DG and son of B.M. Shukul)

Rustamji became SP, Khandwa in March 1943 at the age of twenty-six. He succeeded an Englishman.

The police constables in those days wore blue uniforms. The constables and Sub-Inspectors wore a *safa* (turban.) When Rustamji became the chief of Madhya Pradesh Police in 1958, he standardised the uniforms of all the amalgamating states of Madhya Pradesh, Madhya Bharat, Vindhya Pradesh and Bhopal. He introduced side caps for the constables and beret caps for the Special Armed Force (SAF) and full trousers instead of shorts as working dress.

Rustamji found that in Madhya Pradesh, a constable was receiving less average pay than a government sweeper. He worked hard and in 1960, got the government to grant a pay of Rs 65 per month to the constable. In 1943, the constable drew a pay of Rs 16 per month, which was later increased to Rs 35.

(Photo courtesy Cyrus Rustamji)

Rustamji got married on 7 March 1945 to Naju Kiash of Bombay, when he was SP of Khandwa district. In those days, an SP with less than eight years service wore three stars on his epaulette. After eight years, he wore a crown. On getting the selection grade, he wore a crown and a star.

It was probably because of the three stars, an SP in Madhya Pradesh was popularly referred to as "Kaptaan Sahib".

(Photo courtesy Cyrus Rustamji)

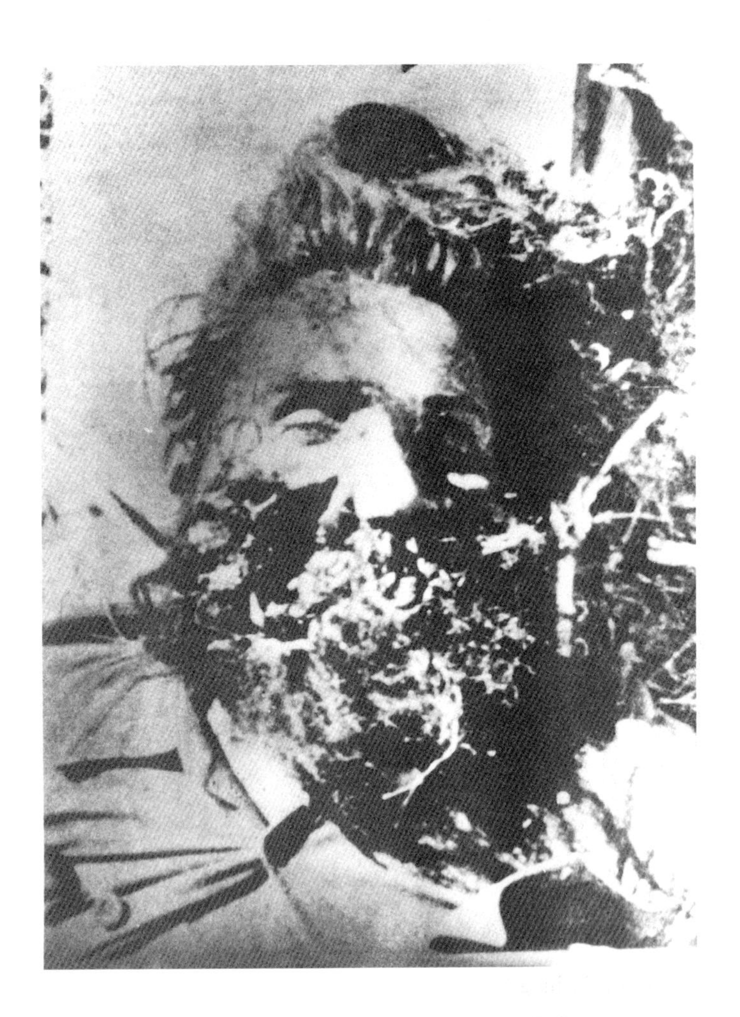

On the evening of 13 November 1959, in a daring encounter and in full view of hundreds of people, Gabbar Singh, who has now become a household name after the film *Sholay*, was killed. It was a hand grenade that blew off a part of his face.

Madhya Pradesh had declared a reward of Rs 20,000 on him. Uttar Pradesh had declared another Rs 20,000 and Rajasthan Rs 10,000. Gabbar was popularly known as Gabra.

(Photo courtesy K.F. Rustamji)

(*Top*) R.P. Modi, the dashing twenty-six-year-old police officer who was responsible for killing the infamous nose-chopping dacoit, Gabbar Singh. Modi also took part in the encounter in which Lakhan Singh was killed. He was a member of the police team which killed the 'bandit queen' of Chambal — the one-armed female dacoit Putli Bai in 1957. The above photograph was taken a day after the Gabbar Singh encounter.

(Photo courtesy R.P. Modi)

(*Bottom*) Madho Singh, another daring police officer who took part in all the above encounters and also several others. He is seen in the centre in the front row.

(Photo courtesy P.V. Rajgopal)

In February 1961, communal riots broke out in Jabalpur after a Hindu student, Usha Bhargava, who was allegedly raped by a Muslim boy, committed suicide by setting herself on fire. Prime Minister Nehru visited Jabalpur after some weeks.
"JN went round Jabalpur. As usual I sat in the front seat and from there I cast little bits of information at him about the number of houses damaged, the cost of repairs. We stopped in one area. The damaged roofs showed up, new red tiles had been placed on them. Small little huts grouped together in close proximity — so easy to damage and easy to repair.
"JN could not resist the grand gesture...the disagreement with authority.
"He said, 'What I can't understand is why they were re-built exactly as they were. They should all have been pulled down — all the slums must go and new blocks put up.'
"'But what about the cost, Sir,' I weakly murmured.
"'Cost? My dear Sir, it is human beings who live in them... human beings!! What does cost matter?' JN shouted.
"I shut up." (Entry in Rustamji's diaries)

(Photo courtesy K.F. Rustamji)

Gen Manekshaw addressing BSF officers. The others in the photograph are (from left) Golok Majumdar and P.R. Rajgopal, both then Deputy Directors in the BSF. Rustamji sitting on the other side is not seen in the photograph.

I heard from some BSF officers that Gen Manekshaw was asked to remain seated while addressing the officers, but he preferred to keep standing saying, "It would help me to look down upon you." This might have been a typical light-hearted remark of Gen Manekshaw, but not all took the remark in that spirit.

Rustamji wrote in an article, "Sam, the Chief of Army Staff, and I had a clashing relationship all through those stormy days till the Bangladesh war ended. That day I rang and congratulated him on the victory, particularly the strategy that had been devised, which had led to an early victory. After that I said, 'Chief, do you realise we haven't quarrelled for 12 days?'"

He laughed and said, "You bloody Parsee."

(Photo courtesy Golok Majumdar)

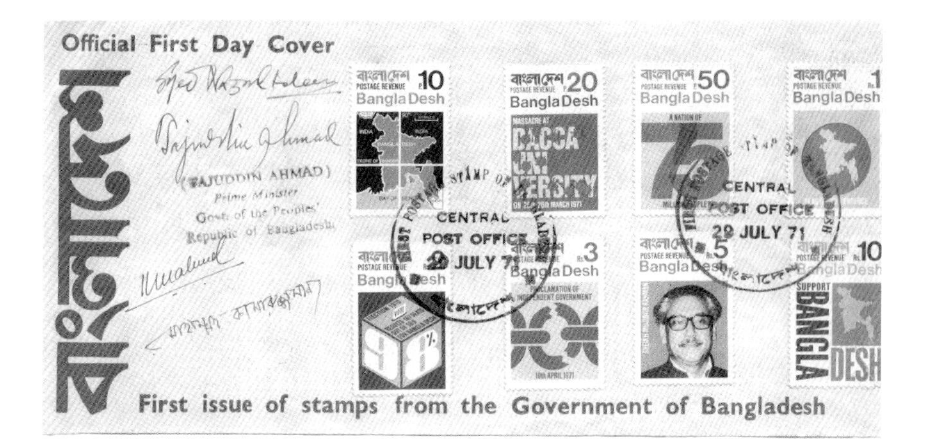

The first day covers with the eight stamps issued by the government-in-exile on 29 July 1971, which were presented to Rustamji by Prime Minister Tajuddin Ahmad. They carry the signatures of Syed Nazrul Islam, Tajuddin, [AHM] Qamaruzzaman (in Bengali) and Khondakar Mushtaq Ahmad. The first three were arrested immediately after Mujibur Rehman was assassinated in August 1975 and Khondakar took over as President. They were brutally murdered in jail in November 1975.

Bangladesh has been spelt as two words — Bangla Desh — on the stamps.

(Photo courtesy Cyrus Rustamji)

Rustamji receiving the Padma Bhushan from President V.V. Giri in 1972. I was told by senior BSF officers that Rustamji was unhappy with the award of Padma Bhushan. All the three service chiefs were awarded the Padma Vibhushan and since his own contribution and that of the BSF was singled out for praise by the Prime Minister and the Defence Secretary in their letters, Rustamji also expected the Padma Vibhushan.

(Photo courtesy K.F. Rustamji)

Photograph taken after the Padma Bhushan investiture ceremony. The garland that Rustamji received, he placed round his mother. Also in the photograph are Cyrus (son), Kerman (daughter) and Mrs Naju Rustamji.

Rustamji had high regards for his mother and before he went out on any difficult mission, he sought her blessings.

Though all things were organised and ready in November 1965, Rustamji fixed 1 December 1965 as the Raising Day of the BSF as his mother's birthday fell on that day. This information was given to me by Cyrus.

(Photo courtesy Cyrus Rustamji)

Rustamji reached the age of superannuation on 22 May 1974. He was given a two years' extension in service and made Special Secretary in the Ministry of Home Affairs. As there was a delay in the appointment of a successor, he continued to look after the charge of DG BSF. Further, on the orders of the Prime Minister, he was monitoring the on-going All India Railway strike called by George Fernandes. BSF battalions along with territorial army units were deployed at various places to "keep the wheels moving".

There were two officers in the reckoning as Rustamji's successor — Ashwini Kumar, an IP officer of 1943 seniority, and another officer of the IPS cadre, who due to the benefit of his army service had 1942 seniority. Ashwini Kumar, who joined the BSF at its inception in 1965 along with Rustamji, was considered the natural successor and appointed DG BSF. Photograph shows Ashwini Kumar taking over charge from Rustamji on 30 September 1974. The person standing on the left is Harish Soneja, Private Secretary to DG BSF.

(Photo courtesy BSF)

Rustamji was pleasantly surprised when he was informed by a friend that he was on the honours list on the occasion of Republic Day 1991. Since he had already received the Padma Bhushan, he thought that it could be a Padma Shri recognising his talents as a writer, and felt elated. When it was confirmed that it was the nation's second highest award, his reaction as recorded by him in his diaries was, "For years I strove for recognition, nothing came my way. Now when I have turned my back to it, it came in abundant measure. I wish I had not got the Padma Vibhushan."

(Photo courtesy Cyrus Rustamji)

(*Top*) The Jal Mahal palace at Tekanpur, near Gwalior, was acquired by the BSF for housing its Training Academy. The palace and the huge area of land was given away by the Maharani of Gwalior for a token amount of Rs 6,41,000 only in October 1966.

(*Bottom*) After retirement, Rustamji was able to get a grant of Rs 3 Crores from the Dorabji Tata Trust for establishing the Rustamji Institute of Technology (RJIT) for the children of BSF personnel at Tekanpur. Rustamji also gave an amount of Rs 4,00,000 from his own savings for providing scholarship to a female student. The RJIT was inaugurated by him on 2 October 1999.

(Photo courtesy BSF)

In October 2000, Rustamji was invited by the NPA, Hyderabad, where I was the Director, to take the salute at the Passing-out Parade of the IPS trainees. At the mess night on 30 October 2000, Rustamji made me stand in between him and his wife for the photograph.

At the age of more than eighty-four-years, he stood erect and went through the drill the next morning. Standing behind him are myself and P.S.V. Prasad, the Additional Director of the NPA. It is probably the last time Rustamji has been photographed saluting.

(Photo courtesy P.V. Rajgopal)

PART – 1

1916–1938

FAMILY TREE

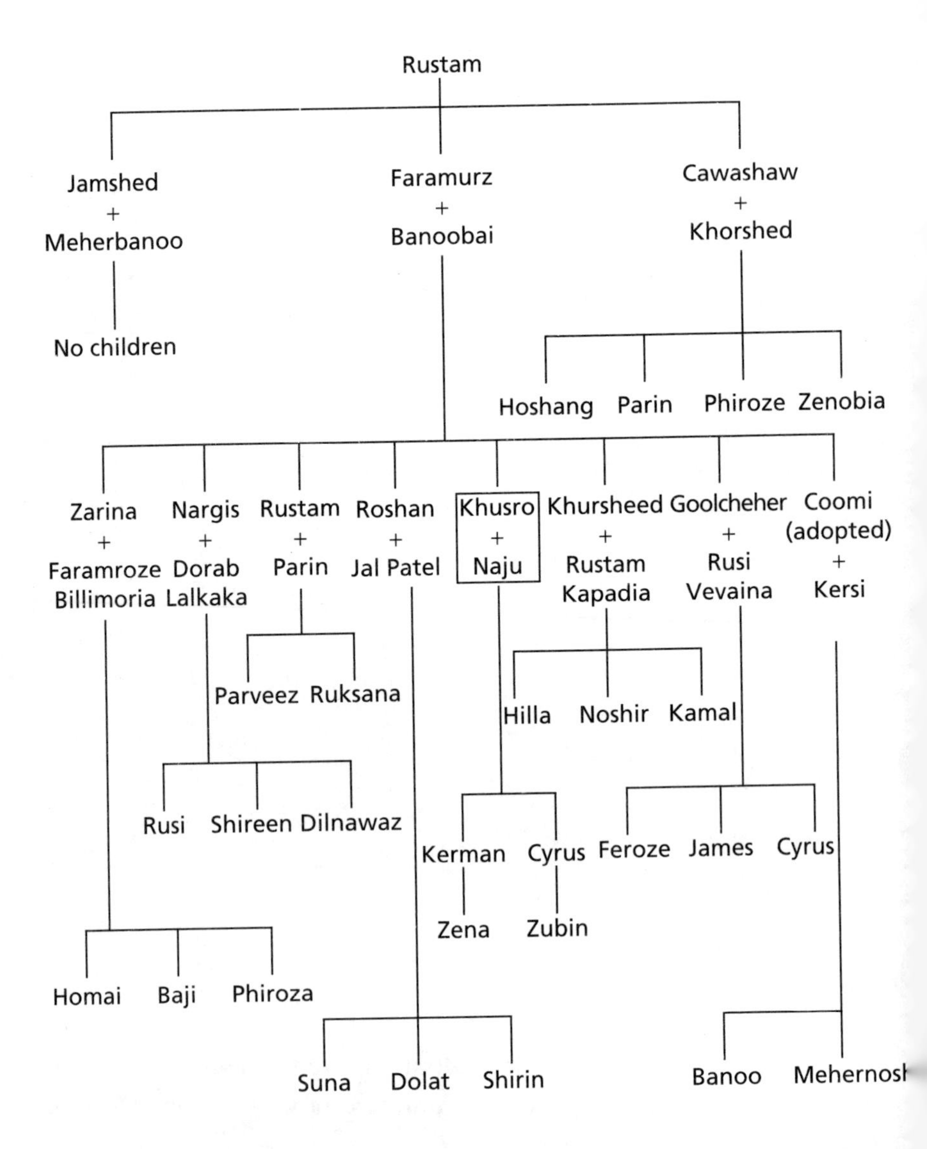

Rustam
Jamshed + Meherbanoo
No children
Faramurz + Banoobai
Cawashaw + Khorshed
Hoshang
Parin
Phiroze
Zenobia
Zarina + Faramroze Billimoria
Nargis + Dorab Lalkaka
Rustam + Parin
Roshan + Jal Patel
Khusro + Naju
Khursheed + Rustam Kapadia
Goolcheher + Rusi Vevaina
Coomi (adopted) + Kersi
Parveez
Ruksana
Hilla
Noshir
Kamal
Rusi
Shireen
Dilnawaz
Kerman
Cyrus
Feroze
James
Cyrus
Zena
Zubin
Homai
Baji
Phiroza
Suna
Dolat
Shirin
Banoo
Mehernosh

1

My Family

On the hot summer night of 22 May 1916, a big, black, hairy scorpion appeared on the veranda of our house in Kamptee, near Nagpur. With a hurricane lantern in one hand, my father went after it and killed it with his slipper. Moments later I was born.

My brother and sisters could recollect details of the scorpion with great exactness for several years thereafter, though they had no remembrance whatever of my arrival into this world. When twenty-two years later I was selected for the prestigious service, the IP, the joke in the family was that though I had the appearance, the bearing and the mental make-up of a venerable professor, I was destined to join the police because the soul of a scorpion had entered me. I would like to think that it was a good scorpion which had itself inherited the soul, in upward transition, of a noble man, who had led a life of piety and continence, respected in his community and family; literate and industrious. The noble man in his avatar as a scorpion, offered himself as a sacrifice to a slipper, merely in order to make it easier for my mother to deliver me.

My parents kept on doling out children at regular intervals. We were five children — three girls and two boys — Zarina, Nargis, Roshan, Rustam and I, and still they kept coming. The twin girls, Goolcheher and Khursheed, were born when I was three. There was always one more dependent relation in the house, making it a figure of eight.

My parents were both Parsees who hailed from Bombay. My father, Faramurz and his two brothers lost their father at an early age. He died in the great Bombay plague at the end of the nineteenth century. The young widow and the three boys were taken to Jhansi in Uttar Pradesh, by their uncle who was himself a low-paid railway engine driver. He supported them through school and college, where they also earned scholarships. They were among the first double graduates from Agra University. They set out on their careers. As they had no influence and as career examinations were unknown then, the three brothers, in spite of their high educational qualifications, were able to get jobs only in the lowermost rungs in the Indian princely States. The eldest, Jamshed, rose to be the *Dewan* (Prime Minister) of Jaora State (now in Madhya Pradesh); the youngest Cawashaw became Finance Minister, Bikaner State (Rajasthan). Both were given the titles of Khan Bahadur by the British.

My father joined service as a *Naib Tehsildar* (Deputy Revenue Officer) in the princely State of Jhabua (now in Madhya Pradesh) as his uncle was then posted in the railway station at Meghnagar, which fell in that State. For years he struggled in the lower rungs of the revenue department as he was charged with looking after famine relief work. The first signs of a famine are seldom noticed in time. The warnings of the young *Naib Tehsildar* were treated as the outpourings of one of those damned 'educated natives'. Then suddenly the whole population seemed to be on the move — walking, begging for food, walking to get to some place where the government had established a camp and food was being doled out. Often there was a riot, as hungry men and women fell on the cauldrons of rice to grab whatever could give them another day's life. Years later when my father talked of that famine, I could see that it had left one permanent mark on him — a foreign government cannot feel the people's suffering. Only an Indian government could be fair and just to the poor.[1]

Some years later he was able to get into the provincial services in the Central Provinces (now Madhya Pradesh) as a *Munsiff*

[1] Administration of the princely State was under the British Resident at Indore.

(a Judicial Officer). Gradually he rose in the department to the rank of Additional Session Judge, a position which few Indians were allowed to reach in those days. Throughout his service career, my father maintained a reputation for honesty and impartiality which continued steadfast. Gentle, kind and loving, he had passed his life in service to government and his family, doing good to all who came to him. He had a favourite quotation and this he fulfilled to the letter, "I expect to pass through this world but once; therefore, any good that I can do or any kindness that I can show to any fellow-creature, let me do it now, let me not defer or neglect it, for I shall not pass this way again."

While my father, in many ways, was a dreary visionary, my mother made up for it with a store of practical common sense and drive, which helped him considerably in life. She was my father's first cousin and she had lost her parents in the influenza epidemic in Bombay. She was married off to my father when she was just fifteen.

My mother was the one who pulled all the strings of family life in the Rustamji house. She arranged the marriages, looked after confinements, planned the future of the boys, hustled, encouraged and kept things moving. A word from her was dreaded more than any other form of censure. A Parsee mother is a seemingly inoffensive woman, with some education and a lot of charm for outsiders, but, when it comes to her children, she lays down the law, like a dictator.

I still remember the trembling with which I used to face her mighty lectures, which were my lot in my college days when I was late for dinner. After cricket on the Science College ground, a group of us always wound up at old Banta Singh's shop for tea and toast. At the beginning of the month it could even be potatoes and parathas. It appeared as if some devil in the Parsee community turned the hands of the clock to nine when it was only eight. As a consequence, I was late in reaching home and as I wheeled my bicycle into the rear bathroom, called *karimori* for short, I wondered what the storm would be like.

As expected, it came like a stroke of lightning. "Where have you been? Again at Banta Singh's shop, running up a big bill while the food goes waste at home? Who was with you? Were there any girls too?" (In those days, the company of girls was allowed only on badminton court, picnics and weddings, in which you looked at them from a distance and fixed your gaze at their bosoms.) And then a change of attack, "Son, why do you like cold food?" If I said that the temperature of the food hardly mattered, she kept muttering to herself about the black history of my good-for-nothing ancestors on the father's side who were known to be gamblers and came home late and never bothered about cold food. So from my early days, I learnt how to keep quiet when I was not losing anything. Suddenly her mood and her tone would change, "My *dikra*, why can't you come home in time to eat with us all? Come here, you don't know how much you mean to me." There was constant friction with her because she would not increase my allowance (Rs 2 per month at that time).

Mothers usually take upon themselves the spiritual education of their children. My mother's main teaching was hardly anything about Zoroastrianism. She probably knew very little of it herself. She insisted on one rule of life, like all mothers of this faith — no lies. She was roused to frenzy if she caught any of her children telling lies. I can still feel the sting of a smack I got for something trivial. "Telling lies, telling lies," she said with such a frightening scream that to this day, whenever I tell a lie (and how can you avoid it when you are married and are a policeman), I cross my fingers and say to myself, 'Mummy, forgive me wherever you are.' The one other time I got a beating was when she found two cigars in my coat pocket. In the thirties, the American films showed gangsters smoking cigars. Mother was convinced I was showing signs of becoming a gangster and I had to face her wrath.

For years she kept me under her thumb. I rebelled, I shouted, I hurt her badly. One day, when I was about ten, she said to me, "You don't kiss me nowadays when you go out?" I was so confused by the question that I said, "I don't feel like it," when all I wanted to say was, "Mummy, I've grown up." I saw the hurt it caused her.

Years later, when I was in job and there were times I was alone in a tent in some interior village, I would think of her. It would come to me as a revelation that her strictness had saved me from so many of the disasters of youth. What a lot she had done for me and how badly I had behaved with her. All through my life I have borne the guilt of my insults to the mother who cared for me and disciplined me, and forced me to study and top the university so as to achieve something in life.

The day I stood by her lifeless body in 1974 and the firelight from the urn lit up her face, I felt such a gust of affection and regret that tears came to my eyes for the first time in many years. As she lay serene in death, and we lowered the coffin in a hillside grave in Nagpur, the words of an old song came repeatedly to me — *Love's last word is spoken, Cherie...*

A lot of changes occurred in the family. Father built a new house in Nagpur which was named 'Banoo Lodge' after my mother. Papa would never have built the house if my mother had not fussed and fumed and got things done. She had a remarkable talent for getting things done. For the first time, I had the luxury of a room to myself and in which I could study, sleep and dream of the Anglo-Indian girls who abounded in the locality. Only one girl from the ruling race deigned to talk to me. She and I went out together on bicycles to a park, and when a group of youngsters threw stones at us, we quickly retreated. It was so odd in those days to see a boy and girl sitting together, more so an Indian boy and an English girl.

Ours was a singing family. Father — we called him Papa — was a Persian scholar and loved the poetry of the Iranians and Muslims. My mother — Mummy — sang in the thinnest voice I have ever heard. English music, Indian music, even some French songs came to us from the convent. Songs like *Oh dear! What can the matter be, Johnny's so long at the fair*, *She was wearing blue pyjamas when she comes* and *Three old ladies locked in a lavat'ry...*were the popular ones in those days and sung with gusto. There was no film music as it was still the era of silent movies. My sisters played the *dilruba* (a stringed musical instrument which is played with a bow) and the sitar. A wizened old music master who seemed to have stepped straight out of a Mughal miniature came to teach the girls the *dilruba*. We only stayed by him because Mummy shouted at us when we showed any signs of restlessness. All of us put a hand on the harmonium now and again. I learnt to play the violin, and had reached the stage of *Won't you buy my pretty flowers* when I gave it up. Throughout my life I have lacked persistence.

Our house was always busy with examination or study. And if we were free from exams, we were busy in interminable wrangling on God, sex and Greta Garbo, the film star. Those nightly discussions, when we tried to see things without prejudice and bias are a delightful memory of my youth, and I think have done a lot in making my attitude towards life humane and systematic.

We were like a club in our own house. The most interesting people, the most loveable, happy and rowdy people were not to be found in other people's houses but in our own. That was why we rarely went out for company. And because we were such a compact group with our own jokes, signs and signals, an outsider found it difficult to muscle in. I therefore decided to find a wife who would not raise an eyebrow when we tended to border on vulgarity and who would not consider all our fun cheap and undignified. Yes, sir, she would have to be one of us and she would have to be cheerful, loving, talented and slightly mad.

As a family we scored only one distinction. One or more members of the family won the prize for elocution in the university's elocution competition continuously for thirteen years, all because of the tuition of Rustam, our brother. He had become a well-known speaker in the University Union, and represented Nagpur University in a debate with Oxford University on the subject 'India is not yet fit for Independence'. Since the earliest years, Rustam leaned towards politics, while I had a kink in my brain, which forced me to write from an early age. I began with essays. Later I tried my hand at short stories, which, although began well, would never come to a satisfactory end.

The whole family was intensely nationalistic. My father, who had come under the spell of Gandhiji and Dadabhai Naoroji, was a true nationalist and he strongly believed that British rule in India must end and Indians should self-govern. While we were growing up, our main topic of discussion, on the dinner table where we all met, was about the atrocities of the British. The lathi charges by the police stirred Rustam to agonies of excitement. In fact, the main theme of the early years of Civil Disobedience Movement was hatred of the ruler. They are bloodsuckers, they looted India, took away the Kohinoor diamond, and even raped women (it had to be said, even if unproven because hate manufactures stories easily). At that point in our lives, the only topic was hatred. The good that the British had done to India was never mentioned.

At home we talked endlessly against the British Raj. In school we learnt to admire their ways. We lived in a sort of duality — never praising the British at home and never railing against the British education in school. That I suppose is the way all subject races live and learn to be like their masters, and finally rise against them when they begin to consider themselves equal.

Details of my family would not be complete without the mention of our cook Noor Muhammad and our ayah Posamma. Noor Muhammad served the family for forty-nine years, from 1920 to 1969. He had innumerable wives and the last time I saw him was with a little child. Often the talk at the dinner table was about Noor Muhammad's mistake in double-salting the food and Posamma's fondness for drinks. When we would offer her a small peg she would protest, "*Kya, Baba*, this is not even sufficient for dropping in my ear." When I look back, I suspect the relations between Noor Muhammad and Posamma, who lived in the servants' quarters, was something more than friendly. It was an example of perfect Hindu-Muslim unity.

Golatoris 39
22/7/41

College Days.

In 1932 we went to Poona for a summer holiday. I had just passed my Senior Cambridge and I had in me an eagerness to see places and peoples, which amounted at times to agony. I felt that the whole world was before me to see and experience and I was being held back by the parsimony of my parents. We had rented a house in Modi Bagh near the Agricultural College and there we spent three months of laughter and song. Among the several others who lived in the same compound was a Dr. Cheema, a Professor English in the Deccan College, who persuaded my father to make me a dentist, and infused me with enthusiasm for the idea. Now, when I come to analyse it this enthusiasm was not so much for the dental profession, but for a longing to see and live in Calcutta. It was agreed that on our return to Nagpur I should find out all particulars about the Calcutta College and join it for the next session.

But on our return to Nagpur the bogey of expenses again came up and it was decided that I should for the present join the Science College in Nagpur. For me it was to be Science because Rustam had already been to

Rustamji started writing his diary in November 1938. Later on, he wrote extensively on his life prior to 1938. This is an account of his college days written in 1941.

2

School and College

I remember my first day in school because of the horror I experienced at finding that I had lost the hefty bribe of two annas (12 paise) that had sent me there in January 1921. I started crying on discovering that the two-anna coin was not in my pocket when I entered the classroom.

The St Joseph's Convent in Jubbulpore (now spelt as Jabalpur), where I began my schooling, was a girl's school and therefore a disgrace for a boy to be in. The day was livened up by a prank-loving boy, Adi Patell. Five of us boys and girls went in a *tonga* (horse-drawn cart), shouting insults at the fat and the old.

In Jubbulpore, we lived in a house in Marhatal, which had St Joseph's lilies in the garden. I was the proud owner of a tricycle and I remember my jaunts with Adi and Kazi. My years at school were uneventful but for the awful sceptre of Arithmetic, which kept intruding into my life. I remember the years in Standards II, III and IV when successive female teachers, aided by an autocratic home tutor, Wahab, tried vainly to instil the love of mathematics in me. But the interest in reading and writing was cultivated in Standard III.

My memories of Jubbulpore are rather vague, but I remember a procession my father had taken us to see. That was in 1923 or 1924. The Ali brothers of the Khilafat Movement had come to Jubbulpore. A huge crowd had turned up to see them being taken in a procession.

In November 1924, we moved to Nagpur and I can remember every bit of my life from then on.

With passing years, my life grew happier as I grew older. I was admitted to St Francis de Sales High School at Nagpur run by the Jesuit order. That school was publicly criticised but was full of politicians' sons. At the school they gave me hours of instruction on the Old and New Testaments. They insisted on my acquiring full knowledge on the history of Britain and learning world geography. As a concession, they threw in 'higher Hindi' which was the *Ramayana*, taught to us by a man who made us hate him and take no interest in the book. There was nothing in our curriculum about Indian history or geography. Any mention of Gandhi, pronounced contemptuously as 'Gandy', was unthinkable in an Anglo-Indian school. I was ignorant about vital subjects like caste, untouchability, the tribes and sects, the impact of Islam, or any subject closely connected with the Indian people or with Mughal rule.

Yet, except in the lower classes, where I was invariably the youngest and was bullied and pushed about, the school gave me an opportunity I relished — learn about the world and develop my senses. Perhaps, it also taught me the rudiments of discipline. All the teachers carried canes and whacked us for any instance of infringement of the rules with a vigour that left red weals on our hands. One Reverend Father, disgusted with the habit of boys coming late to class, passed an order that whoever came in first after the bell rang would get one stroke of the cane; the rest would follow in serial order to get one more swish. Two of us loitered outside for no reason and came in tenth and eleventh. To this day I feel proud of the fact that I let him go in first. I took eleven savage cuts on my palm and could hardly hold back the tears at the pain and the humiliation.

Our best teacher was Peter D'Souza, who took the last two classes in school. He certainly knew how to make his subjects interesting. He encouraged me to write, and made me read out my essays to the class. He opened up the whole world of English literature to me, revealing the beauty and the grandeur of poetry and drama.

How do I say I am grateful? Such a teacher deserves a memorial; not plain words.

It could be said that I was educated to uphold the rule of His Majesty King George V, but that was the way all education was designed in India at that time — to get us out of our depraved ways of the past and put us on the path of Christian virtue. It was not as if anything was taught to us directly, but all the influences that came to us were in favour of parliamentary rule, justice, in playing the game and heroically going down with the ship. At the same time there were glimpses of the common man, like the poetry of Oliver Goldsmith, the explorations and the adventures of soldiers, and the emphasis (never intended, perhaps) on justice and equality. I think we learnt to see India better because we saw her from a distance; we hated the ruler, but admired his culture.

I was called a 'pagan boy' in the Christian school. I might have been bullied and insulted because I was not a Christian, but I was slowly moulded in their image. I take pride in the fact that I read the *Bible* through all the years of my schooling and even afterwards, as I felt that to write good English, a thorough reading of the *Bible* was essential. I take consolation from the fact that most of the prominent national leaders of my time were products of an English education and Western influence. Gandhiji was like a saint who came from England, educated by them and considerably influenced by British laws and history and the missionary influences of those who sympathised with Indian aspirations.

When we came to Nagpur in 1924, there were few signs of the impending storm of Civil Disobedience Movement. I remember standing outside the Council Hall near our house, when the Governor, Sir Frank Sly, drove past in a carriage drawn by four white horses. The crowd bowed and waved to him respectfully, and he acknowledged the greetings with a hand raised to the head in an Indian salaam. I was too young to know that India had been shaken by a severe revolutionary movement in Bengal and Punjab. Governors had been shot dead, some by women; a bomb was thrown in the legislative council in Delhi; several armouries had been looted; and the jail in the Andaman Islands was full of revolutionaries from Bengal, Punjab and Maharashtra, many of them Muslims.

In the twenties and early thirties, the main topic of the family's discussion was the Civil Disobedience Movement and the various agitations for Independence taking place in Nagpur. We used to read in the newspaper almost every day about the Congress leader of Nagpur — a Parsee named Manchershaw Rustamji 'Awari', who was given the title 'General' by Mahatma Gandhi. One of my earliest memories is that of General Awari who went and put up the Congress flag on the High Court building.[1] I remember seeing the procession going to the High Court and what remained as a distinct and indelible memory was the mounted police chasing away the people after the flag hoisting. He was arrested and the procession was dispersed. I can still see my brother, Rustam, fulminating as the mounted police charged opposite our house on Palm Road.

The main effort of the early years was to build up pressure for freedom. Millions came out to help in the struggle. Men and women responded to every call for volunteers with a fervour and self-sacrifice that I have never seen again in India. It was India's finest hour. The student community was naturally the most agitated by what was happening and was at the forefront. Every one of us, brothers and sisters, came in that category.

It is a fact worth mentioning that in the early years of Civil Disobedience, there were a large number of Parsees and Muslims in the movement. Gradually they began to decrease in number, and when Independence came, only one or two remained and were given ministerial posts. It may be that they were no longer required; it may be that the Parsee spirit that is quick to take on a challenge is reluctant to make capital out of it. Or what may also be true, especially in the case of the Muslims, they felt that the movement was taking a turn towards giving more powers to Hindus, whom they distrusted.

While in school, we formed a friends' club, which met at the house of the Parakh boys. Its members consisted of Boman and Ratru Parakh, Ramdas, Hoshang and Nawal Doongaji, Shekhu Ahluwalia and George. The activities of the club were hockey every evening, a

---

[1]This happened on 13 April 1926.

war with another club every third day, a battle of fisticuffs on the premises quite frequently and a not infrequent discussion on sex and morality.

I cannot say when I first heard of sex. I had heard sly references at school but I had never given it a thought. At about the age of twelve, Nawal Doongaji's driver explained the act to us. Although I knew how the act was done, I had never associated it with reproduction. I had gathered it was a low sinful act of immoral and *chalak* (unscrupulous) people. But one Sunday afternoon, when we were in the Parakh stable, Boman Parakh told us in a confidential whisper that, all mothers and fathers did it and that was how children were produced. I was greatly shocked and I still remember the days when I tried to reconcile my father's and mother's innocent faces with the atrocious and shameful act they had been accused of.

In 1932, I appeared for the Senior Cambridge examination and came sixth in a class of fifty. In a sense, I was educated abroad, knew little about India, and nothing at all of science. Soon after our Senior Cambridge results were declared, we went to Poona for a summer holiday. Dr Cheema, a professor of English in the Deccan College, persuaded my father to make me a dentist and infused in me the enthusiasm for the idea. I was excited at the idea of studying in Calcutta (now known as Kolkata); joining a Dental College was secondary. On return to Nagpur, the bogey of expenses came up and it was decided that I should join the College of Science. For me it had to be science because my brother Rustam was an arts student. The date for application had expired and so Rustam took me to Dr Krishnamurti, who was then officiating as Principal. I walked sheepishly into the Principal's office, clad in my only suit of light brown Havana. The date was condoned for my benefit and I was told to appear for the interview.

The College of Science that I had joined was a tough testing ground for me. As I had not taken science in school, I found I was totally out of depth. The backwardness made me lose interest in chemistry. A friend and I decided to study together, and what the professors had not been able to teach me, Balwant Rao did for me. Physics and biology were the subjects in which I was on even ground with the others, and I shared the first place in the intermediate examination with a friend.

The other testing ground in college for me was the University Training Corps (UTC). About two months after we had joined college, we appeared for an interview for selection to the UTC. I was nearly rejected by Captain Cox but for the timely intervention of S.M. Bormaunt who said that though young, I would grow up and hence deserve to be taken. I was a lean, lanky youth of sixteen years. The UTC uniforms which were issued made us look like clownish survivors of the Great War — a cork helmet that shook crazily every time we saluted, and boots with yards and yards of woollen *puttie*s (strip of material) which had to be wound round rough woollen socks. In addition, we wore flannel shirts. In Nagpur, where the temperature goes up to 47°C in summer, some of the tough Maratha boys even fainted during parade. On one convocation day, when we had to present the guard of honour to the Governor, I nearly passed out and only came up standing because I had drunk a full glass of water under the strict orders of the commander, who had said, "I don't care if you pee on the parade ground, but no passing out."

I was promoted as Under Officer and could wear a Sam Browne belt and an Australian hat. My platoon threw me up in the air when we won the drill competition. We filled the big cup with beer and passed it round till two boys who were teetotallers, led us away to our ground-sheets, blabbering drunk.

Hockey and cricket were the games we played most in our college days. Prof Vaidya gave much of his time to coaching us in cricket and probably laid the foundation of my health. My wrists were too weak for batting and I refused to wear glasses although I needed to. But I could twirl the ball in leg-breaks, which seemed easy to play, and got wickets. Prof Vaidya was a dedicated coach, who would put a coin down a bat-and-a-half distance from the crease, and I had to pitch every ball on it. That made me a bowler. In my last year, I captained the university cricket team.

One of the most memorable moments of my college life was seeing Gandhiji from close quarters. I was a member of the college union. In November 1933, we sent out an invitation to Gandhiji, who was at his ashram in Wardha, fifty miles (eighty kilometres) from Nagpur, to come to the college to deliver a lecture. In order to get some publicity for our union, we sent notices to all the local colleges. Every student in Nagpur seemed to have responded eagerly to have a *darshan* (view of a revered person).

Two hours before he came, the Convocation Hall was packed to the brim with thousands outside clamouring for admission. I nearly broke my arm trying to prevent them from storming the door from which we wanted to bring Gandhiji in quietly. From the main entrance, C. Rajagopalachari entered first and the people in the upper galleries mistook him for the Mahatma and showered handfuls of flowers on him. Then suddenly from the side door Gandhiji entered. It is difficult to describe the emotions that overwhelmed me. There he was, three feet from me, smiling at me. Instinctively I lowered my head in a *namaste* (salutation), trying hard to keep myself from falling on him because of boys pushing me from behind. There was something childlike in his toothless smile. It is difficult to explain why I could not keep staring into his eyes. Somehow, the charisma dazzled me and therefore I lowered my head upon seeing him.

Part of the time in the meeting was taken up in a senseless controversy whether he should speak in Hindi, as some people wanted, or in English, as others vociferously demanded. He spoke both in English and Hindi, but the loudspeakers of those days could hardly carry his voice beyond the first few rows. The reverence for the man was so great that not a single person moved from his seat till he left. The tumult, the uproar, the acclamation, the worship and the idolisation was something that is impossible to describe. Each person felt that he was in the presence of a mighty being and stamped the meeting in his mind as a moment to remember.

I got a chance to see and listen to several other luminaries. My brother took me to hear Dr Annie Besant in the Old Town Hall. In the early thirties, I had attended a lecture by Pandit Jawaharlal Nehru. The personality of the man was indeed striking. There were numerous other people who were invited by our union —

Bhulabhai Desai, V.S. Srinivasa Sastri, Dr S. Radhakrishnan and Dr C.V. Raman. A lot of Muslim leaders too came but not Mohammed Ali Jinnah. I heard him later in a public park in Nagpur. The standard of their speeches was very high. They spoke from the heart and one took note of what they said as they were heartfelt feelings and not just lip service.

College life with its liberties, its orgies and its energy was more attractive than school life. Despite all the drawbacks in the initial stages in college, I stood first in biology in the Intermediate examination. I came under the spell of Prof Moghe, who was Head of the Department of Zoology and did my B.Sc (Honours) under him, again securing a first position in the university in the year 1936. But more than the instructions that I received in the classrooms, the experience I gained from life in the college helped me to grow out of the glorious, wistful, charming and agonising delusions of youth into the staid, *pucca bada* sahib.

As per the practice in those days, I earned my M.Sc degree after one year. In 1937, I was selected to be a demonstrator (lecturer) in zoology. I worked for about six months in my college on a salary of Rs 150 per month, when I was suddenly lifted into another world on my selection to the IP.

The competitive examination for qualifying for the ICS and IP was entirely different in those days. It was not held on an all-India basis, though the examination was held simultaneously in India and England. It was restricted to the provinces as per the vacancies available. My province, then known as Central Provinces and Berar, which comprised of what is now parts of Madhya Pradesh, Maharashtra and Chhattigarh, had not taken anyone into the IP on direct recruitment for the previous four or five years. The new government came into power in 1937, consequent on the Government of India Act 1935. It felt that the All India Services should be abolished. It therefore did not give any notice of the examination till nineteen days before the due date.

A friend of mine, Torun Mukherjee, brought two sets of forms. I was not keen on joining the police. In fact, I did not want to appear, but my brother, who was intensely nationalistic, said that the only way in which one could change factors, which were against India, was to go into the services and handle things ourselves. He persuaded me and therefore I filled up the form. For nineteen days, I had to work night and day because of some subjects which I had never studied either in school or college, one of them being Indian history. I devoted all my time to it and worked really hard. I hardly slept for the last two or three days before the examination. To my surprise, I stood first and that year only one person was taken into the IP from my state. My friend, who was largely responsible for my appearing in the examination, got left out. He joined the army and rose to the rank of a Colonel.

I must admit that one reason for my success could be that a substantial number of marks (400) were allotted for the interview. The largest amount of help that I got in the interview was from my own Principal, Prof Morris Owen, who spoke for me even while I was there in the Hall. He said, "He was one of my best students. He deserves to be in the IP. And mark my words; this young man is going to go very high."

PART – II

1938–1947

The Adventure Begins — G'Kota. 2/ 8th Nov '38.

At 2 o'clock in the afternoon the "saman" was brought out from the bungalow and spread in romantic confusion on the drive. Packing had been postponed till the last minute and then to make sure that nothing had been omitted I made them put out everything. I am now a convinced believer in mummy's policy that unless everything is laid out on the verandah about 6 hours before departure something is sure to be forgotten. So there they all lay — portmanteaus & hat-boxes, deodar petis, a meat safe, a mattress, mosquito-curtain poles, a biscuit tin and all else. It only needed a bird cage with a miserable yellow bird inside to complete the picture of a Chinese refugee's kit. The ~~mattress~~ meat-safe seemed to be clasped in an eternal embrace by the mattress, and I could see ~~the~~ my mellow old portmanteau turn up his nose with disgust, as he rubbed shoulders with a dog basin. There they all lay together, from the drawing-room and the bath-room, kitchen goods and a gramaphone all mingled in terms of socialistic equality.

"The Adventure Begins" — the first page of Rustamji's diaries dated 8 November 1938, the day after he joined Police Station in Garhakota for on-the-job training as an officer incharge of a police station. He continued writing for all the thirty-six years of his service. He told me he had misplaced several diaries and some were lost during his transfers from one place to another.

3

Training Period

With the appointment order of the Secretary of State for India in hand, I joined the IP on 7 March 1938. In those days the practice in the Central Provinces was to post an officer to a district to begin his training on the job. I was posted to Saugor.

There was a large military cantonment in Saugor and that was probably one of the reasons Saugor was considered a good district for training. Maybe the intention was that the civilian officers of the British Empire should develop harmonious relations with the army officers from the start or it was because the government felt the young civilians would have good company.

A large number of officers, including some Englishmen, were posted in Saugor for training. There were three ICS and one IP officer — Jai Kumar Atal, K.B. Lall, Ronald C.V.P. Noronha from the ICS and C.T.L. Hakewill, an English IP officer. A great friend of all of us was Benoy Kumar Chaudhuri, the Additional Sessions Judge. The Indian officers looked upon Sreenath Mehta, ICS[1], the

---

[1]Jai Kumar Atal of 1937 seniority was seconded to the Indian Foreign Service after Independence. K.B. Lall (1937) rose to become the Defence Secretary. R.C.V.P. Noronha (1938) became Chief Secretary, Madhya Pradesh. C.T.L. Hakewill (1936) left India in 1947. S.N. Mehta (1928) refused to become the Chief Secretary of the State as it was a desk job. He was largely instrumental in getting the Government of India to start a steel plant in Bhilai and preferred to remain as its head. B.K. Chaudhuri later became a judge of the Madhya Pradesh High Court.

Deputy Commissioner (DC) of Saugor, as their head. This group was so intensely nationalistic and so keen on supporting each other against the British officers that we acquired a certain cohesiveness. At times we were joined by some Indian officers of the army who were anti-British.

Pre war Saugor had a unique English atmosphere of its own because of the Army Cavalry School, probably the biggest in the world. At that time Saugor had one of the biggest collection of army officers. The Englishmen there posed as superior. On my part, I felt inferior because I was unused to their ways. The distance between us was not only because they were English, but because they were from the military. And as it happens, even now, an army man tends to look down upon civilians.

When I reported to the SP at Saugor, an Englishman by the name of R.H.A. Burrell, he asked me, "To sit quiet for a week and just look around." I knew after a day what a terrible sentence he had passed on me. Here I was among unfamiliar people, without even a book to read. Just at the time when I was keenest and thought most of myself, I was forced into a period of solitary confinement. I passed through a furnace. I emerged from this period a different man. I developed such an intense loathing and dislike for official life that it took me a very long time to recover.

After a week, I had to begin my training by doing the work of each rank of the police for a specified period, depending upon the importance of that rank. I did treasury guard duty for one week and wondered how the men kept their sanity doing it. What a difficult job it is and how we take it for granted and freely punish the men doing such duties for minor lapses. I had a brief stint in the Police Training School at Saugor, where I was clubbed with the subordinate staff, to learn Physical Training (PT) and parade.

For my training, the SP had laid down a ride every day, a game of hockey in the Police Lines as often as possible and a check of night patrolling in Saugor town once a fortnight on a bicycle. The SP told me that the main idea of the game of hockey in the lines was to enable me to know most of the men by name. He said that, that would help bridge the gulf between officers and men.

I was detailed to do a cavalry course in the Army Cavalry School. Although it was a civilian course, it was extremely tough for me because I had never ridden a horse in my life. I had an average of about three falls a week, but luckily the ground was covered with sawdust with the result that the humiliation was more than the hurt. The course started with making us ride without stirrups on the very first day. At the end of the course, we were jumping over hurdles, going down slides, doing long canters and gallops. The certificate awarded to me on the completion of the course only said that I could ride over broken ground. The ordeal of the course left me with a lifelong addiction to riding. I rode regularly for fifty years and only gave it up because a wanton horse, probably a hound from hell, threw me on the race course in Bombay in 1989.

When I joined service in Saugor, it took me some time to get acclimatised to life in a cantonment. I lived in a house with Atal and Hakewill. Both of them used to have animated discussions on shooting and horses all through the day. When we went to the club, people asked me if I had done any shooting; same was the case if I called on anyone. They asked me to come out riding with them. We saw polo matches and jumping competitions. We went out riding in accordance with the accepted rules of conduct of a gentleman.

At first I thought that these tastes had to be cultivated. Perhaps, one couldn't enter the 'Horseback Hall' until one could jump the hurdle at the gate. Perhaps, there were joys in *shikar* (hunting) which could not be experienced until one was an expert. I took to these sports with keenness. I went out riding everyday and on *shikar* every weekend, to the nearby Ramna forest, in rain and sunshine. But, though I became a good horseman and a tolerably good *shikari* (hunter), I could not find those hidden joys that were so loudly trumpeted. I admit I found something to talk about with a zest that amused me. Now when I look back, I realise that we all indulged in small talk because discussing the political situation prevailing then was taboo. Discussing official work after office hours was discouraged and there was absolutely no question of commenting upon another officer, senior or junior, behind his back.

Apart from riding and *shikar*, the other prime interest was golf. In fact, golf for us, in those days, was a religion. If a man disparaged golf, we thought the worst of him. For, if a man disparaged golf, we were assured he was also a wife-beater and read other people's letters. Golf, we were told, cultivated the virtues of forbearance, perseverance, honesty, a sporting spirit and concentration.

As I loved cricket more and had played the game since childhood, to my mind, it appeared golf is essentially a game for a person who is no good at games. It is, as A.A. Milne says, "The best game in the world at which to be bad." Whereas a bad player in tennis is always shunned by the opposite player and cursed by his partner, a bad golfer can back away in solitude. And in a few years he can attain a tolerable standard. A great deal depends on the concentration with which one plays golf and as these players can supplement the lack of dexterity with a great deal of concentration, they gradually lower the handicap and retire at sixteen.

It took me long to discover the sterility of life in a cantonment. When I joined, I was so dazzled by the hollow pomp and glitter that I could not see the human essentials. It took me a long time to pigeonhole an Englishman. In the beginning of my service, when I had met few servicemen and fewer Englishmen, I believed, in my innocence, that every army officer who walked with authority was a symbol of efficiency and courage. I was shy of Englishmen and afraid of their wives. But with the passage of time, I learnt to concoct stories to show-off. I was able to narrate stories illustrating my experiences in *shikar*, or my friendship with celebrities or my noble descent. Three years later, I kicked myself for the hypocritical attitude I had adopted earlier. I was not able to forgive myself for narrating those stories. They came back to me and made me wince at the stupidity of the callow youth, who concocted stories to show-off. Though I was mostly to blame, I shall not forgive the ignorant, stupid, pompous men and women of Saugor, who tried to embarrass me as much as they could by forcing me into their own pattern of life. If I had escaped, it was because I had seen more Englishmen.

Saugor was my first contact with the world of our rulers which I had seen from a distance. How I envied Jai Atal and his Oxford manners! How I tried to imitate that manner in speech; the careless banter, that self assurance! I tried to observe closely the young Indian and British ICS officers who were posted in Saugor after their training at Oxford and London. I listened to their speaking with a drawl about the 'old school *taai*' and 'trends in modern *aart*'. Alas, they would be dumped in villages, miles away from anywhere and all that they would be asked to do was to "issue a permit to a bus to go along an unmetalled roadway" or "sanction odd items for the *patwari*s (land record keepers)." It would come as a rude shock for these gentlemen — the cream of India's educated youth, who were intended to rule the "two-thirds who lived in villages." Preposterous! They had come with rosy dreams about overhauling the land revenue system, and establishing a new economic system of their own that they had formulated in the classrooms of Oxford.

When I joined service, I credited the ordinary official with efficiency and intelligence. At first I mistook the pomp and bluster for efficiency. I mistook the claptraps of discipline for the natural obedience inspired by a leader. But after two years of service, I began to see the official world through the haze of prestige and dignity. I realised with a shock that the majority of them were the shallowest routineers, with the exceptional ones dubbed 'a crank' or 'a clever chap'. The really capable officer, who shunned the crude flattery of confidential reports and struck out an original and efficient line of work, was relegated to an inferior assignment and made the butt of a conspiracy of lies. Unfortunately, this repudiation of efficiency made 'anti-change' the slogan of the services. The capable officers, who believed that the problems of administration could only be solved by drastic changes were discouraged and defeated. The new concepts of work and discipline were ridiculed and consigned to limbo.

My joining instructions specified what I had to get in the shape of clothing, and in the lot was mentioned: *One dinner suit — with bow, not tied like waiters' bows.*

I bought some bows from the shop of Moses David in Bombay and hoped that the diagram given on the envelope would enable me to tie the bow when the time came to wear it. The time came suddenly one evening. A Captain in the Equitation School 'threw' a cocktail party. Jai Atal insisted that I should go with him. The thrill of it was so great that I agreed to accompany him even without an invitation.

The entire afternoon I spent in learning to tie the bow on my thigh with the help of the diagram. Jai's dog thought this was a lovely game and repeatedly tried to pull away the ends. For hours I tried every conceivable knot but the bow would not tie. In fact, it ceased to look like a bow. Eventually, in the evening, Hakewill tied it for me, but it was so loose that it hung down the collar, like a bit of dog's ear used as an ornament.

Moses David had prepared the suit with shoulders padded so heavily that I seemed to be carrying a big load on them. When I tried on the jacket in Bombay, it looked grand. But the moment I wore it in Saugor, and appeared in the drawing room of our house, there was such a loud shout of laughter that I could feel hot, bitter tears fill my eyes. They called me 'Eastend gigolo' and other names. By the time we set out for the cocktail party, I was in utter ruin. With the bow tie flapping widely in the breeze and the shoulders growing larger and larger, I was in no condition for any party. I sat moodily in a corner, trying to spend my time without looking at the suits from Saville Row and Rankin. Then I made the terrible discovery that my shoes (patented leather, black, according to prescribed standards) were far more pointed than was necessary. That was an additional defect to conceal. With one hand I tried to make the bow hang as little as possible, and with the other, I repeatedly pulled the trousers lower and lower to conceal the shoes. I decided to get up and stand in a corner, in a drooping sort of way to suppress the padded shoulders, but was so afraid than an elegant man or woman would mistake me for a waiter that I did not dare to get up.

I brooded over the cocktails, afraid even to imbibe so much that my grief would give way to levitation, till we returned home and I buried myself in a book to forget all the humiliations that I had heaped on myself.

I ran into the officer, whose party I had gatecrashed, twelve years later at Aurangabad, where I was Deputy Inspector General. He had become a high-ranking army officer and was quite a different man. He had dropped the cavalry manners and eschewed alcohol completely. He came to my house in a white bush shirt. He had become himself — a de-naturalised Englishman, but there was something missing in him. The keenness, the verve, that air of courageous dash, had faded away. Perhaps it was the war, or perhaps it was because India was no longer a part of the Empire that had enabled him to find himself.

But what I remember fondly of those days was the attitude of young officers, both from the civil and military side. What they wanted most were 'beat ups' — a display of youthful high spirits, a tiger shoot, a polo match, a whirlwind affair with the old colonel's wife, all temporary, small-time diversions. Their attitude was 'who knows what tomorrow would bring!' Even those waiting for freedom wanted to live for that day. Strange as it might sound today, the in-thing in those days was to boast, "I don't know what my pay is", or "I don't know how much I received this month."

Four months after I joined service I had my first exposure to the eccentricities of people at the top, which in other words means the eccentricities of the Englishmen. The IG of police, Sir Charles C. Chitham came for inspecting the work of Saugor district police. The SP had gone away to Nagpur for some work. I was incharge. The inspection routine started with the parade in the Police Lines. After taking the salute he started inspecting the men lined up. When he came to the squad comprising of recruit constables, he said to me in anglicised Hindustani, "*Sab ko jhad pey chadadoh.*"

I wondered what sort of an order was that. '*Sala pagal hai kya*?' (Is the bounder crazy?) I thought or has he fouled up his Hindi. I said, "Sir? ...... I could not...... get you, sir."
"Young man, don't you understand Hindustani?" And then he growled, "I said......PUT THEM ON THE TREES."

The recruits scampered up the cork trees that lined the parade ground.[2] After a detailed inspection of the Police Lines, he went back to the Circuit House. The Reserve Inspector (RI) — the officer incharge of the Police Lines — asked me, "What do I do with the recruits who are up on the trees?"

"You ask the IG," I said.

"You ask the IG," retorted the Anglo-Indian RI. The RIs were mostly Europeans or Anglo-Indians. In those days there were no Deputy SPs in the smaller districts. Next to the SP, the most important person was the RI. The Inspector level officers having long years of service never thought much of young entrants to the IP because of their own close equation with the senior officers.

So I cycled up the hillock to the Circuit House and saw the IG lying in the veranda on the old type of planter's chair with his legs up on the sleeves of the arms of the chair which were drawn forward. I saluted him and said, "Sir, the recruits... sir, the men you put up in the trees...sir, the men are still up in the trees."

Sir Charles gave out a loud laugh and said, "Goddamn, man! Haven't you got any initiative? Haven't you chaps got a mind of your own? I was trying to test you — to see what you would do. Go. Use your brains."

I nearly knocked off my *sola topee* with an extra smart salute. As I was leaving he said, "Join me for dinner."

When I came back to the Lines, the RI asked me, "What are the orders?"

"Use your brains." I told him in the same tone as the IG told me.

"You use your brains." The insolent fellow shouted back.

Just as the sun went down, I reached the Circuit House to have dinner with Sir Charles, who behaved in a totally different manner. He had a pleasant conversation with me over drinks. He spoke about his passion — building roads, police stations, quarters for the constabulary and laying out parks and gardens.

As I was leaving after dinner, he said, "I am going to Sanauda tomorrow morning. Come with me." I went with him in his car for

---

[2]The parade ground referred to in Rustamji's diary is the one which falls on the left side as one enters the Police Lines, Saugor.

the inspection of Sanauda police station. In one hour he inspected the police station work thoroughly. He could get a grip of the crime and the way the Sub-Inspector had worked. After the inspection, he said, "I am going to Damoh on my way to Jubbulpore. You walk back to Saugor. It will be good for your health." I marched all the way back on the deserted road in my full ceremonial dress cursing him all the thirteen miles.[3]

Sir Charles gave me his camp cot, saddle and his kitchen utensils when he handed over as IGP Central Provinces and Berar a few months later to take over as Chairman of Federal Public Service Commission (FPSC), forerunner of the Union Public Service Commission (UPSC). Though I mentioned in my diary of those days that, "I bet the old man must have forgotten about the recruits sitting in the trees and was making up for it by shouting at me," now I feel it might not be so. He did it deliberately. It was a typical British way of training youngsters to take decisions on their own.[4]

I remember in 1941, when I was posted as Sub Divisional Officer of Police (SDOP) in Narsingpur, I sent up a case to the DIG at Jubbulpore. The evidence in the case was equally balanced and I asked him for guidance — whether to prosecute the accused or set him free. He sent back the file to me with the brusque remark, "I am not paid to do your job." Here again, the senior officer wanted me to take a decision and not get into the habit of looking up for direction. A similar instruction was given to me by my SP. I was sent to the rural police station of Garhakota for undergoing the next stage of training as SHO. When I went to report my departure to him, he bid me goodbye with the words, "I don't

---

[3] I drove down from Sagar (erstwhile Saugor) to Sanauda in October 2006. Except for a stray vehicle, there was hardly any traffic even sixty-eight years later.

[4] The well-known management guru, Peter Drucker has, in one of his articles, mentioned that the officers of the ICS were the best managers. They were recruited at a young age, put through a perfunctory training and posted in independent charge and made to take their own decisions. This developed them into good managers. In fact, Drucker praised the East India Company as a huge company run by a small number of people having all information at their disposal and taking decisions independently.

want to see your face for the next six months." What he meant was that I should not run to him every now and then, seeking guidance on how to do things. He wanted me to do the work myself, make mistakes, learn from the mistakes and develop confidence to do the work on my own.

I hired a bus to take me to Garhakota which was thirty miles from Saugor. At two o'clock in the afternoon of 8 November 1938, the *saman* (luggage) was brought out from the bungalow and spread out in romantic confusion on the drive. I became a convinced believer in Mummy's policy that unless everything was laid out on the veranda about six hours before departure, something was sure to be forgotten. So there they all lay — portmanteau and hat-boxes, deodar *peties* (boxes), a meat safe, a mattress, mosquito net poles, a biscuit tin and other things from the drawing room and the bathroom, including the 'throne' (commode), kitchen goods and a gramophone, all mingled in socialistic equality. It only needed a birdcage with a miserable yellow bird inside to complete the picture of a Chinese refugee's kit.

The driver had promised to come at three but came at five. It was loaded and lazily we crept out of Saugor. It was quite elating to sit in the front of the bus with Cheeky, my Pomeranian, and think of all my goods packed in the rear. Wahab, my orderly, was rather disappointed in my taking all the kit in one bus. He held that the villagers would not be impressed. They will shake their heads when they see my bus and say, "Oh! It's just a Head Constable going on transfer." He was of the opinion that I should have at least two to three empty buses follow me and blow their horns together when we neared a village. As we crawled along, Cheeky thought he was sitting in an armoured personnel carrier and kept barking at the ferocious roadside dogs. By the time we reached Garhakota, there was brilliant moonlight. Sub-Inspector Jaswant Singh was there to receive me.

The first case I had to look into was against Ramlal, a habitual cheat. The modus operandi of this man was that he would go to a village posing as a great sadhu who was in direct contact with the Almighty. He would go out to where some villagers were seated and perform some wonderful feats of *jadu* (magic), like taking a bit of dust, throwing it in the air, muttering some incantations and then producing a coconut or a bone out of his palm. The villagers would be very much attracted to the great saint who claimed infallible powers of treating every known disease, from impotency to malaria with his prayers and *jadu*. Damrulal, a poor cultivator, had not been blessed with a son. The villagers dinned into his ears that his wife Sukhraini had a *bhoot* (evil spirit) in her and unless this was cast out, the problem of a son and heir would not be solved. So Damrulal approached the so-called saint Ramlal and begged him to intercede with the Almighty on his behalf to drive out the *bhoot* from his wife. Damrulal could not produce much, so for two pice (about four paise) the saint agreed to cast off the demon. He closeted himself with Sukhraini. Damrulal waited outside. He could hear a *bhajan* (prayer) being chanted inside. After the prayers, the sadhu made various 'passes' at Sukhraini and anointed her feet with sacred ghee. Next he asked her to lie down flat on the ground as he had to anoint her from tip to toe. There was a scuffle as the saint tried to pounce on her. Sukhraini rushed out and Damrulal thrashed the saint with his shoe.

In trying to study the crime in an Indian village in 1938, I found that two guiding principles had to be borne in mind. One was the poverty of the people and the other, the so-called innocent character of villagers and the complete absence of guile and malice.

Seldom was there money in the house of the villager. The entire wealth of the family was in the form of ornaments and cattle. The ornaments were very well safeguarded because they were always on the woman of the house and it was a dangerous game to steal from a woman. Cattle, however, were the real mirror of a man's financial position and *izzat* (honour).

The most common item of village crime was the petty theft of agricultural foodstuff or fodder. A few ears of wheat costing perhaps a pie (about half a paisa) or so would be a great temptation to a man whose monthly income was Rs 8. Added to that was the sun and rain, the *malguzar* (landlord) and his *karinda* (assistant), the deer and the panther, all seeming to be in a conspiracy to deprive the poor villager of whatever little he harvested from the soil. Then, when his crop came up, the birds attacked it from the air and his fellowmen stole or let their cattle in shamelessly to graze on the fruits of another's arduous toil.

I found the villagers in those days had very peculiar ideas of morality. The woman even changed her husband on the ground that the husband was weak — *chhota padta hai*, as she put it, which meant he was unable to satisfy her sexually. There was no great social stigma attached to having a 'keep'. It was quite common for a widow to go and live with some young man whose wife did not have any great objection as she considered the addition as another helping hand in the house and in the fields. But the most peculiar feature of the marital arrangement was that a husband was willing to be compensated or pay the fine in rupees, annas and pies for any lapse of marital fidelity.

A woman came and reported at the Station House that a man had assaulted her and outraged her modesty. Her case was one of the legions of that variety that kept pouring in at the Station Houses. A man and woman are caught in a compromising position and then immediately the woman takes up an attitude of injured virginity. It was the same in rape cases also where adult women were concerned. The woman gave her consent but when caught in the act, she immediately changed and trumped up a long story of how she was forcibly thrown down and raped.

Due to the poor means of communication, I did most of the touring either on foot or on a bullock cart, which covered a distance of five miles in an hour or sometimes on horseback over the countryside, which did not permit a bicycle. Invariably the road was just two small ruts running through the jungle. The cart would jump like a thing of life. At times, fearing a rupture or some such thing, I would get down and walk the rest of the way. The cart for touring was the first step to becoming rustic — to imbibing the life of the villages. I used to do fifteen miles a day and after that a bed was a luxury too great to be appreciated in words.

One got used to these little things and a delay of an hour or two did not matter in life in the rural areas. In fact, there were only a half a dozen people with watches in Garhakota and all the watches seldom showed the same time. The watches had to be wound every twenty-four hours. Once I found that the Sub-Inspector and I were forty-five minutes behind the doctor, who had set his watch the last time he had been to Saugor. There was no train to catch in Garhakota, so we did not have to worry about a standard time.

The village scenes were a bit like the ones from an Indian talkie[5] — the sun setting beyond the river in a glory of orange and amber, the trees throwing romantic shadows into the water, the cowherd driving his flock home and singing in sheer exuberance of youthful spirit. It was the sort of simple rustic panorama that filled your heart with gladness, a scene that somehow made you feel happy without any rhyme or reason.

Most of the villages were a collection of crude mud huts. The inhabitants were semi-naked, grimy men and women — nothing to live for, yet afraid to die. I tramped through the wilds of Banda *tehsil*. The people there were even more primitive. Many of those I met had never seen a train in all their lives. Once I gave an orange to a small boy. He looked at it and refused to take it. He had never seen an orange before and did not know how it was eaten. The government statistics placed the average income of an Indian villager in the beginning of 1939 at Rs 6 to Rs 10 per month.

I have often wondered why there was so much somnolence in rural India of the thirties. I think they knew nothing better. Their fathers, grandfathers and generations beyond had endured tyranny and deprivation, raids by marauding armies, and the atrocities of thugs. The ruler seldom cared for the welfare of men and women in the remote villages and they were left to fend for themselves. In any case, India, for 150 years before the British came, was in turmoil, ravaged by thugs and *pindaris* and robber bands of various hues. Survival depended on the ability to bear the misfortune without complaint. It was the prospect of Independence

[5]Films in the thirties were referred to as 'talkies', because the transition from silent to talkies took place in 1931. Rustamji referred to movies as talkies in his diaries of that period.

and the hope of a way out of poverty and want, as held out by the politician, which slowly began to affect the rural areas.

I always got on very well with village folks. Many a time, in the remote areas, the villagers mistook me for an Englishman because of my fair skin and were thus more forthcoming. It was really great fun to sit round a campfire in the evening, talking with them. There is a native charm about some of our villagers. I found that they were not as ignorant or stupid as they were said to be. I observed that they sat in groups according to their castes and status in the village. When an Englishman went on tour to the village with his wife, the number of people at the campfire was more. The village women would keep staring at the Englishwoman wearing a frock.

It was most interesting to observe the villagers at some of the joys and sorrows of village life. I shall never forget the week I spent in a village where the rains had failed. Dry parched soil looking up in hungry crevices, cattle moving about uneasily and loudly crying for water and the poor villagers distracted to despair at the starvation that faced them. Thus things went on for days and the agony and suffering went on increasing. At last, when hope seemed to have been abandoned, a stray cloud appeared on the horizon. It rained. I had seldom seen rain greeted with greater emotion. Old men and children, men and women, all ran out into the rain with their faces uplifted to receive the cool lash of the precious water. Children rolled in the mud, boys shouted in exultation, old men prayed; for them rain and the soil are the true gods of India. They are the fountains of all life; the givers of our existence.

One evening, I went to the Garhakota village and found a man wringing his hands and jumping about. He told me that he had been bitten by a scorpion. I brought him to my tent in the *thana* (police station) premises and injected potassium permanganate and Iodex into the sting. The pain subsided after four hours. Next morning, the *paan wallah* (shopkeeper selling betel leaf and areca nut, etc.) opposite the *thana* came running with his little son in his arms. The son had been stung by a scorpion about five minutes earlier. He was shouting and crying with intense pain. I took my *shikar* knife and made a deep cut till blood began to flow freely. Then I injected a little potassium permanganate and Iodex into the wound. The result was almost miraculous. The pain eased off immediately. I was surprised at the wonder cure. My fame soon spread in the village. Infallible powers were attributed to me. One man wanted a *taviz* (talisman) from me to tie round his child who had got measles.

But a surprise awaited the day after. In the morning, when I came out of my tent, a big assemblage of patients greeted me. About fifteen persons had collected to be treated by the *Chhotey Kaptaan* Sahib (ASP), who was also a doctor. Many of the cases did not come 'into my ken'. One fellow had severe pain in his right chest. His pain miraculously healed with two Aspro tablets. He blessed me till the fifth generation. I felt I would have to enlarge my medicine chest if I was to continue to be on the pedestal.

I once accompanied Sub-Inspector Jaswant Singh and the *Naib Tehsildar*, Dave, to the *mutt* (monastery) of a well-known sadhu who lived a few miles away from Garhakota on the Patharia Road. He was a prominent figure in Garhakota society. Everybody paid him a visit and his 'not-at-home' box was full of visiting cards. It was a small mud hut with tall poles carrying sickly-looking pink flags. Jaswant Singh explained to me that tall poles with the worn out flags were donated by people, whose desire for a son had been sanctioned by the Almighty. When the Prince of Wales had visited the country some years earlier, those who did not have a male offspring suddenly decided that they too should have a 'Prince of Wales'.

In the course of my stay in Garhakota, I came across several *baba*s (ascetics) — some with criminal records who played upon the 'faith' of the people and found God a very profitable profession. One *baba* confessed to me that he had a great desire to travel the length and breadth of the country but was penniless. The garb of a sadhu helped, he said, in travelling free in trains and buses and getting free meals at wayside food stalls and in the homes of wealthy people.

During my tours, I came across several European missionaries settled in the remotest of areas for long years. I saw a decent looking house in Khurai and when I reached the gate, a European gentleman came out to meet me with outstretched hands. He took me inside. His old-world cordiality was a delight. It transpired that he was a Swedish missionary. We sat down. After spending months in *dak* bungalows and tents, it was a pleasure to sit in a drawing room with pleasant curtains and carpets; with pictures and flowers. And there was such an indefinable atmosphere of peace about the place. There was an appealing simplicity in that house — a beauty not to be found in any palace. It had the atmosphere of crinolines and lavender about it. I then heard footsteps coming down the wooden staircase. I hoped it would be his young daughter. I thought I would ask her to come with me and explain to her everything about India. It turned out to be the missionary's wife, who brought me a bunch of bananas. He came outside and left me at the gate. While I walked back, I mused about the difference between the mellowed old missionary and the sadhu *baba* I met in the company of Jaswant Singh and Dave.

I came across a most amusing festival called *Phag*, which is celebrated at the time of Holi — the festival of colours. In the middle of the village, a long pole had been planted and from the top dangled a bagful of *gur* (jaggery). All the women of the village were armed with long bamboo poles and dared any man to climb up the pole and get the bag. If any valiant reached the pole, he was assaulted by all the women and had to beat a hasty retreat. There was a good deal of healthy banter and it was most interesting to see how the men and women behaved with each other. There was none of the shyness or reserve. The women boldly ran up and dealt a few light-hearted blows on anyone they wished. Unfortunately, I was also a victim of feminine fury and had to pay a very heavy fine of one rupee to be allowed to go home. It was left to a burly *Kabuli* (men from Kabul who were in the money-lending business all over India) to keep up the honour and prestige of the men. He crawled up the pole in spite of a heavy fusillade of lathis and brought the bag down. But on coming down, he hugged the bag and fainted.

While camping in the villages on tour, there was always the possibility of *shikar*, which helped to get us out of the monotony of rice and potato or egg curry. A village *shikari* took me to his field which, he said, had been invaded by a herd of wild boars. He clapped once and about twenty wild pigs came rushing out all round me. I fired at the herd with a 450/500 rifle and missed. The *shikari* looked at me with the look of someone who had deprived him of a year's food. I was never a good *shikar* shot, though I was good with a 303 rifle on the range. A *sambhar* (stag) that I shot looked at me with such pitiful eyes as it lay dying that I felt *shikar* was not quite my line. Presumably I took to *shikar* just to pretend to be a *burra* sahib in the villages. When the British left, the desire to kill animals went with them.

When I reached any village, I was invariably welcomed by the village *kotwar* (watchman) in his uniform — blue overall, a broad belt and a lathi in hand. He was a computer of information. He knew all about crops, land revenue, village factions and feuds and when we were alone, he would tell me, in a hushed tone, how a widow was having an affair with a Head Constable; how a girl had been raped and the village panchayat had hushed up the matter by making the boy marry her. He even described the case of two women living together and suspected of indulging in lesbian practices. They were called to the police station and in order to make them atone for their evil ways, they were raped by the Sub-Inspector and two of his constables. The *kotwar* did not find anything wrong in that. He felt it served them right.

In 1938, a year after the Congress took office in the Central Provinces, a report about the achievements of the Congress ministry was published in the newspapers. The list was very impressive. They had granted a holiday for the Tilak anniversary, the name of Mr Gandhi was changed to Mahatma Gandhi, the *vidya mandir*s and prohibition had been introduced and the police were made to send their case diaries to the magistrate on a daily basis. But to me it seemed that their greatest achievement was something different. At the time they assumed office, the city was the point from which all centrifugal activity began. After assuming office, there was a tendency to concentrate more on the villages, maybe due to the pressure of the Members of the Legislative Assembly (MLAs), who represented the countryside. The countryside was asleep, content in its poverty and which, they felt, would never change and neither was there the desire to change. The villager at last started receiving that modicum of attention that he deserved. The Congress also affected a miracle in the minds of the villagers. Hitherto the villager thought that a thorny life was his fate and his was not to reason. He went through life as a chastised, hungry, downtrodden; yet a content individual.

After a year of the Congress rule, a new spirit of enquiry was seen. Men's minds were awakened. They wanted to know the whys and the wherefores. They had at last realised that future prospects for the menfolk lay in their own hands. The villager gradually started becoming aware of his neglected condition and the possibility of succour. This was indeed the greatest achievement of the Congress. They had opened the minds of men by spreading a new spirit of enquiry, which is the basis of all education. As the thirst for knowledge increases, men are tempted to read and write. This is the first step in progress.

In the innermost villages, it surprised me to observe the deification of Mahatma Gandhi. During the elections to the local bodies in 1938, I saw the villagers rush up to the polling stations, fold their hands in obeisance before the boxes and vote for Mahatma Gandhi — the Congress candidate. The villager talked about Mahatma Gandhi with awe. He did not have the respect and admiration that an educated man would have had; he had the fear and reverence which is inspired by a deity. Portraits of Mahatma Gandhi and Jawaharlal Nehru were carried in certain exclusively religious processions and the Congress flag was flaunted by many a dilapidated shrine. This had its own effect on the mind of the Muslim villager.

The British were blamed for creating communal discord in India. It was said that creation of separate electorates was responsible for the trouble and that Hindus and Muslims had lived as brothers prior to this. But the verdict of history is otherwise. From the day the intrepid Muhammed bin Kasim set foot in Sind in AD 712, religion has been the *causus belli* of every war that has been raged. Untold atrocities have been committed in the name of Allah and *Aum*.

The hatred that blazed in those bigoted times has come down to us through years as dying embers. It appeared to me at that time that the problem was gradually working up to a crisis and within the next few years, was likely to explode. I recorded in my diary as far back as 1938 that so long as politicians introduced religious considerations into politics, so long as they depended on heavenly inspiration and sought to translate ancient ideals into a modern world, communal strife would continue to sully the fair name of India.

After two months in the village, I got fed up to the gills with it. Going about from place to place had a monotony — more terrible than staying in the tent in Garhakota. An intense depression seized me. I thought of the blue-eyed Empire-builder who had at least the consolation that he was 'keeping the good old flag flying', 'looking after the empire' and all that. But what about me? I had no such noble motives. I had to only 'learn to labour and wait for the 1st'.

I was asked to be present for the Police Week celebrations at Saugor Police Training School where all the senior police officers were to be present. The trouble with such gatherings is that the crowned heads do not step down from their thrones. In my case, I was a little diffident to step forward on the red carpet. But there were some compensations. The food oftentimes was good, the women charming and the atmosphere festive. But I had a sneaking suspicion that they could have done without me, and I without them.

I looked back at the period of six months spent in the villages. I discovered that my rural police station training had taught me more of police work than years of city life could have done. Moreover, I learnt to view India in a correct perspective. Living in cities, we are rather inclined to view things in a narrow, prejudicial manner. We know nothing of the problems of rural India. In my case, life in the villages had meant one endless record of new experiences, because I was always moving from place to place. At one place, Mirpani, my tent was pitched in a cremation ground because there was no other shady place to do so. I camped for the night in village schools and wayside huts, the outer verandas of *malguzar*'s bungalows and under bridges. In a village in the princely State of Bhopal, I slept in a godown (storeroom) of tobacco leaves and jute bags. I could hardly sleep as I kept sneezing the whole night.

Officially, my training, which started on 7 March 1938, finished on 15 June 1939. But when I looked back at the fifteen months of my training, I was surprised at the little I had learnt, and the lot more I ought to have learnt. What little I had learnt had been a result of my own endeavour and curiosity. No one appeared to have been interested in my training and none had told me what to learn. So when I was about to put my foot on the second rung of the ladder, I viewed the prospect ahead with misgivings and fear. Frankly speaking, I felt I would have been hopelessly at sea had I been asked to investigate a murder case or even a case of theft. Communal riots were not so much as mentioned in my training schedule. Yet if a serious situation cropped up in my charge, I would have had to deal with the whole show on my own without, perhaps, even the advice of a second person. The responsibility would have been so great and the stakes so high that one could not risk committing a mistake. One must do it correctly the first time one is up against such a problem without the slightest knowledge or experience.

One great weakness of all IP officers posted as SPs was dogmatism, untempered by experience. We propounded grand schemes for the control of burglary; we instructed investigating officers who had spent a lifetime in investigation; we laid down policies and made the staff adhere to them and all this was not based on experience and experimentation. Hardly any of us had written more than one case diary, and that too to show to the examiner of our practical test. Yet with all the shortcomings in our training and experience, we were selected to supervise the work of a district which had a population of several thousands of people, and which in extent was equal to or bigger than some of the smaller independent states of Europe.

In police work with the criminals working against you and where you have to be wary of your own subordinates, first-hand knowledge is absolutely vital. This is another lesson which experience has taught me. Yet another fruit which I gathered from the garden of experience was the avoidance of hastiness. Unless it is absolutely imperative, do not take important decisions on the spur of the moment.

It is only a hasty man who takes an irrevocable decision, without care and thought, and calls it a quick decision. Another danger of youthful impulsiveness is to exaggerate trifles because one has not had the time to get used to that particular incident, or to think over it calmly.

Fortunately for me, when I was having all these misgivings about my imperfect training in July 1939, F.C.S. Quinn-Young was posted as SP Saugor. Freddie Quinn-Young was a red-haired half-Irish, half-Channel Island officer who looked like a gollywog. The amount of interest he took in my training was more than what I have seen Indian officers take in new entrants to the service. Quinn-Young took me with him on all his tours. We inspected police stations together; we walked miles and miles in the evening and had our drinks and meals together. I learnt a lot from him. His words of wisdom continued to be of interest to me all my life.

I had come to the IP straight from college. Due to my scientific background, I felt all the time that there seemed to be no basic rule or formulae or equations for policing. What is policing? How is it done? How should it be done? Quinn-Young was the first to tell me that policing means knowing your area, knowing your staff, knowing the criminals, understanding the crime and how it was committed and finally, connecting the criminal with the crime. His emphasis was not on connecting the crime with the criminal, but the other way round.

Quinn-Young worked on the simple but remarkably efficient system of "knowing the criminal". Instead of beginning from the crime by working out clues as clever detectives do in fiction, he believed in starting from the criminal and connecting him with the crime. The former system was perhaps more spectacular; the latter required hard work and patience. It was the same system that Col Sleeman followed to track the thugs and get rid of the thugee problem.

He told me that the fundamental principle of police work is information which could be obtained by intensive touring in one's *ilaqa* (beat). He said, "If you know your area well, the detections will come on their own. There is no need for torture or illegal detentions. Information will come from friends because in almost every crime someone would know who committed it. The ability to get information is vital and that would depend on the faith people have in you." Quinn-Young devoted a lot of time to talk to me about the police, their faults, the intrigues, which are part of any service and drilled in me the fact that there was a system in policing which few care to understand or follow. He said that the officer-incharge of the police station was the kingpin of the system and any attempt to bypass him would not work, nor would any attempt to give him an impression that he would be relied upon completely.

After the training, I had to clear the departmental examinations to be confirmed in the service. I had failed in my first law examination, although a friend, who was incharge of the examination hall, had slipped a copy of the Indian Penal Code (IPC) to me. When I asked the DIG, an Englishman, who had set the paper, why he had failed me when I had done fairly well, he replied with a wicked smile, "First time I fail everyone; never even see the paper; makes them study more."

In the first week of September 1939, I was at Parsonia, inspecting the police station when the international situation began to take a serious turn. A copy of a few days old *The Times of India* newspaper came through to me and from that I learnt that Germany had concluded a pact with the Soviet Union and the German press had complained of the treatment meted out to her nationals in Danzing and the Polish Corridor. The situation had suddenly taken a grave turn. I have seldom been as worried as I was that day at Parsonia. The news, though it made my blood tingle with visions of youthful valour and comradeship, gave me a premonition of an awful disaster. I could not sleep. I got out of bed and sat on the easy chair in the veranda. A cool breeze whistled through the trees and moonlight suffused the air. Far away I could hear the tom-toms celebrating a village festival. How still and quiet, I thought; so much India-like. While the world was in the grip of an agonising upheaval, the spirit of India slept in philosophic disregard. There I sat and wondered about the war before dropping off to sleep at two o'clock in the morning. I woke up early to get back to Saugor and consume all the latest newspapers and have discussions with my friends.

All of us still hoped there would be no war. On 1 September 1939, at ten o'clock in the morning, German planes bombed Polish towns. Hitler had decided to opt for a war. On 3 September, Britain declared war on Germany. Soviet Union had mobilised and invaded Poland to reclaim the Polish Ukraine and establish a buffer zone between her and Germany. The future felt uncertain. A momentous war was in store. Reports of daring moves started coming in from all sides. A Polish aviator crashed into a German plane; a German aviator plunged into an enemy ammunition store. Youth, as ever, was to the fore. As a twenty-three-year-old, I felt it was the spirit of youth that made a nation — and a nation is born in war. No suffering attracts me and no sacrifice thrills me as much as the heroism of a soldier on the battlefield; no death seemed to me greater than death on a battlefield.

News continued to pour in about the war. At Saugor, it generated greater interest as the officers that I met in the Cavalry School, both British and Indian, were soon drawn into the war. Many of them fell on the battlefields; some rose to high ranks and were richly decorated. One IP officer, D. Ellis joined the Royal Air Force to defend his country in its dark hour. It appeared Britain was paying a heavy price for saving the world against Hitler.

I finally cleared my departmental examinations. I was "ripe for a subdivision". In March 1940, I was posted to Narsingpur[6] as SDOP.

---

[6] As an economy measure the three districts — Narsingpur, Damoh and Seoni were reduced to subdivisions in 1932. They again became full-fledged districts in 1956.

Camp Amgaon 135
7/1/42.

1941

The Year of Struggle.

For me 1940 was the year of quiet confidence. I had everything I wanted, my services were appreciated, and I was confident that with the talent I have I will be able to do well. But 1941 shattered all those delusions. The quiet confidence was replaced by grim despair and then by hard determination. The dream of efficiency still exist, though they have become hazier. But out of the struggle arises a cold determination to fight. "Bind up my wounds. Give me another horse." This time I will strike hard and give no quarter. When the world thought the D.I.G. had me down, they gave me no sympathy and encouragement. Now when I come out again I will give the world a taste of the stuff I am made of. I will not let consideration come in my way. I have learnt that it is not the fighter who gives consideration. It is the victor who can afford it.

At the beginning of every year, Rustamji made an analysis of the past year and his projections for the next year. This practice, which he started at the beginning of 1940, continued for all the years he maintained his diaries. The four-page analysis of 1941 includes an in-depth analysis of the World War II situation, the freedom struggle and his strategy of how he should conduct himself in the coming year.

4

Pakistan Takes Shape

The first thing I did upon taking over in Narsingpur in March 1940 was to buy a second-hand car — a 1938 model Morris Cowley Y8-22. I got it for Rs 250. The price broke my back as my salary was Rs 350 per month. I was forced to buy it as the rules required that an SDOP maintain a vehicle. I named the car 'Oscar' as per the fashion in those days to give names to one's conveyance, just as one gives names to a horse or a pet.

Narsingpur was a quiet and interesting place. It had the typical gentry of a small town — an old British judge, a young doctor, the outspoken wife of the SDO (Civil), a Bengali headmaster of the local high school and a curious Sub Judge. On my first visit to the club, I met a lady who was surprised to hear that I played hockey.

"You don't look like a hockey player," she said.

"Then what do I look like?" I asked her.

"A mischievous schoolboy; a scholar with a sense of humour."

I was taken aback. A mischievous schoolboy was a hard bit. For years, even before joining service, I had been trying to cultivate that air of detachment, that superb sense of dignity, that sinister raising of the right eyebrow, which seemed to be a nonchalant possession of British Governors of the provinces and Gary Cooper, the Hollywood star. The irresponsible woman smashed the illusion with one wretched sentence. Never again will the right eyebrow go up in the mocking, sinister look, which I thought was the way I would be looked upon — as a terror by my subordinates.

After two months in Narsingpur, I was shifted to Damoh. I replaced J.P.C. Coventry, the hardworking young officer, who I found had written a ten-page note on the distribution of duties among the two Head Constables and six constables of a police station.

In the two months of my stay in Damoh, I read a lot. I found Damoh to be a place which encouraged reading and writing, though I cannot tell why. There was a gentleness and dignity in Damoh. All the delightful memories of youth come rushing back to me. I discovered my interest in the plays of George Bernard Shaw. I have not read any author as systematically as I have read Shaw. I finished most of his plays and prefaces in those two months and the effect on me was that it strengthened my confidence in myself. I had a sneaking distrust of my opinions and decisions. Often I accepted the decisions of another because I was doubtful of my own. But when I found I agreed with Shaw, where others would not, I came to the conclusion that Shaw would agree with me where others often would not. And in that curious psychological manner, my confidence in myself increased. Above all, there was one thing that Shaw had taught me — nothing justifies life except humanity; nothing satisfies life except truth; and nothing fulfils life except nobility. To live well, one must be sympathetic, truthful and confident.

I got posted back to Narsingpur after two months. The loneliness in small towns like Narsingpur and Damoh, where I was stationed at that young age of twenty-four, produced in me a craving for companionship, a desire to share life and jokes with someone who might not be fairer but certainly dearer than all the rest. I must blame Timi for a part of that longing. She was working as a young doctor in Jubbulpore and was introduced to me by Didi, wife of B.K. Chaudhuri. Although I had never given a thought to marrying her, I always felt a girl like her would make a grand wife. Timi was a most unwomanly woman. She had none of the meanness of a woman; none of that spitefulness which added a 'but' to dilute every compliment. She had a sympathy and a cheerfulness which raised her miles above many of the women I had met. There could never be a dull moment in the company of a woman like her and strangely enough, she would never be bored with you. She preferred to call me 'Rusty' and not Khusro. She taught me dancing. How well I remember those long lazy afternoons in her room when we were friendly, but she would always resist my advances. "For the which," as Samuel Pepys says of the shipwright's wife, "I did respect her."

Timi got married to an army officer. Several years later, when I was DIG in Aurangabad, I saw her at one of the small airstrips. She ran towards me and I took her in my arms and kissed her in full view of her irate husband, with the subordinate staff that had come to see me off, wondering what was going on and who would shoot whom. Such I suppose is what true love is all about. It is difficult to forget the first woman you fell in love with but didn't get married to. That love never dies; it lies tucked in one corner of the heart forever.

I shall remember Narsingpur for two things. First, it was my first independent charge and secondly, my differences with the DIG, Northern Range at Jubbulpore, B.C. Taylor.

Since I was incharge of the subdivision, I applied Quinn-Young's system of detection with slight modification. It produced grand results. It made work in the subdivision systematic and it became my credo. Based on the methods I adopted, I wrote an article on detection of burglary cases which was published in the *Indian Police Bulletin*[1] in two instalments and earned me a lot of kudos.

I followed the Englishman's practice of spending the winter months in touring. I was out on the road for days on end, galloping for miles over the delightful countryside with the rich, fertile, green fields below and the glorious clouds above. Of course, touring had its own inconveniences and annoyances. You had to depend on the villagers for the carts to carry your tents and rations for the followers. When my men would go for the carts, the persons who had them would go

[1] This was the first police magazine. The publication was discontinued in 1946.

into hiding and their womenfolk raise a wordy barrage, unequalled in tone and ferocity. Pitching the tents also required help. At one place the locals were watching a *Ramlila* show at eight o'clock in the evening and told my men to go to hell. At many places, I had to depend on the local *malguzar* to provide dinner and a bed.

I got used to village life and started taking interest in the day-to-day life of the people of rural India. In the villages, in the early forties, a volleyball tournament attracted a large crowd of locals, just as cricket does today. You could see the people merge into the spirit of the game; you could see them forget their starving crops and sickly families. They were immersed in the game and were able to escape, if only for a while, from the dull grind of agricultural work. And they would go back to their fields with something learnt — a new spirit; a spirit of work and achievement.

The other most interesting aspect of village life was the village fair. It actually combines a holiday with some religious function. On a visit to Burmaan on the banks of River Nerbudda (now Narmada), in January 1941, I went to see the local fair. If you want to see the Indian village folk at their best, go to a fair, see the huge concourse of men and women, all attired in their gala clothes, laughing and singing and gaily going round the booths; see the clown advertising the *nautanki* (drama), or the yogi tying himself into knots; see the village virgin and the harlot (who does brisk business during the duration of the fair); and see the sea of humanity merrily breaking over the shores of pleasure. It seemed to me that the religious side of fairs was gradually becoming less important and except for the aged, or the infirm, who visited the fair in the hope of a cure or salvation in the afterlife, the majority of people went to it for the pleasure of a change. Besides enjoying the shows, they could assure themselves of divine favour by bathing in the sacred river. After bathing in the river and donning their best clothes, people went round the shops buying, for it was considered auspicious to buy after the *snan* (bath).

In all fairs, loudspeakers playing popular songs were a common feature. I moved about in the crowd, watching amusing cameos of life — a peasant and his wife gravely discussing the new ornaments for their girl's marriage; one buying a trunk; a couple with two kids haggling over the price of a rattle for their youngest child, who must have been promised a present if he stayed at home and obeyed grandpa; the young gallant selecting a *dholak* (a small drum) for the dancing parties; or a young wife buying a coat for her baby.

Standing in a corner were three women, quietly singing with rapt and serious faces. They were then joined by three more — a little younger and gayer, discussing the new romeo who had been swaggering up and down in tight *jodhpuri*s (breeches) and a khaki coat. The woman with the 'come hither' look was the local Mae West, looking very ornamental and oiled, and I noted the envious glances of all the other women, very curious to find out all about the 'other type'.

After a few days they would all go back to their villages with their stories of the fair. And for a year they would work and sweat with the prospect of another Burmaan, when the crops are rich and prices high; when the poor peasant can buy all those little luxuries which he always looks forward to, but can never get.

I came away from the fair with a sense of satisfaction. 'These,' I said to myself, 'are the heralds of the future.' The young student, with zeal and keenness to help the *kisan* (farmer), the *kisan* willing to learn and work, the *malguzar* mindful of his peoples' welfare, the women emerging out of the petty thrills, the children happy and the old people contended. These are the people who will build the new India, and in fact they had already begun by getting rid of their apathy and ignorance. And once that was done, they would have begun to rebuild the mind of the country; and once that too was done, the country itself would be rebuilt.

Due to the fertility of the soil of Narsingpur, the living standard of the average man was relatively high. The people were more educated and hence their political awareness was higher. But it would be wrong to suppose that the average villager was also interested in politics. In those days, a villager thought as much about local politics as he did of the American presidential elections or the World War. The villager was so busy with his crops or his daughter's marriage or the problems caused by the *patwari* that he had little or no time for the Independence movement or the war going on in faraway Europe. His world was the village and his family. But the government held the impression that agitators were pouring into the villages, and the Congress' individual *satyagraha* campaign would develop into a mass movement. We received instructions to ensure that the match does not reach the rural dynamite and were also asked to monitor the people's contribution to the war effort.

I went on thinking as to how we should deal with a *satyagrahi*. Arresting him would make him a martyr and martyrdom is propaganda. It served no purpose and only increased the agitation against the war effort. The policy of ignoring *satyagrahi*s proved more useful than lathi charges, heavy sentences and fines. The government also realised that the only answer to *satyagraha* was *satyagraha*; the only answer to passive resistance was to ignore the passive resistor. For *satyagraha*, like religion, thrived on persecution, and an ignored *satyagrahi* was like a dismissed constable — an object of ridicule rather than worship. When a local leader, B.P. Pachauri, offered *satyagraha* in Narsingpur and another one in Tendukheda, large crowds collected to see what the police would do. We stood there the whole day and in the evening, we smiled at them and turned our backs. The crowds also turned their backs. The *satyagrahi*s felt deflated.

Thus time passed. In early 1941, within three years of joining the police service, I started feeling frustrated. I came to realise that officers in the IP were mediocre men, with middle-class morals and 'ruling-class' minds.

At that early stage of my service career, I realised with a shock that promotion in the police department did not depend only on efficiency; it depended on intrigue, sham and in some cases, the worst type of nepotism. In the police department, I observed, personal likes and dislikes played a very important part, and it had become so well established that no one objected to it. The first act of Mr A.G. Scott, when he was promoted as IGP in 1940, was to post a particular Circle Inspector, who was in his confidence, to Nagpur so that he might always be available.

The Englishmen thought if the Sub-Inspector was a good detective, produced good results on paper, was a strong disciplinarian and got all his enemies mercilessly punished, then he was fit to rule over men by being made a Circle Inspector. I found that since the Sub-Inspectors were always in contact with criminals in their circle, and scheming lawyers in courts, they had acquired some of the habits and characteristics of both these classes.

Another interesting aspect of promotions in Central Provinces was the preferential treatment meted out to north Indian officers. Taylor once told me that he preferred these officers as they could enforce discipline better than the 'native' officers. In actual fact, it was so because those officers had better *intazam* (organising) ability — they could drive villagers and arrange camps and delightful *shikar*s. Such officers were also able to concoct good figures of detection of house-breaking cases and, the thing that impressed the Englishman the most, they were able to show an impressive increase in the number of cases under the preventive sections of law and arrest of proclaimed offenders. There were innumerable instances of Sub-Inspectors, who showed a meteoric rise merely by pandering to the tastes of the Englishmen.

My own problems in the subdivision arose out of my Circle Inspector's proximity to the DIG. I suspected his integrity and his tendency to instigate the Hindus against me, stating that I was pro-Muslim. I recommended him for punishment in a gambling case where he fudged the figures of the amount seized, but the DIG wrote back, "I am not going to punish an experienced Inspector on the recommendation of an Assistant Superintendent of Police (ASP) with three years' service." This emboldened the north Indian Inspector and his tantrums increased. He kept punishing subordinates and recommending others, whom he was not empowered to punish, to me. If his recommendation was not accepted, he dubbed them as my favourites to the DIG. Taylor, on his part believed that it was the right of a Circle Inspector to *shikar* (go after) any subordinate who tried to oppose him. I also got the impression that he considered it good to *shikar* young ASPs for the good of their soul. He probably thought that unless ASPs got their corners rubbed off in the early stages, they were not likely to fit round holes.

The finding of the DIG in the Departmental Enquiry against the Circle Inspector, in which he passed severe strictures against me, was the most shocking pack of lies I had ever heard. The Circle Inspector confessed his guilt before the SP, R.F. Mckeevar and me, but the DIG acquitted him. What took my breath away was the absolutely false and undeserved strictures he passed against me, in which he suspected my motives, criticised my ability and damned my character.

I was able to get over the feeling of despondency to some extent, although the fact that I was deeply wronged was uppermost in my mind all the time. I got used to the fact that I had lost; I could not fight the referee. I was prepared to slip away to some hole to lick my wounds in silence. I was fed up with the sordidness of the whole thing, the petty meanness and the indignities. Then, one evening, when I was on a walk, a line from an old song by Maurice Chevalier suddenly occurred to me,

> I have learnt life's lesson,
> It's fighters who always win...

This was my slogan when I went into the hall for my examinations. The man who loses is not the man who refuses to fight, but the man who doubts his ability to win, who hesitates and flags and finally surrenders. If I had entered the fray, it was my duty to fight to the last, and if necessary, go down fighting. I decided to go to the IG and complain to him against the DIG. I decided to tell him how I had been framed and how it had affected me. I decided to tell him, 'Sir, there was a time when I was prepared to die for the department. Now I shall live to get out of it at the first opportunity.'

I went to see the IG in the Circuit House in Jubbulpore with a lot of trepidation. I always felt awkward in the company of Europeans or non-officials or any other whose way of living and thinking was different to my own. When he came out and saw me, he said, "Well! What are you doing here?"

"I came to see you, sir."

"You came to see me?"

"Yes, sir. I came to see *Gone with the Wind* and I thought I'd see you also."

"You haven't been getting on too well in Narsingpur lately. You can't quarrel with your subordinates; bad for discipline."

"That is what I wanted to explain, sir."
"No. No. I don't want to hear anything. I've read reams and reams about it. However, come and see me at 10:30."

I shoved off with a sinking feeling. It wasn't going to be easy.

The IG had apparently formed his ideas from what the DIG had told him and that would not be helpful to me.

I met him at eleven o'clock and began the sad story of my wrongs. Gradually I warmed up to the task. It did not take long to see that the IG did not see eye to eye with the DIG, though initially he had felt that I had not managed the situation tactfully. We had a long talk. During the latter part of it, when I noticed that he was inclined to back me, I took the attitude of the officer who had been wronged and humiliated. I told him about the slow torture. He told me not to worry and continue working hard as before, "I know you are a hardworking officer and have got the place in good order. You managed the Gotegoan riots very well indeed...You must not worry." He said an officer was transferred on complaint if he committed the same mistake again and again.

For days my conversations with the IG kept on recurring in my mind. In fact, one of the greatest lessons I learnt from the DIG episode was that a personal touch and appeal carries more weight than any amount of well thought out logic on paper. I felt if I had not put forward my case clearly and forcibly before the IG, he would have believed all that the DIG had told him. So the lesson was that first establish your reputation with your superior officer, then undertake moves after sounding him out on them, without leaving anything unaccounted.

Taylor left on deputation to Hyderabad and D.G. Watson replaced him as DIG, Jubbulpore. My spirits soared high. I worked hard at my work and I read all that I could find. All the time my maxim had been, 'Prepare yourself for action. When the time comes you should muscle your way upwards and establish yourself. The going would be tough, calling for courage and tenacity.'

In December 1941, I was camping in a tent pitched under the shade of two trees in Suatala village. Dogs barked at the rising moon.

Suddenly the voice of the radio announcer said: "The Admiralty regrets to announce the loss of the battleship *Prince of Wales* and the battle cruiser *Repulse*."

"A world at war," I said aloud. The mad grappling of steel in Europe and Libya had now been supplemented by a war in the Pacific. The Japanese had suddenly attacked Pearl Harbour and American possessions in the Pacific before invading Malaya and North Borneo. The warlords of Japan had run amok. This action of Japan would lead to wars being declared between America and Japan and between Britain and Japan.

Although the threat to India was more dangerous, conditions in the country in 1941 did not favour the setting up of a popular government. The Muslim League continued on its obdurate course of preventing the Congress from taking power. The restlessness among Muslims from the Central Provinces was palpable right from the time I joined the service. To my mind the relations between the two communities began to get strained after the 1937 elections to the provincial assemblies when the Congress came to power in the Central Provinces. Small, insignificant incidents were given a communal colour. The Muslim Sub-Inspector, who was punished on a Hindu Circle Inspector's report, would always ascribe wild motives. The municipality at Gotegaon that had refused to open an Urdu school because there were only ten Muslim children was dubbed tyrannical and anti-Muslim. The Hindu judge, who had given a decision against a Muslim, was considered biased and corrupt. The religious bond among the Muslims found strength with distrust of the majority. Personally I was of the opinion that the Hindu leaders had shown great sympathy for the Muslims and if there was any man who ill-treated them, he was the exception rather than the rule. But the idea of having been wronged always arose when a decision was given against a Muslim.

During the war years from 1939 – 42, the hatred of the average Indian was directed towards the members of the rival community, be it Muslim or Hindu. And what little hatred that was left was directed at Britain. The emotions were so charged that had recruiting depots been thrown open for Muslim and Hindu armies with the object of fighting each other, there would have been no dearth of recruits, with very few at the recruitment booth opting to fight the Japanese.

The Muslim
thinks the Hindus have come into
power and the establishment of a
"Ram Raj" is not far distant. He is
told scare stories by vernacular papers
about the introduction of things called
'Vidya Mandirs'. He gets the impression that
all young Muslim boys are to be forcibly
converted to Hinduism. He reads the
vernacular papers and thinks the
whole of India is seething with
communal discontent.

It seems to me that the
problem is gradually working up
to a crisis and within the next
few years will explode

If today the
Congress adopted Atheism as a creed
(and got away with it) the problem of
a divided India is solved.

At the young age of twenty-two, Rustamji could foresee the consequences of the gradual build up of feelings between the Hindus and Muslims. According to him, the 1937 elections and the formation of the Congress ministry was the start of the communal divide. I have culled out the relevant lines in the lengthy diary entry of 8 December 1938. The last paragraph reads, "If today the Congress adopted Atheism as a creed...the problem of a divided India is solved."

Mass evacuations are a common feature in Indian history — and strange it is — that the originators of the Pakistan scheme do not consider the suffering and tragedy of those rash moves, when they propose their scheme for an exchange of population. There is the example of Muhammad bin Tughlaq, the ill-starred genius, who moved man woman and beast from Delhi to Daulatabad, and caused untold suffering during which several died on the way. In recent years there was the Hijrat which ended in disaster. It is easy to delude public people with hopes of wealth in another town

Camping in Gotetoria village in Narsingpur subdivision, Rustamji wrote in his diary in March 1941, about the originators of the Pakistan scheme not considering the consequences of their proposals for exchange of population.

The 'Hijrat' (Flight of the Faithful) that he has mentioned, probably, refers to what happened in August 1920 when about 18,000 Muslims, instigated by the leaders of the Khilafat Movement, tried to migrate from the then India, which they regarded as the land of infidels (Dar-ul Harab) to Afghanistan, which they believed to be the land of Islam (Dar-ul Islam). The crowd, chanting religious slogans, marched from Landi Kotal in the North West Frontier Province (NWFP, now in Pakistan), through the Khyber Pass to Afghanistan. They were mercilessly driven back by the Afghan government.

Fighting the war with Japan, I felt, would have had a tremendous moral effect. We could have forgotten the past ten years of communal bickering and strife. I felt that by fighting side by side and facing the future together, a tremendous moral force would have united us into a new people. It could have shaken us out of our torpor and hardened and tempered us into a world power.

The enthusiasm for the creation of Pakistan even affected the Muslim officers in the police and other services. During those years I found they would discuss openly and endlessly the accelerated promotion they would get once Pakistan was formed.

The Congress had vowed itself to non-violence and *satyagraha*. The masses were starving and were in no position to subscribe money to any war effort. We had reached a situation in which one party did not want to defend the country because it believed in non-violence, and another believed in fighting its rival rather than its enemy, and the masses were tense because of the danger posed by a total war. There was a general feeling that the war had come perilously close to India and to play with ideals at such a time might prove disastrous.

❧

In June 1942, the post of SP, Chhindwara fell vacant. Being the seniormost ASP, I thought I would be sent to officiate as SP. But Vilayat Hussain, the Deputy SP from Jubbulpore, was sent. Bilaspur too fell vacant subsequently, but I was not sent to officiate there either. There was a sneaking suspicion in my mind that the IG might have found me too junior or too hot-headed to be incharge of a district. I was asked whether I would be willing to go as Aide-de-Camp (ADC) to the Viceroy. I gave my willingness very happily. I wanted to experience the grandeur of the viceroyalty, but after two months, I was told that the proposal to have a police officer and that too, an Indian had been dropped. In sheer frustration, I applied for three months' leave which was sanctioned post-haste. I planned to go to Nagpur and from there proceed on a long vacation to Kashmir with my friend Jal.[2]

---

[2]Admiral Jal Cursetji, who later became Chief of the Naval Staff.

Nagpur 1939
15/8/42.
3 AM.

A Personal Diary of the
Satyagraha Riots - August 42.
12th - 14th

Lale and I came to Nagpur from Narsinghpur on the 5th and till the 10th, when Lale returned we had an extremely gay time. On the 11th I was recalled to duty as the situation in the city had taken a serious turn, and I was asked to report to Trigenza TRIGENZA (DSP) as soon as possible. I was not pleased with the posting because it would mean living and working in Nagpur. However, as there was no option in it, I reported to Trigenza on the evening of the 12th and he sent me off immediately (in my grey bags and the old tweed coat) to take charge of the Kotwali and to be a liaison officer with the troops.

We left in a military convoy in which there were about 7 buses. When we reached the Jumma Talao, the Captain in charge with copy-book efficiency said that there was a crowd in front and it was not possible for him to ~~take~~ take them travel

Rustamji wrote his diary regularly even during the period of the Quit India disturbances.

5

Quit India Disturbances

Jal and I reached Nagpur from Narsingpur on 5 August 1942 and till the 10th, we had an extremely busy and enjoyable time. On the 11th, a mounted constable came to my house with a note saying that I was to report immediately to the SP, E.L. Treganza. I was recalled to duty because the situation in Nagpur city had taken a serious turn as a result of the resolution passed by the Congress at Bombay on 9 August, asking the British to quit India and the subsequent arrest of the national leaders. I met the SP on the evening of the twelfth and tried to get out of a difficult situation by saying that I did not have my uniform with me. But Treganza, who was my SP in Saugor for a few months, would have none of it. "Don't worry about small things, my boy," he said, "This time the Congress has shown its true colours and we must put an end to it." He sent me off immediately to take charge of the *kotwali* (the main police station of Nagpur) and be a liaison officer with the army troops.

We left in a military convoy in which there were about seven buses. When we reached Jumma Talao, Lt Curtis, who was incharge of the army platoon, said it was not possible to take the bus through the crowd in front. Far on our right we could see the Cooperative Bank in flames. We encountered a few roadblocks on Walker Road but we managed to remove them. From the Tilak statue onwards, the obstructions were many and we were constantly stoned. Telephone wires had been cut and tied across the road.

Our plan was to break through to the *kotwali* and then push on to the *tehsili* (office of the *tehsildar*) which was reported to be burnt down. Despite the objection of the senior officers of the Mahar regiment, Michael Sullivan (an ICS officer) and I were able to get two platoons and a few policemen together. We pushed on with them and on arrival at the *tehsili* found it was safe and the attackers had been beaten back by firing at the crowd.

On our way to the *kotwali*, a couple of stones were thrown at us, and the Mahars were so upset that they began to take pot shots at people in the windows. This 'accidental shooting', which Sullivan claimed had done a lot of good, was stopped by me.

At the *kotwali*, I was appalled to see the confusion among the police. There was no account of the men on duty. Incident upon incident was reported, but none was recorded or acted upon. There was no plan of action. There was absolutely no system at all. Anarchy prevailed all over the city. Most of the police outposts had been burnt down and the men manning them had fled in terror. Nothing was known of the men in the Police Lines in the city. The whole city had been left at the mercy of the revolutionaries. Government servants were attacked and police constables were badly beaten up in several places. The crowd was very violent and the police was not adequately equipped to face them boldly. Since the police outposts in Itwari were burnt down and no alternate arrangements were made, the mobs had a free run of the area.

I found my position most peculiar. Kesar Singh Kuckreja continued to be the City Superintendent of Police (CSP) and I was unable to decide what my position in the whole show was. I had no authority and Treganza had said that I was to be a liaison officer with the army. Kesar Singh, the elderly and experienced officer, who rose from the ranks, disliked my interference and wanted to continue in his own way — a way which I knew to be wrong but which I felt powerless to counter.

At ten o'clock in the night, we learnt that a big crowd had begun looting a grain godown situated behind Maneck Talkies. A short distance away from the theatre, we saw a few people take grain away. We found a gang of at least 150 people looting a nearby godown. A constable, Kedar and I rushed in. The looters tried to get out, and with the police at the door and the looters pushing from inside, the door got jammed and we were locked in with about sixty men. We were face to face with the looters. There were a few scraps and then we were all on the floor in a grand melee. Meanwhile, the police burst the door open and came in. They began to beat about indiscriminately with their lathis. One savage blow landed on my ankle which left me limping for the next one week or so. Just then, the Mahar Regiment boys rushed in and Lt Curtis started firing with a Tommy gun.[1] Three shots whizzed past us. It was a very near miss. I crouched against the side of the wall and shouted, crazy with fear, "Curtis, what the hell are you doing? Stop it!"

Fortunately for us, the man realised his mistake and ceased firing. Curtis was most apologetic. Again and again he said he had made a bloody mistake, and thanked God that nobody had been injured. We arrested eighty-one people.

Thereafter, Curtis behaved with exemplary courage and restraint. Once he and his platoon along with me were cornered in a blind alley by a violent mob. He fired two shots in the air and the mob dispersed. We came out alive. We opened fire at a few other places, dispersed crowds mainly near the grain godowns but fired always in the air to frighten the crowds away. Not one man was killed. Curtis entirely agreed with my action, but there were messages from senior officers alleging that we were soft on the agitators and that the city would soon go out of control.

The next day we went to the Pachpaoli Police Lines and then to the *tehsili* despite being stoned all along the way. Sullivan took a rifle from one of the policemen on duty and started firing at a group of youngsters who were erecting roadblocks. I snatched the rifle from his hand. Another defender of the Empire, a military officer, opened fire with his revolver at a woman who had thrown a stone at him. I presumed he had hit her because we heard a scream and moan. We saw a pool of blood. I tried to warn the defenders that clumsy fire in revenge would not help to bring the situation under control. In fact, it would have just

[1]Thompson Machine Carbine (TMC), a deadly weapon.

the opposite effect. They probably reported to the Governor that I was too weak to deal with the situation.

The next day when we were at the boathouse on the tank, a convoy came through with A.G. Scott (IG), G.W. Benton (DIG) and T.M. Collins (DIG) to review the situation. Since Benton was in the group and he knew me well, I made a complaint against Sullivan that he had snatched rifles from the men and fired at crowds blindly. I tried to explain my action in trying to save the grain godowns rather than open fire and kill people on the streets. I pleaded for time and patience, while they talked about the war and dangers of a Japanese attack. I told them all that I was interested in was using minimum force and allowing the return to normalcy after which we could take legal action. The use of unlimited force against the people tends to embitter them. Mass movements of disorder should, of course, be brought under control, but indiscriminate suppression should not be used. The average Indian mob cannot maintain its frenzy for more than a week. Lassitude and laziness assert themselves. The proper action to take under such circumstances was to allow the frenzy to die down and then take the usual legal action to punish the wrongdoers. I ended by saying, "The economic compulsions of poor people are such that no breakdown of law and order can continue for long."

They however, did not agree. There was no word of encouragement; no credit for my action. A lack of system and the apparent muddle were made much of. I was told that I would be replaced by another officer who would "batter the bastards into submission."

I suddenly felt disheartened and devoid of energy. Had they uttered a couple of encouraging words, I would probably have had a different feeling, as, from my point of view, it was a wonderful experience. I saw what a big city looks like during a major disturbance. I faced the music and came out of the ordeal with confidence in myself. Every step I took convinced me that it was my judgement which was always proven right.

The senior officers lost no time in carrying out what they had threatened to do. I was shifted from the charge in the city. It fell to my lot to control the situation at Maudha, a small station house situated on the bank of River Kanhan, about twenty-two miles from Nagpur.

The disturbances that occurred were initially confined to Nagpur city. When stern measures were adopted in the city, it gradually spread to the interiors. Reports of destruction in Ramtek, followed by Umar, Khapa and Maudha poured in.

We started in a police bus with a small force of eleven men at four o'clock in the evening. Some time was spent in removing the roadblocks on the way. The mob attempted to burn down the Station House but could only partially succeed because the building was solid. But every scrap of paper and every stick of furniture was burnt down. We spent an uncomfortable night in eerie silence expecting to be attacked at any moment by a superior force, which we would not be able to face confidently because we had only six muskets at our disposal and the rest of the men were newly recruited constables armed with lathis. In the morning we pushed towards Baroda village and searched an orange grove belonging to Maganlal Bagri. We were surprised to find a big bungalow set up as the headquarters for the Hindustan Red Army (HRA)[2], known locally as the Hindustani Lal Sena. There was no trace of the HRA men. (Much later I learnt that the HRA men thought we had come heavily armed with a large force and would swoop down upon them in the wee hours of the night; so they had quietly slipped away).[3]

All the disturbances in the area situated on the Bhandara Road were alleged to have been organised by Maganlal Bagri, the leader of the HRA. We seized a photograph from the house

---

[2] Hindustani Lal Sena was formed on 13 April 1939 — the anniversary of the Jallianwala Bagh massacre of 1919. The objective of this Sena was to wage an armed struggle against the British using guerilla tactics. Its leader, Maganlal Bagri joined Congress and became a Member of Parliament from Hoshangabad in present day Madhya Pradesh in 1957. He defeated H.V. Kamath, the ICS officer who had resigned from service in 1938 and plunged into the freedom movement.

[3] According to an article written by a Muslim scholar in the *Indian Express*, dated 7 August 1997, Maudha remained 'free' from British rule for four days before it was recaptured. Rustamji gave me a graphic description of Maudha incident and how dangerous it was. It was his pluck, courage and luck which saved him. After return from Maudha, he prepared his 'will' distributing Rs 1,000 (the only money he had) among his relatives and his books to K.B. Lall and his guns to R.C.V.P. Noronha, the two ICS friends of his.

which showed that he was a tall and well built man, with big eyes, prominent cheekbones and an aggressive chin. Dressed in uniform he stood beside his wife who was seated on a chair.

Two days later I was asked to go to the temple town of Ramtek, where the *tehsili* building was set on fire, the strongroom was broken open and the mob treated themselves to three lakhs in cash waiting to be looted. The frenzy of the crowd knew no bounds. They took some of the money and burnt the rest, as the rioters felt that they should destroy anything that carried the photograph of King George VI. Then they set fire to the station house, the civil court and the warehouse.

The information was conveyed to Nagpur. Maynard, Collins and a troop of men under B.M. Shukul left for the place. There was complete stillness when they reached Ramtek. I was ordered to camp for a few days at Ramtek where some Muslim subordinate police officers had collected a large crowd and converted it almost into a concentration camp. I began releasing them. That again went against the thinking on the subject and I was moved out from there and brought back to the city.

My position with the British was weakened by an official Congress report that said, "Rustamji acted with moderation and had saved the city from much trouble." Added to that were the reports of my brother, Rustam's instigation of the students of the Law College to sabotage. A section of the Muslim officers in the Criminal Investigation Department (CID) had conveyed all sorts of stories to the IG, including incitement by my brother of students in the Law College to rise against British rule. I could sense that the ground was being prepared for my exit.

During the course of disturbances I felt I might get killed. There were situations in which I was placed where life and death were frightfully balanced, and the only thing which pulled me out was my destiny. Luck might not always favour me. I had a feeling I might be caught in a trap and done to death. I might be killed by mistake. I might be caught by a crowd and dismembered limb from limb. Oh yes, death stalks a policeman very close behind. I would hate to die a gentleman. It was my hope and high endeavour that when the call comes, I would answer it with all the fury at my disposal, and rather than surrender I will struggle and hit out till there was life in me.

It was not that I feared death. I just wanted to live. I thought if I die, I would regret that I was not present at the reconstruction of the world after the war. I thought, thus far I have lived life with gusto and if I die, I should die with gusto.

The acts of sabotage were, in my opinion, an expression of resentment over the arrests of popular leaders, leading to accumulation of frustration and hatred over time. But there were indications about what shape the movement was to follow was laid down, in some vague manner, by the Congress Working Committee (CWC), and circulated to the provinces. This was evident from the fact that the disturbances followed the same pattern in all the provinces — disruption of communication, obstruction of government servants and picketing of schools and colleges.

The movement was probably designed by the Congress, but the methods used did not appear to be theirs. They were the methods of violent organisations who had usurped the powers and authority of the Congress when the leaders were put in jail.

The arrests of the members of the CWC led to organisation of meetings, delivering of incendiary speeches and disturbances in the city on the afternoon of 12 August. A big mob attacked the post office and set it on fire, looting the cash and valuables. In the Sitabuldi area of the city, a postal lorry was burnt. Mobs went on rampage in several parts of the city and in the interiors. At that stage when the administration had practically lost control of the city, the Mahars were sent out to strike terror and inspire respect.

In Nagpur city, the disturbances were controlled by three men at the top — Farquahar, Treganza and Wright. The District Magistrate (DM), Farquahar, was an astute and amusing administrator, who was hardworking, efficient and clownish. Treganza, nominally the SP, was struck down with dysentery, and was unable to move about. He was the most intriguing of the three. He had the vision and the intellect, but he was peevish, unsystematic and thoroughly unamenable to reason in discussions. Hard-drinking had shattered his nerves, so that he could not face any situation calmly. He believed strongly in controlling things from the control room and never went out to lead the men, with the result that the city was unprepared for the disturbances or for countermeasures.

The third man, F.G.G. Wright was quite the opposite of Treganza. He was small, precise and always unperturbed. He did not have big ideas, but was exact and decisive in all the things he did. As a policeman, I always admired his grasp of police work, his ability to liven up things without the rantings and ravings which are typical of senior police officers, and more than all of them, I admired the tact with which he handled Treganza. He admirably illustrated the value of discussion. He always seemed to agree and yet things were done differently from the way 'Trigger' (Treganza) had proposed.

The most striking impression of every Indian who was involved in suppressing the disturbances was the utter panic and ruthlessness which seized European officials. Whenever any disorder occurred, the average European official lost his head and ordered an indiscriminate use of force and retaliation. They dubbed it a rebellion. Officials with thirty years of experience of the country behaved with vindictiveness and spite which would have shamed Nero and his satellites. They ordered firing, indiscriminate searches and arrests, beat up all who dared to face the police and the army on the streets, imposed heavy collective fines on villages and meted out atrocious punishments to all those who gave themselves up to the police. It seemed as though all the hatred and mistrust they felt towards the people of this land were suddenly exposed in all their nakedness. Scruples, honesty and 'being a gentleman' were abandoned. They even forgot their invaluable sense of humour, which had enabled them to survive so many shocks. They behaved like panic-stricken savages, resorting to brutal force which plunged the country into a bloodbath of suffering and hatred.

The British were under a certain amount of pressure in 1942. After the ignominious evacuation of the British forces from Dunkirk in June 1940, there were a series of other setbacks like the sinking of the *Prince of Wales*, the reverses in the African desert, the Japanese conquest of Malaya and finally, their advance to the borders of India. It was at this time that the British felt that they were fighting with their backs to the wall and their attitude towards Indian Independence tended to harden. They felt that the freedom struggle was obstructing the war effort and that the Congress leaders were insensitive to the difficulties they were facing back home. The British officers, therefore, wanted stringent action to be undertaken to quell the revolts and the agitations. But it must be said in favour of the British that even the repressive measures taken by them were within limits except at some places where officers lost their heads. The number of casualties, however, even in a mass movement like the Quit India was not very many.[4]

The government published a report under the title *Congress Responsibility for the Disturbances, 1942 – 43*. There was no formal enquiry; no enquiry commission was constituted. The report released by Sir George Tottenham, the Secretary to Government of India, Home Department appeared to have been drafted by the Director, IB. It was a totally one-sided report, incorrect in many details and grossly exaggerated. The report put the blame on young military officers. What Tottenham tried to make out was that the Congress was damaging the war effort in a big way, thus calling for firm measures. The Tottenham report was critical of one aspect of policing and that was intelligence. As a consequence, intelligence agencies in the provinces and at the Centre were expanded and steps were taken to introduce vehicles, radio, etc.

The effects of the Civil Disobedience Movement were felt most by the government servants. There was a conflict of duties and ideas. The father, a government servant attached by duty to his post knowing that the bread of the family came from the government. The son, a hot-headed college youth in whom the firing by the military and the death of a friend or a comrade had caused intense bitterness. It was a strange phenomenon that the children of almost all government servants participated actively in the movement. The position of the fathers who were government servants was

[4]According to records in the National Archives of India, the number of fatal casualties in Central Provinces was eight while all over India it was sixty-three, as quoted by Francis G. Hutchins in *Spontaneous Revolutions – The Quit India Movement*. According to D.G. Tendulkar, "The civilian casualties from August 1942 to November 1942 were over 900 killed according to official figures..." (*Mahatma – Life of Mohandas Karamchand Gandhi* – Vol. VI).

more conflicting. The majority of them had some sort of sympathy with the movement. But they were egged on by people above them to use repressive measures and put down the "rebellion." They knew the agitators whom they had to handle and could judge their reactions better than the Englishmen. They felt that tactless handling of the situation would aggravate it to an extent when it would become unmanageable. But they could not disclose their ideas to their superior officers. It was most uncomfortable to fight on two fronts — one before and the other behind.

I too found myself in a delicate situation. One day, on returning home after facing a tiring and danger-ridden situation, I saw a tall person leaving the house. He avoided looking at me. I asked my brother Rustam, who saw him off, as to who he was as his face looked familiar. Rustam replied, "He is Maganlal Bagri."

I was shell-shocked. I shouted at Rustam, "Why did you allow him to come inside?"

"He was staying in our outhouse for the last few days."

I remonstrated violently with Rustam. The man who was most wanted by the police, the man whose followers could have done me to death, how could he give sanctuary to such a person and put me in an embarrassing situation?

Rustam, who was intensely nationalistic, replied calmly, "Khush, you do your duty, I do mine."

It became a delicate situation at home, one brother doing his best to end the British rule and the other trying his best to preserve it. I seriously considered resigning from service, but my father did not favour it. He said it would be a pity to leave such a good service and such a good opportunity to serve the people. He said I c ould ask for leave and praised me for doing the right thing by saving lives, banks and grain godowns.

Once the disturbances subsided, I requested the authorities to be relieved and allowed to continue with my leave. I devoted the period of leave to reading. On the expiry of my leave period, I was posted as SDOP to Khamgaon and later it was changed to Ellichpur in Amraoti district.

Ellichpur was a small subdivisional town with not much work. A posting in such small places made the thoughts in my mind always run in a groove. If someone had been unkind to me it rankled and poisoned the line of thought. If I read a book, my thoughts were a reflection of the angle from which I looked at it. If I thought of writing, I became despondent, cynical and dull. I always felt an irresistible urge to write but I tried to control it with an absurd objection that writing was really not good for one's career. I had a mortal fear of being dubbed a 'writer'. I felt I would die of shame if someone in the department called me a 'playwright'. I spent my time touring the whole subdivision.

On 24 November 1942, when I returned from a tour, I found an orderly waiting for me with a telegram. I opened it with cold, trembling fingers. Mummy used to say, "Whenever you get a telegram, be prepared for bad news." And the telegram read:

> "My warm congratulations on your well-deserved Indian Police Medal awarded by His Excellency, the Viceroy. — Governor."

I gave a curt, heroic laugh and walked into the house. I went into the dressing room and saw myself in the mirror. No change was apparent, but then, I had always considered myself heroic. I went about the house, from room to room, my jubilation mounting with every step. I looked at myself in the mirror again. Gosh, what a life! What a marvellous world! If only I could tell someone of my good luck, climb on top of the house and shout as loud as I could, and laugh and laugh. But the servants were looking. I hummed, *Yankee-doodle went to town*...the desire to tell someone became overpowering! Yet, all the time I was wondering why I had been awarded the medal.

I got into the car and rushed to the SDO (Civil) Paranjpe's house. He was not at home. A grand feeling of conceit mixed with satisfaction and exhilaration engulfed me. I seemed to be glowing inside; however the kick was missing. No one around to flatter me; no one to say how proud she was of me. For the first time I realised that to get the most out of joy, one has to share it with someone. I sat at the desk and wrote a letter to Kishan (K.B. Lall). Timi seemed to smile at me from the desk. If only I could see her and kiss that delicate neck.

By four o'clock in the evening, I began to feel damn fed up. Here was a memorable day which was being ruined by doing nothing. To find relief from depression I decided to take Paranjpe out for a drink. We shared rum with Tatia Saheb, a kindly old man who liked to feed officials. That little escapade saved the day for me and the redeeming feature was when Paranjpe brought away the half-empty bottle of rum from Tatia Saheb's house, so that we could drink it later on. Then we went to see *Naya Sansar* (meaning 'New World') in the Talkies. I went to sleep, muttering *Naya Sansar* as a whole new world seemed to open before me.

The citation given along with the Indian Police Medal read:

> "Mr K.F. Rustamji, IP, Assistant Superintendent of Police was recalled from leave and posted to Nagpur district on the outbreak of the recent disturbances. He rendered exemplary and courageous service in dealing with several dangerous situations in the Nagpur city. In addition, he led the police relief party to Moudha station house, which had been subjected to an armed attack and burnt, and, visiting village Baroda, the headquarters of the dangerous Hindustan Red Army gangster, Maganlal Bagri, and effectively restored order in that area."

The citation to the medal awarded to Constable No.213, Kedar read:

> "In the course of a raid on a criminal quarter in the Nagpur city during the recent disturbances, he and Mr. Rustamji, Assistant Superintendent of Police, were trapped in a godown, where they were attacked by a violent band of about fifty looters. When Mr. Rustamji was temporarily incapacitated owing to injuries, Constable Kedar grimly stood over him and repelled repeated attacks by effective use of his lathi until help arrived."

I went to Nagpur to receive the medal on 11 February 1943. When I called on the IG Police, Scott, he got up to shake hands and congratulated me, saying, "Rustamji, we made a thorough appraisal of the situation after the disturbances and have come to the conclusion that your tactics were appropriate. The city had been saved from much damage by the restraint that you had urged on us. You were right. We were wrong."

It's only a Britisher who could have said such a thing. My father always used to say that it was a peculiar characteristic of the Englishmen that if you said they were wrong, they disliked it; but if you were proved right, they felt you had merit and should be pushed up.

It's amazing how things work out in the end! I was replaced because I refused to "batter the bastards into submission." I became a suspect in their eyes after the Muslim officers in the CID[5] had reported to the authorities about my brother's attempts to create problems and also because of the report of the Nagpur District Congress Committee. 'God save the King,' I muttered to myself.

In hindsight, I feel the medal was awarded to me because the effects of World War II began to be felt around the end of 1942. Prices rose and many things fell in short supply. Even a matchbox was difficult to get. Food shortages occurred in a big way, leading to the horrible Bengal famine in 1943. All these contributed to changing the whole pattern of administration and people's respect for law and order. My action in trying to save the granaries and the treasuries rather than killing people on the streets appeared to have been appreciated.

The award of the Indian Police Medal and the rumours of a posting to a district made me acceptable to the Europeans in Amraoti district. I drew close to an Englishwoman, who was petite and charming. What I liked best about her was her nature, her sense of humour and her loud, unrestrained laugh. She and I developed a peculiar teasing relationship over which we slipped a cover of formality to avoid misunderstandings. During the New Year's party at the Amraoti Club, while we were dancing, with her deft footwork, she guided me aside to one corner and kissed me. Our love affair lasted exactly one week. She was my boss's wife!

---

[5] In the pre-Independence days, the CID (Intelligence) branch was manned mostly by Anglo-Indians, Christians and Muslims in many of the states.

Khandwa
28th March 43.

— So I became a D.S.P.

On the 22nd March 1943 in the 26th year of my life I became a D.S.P. of the district of Khandwa C.P. This was about a year after I should have become a D.S.P., but having shown intemperance acting in Narsinghpur I was held back, and now that I have settled down and become a "pucca sahib" I am considered fit to hold charge of a district.

Being a D.S.P. seems to have made a few changes in me. It has sobered me to some extent. I hold myself in check. I stifle the brilliant remark which would have evoked a guffaw in former days. The work being greater I feel less buoyant in my free moments. I look more dignified. I feel less confident. I think time is precious. I don't want to meet un-intelligent people. I'd rather keep to myself.

In the erstwhile Central Provinces, the police chief of a district was known as District Superintendent of Police (DSP). Later it was shortened to SP. I have used the later designation all through the book to avoid confusion with Deputy Superintendent of Police.

6

Effects of War and Famine

On 22 March 1943 in the twenty-sixth year of my life, I was promoted as an SP. My subconscious kept on saying, 'They have given me an important district like Khandwa; I must be a damn good fellow.' As an ASP, I looked upon myself as a callow, sumptuous, self-assured, theoretical and ignorant youth. Becoming an SP brought about a few changes in me. The promotion sobered me to some extent. I started holding myself in check. I started stifling the brilliant remarks which would have evoked guffaws in earlier days. I felt less buoyant in my free moments; looked more dignified and felt less confident. I did not want to meet unintelligent people. I distrusted people around me. I felt older, balder, less attractive but very wise. I realised that brilliance is flashy, and what was required was hard work, tact and thoughtful insight. Being an SP was infinitely more fun than being an SDOP, it was a grand feeling! One felt independent, more free. The exhilaration of promotion proved to be heady.

Having got an important charge at a young age, I began presuming that after a time my plays would be produced, my books would be read. I would be known in the country. I would go as the IGP to a princely State or become DIG in the Central Province.

Then when I would be nearing fifty, I would be among the greatest police officers in the land[1]. All those thoughts came to me either because the promotion had disturbed my ego or because Ethel Mannin's book, *Confessions and Impressions* had made my mind go topsy-turvy.

I was given a warm reception in the club, which was the centre of all activity. All gathered there, from the civil to the military. From the military side came the high-spirited officers of the Hyderabad and Patiala Lancers. On the civil side, there were Daddy Chelam, Tasdiq, the District Forest Officer (DFO), Abraham, the Civil Surgeon and all led by the DC, Khan Bahadur Fazle Karim Khan, who happened to be an old family friend.

The club was our main site for interaction in the field of administration. I could discuss with the Sessions Judge some case while we awaited our turn to play tennis. He would tell me about his suspicions about an investigation. The Colonel would tell me informally about his suspicions regarding a case in which one of his men had run amuck. Several rainy days were spent in playing dumb charades and gambling; we even produced a play written by a Hindi teacher for us. There was cricket sometimes. Often the entire club would go to the local cinema, and at the request of Khan Bahadur, all the reels of song and dance would be shown again while the crowd below cheered.

In Khandwa, I got on well with Riaz Naik, a young ICS officer who hailed from Punjab. Both of us were bachelors and he used to discuss his love affair with a non-Muslim girl. Riaz and his friend Maqbul often gave me impassioned readings of the poems of Mohammed Iqbal, the great Urdu poet and also explained the meaning of the poetry. Interesting sidelights on the life of Iqbal were thrown in by Riaz who had met the poet frequently in his lifetime owing to his friendship with the poet's son. Riaz said that the poet was allergic to anyone using his toilet and on one occasion

---

[1]Rustamji became Director General of the BSF in August 1965, at the age of forty-nine. His thoughts mentioned in the diary of 28 March 1943 appear very prescient.

he stopped Riaz and told him to advise his friend, (the poet's son) not to urinate in his toilet. Riaz said he had the unique distinction of having kicked a football straight at the poet's head and that drew out a stream of abuses, which were far from being poetic. (Riaz went over to Pakistan after Independence.)

Our tours to the tribal areas were full of colour and costume. The villagers received us with pipe and drum, followed by firing of two shots in our honour before we were shown a dance recital (which the Sub-Inspector had arranged) and which went on till the wee hours even after we had asked to be excused. The celebrations still went on and when we woke up in the morning, we found the drums pounding away still.

The effect of the war was not quite apparent at first. By the fourth year of the war, in October 1943, people became tired of it and began hoping to see it end soon. The prices of all commodities shot up. Travel was almost impossible owing to the rush in trains. And above all, there was the constant dread that the Japanese would break through Assam and invade the country. In Bengal, thousands lay dying of starvation.

In normal times, India produced enough grain for her own requirements, but the war caused a shortage in most parts of the country. As soon as the war began, prices of essential commodities began to rise. Profiteers hoped that prices would rise still further and hoarded their stocks. The withdrawal of grain from the markets created panic. The average man in the country stored grain to provide for emergency. The demand for grain being great and stocks in the market being low, prices began to increase alarmingly. The government decided to fix the prices of food grains in accordance with the prices prevalent in the Nagpur market.

The thin trickle of grain soon ceased altogether. The middle classes had stored enough grain for emergencies of this nature and could fall back on their hoarded stock, but the poor cultivators and labourers, who had not foreseen the contingency, were suddenly faced with starvation. Large crowds marched to the offices of government servants. Starving people collected at the few government grain shops that were still functioning — a tearing, screaming mass of humanity with each individual trying to climb over his neighbour and get a few grains before the stocks got exhausted. The government came to the conclusion that the best way to handle the situation was to remove price controls and go back to free trade, or a semblance of it. Price checks were lifted and grain again began to flow into the market, but at exorbitantly high prices. Meanwhile the occupation of Burma deprived the country of a large part of its rice imports and paddy prices rose further still. Cultivators, attracted by the fancy prices, sold off most of their stocks. A few months later they could not get any grain at all. In several places the people lived on grass, leaves and roots of trees. A good *jowar* crop was, however, harvested to avert any tragedy. The cultivator became careful and hoarded his grain to save himself. The urban population, and more so in Bengal, did not get enough of it. Rationing and procurement schemes were belatedly introduced, but the rot had set in to become an endemic.

No public outcry was raised against the profiteer but the brunt of the blame was borne by the government. In Bengal, the famine was caused to some extent due to official muddle. Their calculations went absolutely wrong. Thousands succumbed to a horrible death by becoming victims of profiteers, hoarders and incompetent administrators.

The majority of provincial governments showed ample foresight to save their districts from starvation. We owe a deep debt of gratitude to the many DCs, who amidst several baffling problems and hatred of the common people against the Englishmen, worked with untiring zeal and devotion. They faced criticism and ridicule from above and below. They were never encouraged or commended by the people whom they served. Yet they did their best to help the people of the country they served.

As soon as war was declared, the government tried to curb profiteering by passing the Defence of India Act which helped only in driving foreign goods into the black market. The prices of all articles soared but articles, which were not manufactured in India, became scarce. Tennis balls, which before the war were available for 8 – 10 annas (fifty to sixty paise) per dozen were sold for Rs 90; razor blades at Rs 3 – 8 annas per packet; fan belts which used to sell for 14 annas (about 90 paise) could be had for Rs 65; a bottle of John Haig Scotch whisky which was earlier available for Rs 6 could be had for Rs 60. (Before the war, Scotch whisky was priced between Rs 6 to Rs 12 a bottle depending on the brand). With the non-availability of foreign goods, the *swadeshi* campaign died a natural death.

Salaries of government servants became unattractive. As a result of inflation, the power that vested with the government officials led to a staggering increase in corruption among the subordinate officers. It appeared that as soon as conditions returned to normal, a vigorous anti-corruption drive would have to be undertaken.

Because of the war, some English words passed into the vocabulary of rural India. Words like 'bomb' and 'aeroplane' became known to everyone, but the word which had the widest currency and the greatest dread was 'control'. In the remotest villages, 'control' inspired awe and fear because of the manner in which control had worked against the people. Grain control sent grain underground; sugar control swept sugar away from the market; matchboxes were sold only as an obligation owing to the 'control' on them. (Match boxes were imported from Norway and Sweden. The local company WIMCO could not meet the demand). 'Control' rice, 'control' sugar, 'control' cloth signified second-rate items obtained with difficulty.

Before the war, the railways begged you to travel. During the war they dictated to you the terms on which you were allowed to travel. First, you could only travel if you were a military officer, man of the Food and Civil Supplies Department or a person connected with the war effort. Secondly, you must not talk about military matters and the general conduct of war. Thirdly, you must travel light and take your food with you. All over could be seen posters of a soldier pointing a finger at you and saying, "We did it in 1918, we will do it again."

Throughout India, the worst years of the war, 1943 – 45, were the years in which the relations between the Hindus and Muslims were most cordial, as attention was focused on the grim situation due to the war, the famine and the struggle for existence and the threat posed by Japan.

In 1943, I invited my parents and family members to come over to Khandwa. Mummy brought up the question of my marriage with superb artistry. For the first few days nothing was mentioned. I was tactfully told what a good house Rusi Vevaina kept and what a bad house mine was in comparison. The next phase of the campaign was mainly propaganda. I was given vivid descriptions of all the marriages which had occurred in the recent past and how prospective brides were all disappearing, girl by girl. I was told there were very few left and even they would be snatched up in the sudden rush that had occurred owing to the war. Then I was told that all the people whom I knew were anxiously waiting to see me get married and after all, they all wanted my good. The last phase of the campaign nearly brought me down. I was tactfully informed that my good looks were fast disappearing, that I wasn't as handsome as I thought I was, and it might come as a rude shock to my pride if I found that I had been rejected by the girls continuously owing to my baldness and my incipient paunch.

It would not be true to say that the propaganda did not affect me. It did. Inwardly I felt that I could not have friendships with women without loss of face in a small remote district place. A conflict raged within me. At times I thought I was not yet fit for marriage and other times, I thought I was getting old and bald and if ever I found the person I was looking for, she might not approve of me. So later that year, for the first time in my life, I agreed to appear for a marriage interview in Bombay. When we reached the house, we found the whole family standing outside to greet us. We went in. There were so many girls sitting around that it was difficult to tell who was the girl intended for me. I was so rapt in talking to one of the married girls whom I had met before her marriage and found very attractive that I completely forgot that I was there to make the all important choice. Cakes and drinks were served. I was babbling merrily when suddenly there was a terrific crash as though a whole set of china had been thrown on the ground. The family was quite calm and took it very well.

If such an incident had occurred in our house, all of us would have rushed inside to see what had happened. Papa would have shouted, "What's happened? Is anybody hurt?" Noor Mohammed and one of the sisters would have accused each other; Mummy would have added her bit and finally one of the girls would have burst into tears. But here, the host said it was the Frigidaire tray which had fallen and merely laughed it off.

For a few days nothing more was heard and I assumed that I had been rejected. A year later, in April 1944, I was asked to go over to Bombay to see a girl. I took leave for a few days and left Khandwa on 29 April. If I had delayed it by a day, I would not have been allowed to go as on that date Mr Gandhi was released from jail and his condition was bad. The government was apprehensive that in case of his death, there would be large-scale unrest in the country.

The train was three hours late when I reached the station. I went back to the club and was drinking with the crowd when I heard the *Peshawar Express* steaming into Khandwa. I said goodbye hurriedly. Khan Bahadur Fazle Karim, the DC, shouted from a distance, "*Aur agar koi aachhi chokri mil jaye, toh saath mey ley aana.*"(And if you find a good lass, bring her along with you).

I shouted back, "No fear. There is no danger of that," and drove out of the club. Near the rest house, the fuel ran out and I began to run to the station. However, I was given a lift in his jeep by an officer of the Patiala Lancers and he drove at breakneck speed through the town to drop me at the station on time.

In Bombay, Gooly (Goolcheher, my sister) very obligingly told me that there was an awfully nice person whom she knew. Would I like to meet her? I said 'yes' and she told me that she had phoned her up and she had agreed to come out with us the next day.

On 1 May, at about 5:30 p.m., Papa first came and informed me that the visitors had arrived, one of whom was a charming young girl. I pulled down my tunic, patted the remnants of my hair to conceal the bald patch and strode into the 'West End' of the Sanatorium (Parsee *dharmshala*) from our end. I saw a fair girl dressed in white, sitting very demurely on a chair — 'good looking — yes; seems good natured too; nice laugh; speaks with a good accent; nice eyes; very interesting,' I said to myself.

Since none of the others broached the topic of going out for a drive as we had planned, in utter desperation, I suggested it myself. It was reluctantly accepted. Rusi Vevaina and I sat in front, Gooly, Homai and 'the girl' behind. At Juhu, we sat for a brief while in Vevaina's house and then went for a walk on the beach. I was surprised to find all my companions slipping away and leaving me alone with the beautiful girl in white, who had a fascinating aura around her. I was irresistibly drawn towards her and followed her throughout the evening.

After we returned home and had finished dinner, Gooly said, "And how do you like the girl?" I said she was charming. I was asked to decide whether I would like to marry the girl or not. The decision was a difficult one because I had fought against the idea of marriage relentlessly for several years. I tried to play for time but was informed that I had to make up my mind at once. If I saw the girl a few more times and took her out, it would be difficult for the girl and embarrassing for me. I told them I would sleep over the question and give them my decision the next morning.

I spent a sleepless night, with a relentless struggle waging within. One part of me seemed to be all for the girl and a happy married life; another part wanted me to travel, see the world, have a good time before I settled down into the rut and began doling out babies with precision. It was impossible to sleep. At two o'clock in the morning, I got up and sat in the balcony. Moonlight revealed the tall palm trees swaying beautifully. I could hear the surf beating breathlessly against the rocks of Cumballa Hill. I was immersed in deep thought. Bombay had begun to stir from her sleep. Occasionally a car drove along the road. I could hear the trams moving. The milkman walked past the door with his squeaky boots and the clanking bottles. It was another day for so many people — a day like any other day; for me it was the beginning of a love.

To decide was to act. There was no time to lose because I had only seven days' leave. I, therefore, informed them that I had made up my mind to marry the girl, provided she was willing to have me.

Since I had made up my mind to marry her, there was nothing to stop me. I rang her up and asked her whether she would be willing to come out with me for lunch followed by a matinee show. She agreed. I went to Ness Baug in Grant Road and asked an old Parsee woman where the girl named Naju, whose surname I did not know, stayed. She told me to go to the fourth floor. By the time I reached there, I believe, she rang up Naju's mother and told her, "A tall man wearing shorts is coming to meet your daughter. Be careful." (I always wore shorts when I went to Bombay. In those days people looked at me curiously, wondering who I was and where I came from).

We went to the Sea Lounge restaurant in the Taj Mahal Hotel. I looked into the huge mirrors to see how we looked as a couple. After lunch, we went to see Mickey Rooney in *Girl Crazy* and I continued the onward march. Before the end of the picture, I held her hand and kissed her tentatively on her hair.

On 3 May, we again lunched at the Taj and went to see *North Star*. Both of us seemed rather withdrawn. When I went to drop her to her house, she said, "Please wait. I want to return you your money." I told her I would take it later on. She replied, "Maybe I won't see you again."

I was aghast. I had another sleepless night. In the morning I was told that she had got the impression that I was playing the fool and was only meeting her as part of a pleasant holiday. Early next morning, I rang her up and asked if she would come out for lunch. There was a little urgency in my voice. When we met I said I was sorry and she also apologised for her behaviour. It was over in a trice. We started competing with each other in saying 'sorry'.

We went to our church on the hill and sat on our favourite seat. I started off in a typical bureaucratic fashion. I said, "I've got something important to say to you, Naju. I'm going to ask you to marry me, but before I pop the question, I am going to put the pros and cons before you, because we must not have any illusions or delusions about this business. Cons first, then the pros...the first con is that you will probably have to spend most of your life with me in the districts — small places, where there isn't much to do. There are very few people. There aren't any cinemas, or hotels, or dances or races. You'll have to decide whether, after being born and brought up in Bombay, you will be able to live that sort of life with me. The second con is that I am by no means a rich man. My pay is Rs 675 per month — enough to subsist on, but nothing very much when you consider the number of things you will have to do without. As for the pros, I love you. I feel that we can be happy together and I will try my best to make you happy. Now, will you marry me?"

She said she would say 'yes' for herself, but would ask her parents. So I kissed her and she kissed me and I kissed her and so on.

We got engaged. I presented her with a pendant watch, which she treasured for a long time.

Being engaged is no pleasure if you have to live hundreds of miles away from your fiancée and depend on letters for intimacy. An engagement is a link between a kind of life that is dying and another that is struggling to be born. Naju and her people were originally of the opinion that the wedding should be in December, but Papa and Mummy did not find the time suitable. Mummy's idea was to have the whole family for the wedding and combine the visit to Bombay for the summer and Papa's eye operation with the festivities of the wedding. The others heartily approved of the idea because it fitted with their plans for celebration. I was relegated to the position of a mere bridegroom — a pawn in the game. The uncertainty and the delay became depressing.

There are a few things I dislike more than waiting — I cannot wait for food, or for a report; I cannot keep a file pending, or delay in sending reports; I never keep anyone who comes to meet me waiting and yet I was kept waiting for almost a year for the most important event of my life — marriage. Since May 1944, I kept counting day after day, and week after week, like Robinson Crusoe knocking the days on a pole. I saw the seasons change, friends come and go, strange events take place and each time I felt an unutterable longing to have Naju by my side. It was an expectant, impatient, anxious sort of period of waiting. The loneliness became more acute. Out of this strain of anxiety arose our first problem — jealousy. In some letters Naju wrote that she had been out to dances and parties. In normal moments that would not have struck me as unusual, but my undiluted concentration on work made me oafishly saintly. Loneliness had warped my outlook and a curious sort of restlessness regarding marriage seized me. I wrote a nasty letter to her and she replied that she had not meant to tease me.

At about the same time there was a report of murder in one of the police stations. A tribal walked into a police station in the dead of night with an axe in one hand and a human head wrapped in a towel in the other. He placed both on the table, stating that he had murdered the man. Seeing such a ghastly sight in the dim light of a wick lamp, it took some time for the Head Constable to regain his composure. When asked why he had killed the person, the tribal, pointing towards the head, said innocently, "He cried profusely at my wife's funeral." At other times, I would have considered it as the weirdest motive for murder, but in the condition I was, I could understand his jealousy.

Almost a year went by. There were the usual inspections, the usual touring, the same old camp fires, and all the time, in every file and flower, I would see Naju's face, and feel jealous at her letters about parties she had been to. My father wanted the wedding to be in June. I was furious that the marriage had been postponed. I wanted it to be in March. While camping in Harsud in January 1945, I wrote a long letter to Mummy and ended it saying, "Much time has already been wasted." This sentence caused annoyance to Mummy but became a never-to-be-forgotten family joke.

The wedding finally took place on 7 March 1945 in Albless Baug, Bombay. I was granted only five days' leave. There were only twenty-five guests as all entertainment was restricted due to the war. Soon we were in a train bound for Khandwa.

At the Khandwa railway station, my friends of the club — army and civil, staged an unforgettable reception. A village band on the platform played *Main to Dilli se dulhan laya re*...two tribals fired their guns in a welcome volley that frightened the pigeons and the children; there were garlands enough to smother us; and then a subaltern dressed as a convict read out an indictment against the tyrant Rustamji and pronounced the sentence of imprisonment for the charge of kissing his wife. Naju was so bewildered that she almost refused to come out. All the passengers of the train looked out to see the strange happening at the railway station. We were carried with great pomp and ceremony to a breakfast arranged by the army.

The day I brought my wife to Khandwa, the IG and DIG — both Englishmen, were camping there. When I met them at the Circuit House, they said that they would like to come and call on my wife. When they came, Naju served tea and biscuits and they paid lavish compliments at her beauty and dress, trying to put her at ease.

In April 1946, the popular government took over. During the autumn of 1946, I was planting green peas in the garden when I received a curt wireless message stating that I had been transferred to Chanda (Chandrapur). The transfer from Khandwa came as a bolt from the blue to me. I felt that it was a punishment — being exiled to the forest district of Chanda and that depressed me more. A transfer from Khandwa to 'Chanda, of all places'! Naju succeeded in getting me out of the idiotic frame of mind that made me feel unwanted. For the first time in my life I tried to pull strings for stalling the transfer but the orders stood and my supplications proved to no avail. I was told that most of the British officers, who formed the majority in our cadre, would be going away and hence the shifting. However, my grudge was that the better and more important postings were reserved for relatives and friends of the political powers that be.

The failure to get the transfer cancelled strengthened my resolve not to make use of influence in future. I decided to stick to the path of honesty.

So on 26 August 1946, we stood outside the railway station at Khandwa, bidding goodbye to all the friends who had come to see us off. The Parsees were in great form and one felt a little touched at the kindness of Dave, Sayed and Kapur. Old Ishwardas stepped into our carriage like a little elephant and grandly presented us flowers, and a permit to have all our meals free of charge in the refreshment car. As the train slid out, I thought of all the good times and the anxious times I had spent in Khandwa. 'Good old Khandwa, I will always have a soft corner for you.' I will remember all the grand times we had — Naju, my wife, arriving amid rockets and crackers; the way we loved and worked. I think we must have laughed more in Khandwa than at any other place.

When we arrived in Chanda, we were dejected and dispirited. The climate was awful and there was absolutely nothing to do. We hated the place. We planned to spend as few months in it as possible and then apply for leave. But when we left the place in March 1947, both of us felt sincere regret. In that district of wilderness and aboriginals who lived in abject poverty, malaria, dysentery and blackwater fever, we had a most enjoyable time. First we were lucky to make friends with the Drivers at whose place we often dropped in and laughed with. We played tennis together and almost every alternate day when we were at the headquarters, we dined together. The friendly joviality of that couple did much to make us enjoy life at Chanda. And then, when the cold weather came, we went out into the glorious jungles of Chanda — those beautiful jungles of teak and bamboo, with plenty of game. In no other district did we see such a large assortment of animals, including a bison that looked like an old gentleman in white socks, standing in the middle of the road.

My sophisticated bride, who had never been out in the jungle, had to spend days in tents, walking from camp to camp, or riding in a *malguzar's* two horse *tonga*, living on a diet of rice and withered brinjals, and wondering why we felt so good in the wilderness where there was no film, no dance and no party. Once when I was told that *jungli murgi* (wild fowl) abounded near a stream close to our camp, I thought it a good opportunity to get something better for the table. The two of us sat down on the ground and waited for the beaters to come up. A constable who was sitting in line with us on the right as a *rok* (stop) shouted in a quivering voice, "*Sahib, aagey sher hai.*" (Sir, there is a tiger in front.)

Naju, a Bombay girl, had never climbed a tree in all her life. But the speed with which we scrambled up the tree would have put squirrels to shame. We sat on the first fork. The tiger had probably seen us but had been told by God to leave us alone this time because we were in love. He came back with a roar that nearly blew us off the tree. Naju felt that I had probably forgotten to shoot. She, who would bring the house down at the sight of a small rat, whispered quietly, "Shoot him, shoot," looking very brave. I had to tell her, after 'His Majesty' had left, that I had only two cartridges in my gun and that too meant for shooting birds.

After seven months in Chanda, I was transferred to Saugor as Principal of the Police Training School. I took charge on 1 April 1947. After four months, I was again transferred as SP of Amraoti. I handed over on 1 August and proceeded to Amraoti to take over charge from Martin Wynne.[2]

Prohibition was to be introduced from 15 August 1947. It was therefore decided that all the liquor in the Amraoti club would be consumed at the farewell party to the Englishmen and their wives on the 14th night. It turned out to be a rash decision. All the English people were in high spirits, probably to conceal their gloom at leaving India. Most of them loved India, loved life in the jungles and the hill stations, and loved touring rural India in the winter months. There was some dancing and much drinking and boisterous fun. At the end of the evening, the Commissioner, Amraoti Division, rose to make his farewell speech. He was a little incoherent, and I, rather sleepy. He wished India well and the Indians smiled benignly. Then he said something about thugs and *pindari*s and wished us well again. We smiled some more. Somehow Clive and Hastings came in and yet

---

[2]Martin Wynne wrote a very readable book on his days in India entitled, *On Honourable Terms*.

he wished us well. I dozed a bit, luckily missing something about the Simon Commission and yet again he wished us well. By the time he finished, we were all wishing each other well.

Naju had some bitter words for me, "Khush, you are drunk. Now stop it. Remember you have to command the parade in the morning."

As she dragged me home, I kept on wishing her well.

I commanded the parade the next morning though it was not necessary for the head of the district police to do so. I did not want to miss the momentous occasion. As the flag went up, a lump arose in my throat and tears welled in my eyes. I was choked with emotion. It appeared as if the whole of Amraoti had turned up to see the Indian flag go up. The struggle for Independence had at long last ended.

The Disaster of partition.

I have no doubt that the whole process of partition was so badly planned and executed that millions were killed, millions were uprooted, and for atleast a hundred years neither India nor Pakistan will be able to recover from the setback they received in 1947. But first let us see the setting of the drama in which war weary Britain at last decided to hand over power to their worst enemies, the Indian Nationsl Congress. Although Britain had won the war, it was weary and in a mood of joyous celebration. The world would be different. The victors would be its masters. Economically they had received a severe blow but they were sure they would not only recover but be able to form a new world economy in partnership with the United States. Winston Churchull was no longer needed. His party was defeated in an election that Labour won comfortably. The people wanted an end to war and privations.

Like all great empires before them the British in two centuries of science and industry had developed great wealth and power. The wealth was all lost in the war. But their ideas, their ethics, the manner in which they ran their democracy their laws and police procedures, even the way they spoke, lived and ruled was to taken up by the world. Like the Persians the Greeks and the Romans, the British empire was moving into history.

Prodded by their intellectuals, by the Americans who had seen the support that India had given in the war, and most of all by their economists, the British wwanted to perform the good deed of of granting freedom to India with grace and within a time limit. Thw Labout Party had under Clement Attlee was looking for the person who would be able to put the decision through. Churchill they were afraid would blow up the plan in the Hpouse of Lords where the Convservatives had a majority. Hence the need to find someone acceptable to him.

The selection of Lord Louis Mountbatten to do the job was perhaps a mistake. He had all the charisma, the name, the poewer of command, the courage to face dangerous situations and take bold decisions, and he had a wife who could be an asset anywhere. It is true that he even developed a political instinct, and he always had a love for India which the best Englishmen always had. What he lacked was the ability to see what impact his decisions would have on a land in the throes of a communal hysteria deliberately generated by the Muslim League. He feared the mob more than everything else, but like the good soldiers both of them were, they went into hostile areas and returned victorious. He had one serious defect -- he did not have that feel of disorder which ways of dealing with it which the situation required. He had developed an obsession that India was on the verge of an uncontrollable civil war, for which the British would be held accountble by the world. Yet a man like him, with all the power and goodwill that he had, could have transferred power in the orderly way he so much desited, if he had not been given a dateline to complete the task.

In 1994, Rustamji tried to write his autobiography while staying with his son, Cyrus in Toronto. He typed about eighty pages himself on a manual typewriter and then got a fair copy made on return to India. He called it 'The Auto-B.' I have included some extracts from his write-up. He did not have his diaries with him and hence there are some discrepancies.

7

Independence and Partition

We, who were witness to the freedom struggle in the thirties and forties, never dreamt that Independence would come in our lifetime. It may be true to say that, but for the war and the price that Britain had to pay, the freedom struggle may have gone on much longer. It is interesting to study the setting of the drama in which the war-weary Britain decided to hand over power to her most hated enemy, the Indian National Congress.

Britain had won the war. She was exhausted. The people wanted an end to even the thought of war. They were in a mood for celebration. The world would be different. The victors would be its masters. Economically, the country had received a severe blow but they were sure they would not only recover but be able to structure a new world economy in partnership with the United States.

Further, prodded by the intellectuals and by the Americans who had seen the support that India gave to the war (roughly two million soldiers), and most of all by their economists, the British wanted to grant freedom and quit with grace within a time frame. The Labour Party, led by Clement Attlee, was looking for a person who would be able to execute their decision. Churchill, they were afraid, would obstruct the plan in the House of Lords where the Conservatives had a majority. Hence, there was the need to find someone acceptable to him.

The selection of the man to do the job zeroed on to Lord Louis Mountbatten. This was a wrong choice. Mountbatten had all the charisma, the name, the power of command, the courage to face dangerous situations and take bold decisions, but he lacked the ability to see what impact his decisions would have on a vast land caught in the throes of communal hysteria. He perhaps had never seen the types of frenzied mobs that come out to kill. He had a typical military officer's fear of disorder and mob violence and did not know the ways to deal with them when the situation went out of hand. He was not aware of how the police in India dealt with all forms of rioting with the use of curfew and firing. He was totally ignorant of the simple truth that if the armed forces and the civil services adopted the right approach and right attitude, nothing could be irretrievably lost. He had developed an obsession that India was on the verge of an inevitable civil war, for which the British would be held accountable by the world and that the British had to get out at once to avoid the blame. Yet a man like him, with all the power and goodwill at his disposal, could have transferred power in the orderly way had he not been given a deadline to complete the task.

Now in retrospect we can say that there was nothing in the situation in 1947 which could not have been contained by curfew and show of force. The only condition precedent was that the administration should have the will to enforce the law. It came as a surprise to him that a Gandhi could walk into Noakhali, an area where the mob was mad with hysteria and panic, and bring peace at once.

Mountbatten had collected an able team, mostly from among the military officers, who had worked with him during the war. There was no civilian or police officer in that group of close advisors. It may have been difficult to find anyone knowing India who would accept the new ideas he had been ordered to execute. All the British officers were of one mind, except a few who came later. What was lacking in the team was the sort of man, civilian or policeman, who knew how to deal with violence that broke out in the NWFP and Punjab. It was sponsored by the Muslim League and was designed to turn unwilling provinces into supporters of the Partition.

On the British side at that time were the officers of the ICS and IP, the odd academic and merchant, all of whom were inherently suspicious of the Indian leaders. They constituted the vast majority of British nationals in India, who had loved and slaved for India and had tried to unify and pacify the land. They were the ones to fear that all would be lost in the first month of 'native' rule. Reduction in their retirement benefits had made them fear that they would get much less than what had been promised. It was wrong to turn the entire administration which was 80 per cent British at the time into enemies (against us). What was also not perceived was that in consequence, many drifted towards the Muslim side, to bring Pakistan, from the start, into the British orbit. Earlier it was called the 'divide and rule' policy. In the context of 1947, it amounted to 'ruin and quit'.

The Civil Disobedience Movement of 1942 made the Muslim League think for the first time that when Independence was granted, it would be unable to assert itself to support its interest. There was a sense of alarm in a section of the Muslim populace that following Independence, there would be Hindu rule and they would be submerged in the vast ocean of India.

On one side were the Muslims, a compact community, united by the ideal of Pakistan, capable, as so many communal riots had shown, of holding their own against a large body of opposition. Their desire for power and their hate was as acute as that of the early Mughals. They felt that they had the strength to be rulers and, 'no power on earth can deprive us of it'. On the other side were the Hindus, scattered amongst various political organisations, determined to have the power which numbers should give them. The failure to win over the Muslims had created intense frustration which was more dangerous than hate. They would, it was apparent at that time, violently oppose any attempt to divide the country, and if they agreed to it, it would only be in order that the British should be ousted first.

In the line up for power, the Congress stood, at that time, as a bewildered spectator, unable to support the Muslims, unable to contain its sympathy for the Hindus. The younger Muslims had already deserted it. The younger Hindus were beginning to feel that the Congress had wasted the energies of the people in useless demonstrations and futile programmes.

The truth was that upper class Muslims were yearning for the power that they had wielded in the centuries of Muslim rule. Till the early years of the twentieth century there were men alive, mostly in and around Delhi and in Uttar Pradesh, who had heard the stories of their ancestors who were servants of the Mughal rulers. As a race with a dominant past they had yearned to come up again. As a consequence the communal feelings first manifested in Uttar Pradesh and to a certain extent in the Central Provinces and Bombay. It was only afterwards that it began to appear in Punjab. The Muslim League agents went to Dera Ismail Khan, Dera Ghazi Khan, created trouble there and Hindus began to move out. Later on, it happened in Sind. It was this creation of communal trouble there which led people to believe that Partition would be a good thing or that it was inevitable and was coming.

The crucial point that the Congress missed at a critical juncture in the freedom struggle was that the British had made up their minds to leave India. During the years when Lord Wavell, Lord Pethick-Lawrence and Sir Stafford Cripps conducted negotiations with Jinnah and the Congress leaders, the latter could not discern that the British were prepared to leave. They felt they were at their old game of 'divide and rule'. Jinnah was the only one among the politicians who had read the British intentions correctly. They were going. It was the right time to show that he would be able to make Pakistan a West friendly nation. He had the added advantage of never having to spend a single day in jail which helped him to remain in constant touch with the people and with events as they kept unfolding.

The Muslim League, therefore, decided to change course. It decided to secretly support the British, but still keep its demands for Pakistan open. On the other hand, the Congress failed to realise the exhaustion that war had brought upon Britain. It feared that the British would never part with their hold on India. Also the Congress was not adequately prepared for what I would call the terror tactics of the Muslim League — violence and communal rioting — and capitalising on the Congress dislike of violence.

The leader of the Muslim League was a favourite son of the Congress till he moved out because he found the unique opportunity not only to come into limelight but also to become one of the important players in the freedom game. He expected and got support from the British and worked arrogantly for and got concessions from the Congress. He wanted separation at any cost.

Till about 1945, the most important Indian leader was unquestionably Mahatma Gandhi. He towered above all the other leaders. The country had supported his call to the British to quit India and the disturbances that followed all over the country convinced all that freedom could not be denied to us. But in the parleys held after their release in 1945, Nehru, Sardar Vallabhai Patel and J.B. Kripalani (Congress President) began to feel that there was a difference between them and the Mahatma. In all the discussions the mood of the Mahatma was to stall freedom if it meant Partition. Gandhiji's proposal that Jinnah should be made head of the interim government was not accepted even for a full discussion. Maulana Azad was strongly of the view that Indian integrity had to be maintained and formation of Pakistan spelt disaster for the Indian Muslims. The majority of Congressmen wishfully felt that Pakistan would fail and all Muslims would return to India in no time. Gandhiji had brought the war of Independence to victory, but in the final hour he failed to carry with him the Congress, which gave in to the division of the country to appease the agitating Muslims. He accepted with tears the sadness of Partition. He acceded to the views of those who felt that power was within their grasp and they could easily change the face of India, even if Pakistan was created.

The questions that we would have to ask are: Why did Gandhiji not take a more stringent line? Why did he not undertake a fast unto death as he had done in the past to convince his own people about the rightness of his cause? Why did he consider that the more important task before him was to go to East Bengal and quell the communal fires that were raging there? I am of the opinion that during the prolonged period of two years and eight months when all the top nine leaders of the Congress were under arrest inside the Ahmednagar Fort Jail serving out their term after the Quit India call, they must have discussed the course of action to be taken on coming out of jail.[1] They were getting old and wanted to enjoy the fruits of their struggle. They must have decided to go against Gandhiji's desires and dictates, if they were contrary to their own desires. And Gandhiji, a sharp and shrewd person that he was, must have realised that all his top lieutenants were of one mind and since power was up for grabs, they would not be amenable to his wishes.

When the history of our times is written, it might be said that we gave in too easily to the idea of Partition. It is because, as a nation, we are deficient in one measure. We are unused to bloodshed. We cannot tolerate the sight of blood. It was the Calcutta riots of 1946, what is known as 'the night of long knives' that led us to believe that working with the Muslim League was impossible. We came to the facile conclusion that if there was Partition, there would be no further communal trouble.

There was a weakness in the government at the centre which the Congress could not see. In the interim government formed in September 1946, the Congress and the League had different objectives and different methods. One side wanted peace. The other side wanted to force a breakdown which would lead to Partition. Then there was the unuttered wish of the British officers of the ICS and IP to "let the bastards go to hell". The Congress had never been able to gauge that their servants, in the interim government, were not loyal or dutiful. The military was divided between Indian and foreign officers, though Jinnah and Liaqat were trying to locate Muslims of senior ranks who would help in the process of division. Governors like Olaf Caroe in the NWFP and Jenkins in Punjab were so well entrenched that if they had said to the District Officers that there should be no disorder, they might have woken up to their duty. But many of the senior men in the civil and armed services had a hatred for the Congress, and they angled for jobs in Pakistan with promises to do whatever the League wanted. The men who were pro-Muslim by nature, with a certain amount of leaning towards the underdog, were well-known. They ended up in Pakistan, but eventually left in disgust.

[1]The Congress leaders were in the Ahmadnagar Fort Jail from 9 August 1942 to 28 March 1945.

The muddled reaction of authority to the outbreak of violence in the two northern provinces led to a struggle between the haves and have-nots — the Hindus being the haves and the Muslims being the have-nots. "Take possession of their houses and fields" was the battle cry that started Pakistan. The government that could kill 379 and injure more than a 1,000 in just ten minutes of rapid fire at Jallianwala Bagh in 1919 did not open fire at all to subdue a disaster worse than any in the British Raj. There was a total loss of nerve and determination on the part of the administration. The Indian leaders and a trusted Viceroy could not make the District Officers perform their duty in the right way.

The quandary in which the Congress found itself was mainly due to its own attitudes in the past. Those who had criticised the hated foreigners, day in and day out, for firing on unarmed crowds, could hardly make a quick about turn and say, "Kill to stop the rampage." We were mute spectators to the massacre of Muslims here and of Sikhs and Hindus in the north.

The people of India were misled by the pictures of Nehru attacking looters with his two-foot baton. They felt that if Nehru could do it, the administration must be active too. What history will question is why he did not hurriedly take steps to reform army units, put them under competent officers and force them to bring peace to the land by a combination of pressure and curfew. There were many Indian Army officers of proven merit, having won high honours in the war, who could have saved people on both sides from the savagery that followed.

The tense situation that came up in the two nations is difficult to visualise. Total anarchy prevailed in large parts of the country that had known peace for a 150 years of British rule. It was a slope on which nobody could stop the stampede. The whole world could only watch the biggest disaster of its kind. Then started the caravans of misery from both sides. They were miles long, fleeing from their homes which had been looted and taken over, from their fields that generations of labour had made fertile, running from the savagery of man. If the proper study of mankind is done, we must consider the man-made disaster of Partition as one that is the most important of all for study.

Some part of the blame undoubtedly must go to Clement Attlee and the British Government. They could not visualise the passions they were encouraging in their studious desire to appear fair and impartial. Perhaps they did not even know what had happened. The British Government tried to do the right thing in the wrong way. Churchill said in the House of Commons, "Many have defended Britain against her foes; none can defend her against herself. But let us not add to the pangs of sorrow so many of us feel, the taint and a smear of shame." The Conservatives pleaded for time for the wrong reasons, hoping that some new development may prevent the transfer of power. They were indifferent to the damage that Partition would do in this subcontinent.

The question that none has asked so far is, did the British intelligence agency, which had such a good reputation, not warn the government that the Partition would lead to massive riots and if it did, why did the government rush through the whole process? My own reading of the events is that the intelligence must have come to know that Jinnah was critically ill with cancer and he might not last long. Mountbatten, therefore, after hurried consultation in London, suddenly advanced the date of Independence and declared the date — 15 August.[2] He gave the specious excuse that he wanted to commemorate the date of his receiving the surrender of Japan. The British Government probably felt that if Jinnah died, Pakistan would not come into being. Hence, the change in the date and the consequent disaster.

The Congress eagerly demanding freedom dare not say that it should be postponed till firm arrangements had been made in the districts. The steely leader of the Muslim League, Jinnah had only one obsession — an independent Pakistan, however small, a "handkerchief" he called it, however weak in every way and yet a platform from which he could dominate over India and the Hindu leaders. Each party was a victim to its own delusions. A part of the blame also goes to some of the Englishmen who wanted to build up Pakistan as a foil against us and also for their own personal or their country's strategic interests.

---

[2] Lord Mountbatten went to London on 14 May 1947 and immediately on his return on 2 June 1947, announced the date when Independence would be granted.

We cannot blame them alone; the fault was also ours. The blame can be divided equally between the British, who advanced the date of Partition and never cared to make adequate arrangements and the new rulers of India and Pakistan who could not foresee the consequences of the same. The massacre that took place was due to our leaders' lack of experience in administration and weakness displayed in taking strong action.

The movement for the freedom of India accounted for the loss of very few lives; but it was the Partition of the country which led to the butchering of millions of people on both sides of the border, making it one of the greatest tragedies of history. This is one black spot on the British rule in India.

Hatred, not love which Gandhi had pleaded for, won the day in the August of 1947.

SERVICE UNDER THE BRITISH

K.F.Rustamji, I.P. (Retd.)

I went direct from the College of Science, Nagpur, where I was a lecturer in Zoology to the Indian Police in 1938. Coming from a family which was very nationalistic, there was an inbred hatred of British rule. It was only later that I began to separate British rule from British Officers. And that came when my contacts with them increased at Sagar, my first posting. Pre-war Sagar had a unique English atmosphere of its own because of the Cavalry School, probably the biggest in the world, and the large number of officers who came there from all over, for training. People rode horses, fell from horses, and talked only of horses. There were races, pig-sticking and polo. An ever-present topic of conversation was 'shikar.' Stories were told with typical British humour, "we sat up the whole night and got a sick jackal." And then there were cocktail parties, where the danger of war was brought up, and a very debatable question was whether the horse would be retained against the tanks which Hitler was amassing in Germany. The officers of the time loved horses, and felt they must be retained.

The interaction between the British army officers and civilians and the Indian officers of the ICS and IP was a striking feature of those times. I think that both tried to understand each other, and at the same time talked a lot

S.V.P. National Police Academy Journal *1 - 22*
Volume No.53 No.2 *Jul- Dec. 2001*

When I was Director, NPA, we had requested some IP officers to write about their experiences of serving under the British. The gist of their articles was published in the July-December issue of the Academy's journal. Rustamji contributed a long article on his experiences. I have used some excerpts from his original article in this book.

8

Analysis of British Rule in India

In a short span of nine years in service, I saw the awakening that took place among the masses. In my own limited way, I saw the panorama of Indian history as it passed before my eyes. My analysis of the British rule is based on what I saw, what I experienced and what I noted in my diaries.

In September 1943, while camping in Mandhata (Khandwa district) and after observing the rituals being followed in the temple there, I recorded in my journal that when the history of India is written dispassionately, and the injuries which Britain had inflicted on India are forgotten, historians will come to the conclusion that the British occupation of India was the most salutary influence that had ever affected this land. It is not in reference to the minor advances made in industry, communications, etc. Such advances have been made in several other countries like China, independent of a foreign power. The real achievement of Britain in India was the psychological effect that she produced on the minds of Indians. Back in the early forties, the effect was apparent only on the minds of those who had studied English, but it spread rapidly from them to the remoter minds. This brought about a change in our method of thinking. Our values got altered. Our hopes and aspirations became different. We appreciated with more discrimination. We criticised that which we had.

Now, several years after Independence, when I look back, I am forced to acknowledge the good that the British rule did to India for almost a century and a half. When the British entered India, the land was a battleground, where native rulers and foreign armies were battling for dominance and regularly ransacked the people for supplies. It was chaos that lasted for a century. Thugs and *pindari*s roamed unchallenged over the land and dacoits of every type held undisturbed sway. The British launched campaigns right from 1817 to ruthlessly crush the outlaws who lurked along the highways and made the movement of men and material safe for the people. Step by step the British consolidated their position and established an administrative structure with English officers in key posts. They brought peace to the land by introducing a system which was marked by legal and procedural correctness. They established a system of justice, laid out a uniform land revenue system, modernised the old Mughal administration, instituted military traditions, introduced democracy, set up universities, initiated the English language, science and modern ways of thinking and living, and gave us cricket. Even years after they have left, there is order in the land. The basic structure of financial administration, introduced by them, has worked out competently. Courts are independent and are able to enforce the rule of law.

It was easy to talk about the negative aspects of British rule. We had to exaggerate their atrocities to make the demand for independence stronger. We kept talking ill of the British rule even after they departed and attributed some of the ills prevalent in the country to them. But that is the way any victor would talk of the enemy he has defeated. Before passing a judgement on British rule we have to ask ourselves the question, what if they would not have ruled this country? And one of the big "ifs" of history — what if the mutineers in 1857 had succeeded in driving out the British from parts of north India? Would we have been able to survive the decadent Muslim rulers and other local feudal lords? Would India have been one country as it is today?

I would be on the British side in praising their rule, particularly the manner in which they could weld together disparate groups and bring about total integration in the land. They displayed great administrative skill, from understanding the local people and respecting their religious beliefs to building up a structure of democratic administration on the debris of Mughal rule. It is true that purely for their own administrative convenience and paucity of qualified people, they initially made the whole of what is today India, Pakistan, Bangladesh, Burma and Ceylon (now known as Sri Lanka) as one unit but later separated the latter two countries from this unit.

Making a candid appraisal of the British rule in India, it can be said that in the years prior to Independence, Indians were prejudiced by hatred of a country which treated India as a colony. Hatred was there in full measure. It was necessary; for it enabled us to unite and think of ourselves as one nation. For without it there could be no freedom struggle. The main effort of Gandhiji was to control and channelise hatred. Perhaps he did not know the extent to which it had been diverted into violence by those, including some close to him, who wanted to get quicker results, and could not understand the methods of the Mahatma. The way in which he stopped the *satyagraha* movement after the Chauri Chaura incident of 1922 would indicate that the father did not trust his children completely. About 1930, when the Civil Disobedience movements began, one after another, Gandhiji took strict measures to prevent hatred from crossing the limits into violence. Some British dignitaries were assassinated or murdered; but these acts were committed by individuals who were not members of his party. He called off movements when they degenerated into violence.

A remarkable feature during the freedom struggle was that while the average Indian hated British rule, there was no personal ill feeling against the officers in the districts who were British. I wonder how Gandhiji managed to achieve this. The British hated 'Gandy' but respected Gandhi and perhaps many of them owed their lives to him. If both sides had resorted to large-scale killings, thousands of Englishmen would have lost their lives because they were too few and too scattered to withstand the wrath of millions in case of a violent revolt.

The British also knew that if violence broke out on a large-scale, it would lead from one incident to another, culminating in widespread violence all over India. The Mutiny of 1857 and the Jallianwala Bagh massacre were still fresh in their minds. In fact, the disaster at Jallianwala Bagh always hung like a memento mori over the British Raj — a fact which no Englishman could ignore. The average Englishman realised that the manner in which the firing was resorted to, to teach a lesson to the 'natives,' had caused greater damage to British rule than anything else. Ever since then, the police tried to rely on minimum force, but there were hot-heads who called it weakness and led their men into trouble. Gandhiji's Civil Disobedience campaign, with its emphasis on non-violence, was a development in the freedom struggle which completely baffled the British.

During the disturbances of 1942, there was specific information that a particular Englishman would be attacked. When I asked him if he would mind if a guard were posted at his house, he said, "God, no! I can look after myself." Englishmen and their wives went about with no protection. When I asked English ladies in August 1942 whether they would accept a guard, they turned it down rather rudely. In a vast land seething with anger against the British, you could meet the Englishmen or their women shopping in the bazaar, oblivious to the harsh words being said about them in public meetings. They were confident no harm would be caused to them.

If the British ruled this country for long, one of the main reasons, to my mind, was the courage and fortitude of their womenfolk. The courage of the Englishwoman was no less than those who took part in the charge of the light brigade. This is an aspect of the Englishman's rule in this country which has not been highlighted by any historian. I have observed it.

Some day when all the exaggerations and false reports that have crept into the freedom struggle are swept aside and when historians, free of political biases, write the history of India, they will say with authority that it was a unique struggle — one that could only have occurred in a country imbued with a deep respect for non-violence. The final word will be that both sides overcame the prejudices of the time with a unique spirit of understanding and compromise. The way the British left was the best part of the connection. They left with grace and goodwill; except for the Partition, which, as mentioned earlier, was the work of some Englishmen who wanted to create Pakistan as a balancing force for individual or their country's strategic interests.

Gandhiji was not only saintly in his habits, he was an expert tactician who knew the English and planned the campaign in a way that would hit them at their most vulnerable, that is, the colonial policy of doing good to the natives. The earlier demands for freedom were based on violence which the British were able to contain with the use of force. The real problem for the British arose when the struggle became non-violent and spread to every nook and corner of the land to almost all the 479 districts and the people followed one leader whose dictates were adhered to with respect and reverence.

We are apt to exaggerate the incidents of violence, the lathi charges and the firings, but the real merit of the movement was the restraint that was used by both sides. Actually, as one who had seen the struggle from close quarters, I can say that the freedom struggle in India was the most gentlemanly war that has been waged in history. The verdict of history will be that the freedom movement was a remarkable episode in the history of the human race as a frail, saintly man drove out a firmly entrenched colonial power that had won two world wars and secured from it Independence for India. History had never seen a war of Independence fought by two sides with so much discussion, so much openness and so much understanding. That made it an epic struggle, one that led to similar movements all over the world, and proved to be a method of abolishing colonial rule everywhere.

Why did the British decide to quit India? What made them take one of the biggest decisions in their history — to give away the jewel in the crown? Was it because they felt that India had become ungovernable as the freedom movement had made every Indian turn against British rule? Was it the weariness of the war or was it the poor economic straits the country was in, which made them reduce the size of the Empire? Or was it the unrest in the armed forces and mutiny in the Indian Navy?

It could have been a combination of all. The Civil Disobedience Movement of 1942 or Quit India Movement as it came to be known later was one of the deciding factors. Though some historians have played down the movement and have opined that it did not achieve much as the British were successful in suppressing it completely, but as a person who took part in curbing it, in my view, it is a landmark in the history of India's freedom struggle. The movement proved to British rulers that the whole nation had risen as one man under one leader, even in small towns and in the interior villages. The movement generated fears that there would be total opposition to the British rule once again after the leaders were released. It was after this movement that the government felt that, perhaps the only way to salvage the loss would be to divide India and keep a grip on Pakistan. With all the Congress leaders in jail, Jinnah had a free hand for almost three years to work on the British to accede to his demand to divide the country and create Pakistan.

The British received substantial help from Muslims and communists in suppressing the Quit India Movement. With the German invasion of the Soviet Union in June 1941, Britain became her ally. Probably at a signal from Soviet Union, the Indian communists decided to extend all their support to the imperialist power.[1] The communists became the most important informants of the British intelligence. Since interpretation of history is the first principle of the communist philosophy, the later day Marxist historians of India have, out of loyalty to the party, played down the significance of the Quit India Movement.

Historians and politicians have not given due credit to the role played by the armed forces in Indian Independence struggle for their own reasons. The part played by the armed forces in forcing Britain to grant Independence to India is a subject which is yet to be researched in depth. 1857 was not the first mutiny. There were several mutinies at regular intervals right from the seventeenth century in the west, the south and also in the east. It culminated with the part played by the Indian National Army (INA) and the Naval Mutiny of 1946. Once Britain realised it could no longer command the complete loyalty of the armed forces, it decided to leave the country.

---

[1]The ban on the Communist Party of India (CPI) which was imposed by the British in 1934 was lifted in July 1942, just three weeks before the Quit India call was given in Bombay on 9 August 1942.

Another aspect, which is not highlighted and never mentioned by historians, is the role of the Indian officers of the ICS and police who kept on arguing, insisting, explaining to the British Government that the time had come for them to leave. Several officers had to pay the price for it. But one thing that saved all of us was that the entire Indian official community, including the army, navy, air force, all the officers of the ICS, IP and others, right down to the lowest constable, all of them were of one mind and they wanted Independence. In fact, they supported it wholeheartedly and whenever they had to deal with the protest movement, they acted with a certain degree of restraint when dealing with Indian rebels, which was in many cases contrary to the instructions of British masters. Someday, perhaps, this aspect of the freedom struggle will be brought out — how government servants worked from within to convince the British that their time was up.

A few enlightened hearts in Britain supported the Indian demand for freedom. Though few would admit it, but talking to Englishmen at that time, I felt that many of them did want to "do the right thing for India" at the time when the Labour Party was in power. It was also the hope of intellectuals that granting freedom to India would rid the British of the taint of colonialism, which even their American friend, President Roosevelt, had taunted them about.

Lastly, at the end of the war, there was a feeling that the world would be quite different. There would be hardly any need for armies and there would be peace all around, and the best way for Britain to retain her position would be to get the goodwill of the world and to bank on the credit the world had given her for resisting fascism in World War II.

We must also give credit to the Englishmen in India at that time that they instinctively understood that the time had come for them to leave India. I would say that it was in the year 1946 that the realisation happened. Some of them took it in the right spirit; many felt that they were going to leave the country to destruction. I must also add that the attitude of many Englishmen, whom I came across in service, towards the Independence of India was undoubtedly hostile. The prospect of losing a job which gave them power and position irked them. For hundreds of officers it meant the end of a service, the end of a career, the end of work which they liked, a type of work which they enjoyed doing and quitting it was like throwing away the jewel in the crown and going into an uncertain post war Britain. One of the big questions which was hotly debated at that time among the British official circles, which is now forgotten, was, "Is India fit for Independence?"

They were convinced that Indians on their own would not be able to rule honourably. They believed that 'Gandy' was a hoax and his Congress was a collection of rebellious traitors who needed to be put down with a firm hand and that their own government in Britain was wrong in negotiating with them. They hated the Congressmen, and tried to keep them in check by devious ways, such as winning over a few as informers, or decorating those who blindly supported them with titles. Embedded deep in the British psyche was the belief that Indians are quick to betray their friends or their rulers.

The hostility of the Congress to their rule rankled in the British mind for years. They could not forget that. They were aware of the extent of the loss they would have to suffer in the event of the dissolution of the Empire. They, therefore, began to incite one hostile act after another. Their attitude towards the Muslims, or anyone else in the political field opposed to the Congress was one of fostering and encouraging a separate identity. They seldom sided openly with any community in the communal riots but they saw to it that the members of the Muslim League were rescued from the riots without much damage. In their parleys with leaders, they skilfully played up the opposition of the minorities to Congress rule, hoping that the division amongst the peoples' rank would enable them to postpone the final day when they would have to end their rule.

How did the British rule India? How could so few men control millions of Indians in a turbulent country? How could about 1,000 officers of the ICS and the smaller number of IP officers, and the British Army, which was mainly occupied with the NWFP, control over 400 million people in India?[2] I consider the main reasons for the success of the British were first, the faith and support of the people they ruled over and secondly, the British belief that a good ruler was one who did not hurt the sentiments of the people. The tempo of the past created by the way in which they had established order, had introduced laws and procedures and given a firm assurance to the people that justice would be done after 100 years of chaos following the death of Aurangzeb also helped to gain the confidence of the people.

The other reasons were their ability to review, to face criticism, to encourage and exercise strict supervision and conduct regular inspections. Also at the top were regular reviews, enquiries, commission of enquiry, all types of committees to review the system of work and constantly improve upon it and bring about changes for the betterment of the people in the system of governance. In fact, several of their notes were extremely critical of the manner in which affairs were being conducted by their own countrymen. It is also a tribute to their genius that most of the laws, procedures and manuals drafted by them continue to this day.

A factor which impressed me was a desire on the part of all Englishmen to do justice and this quality translated into the people accepting them as their rulers. The average villager in India wants someone in authority to listen to his grievances. Whether his grievances are settled is not the issue. He wants to pour out his feelings. He wants to be heard. He wants quick remedies to his small personal and other problems. He is averse to going to courts of law or to the officer class in the towns. He prefers officers coming to his village. The British administrators did just that. They went on tours and met the villagers at the camps they set up, or at the campfires in the evening after dinner, to redress the

---

[2] At the beginning of 1947, the total strength of the ICS officers was 939, of which 510 were Indians and 429 were Europeans. Out of the 100 odd Muslims, 83 opted for Pakistan. In the IP, 60 per cent were Europeans. The ICS officers used to trumpet the remark of Josef Stalin of the Soviet Union. When informed that 1000 ICS officers administer a population of 400 million, he termed the situation as "ridiculous". The maximum strength the ICS had at any time was 1,245.

grievances of the villagers on the spot. If the men from the interior came to the Englishman's headquarters, he would set them at ease and strike a chord of intimacy with them by asking, "*Kahan se aaya? Kya baat hai?*" (Where have you come from? What's the problem?) The Englishman loved the rural folk and they in turn had high regards for the *Huzoor* or *Maalik* (Master). I cannot forget the words of Freddie Quinn-Young, the SP who trained me, "There should be nobody in your district who feels he cannot approach the SP personally to tell him of his grievances." The Englishman, no doubt, kept his distance from the townsmen, the educated types and the Congress*walla*s.

These officers from a distant foreign island learnt the language of the state they were posted to. The esprit de corps that was built up by many efficient officers helped them at a time when the whole of India seemed to be in revolt. The subordinates' loyalty to the British officers was exemplary because they had learnt how to lead men. Any relationship based on superior and subordinate can be a trying one but as the Englishmen were used to ruling for 150 years, the power to command came naturally to them.

The average Englishman in service was a hardworking and a rather domineering individual, running a well established system, refined over the years in which all the men in it thought and spoke alike. They came from the same background; they had the same outlook, the same energetic superiority. I was struck by the fact that the younger lot of British officers had uprightness as their prime quality. They retained some of the old colonial thinking which had made them work unitedly to serve India and its people. There was discipline and cohesion in the services. The kingpins were the DM and the District Superintendent of Police who worked hand in hand and maintained order in the country. A striking feature of those times was the close interaction between the British civilians and army officers and the Indian officers of the ICS and IP. Both tried to understand each other. However, it must be added that the attitude of the Englishmen to Indians in the service depended a great deal on the individual. There were also, among them, many who viewed us as 'interlopers,' with distrust and a certain amount of concealed hatred, as we in turn did them.

I must pay a tribute to the English community in India. They had preferred a style of living which isolated them from the traumas and contacts of daily life in India. What they treasured was the home, the garden, the club and *shikar*. They developed an ability to live in isolation which was indeed remarkable. The most trying part of their life, apart from the heat, was separation from children who were schooling in England. Living in isolated houses, many a times without their families, they never showed fear. Business as usual was clearly the English motto.

How was the lifestyle of the Englishman in India? The salary of an SP before Independence was Rs 650 per month. It would be equivalent to about Rs 80,000 or a lakh of rupees today.[3] He had low taxes, could afford to send his wife to the hills in summer. There was not a whiff of corruption amongst any of the senior men. There were many liaisons and love affairs and the Padre was called in for a settlement, but the reputation of the English was jealously guarded. As Warren Hastings had spelt out about the East India Company, "It is on the virtue, not the ability, of its servants that the Company must rely."

What were the thoughts of the English families that were leaving? It was a road back from India for them. They were a bit sad, haunted by a deep depression that Britain had won the War and impoverished itself in the process. It had suffered incredible losses, though it saved the world from fascism. How could the families recover their prosperity? Everything was in short supply in England. There was severe rationing. They felt that the terms of compensation for loss of career were generous, but they still felt sad at leaving their bungalows, the large retinue of servants — cooks, *mali*s (gardeners) and maids to look after their kids — their clubs, all that they held dear and of course, the jungles and the peasantry.

An old English missionary, who was also leaving, said to me, "I was running a home for lepers for the last forty years. I don't know what I shall do in Britain. I don't know whether people will accept me there!" His words summed up the feelings of an average departing Englishman.

---

[3]This estimate was made by Rustamji in an article written in 1996.

PART – III

1947–1958

Nagin and I sat by the radio almost the whole of that night and the next day. A.I.R. stood up to the occasion remarkably well. The chants and hymns, and songs in praise of Gandhiji were lovely. Jawaharlal Nehru spoke ~~in~~ a ~~voice~~ with deep emotion about the tragic deed which had taken away the Father of the Nation. "A light has gone out of our lives" he said, but we will strive to walk in the footsteps the Master had shown to us. In his speech Sardar Patel disclosed that the assassin was a young Hindu, named Nathuram Godse. (The Muslims heaved a sigh of relief) Remarkable among the heartfelt tributes paid to ~~him~~ Gandhiji ~~that night~~ was the beautiful speech of Sarojini Naidu.

Throughout the next day we heard the commentary on the funeral procession to Rajghat. Melville de Mello spoke well. One could almost feel the presence of the tremendous crowd which bore his remains to ~~its~~ their resting place.

In the absence of the D.C., the duty of arranging the functions in Rajgarh fell to me. For the first

Extract of the diary entry of January 1948, where he has written about the assassination of Mahatma Gandhi.

9

Integration of Princely States

The day after Independence, North India especially Punjab, was caught in the grip of savage incidents in consequence to the Partition. My first task as SP, Amraoti was to ensure that there was no flare up of communal violence. The strict preventive measures taken by me made the Muslims feel I was pro-Hindu. The Hindus felt that, being a Parsee, I was not one of them. Rumours were circulated by communalists about my impending transfer. On 22 December 1947, I received a curt wireless message ordering my transfer from Amraoti to Raigarh.

A certain section of the public wanted me out, and it seemed to me they had succeeded. I was terribly dejected at being transferred, within five months, from the divisional headquarters district like Amraoti to a district that did not exist on the map of the State. I was ordered to be in Raigarh, which was situated near the Orissa border, by 31 December 1947 to be in time for the integration of the princely States of Raigarh, Sarangarh, Sakti, Udaipur and Jashpur into the Raigarh district, and their formal taking over by the Central Provinces.

I telephoned Naju who was in Madras, and conveyed the news in such a dismal tone that she burst into tears. She returned by air, missing by an hour the arrival of her sister Coomi's son, Adi, to welcome whom into this world, she had specially gone to Madras. Driving back from the Nagpur aerodrome in the new Chevrolet which I had purchased for Rs 7,500, the blues that had engulfed me on hearing of my transfer, melted away completely. It was good to hear her demolish all my carefully built up prejudices and doubts. What seemed to be a catastrophe in my life began to appear an adventure. We both laughed. How many amusing sights there seemed to be on the road from Amraoti. How much enjoyment there was if only one looked at it in the right perspective!

Within a couple of days, our belongings were repacked and we hit the road. Cheerful and happy, we felt a palpitating tang of adventure in what had earlier seemed like an exile from the province. Rajas and palaces, jungles full of animals, new places and a new kind of job beckoned us. By stages we motored across Central Provinces. We finally reached Sarangarh, where we had our first taste of royalty (still not deposed). The Raja of Sarangarh was good to us. We liked the palace and found his talk of duck and geese very stimulating. Though reeling under the impact of the blow delivered by Sardar Patel barely a month earlier in Nagpur, he did not show any signs of it.

The Raja of Sarangarh put as up in his palace. Both of us went up to the palatial suite that night, very happy and optimistic. If this was the way life was to be in the district, who would mind a two or three years' tenure! Duck and snipe, genuine Scotch, modern sanitary arrangements, a marble-tiled bathroom which Naju had dreamed of — everything was there except for the liberal tips that had to be doled out to the livery of servants. That was the only palace we lived in. The other Rajas were courteous, we bowed to each other deeply and tried to recover as much as possible for the government, while they in turn tried to claim as much as possible of the private property.

By means of a forced march we reached Raigarh on 31 December, and immediately began rushing about to end the State Raj in a decent manner, and inaugurate a new one with bands and jollity. Shankar Dayal Shukul, the DIG and Ramadhir Mishra, the DC had arrived. We tried to make all the arrangements for taking over the five States within the next twelve hours. Gradually the officers of the other departments began trooping in, one by one. Bhawani Mishra, the DFO was followed by my old friend B.K. Chaudhuri, as the District Judge. His arrival was most heartening.

Deputed as we were in a place that did not know us or where the old servants of the State actively tried to obstruct us, we, the officers of Central Provinces naturally had to depend on each other for comfort and advice. The small group of officers was so efficient that it successfully survived the wiles of the Rajas and their minions and built up an atmosphere of faith and confidence. Even the poorest could come to voice their grievances. Gradually we tried to lay the foundation for a popular government. We did not rush them; instead we consulted the leaders and explained the intentions of the government, creating a new sense of responsibility and awareness.

> For forms of government let fools contest
> What'er is best administer'd is best.
>
> – Alexander Pope

The actual taking over of an administration was a curious affair in which I had never before participated. While Ramadhir Mishra went round the treasuries and the important State offices, I was given the lesser task of taking over the livestock and poultry, elephants, a gun which was fired at the birth of an heir, several musical instruments of the State's army bands, the armouries and magazines, dairies, motor garages and other minor State institutions. How we fought to see nothing was stolen or lost. Lynx-eyed, we roamed over all the offices to find traces of hurried distribution of property. The DC asked me to supervise the counting of currency notes that had been taken over. I refused to do it. I knew that however honest one is, even a small, false allegation will stick lifelong. The entire offices of the State High Court and Secretariat had been auctioned off by the rulers. One by one, we went round and bought everything back, to the delight of the anti-*Dewan* party. Smaller things were mostly recovered, but several fields, forests, etc. were gifted away by the rulers before integration and thus were lost to the State.

In the midst of this taking over, Ramadhir Mishra stood out as a man of quick decision, strength and character. Ever cheerful and energetic, astute, clever and diplomatic, he fought the princely State servants with every conceivable weapon and succeeded in setting up the plinth of a new administration with remarkable speed and dexterity. He was the ideal man for a job of this kind. Ramadhir Mishra was the man the district needed on its inception. Unfortunately he was not able to complete the good work begun by him as three weeks after he took over, suddenly he fell sick. Severe colic and entanglement of intestines set in. The case was not properly diagnosed and after his removal to Raipur, he passed away of peritonitis and other complications.

As there was a severe shortage of officers following the departure of Englishmen who were a majority in the State, I was asked by the government to carry on with the work of the DC till a new man joined. In this way I am, probably, the only SP in history to have also functioned as a DC, albeit for only a few days. The Chief Minister, Pandit Ravi Shankar Shukla was scheduled to visit the district and I was put in overall charge of the visit.

A couple of days later, on 30 January 1948, one of the most tragic incidents in my life took place — the assassination of Mahatma Gandhi. The news was communicated to me in an ambiguous note by a CID Inspector who had come to Raigarh to investigate the brutal murder of four Muslims with a hand grenade thrown into a mosque at prayer time.

Our first reaction at the news of Gandhi's assassination was one of incredulity. How could anyone want to kill the most gentle and beloved soul in India? Yet we were aware that a few days earlier, a Punjabi youth named Madanlal had tried to murder him at his prayer meeting. Our doubts and misgivings were further strengthened by the terrible happenings that had occurred in northern India during the first five months of Independence.

We ran to the radio for confirmation. The music was mournful. Then a tearful voice whispered haltingly that Gandhiji had been murdered while he was on his way to his prayer meeting. We were numb with shock. It was too deep for tears. I felt as if a prop had been taken away from me. And yet his death was a vindication of his life. As the doleful chanting came over the radio we felt an unforgettable grief. It was a personal loss for us. That he should be snatched away at the time when thousands of refugees were working their difficult way across the frontiers of India and Pakistan and were being exterminated in great numbers by blood-thirsty fanatics; that he should be murdered so soon after Independence, when his fatherly guidance was most needed, was a supreme tragedy for India. Gandhiji's death closed his life on a dramatic note.

In the first hour as the news came over the radio, it seemed a Muslim had killed him. I went about making massive deployment. Nehru came on air to announce who had committed the crime. He said, "The light has gone out of our lives, but we will strive to walk in the footsteps the master has shown us." In his speech Sardar Patel disclosed that the assassin was a young Hindu named Nathuram Godse. The policeman in me heaved a sigh of relief. But I stood stunned near the radio with Naju consoling me. Tears poured like rain.

Naju and I sat by the radio to hear the commentary on the funeral procession to Rajghat given by Melville de Mello in a brilliant manner. All India Radio (AIR) stood up to the occasion remarkably well. Radios were few in those days, but those who had them allowed others into their houses. One could almost feel the presence of the tremendous crowd which bore his remains to their resting place. Jawaharlal Nehru spoke with deep emotion about the tragic deed which had taken away the Father of the Nation. In her beautiful speech Sarojini Naidu aired her tribute to Gandhiji in a remarkable way.

It was a unique funeral for Gandhiji. Every city, every town, every village witnessed a procession of grief. In the absence of the DC, the duty of arranging the function in Raigarh fell to me. For the first time in the history of Raigarh, the officers of the government and the people participated in the same function. Wearing a kurta and pyjama, I led the procession, singing the *Ramdhun*. Naju and B.K.Chaudhuri followed behind me. On the banks of the River Kelo, the people of Raigarh paid their last tribute to Gandhiji, and on hearing the news over the radio that the pyre had been lit, a wave of anguish passed over the crowd and the cries of "Mahatma Gandhi *ki jai*", "Mahatma Gandhi *amar rahe*" rent the air.

It is strange how unexpected events happen and totally unexpected results follow. Immediately after Partition, killings started on both sides of the border. When the news of these mass murders appeared in the press, a strong wave of communal hatred swept over the land. Riots broke out in many places. What saved the nation from another communal holocaust was the fatal shot that killed the Mahatma. From that day a sudden calm descended upon the land, not only in India but strangely enough in Pakistan also. In the entire history of India no incident has matched the agony caused at Gandhiji's death.

Papa, Mummy and Dolat came to spend a few days with us. We thought the change would do Papa good as he had steadily been losing weight since the previous year. The change would have done him good if only we had not consulted the 'great' doctors of Raigarh. One of them, who prided himself on his experience and knowledge, examined Papa and informed us that he suspected it to be a case of tuberculosis. It was a stunning blow for Mummy; but she bore it bravely. In the light of that diagnosis, we began to revise our plans. Obviously if Papa stayed in Raigarh during the summer the complaint would be aggravated. Papa himself wanted to go back to Nagpur and said repeatedly that if he died elsewhere, he would cause trouble to everyone. Finally we decided that it would be best for them to go to Bombay and stay with Khursheed and get Papa treated by competent medical men. We saw them off at the railway station. I had a peculiar premonition that perhaps it was the last time we would be seeing him alive.

In Bombay, the specialists diagnosed that he was losing weight because of hyperactivity of the thyroid glands. One day when he had gone to the hospital for treatment, he missed step and fell down a flight of stairs leading to the basement. He received a fracture in the skull and within a short time, fell unconscious. He died peacefully a few days later on 3 August 1948. Rustam, Parin, Naju and I reached in time for the funeral the following morning. It was tragic to see him lying on the stone slab with the stillness of death upon him. I was sorry he died in Bombay because he had wanted so much to die in Nagpur. But I was glad that he had passed away in the manner he wanted — without a long illness and without troubling his dear ones. He had lived his life well.

I had worked in Raigarh for hardly five months when I was asked to move again and this time to the other end of the State — to Akola. This was the fifth transfer in one and a half years.

When the transfer order to Akola came, the prospect of a change from Raigarh was most heartening. Even Akola, the second hottest place in India, could not be as bad as Raigarh, we conjectured, and in this we were proved right.

We left Raigarh on 15 May 1948 to motor across the State at the worst time of the year. On the very first day any illusions which we had harboured about the heat were soon dispelled. On the first lap of the journey we reached Raipur at about noon and went merrily to the bazaar to buy some ice. We started from there at three the next morning. We had to stop after every few minutes in the intense heat of the day to allow the engine to cool. We spent the day at Nagpur and started the next morning at three for Akola. We got delayed due to a puncture and crawled into Akola at noon. It was a relief to see Akola and escape into the cool interior of the Circuit House.

We began to rejoice at our escape from the oppressive heat of Raigarh. But what we had left behind was the charming simplicity of Chhattisgarh.

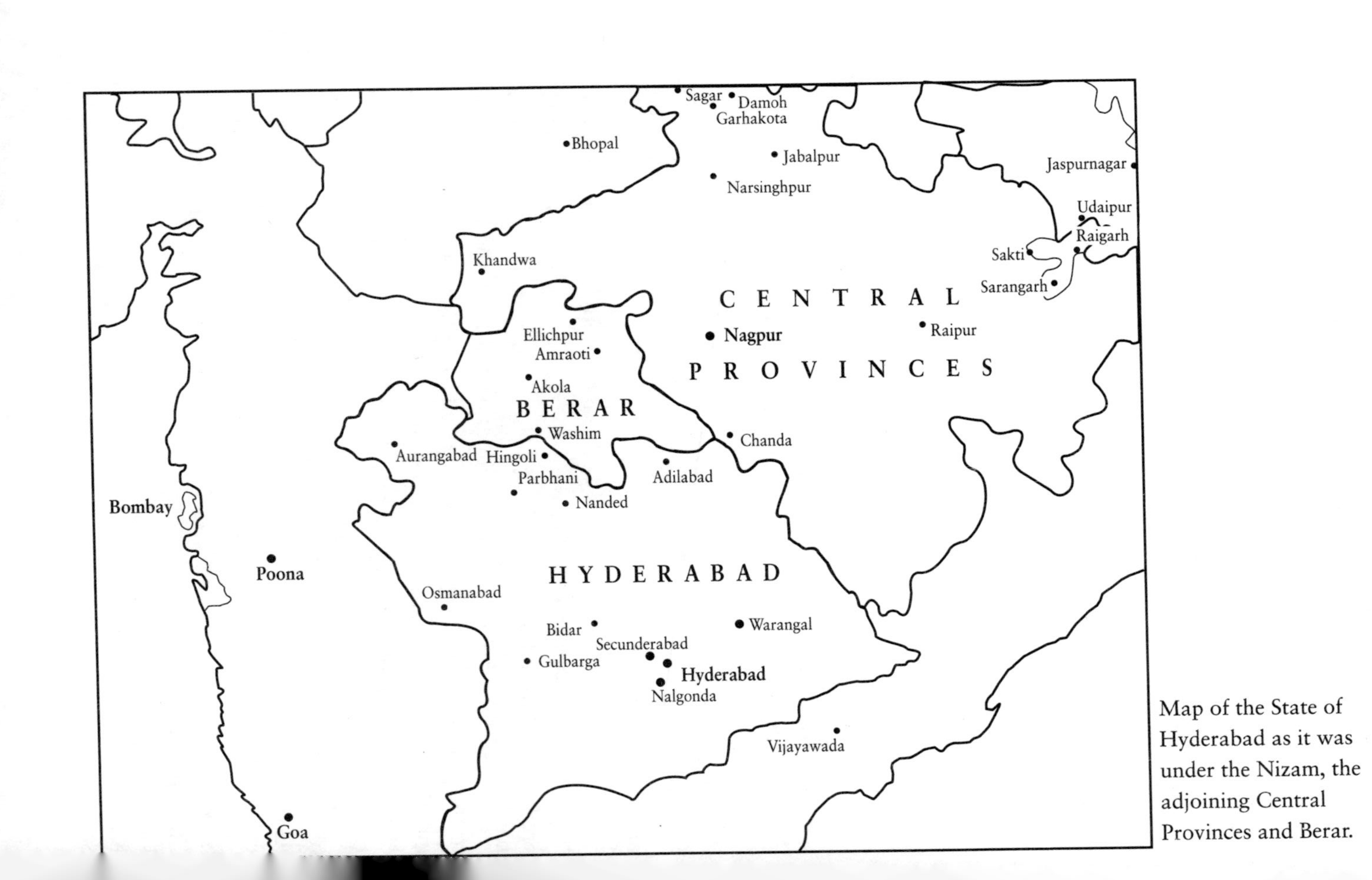

Map of the State of Hyderabad as it was under the Nizam, the adjoining Central Provinces and Berar.

10

Hyderabad Police Action

I took over as SP, Akola in May 1948 and from the first day, I became engrossed with the border problem. The district had a border of about fifty-two miles touching Hyderabad State. The Nizam seemed to be fortifying the State to declare Independence. I was told that my task was to collect intelligence and organise raids by specially armed and enlisted home guards and establish a border belt free of Razakars.[1]

Soon after India achieved Independence, the Hyderabad State Congress (HSC) announced a flag *satyagraha,* which was followed by intense opposition to the State authorities. The State administration took stringent measures to quell the activities of the HSC. In addition to the usual repressive methods of putting down popular agitation, they adopted one which surpassed all in meanness and violence. The cabinet of Prime Minister Mir Laiq Ali deliberately incited the Razakars to attack the HSC volunteers and all those who opposed them.

Conditions inside Hyderabad State had begun to deteriorate. The Razakars, under the leadership of Kasim Razvi, had firmly established themselves in the towns. Gradually they began

---

[1]Razakar is a Persian word meaning a volunteer who protects the government or king. The fundamentalist militia organised by Kasim Razvi to support the rule of the Nizam called themselves Razakars. Their aim was to resist integration of Hyderabad State with the Union of India.

spreading to the villages as their movement gathered strength. Here they were up against the HSC, which was unable to put up much resistance in the towns but was powerful in the villages, where a small war had begun between the Razakars and the HSC. The Razakars denuded the countryside of its wealth. First the livestock disappeared, and then the grain, clothes and utensils were taken. Soon they began to roam over the countryside in gangs, robbing all they could find. The police of the State passively stood by, allowing the atrocities to be committed. They felt that the injustices inflicted on the unprotected Hindus in the villages were a just retribution for the agitation conducted by the HSC for joining the Indian Union. Very soon even the desire for loot seemed to have gone out of the Razakars. They had degenerated into cowardly vandals, raiding a village in groups and committing rape and arson in a hurry before scurrying back to the protection of the towns and their police as early as possible. A steady stream of Hindu refugees kept pouring into our district.

When I took charge in Akola it was difficult to verify the conditions that actually prevailed in the State. Hyderabad was located in the middle of hostile Hindu territory, with an actively hostile Muslim population of 8 per cent within her borders. It was rightly judged that resistance to the Indian Union was tantamount to madness. But the madness which seized the Razakars and swept the Muslims of Hyderabad off their feet was to be seen to be believed.

The main reason why Razvi was able to win over the Muslims was that it was easy for him and the Razakars to instigate contempt for the Hindus, and thereby India. They considered the Hindus cowardly, ignorant and unenterprising, forgetting that the superiority of the Muslims in the State was not due to any special courage or enterprise implanted in them, but due to the fact that it was a Muslim State. When Razvi shouted that he would plant the Asaf Jahi flag on the Red Fort and that the Nizam would wash his feet in the waters of the Arabian Sea and the Bay of Bengal, the Indians laughed to see such sport, but the Hyderabadi really believed he would do it. Added to this traditional impression was the fighting in Kashmir, which had shown Indian troops to disadvantage, and it was felt that India would not be able to stand a war on two fronts — Pakistan and Hyderabad.

In order to prevent any incursions, the Central Provinces government established a border force for the three districts of Yeotmal, Akola and Buldana. In Akola the force was based at Basim,[2] under the command of Antarchand Date, with detachments of one platoon of the Special Armed Force (SAF) each at Rajgaon, Wyad, Risod and Loni. A Sub-Inspector was put incharge of each of them. The entire border force was constituted as an occupation force meant for taking over one district of Hyderabad.

Driven out from their homes, the Congressmen crossed the border and established themselves in camps in Indian Union territory. From there they waged a ceaseless war on the Razakars and the state police. Though the volunteers were not adequately armed or trained, they were fired with the zeal of freedom. From Yeotmal to Buldana, they were able to clear a belt of about ten miles in depth of almost every sign of the Nizam's domination.

The leader of the HSC volunteers in Akola and part of Yoetmal district was a small, well built Maratha named Vinayakrao Chathankar. I was deeply impressed by him at the first meeting itself. Completely unassuming, yet bold and courageous, he was a born leader to whom all the HSC volunteers paid well-merited respect. His greatest asset as a guerrilla leader was his integrity and his fair-mindedness. Even at a time when the organisation was starving for funds, Vinayakrao did not permit a simple dacoity or criminal act to be committed stating, "We are the makers of the new Hyderabad; and people will respect us only if we are honest."

While Vinayakrao was the leader in the field, the behind-the-scene activities were conducted by an organisation guided by Sherwani, a professor of Urdu. He had served in a college in Hyderabad for several years till he was externed for participating in the Vandemataram Movement. The two of them, Vinayakrao and Sherwani combined well, and had great affection for each other.

---

[2]Basim is now spelt as Washim. It was then a subdivision of Akola. Now it is a district.

Events moved fast in the one month I was in Akola. In June 1948, I received instructions to attend a conference in Poona. The conference was a tame affair. No one knew what was to happen and no one was prepared for what was happening. For a few minutes, Lt Gen Rajendrasinghji came in and spoke about the civilian administration of Hyderabad after it was taken over. I asked him what role the HSC would play in the action, his answer was evasive. The conference, like several others convened afterwards, was vague and non-committal. Perhaps people at the top did not know what was going to happen. The remarkable fact was that we were never told that there was to be a police action.

We were asked to provide the army with maps of the townships on the line of attack, together with some information on the strength of the Hyderabad Army and Razakars. I was able to tap a good source of information from inside Hyderabad State. A telephone operator in Nander (now spelt as Nanded) spoke to me regularly after collecting intelligence from other operators and reported how the movement organised by the HSC and its chief, Swami Ramanand Tirth ran, and what trains passed through carrying Hyderabadi troops from time to time. This was passed on to the army so that their plans could be chalked out accordingly. (After the operation was over, when I offered a monetary reward to the telephone operator, he refused saying, "I don't accept payment for serving my motherland.")

Though the army appeared to be fully prepared to march in, I could sense that at the highest government level there appeared to be some vacillation. Earnest endeavours were being made to reach an honourable settlement. The Nizam, on the advice of his Razakar ministers, appeared to be adamant. It must be said to the credit of the statesmanship of Sardar Patel that he tried every conceivable method of avoiding confrontation. Since the army was bogged down in Kashmir, he did not want to open a second front. All efforts at some sort of compromise were defeated by the spate of intelligence reports and rumours about collusion between Pakistan and the Nizam. Rumours were rife that arms were being flown in by the Australian gunrunner, Sydney Cotton, that a deal between Portugal and Hyderabad had been struck and that shipments of arms from Pakistan via Goa were in the offing. When a situation reaches its climax, rumours become alarmist.

It was in this atmosphere of tension that I paid a visit to the Basim border in the first week of September. We all knew that the attack was imminent. The entire nation was on alert. On 12 September, along with the DC, Akola, I met Col Ajit Singh,[3] the Military Commander of the sector for the first time. We had an impromptu conference which lasted several hours. We presumed from his conversation that the attack would begin within a week or so.

Now for a ringside commentary from Basim on the hectic events of the 'Hyderabad Police Action (HPA)', code-named 'Operation Polo'. (The twin cities of Hyderabad and Secunderabad had the highest number of polo grounds in the country. Hence the name.)

Day One, 13 September 1948: At eight o'clock in the morning, the IGP rang up and asked me if I had any news. I said 'no'. I rang up Basim and was casually informed by the SDO that Kanergaon (a town within Hyderabad State) had been attacked. I rushed from Akola to Basim in a truck as soon as I was told that 'Operation Polo' had started. At Basim, the local officers tried to dissuade me from going to the front. "Sir, it is not our business," "Sir, you must at least take a revolver," and so on. Grabbing a revolver and ammunition, V.S. Tambe, the Assistant Commissioner and I got into the same truck and drove into Kanergaon. The action was completed at 1300 hours and troops were busy consolidating their positions and preparing a counter-attack. The little town bore several tell tale marks. On the left we found that the customs *naka* (outpost) had taken a good deal of punishment. The streets were deserted and dead bodies lay strewn all over the place. Tambe and I drove over to see Col Ajit who was having lunch with his officers.

[3] At the time of retirement, Maj Gen Ajit Singh Ghuraya was Chief of the Assam Rifles.

The Colonel told me that the action had been an easy one. At four o'clock in the morning 'everything they had' was thrown across the river at the town of Kanergaon, and shortly afterwards, the attack was launched. In the early hours of the morning, the army under Maj Katrakji,[4] a Parsee, lunged forward to Kanergaon in Hyderabad State from our side. Resistance had been negligible. A few boys with guns who stood up to resist were wiped out. The post was defended only by Razakars and the customs police. The only real resistance in the place was offered by a Pathan, who entrenched himself inside a mosque and fired viciously. The twenty-third hand grenade got him and he was killed with his rifle clasped to his chest, his fair face and eyes set above towards the Valhalla of brave men. He died a soldier's death. I silently saluted his courage. A Razakar chief who used to parade in a swanky overcoat lay in a heap among the dead.

Stiff resistance had been put up by a company of Pathans on high ground a few miles from Hingoli, and that halted the advance for a few hours. Tambe and I saw several gory sights which were rather painful. We could see that fine thread which separates life from death — one moment, the victim was a screaming, praying human being; the next, his mutilated body lay flung in a common heap of the dead. Some deaths were only sounds to us.

A Razakar hiding in an underground cellar with a rifle and a bag of grenades was brought in. He had tried to kill an Indian soldier, who had entered the house with his rifle, but meekly surrendered and walked out when he saw a grenade. Another Razakar was brought in with a sword. Slowly they were flushed out from their hiding places and entrusted with the task of burying their fallen comrades. A few hundred yards away, the Sikhs were engaged in digging trenches and laying out the barbed wire. The widows and the children stood around the common grave with a prayer on their lips. There were no tears that day in Kanergaon. When destiny strikes with hammer blows of extinction, human beings are too stunned to think of those that are dead; their thoughts are confined to themselves; they keep thanking God for sparing them.

---

[4]Maj Katrakji was later murdered in a train.

There was a girl in the group with her mother. Both were injured with shell splinters from the preliminary bombardment. They sat quietly, a few dried tears in their eyes, wondering what we, their enemies, would do to them. When I gave them some bread to eat, they looked at me with such a forlorn look that tears came to my eyes.

We brought back the first batch of wounded to Basim on the return journey. As I drove the truck over the road to Basim, I pondered about the tragedy of that day. I felt that on all the roads leading to Hyderabad State, a similar scene must have been enacted. The same young men must have lost their lives for a Nizam who they never wanted to fight for. The mothers and sisters must be sprawling across roads in the shamelessness of death. What had they done to deserve this?

Jinnah had died two days earlier. The winds of communal hatred that he and the Muslim League had started would make millions of innocent Muslims in India suffer for years to come. Jinnah had lived to be Governor-General; these others had lived merely to be killed, on the altar of communalism and hatred.

Day Two, 14 September: We went to the Circuit House and proceeded to pay a visit to Kanergaon. All was quiet. There had been no counter-attack in the night. There was, however, one incident. Late at night, some women of Kanergaon tried to escape from the horrors of the day by crawling till the barbed wire fence. While escaping through it, the sentries heard them and fired. The screams of women were heard in the dead of the night.

Some amount of wanton killing is implicit in the initial phase of any warfare, but it was good to see that the bloodlust of the troops had been quenched by the next day. Prisoners were being taken. There were signs of revival in the village. Orphaned children stood about in small groups gazing belligerently, yet curiously at the troops. A stream of refugees had begun to pour back into the village from which they had been evacuated a few months earlier by the Razakars. We were welcomed by the people. On a small fort, the villagers hoisted the national flag and cheers for the nation were raised.

I stayed for the night in the village school. Meat and roti were provided by the SAF. I slept fitfully. From the direction of Hingoli we could hear the sounds of firing. Tambe wanted to be present in Wyad when the HSC men went into Hyderabad State. We sat outside in the moonlight, discussing the vagaries of the provincial government and the campaign in Hyderabad. The operation would not last for more than a month, we were sure.

Day Three, 15 September: In the morning, Tambe took pictures of the Extra Home Guards (EHG) as they marched into the State. We returned to Basim. I was a sight — unwashed, unshaved and unchanged with the black cotton soil of Berar pasted all over me.

After a shave and a bath, I went with Ghate for a conference with the Colonel at Kanergaon. We learnt that the Colonel had gone through to the front, so we waited at the rest house. A message came from him that we should send the SAF through to Malhivra. Ghate and I got into a jeep and led the convoy into the State territory. There were a few thrilling moments. The road was infested with struggling Razakars, who took pot shots at people on the road. It was just getting dark. The road was unfamiliar. At last, after what seemed a long distance, but was only eleven miles, we reached the rest house at Malhivra in Hyderabad State territory. There we met the Colonel who was on his way to Hingoli, and needed protection on his flanks. He had asked me for two companies of the SAF to protect his flanks and I readily gave them to him. We posted the SAF as indicated by him and waited till about nine o'clock for something to happen. All sorts of reports of Razakar movement on our right and left along the road kept coming in. The military was slowly building up strength for an attack on Hingoli.

That night, after having some drinks, I had a violent argument on the telephone with P.C. Saxena, the IGP in Nagpur. He wanted to know why I had given two companies to the army. "Not one man of ours must be lost," he said angrily. Perhaps I was a little tipsy, and expected a word of praise instead of abuse. I said, "Sir, I thought we were fighting on the same side." On that he seemed to hit the roof and said something about my always being unwilling to carry out orders.

"What if they are wrong?" I said (rum speaking). I wanted to add that his orders about arresting hundreds of Muslims and putting them in a stockade fortified with barbed wire was the limit in absurdity. However the DIG drew me away from the phone. I am sure he felt that the damned Parsee upstart must be taught a lesson.

We returned to Basim at about eleven o'clock in the night after consuming some more rum in the Circuit House. Partly owing to the additional belligerence of liquor, Ghate and I had a heated argument. My view was that the SAF should be utilised to clear up pockets on the flanks of the army as suggested by Ajit. They could slowly advance into State territory from the border and take up positions inside the State. This was furiously objected to by Ghate, who when arguments failed, descended to the cheap jibes of lack of experience, youthful rashness, etc. I was absolutely fed up. The whole day he had been interfering in my work, in a most provocative manner, and the climax was this row at night.

I went back to my brooding theme of never being able to work with my seniors and it would be best to resign or get out of Central Provinces if I could. I wished I could get away from it all by going as SP to Hyderabad. A lot of rehabilitation work needed to be done there.

Day Four, 16 September: News of the situation at the front was gloomy. The advance had been halted. Not only that, some tactical genius on the other side had drawn the Sikhs into a neat little trap. Under the cover of three hills, an incessant rain of bullets was poured into them for the whole day. The largest amount of damage was caused by some snipers who fired at our men from trees, thus causing more demoralisation than casualties. For the first time the faces of our men looked grim. We left the battle area and returned to Basim at lunch time. At about four o'clock in the evening, a Deputy SP suddenly burst into the Circuit House to declare dramatically, "Kanergaon has been captured. The enemy will attack Basim."

I must give credit to Ghate for maintaining his cool. Methodically all the arrangements were made, with the more heroic among us donning steel helmets, determined to die in such a way that would make for good photographs for posterity. When all the arrangements were made, we rushed out to Kanergaon. I sped out in my victory jeep, telling myself, 'This is life.' The Nizam has probably thrown in reserves to enter Berar at least at one point. At Kanergaon we discovered what had actually happened. A Hyderabad State Army man was sent to fetch eggs. He was astride his horse. The Sikh patrol had chased the man. The men of the Jodhpur Lancers, presuming it to be a counter-attack, had crossed over into Berar, prepared to die, but on the soil of their province. This was the first time I noticed what a significant role morale plays in warfare.

After the commotion settled down, we returned to Basim. Drinks were passed round, a little liberally perhaps. One of the senior officers of the Home Guards rang up all those who mattered in Nagpur to announce the valiant role we had played in saving the province. He made it sound as if a small band of tough Central Provinces men had pushed aside the military and taken over the defence of the country, faced bullets which went whizzing past and stood their ground with courage and determination. The credit-taking exercise had begun. Out in the front, the Sikhs were facing the music; at the rear, noble 'patriots' were doing the victory dance.

Later that night, the IGP in a brief telephone conversation with Ghate, told him that the SAF must be immediately withdrawn from forward areas. I was deeply disappointed — what a stab in the back and what a blow to the reputation of the police force! While the Sikhs were out in front, grappling with the enemy, we could not even hold liberated villages in the rear for fear of being accidentally killed! Never before had I seen an order so wrong, so utterly against the urgency of the moment, so completely lacking in courage and patriotism!

Day Five, 17 September: I went out to Malhivra in the morning for the withdrawal of the SAF as ordered by the IGP. Col Ajit was blunt. He did not care; his men had fallen back for regrouping and refused to release the SAF men.

Meanwhile Gen J.N. Chaudhuri's motorised unit which had entered the State from Osmanabad side, crashed through the poor defences and was well on its way to Hyderabad, when our wireless operator intercepted a message from Hyderabad State Army to its units: "Give three months' pay to all ranks and standby for further orders." At around four o'clock in the evening, a policeman rang up from the Kotwali police station of Akola to convey the information that a ceasefire had been declared. Within five days, the HPA was over. 'Operation Polo' had been almost bloodless for us.[5] Gen El Edroos surrendered to the Indian forces some five miles outside Secunderabad. Gen Chaudhuri, very wisely, did not allow the troops to enter Hyderabad immediately.

The Nizam blamed the Razakars. His army had never fought. The poor, disillusioned Razakars were cut down like corn before the sickle. The Asaf Jahi dynasty had come to an end with a whimper. The Deccan had ceased to be a Muslim stronghold. One hoped and prayed that from ashes of the old Hyderabad would rise a new, vigorous, and well principled Deccan of our dreams.

The police had done nothing; but all were safe. The only thing lost was reputation, but that could be built up in well worded reports, decorations, congratulations to those who could show how 'brave' they had been.

The atmosphere was not in the least festive when I returned to Akola, where Naju had spent her time in anxiety, wondering what had happened. A newspaper of Hyderabad published the news of my death in the HPA and friends from the Khandwa days mourned my passing away. I was tempted to say that I was still alive; only my career in the police had come to an untimely end.

The decision to send me to Parbhani, in the erstwhile Hyderabad State, as SP was cancelled though the original understanding given to me on my transfer to Akola was that I would be a member of the team which was to take over one of the districts of Hyderabad. Instead, I was transferred from Akola

---

[5] Gen Chaudhuri, in his autobiography, has stated that the number of casualties were 1,200 civilians and ten army personnel.

to an inconsequential post in the police headquarters. I felt they wanted me in Nagpur for cremation.

Central Provinces had become unbearable because they did not want to promote me as DIG in the province. What use was a man of no political backing, no party label; not even a Hindu ticket? When my case came up for promotion, the Home Minister, D.P. Mishra (later Chief Minister of Madhya Pradesh) wrote the following reason for bypassing me:

> "From all accounts, Rustamji is a prodigy but after all, an infant prodigy."

Once again, my age had been held against me for promotion. The real reason was that the powers that be wanted to favour their own man — Shankar Dayal Shukul, a Brahmin and a departmental officer was confirmed as DIG.

Getting away from Central Provinces to avoid being humbled by Saxena, the IG was my first aim. It was a very frosty meeting with him. It took just two minutes and then there was such a deafening silence that I picked up my cap and said goodbye. He never said why he disliked me. I applied for three months leave which was promptly sanctioned.

We went over to Bangalore and stayed with Naju's sister Coomi and her husband Minoo. One morning, we went to the railway station to enquire about the timings and were surprised to learn how close we were to Ceylon on the map. Without a second thought, we decided to go to Ceylon with just Rs 500 in our pocket. We went up to Kandy. We never stayed in a hotel. Instead, we slept on benches in parks. We went to hotels and while having tea, took turns to have a wash. We witnessed a cricket match against the West Indian team, which had the famous three Ws – Weekes, Walcott and Worrell.

We left Colombo in a steamer and caught the train at Tuticorin for Bangalore en route to Bombay. When we reached Bombay we did not have a penny in our pocket. When we reached home I was told that there was a call from Ghate, who was officiating as the IGP. I rang him immediately and he told me I had been appointed DIG in

Hyderabad State. Naju and I looked at each other. "Worth it, wasn't it?" I said.

"You bet," she remarked, "now I can buy some new clothes." That day, 7 March 1949 was our fourth marriage anniversary and what could be a better gift? For a time we forgot the penurious condition to which we had been reduced; now with a spring in our step, we went to the shops to buy all that we wanted with some borrowed money. What were debts? I was to be a DIG on a princely salary of Rs 1,950, plus all sorts of allowances. We spent lavishly as has always been our habit whenever we felt we had money.

There was no news in Nagpur of the offer to me from Hyderabad State and several strings were being pulled to send another officer instead. Fate intervened in the shape of a friend. With his help, the order was confirmed and fished out from the Secretariat at just the time when Central Province was sparing officers to other states, including Vindhya Pradesh. A month or so later, it declined to spare any more officers. It was, and it seems so to this day, a stroke of luck. Way back in 1940, when I was a young ASP, the thought that Independence would come in our lifetime never occurred to us. I had noted in my diary, "If disease and pestilence are able to claim those of my brother officers who are senior to me, I hope to retire as a DIG." I became a DIG at a young age of thirty-two, after eleven years of joining service.

On 18 March 1949, we arrived in Hyderabad, the city of Nawabs and cemented roads; of fez caps and bicycles and the Osmania University; of the Nizam; of the communists and of women in purdah; of grand buildings; and all the window dressings of a first class state. At first it was difficult to get used to it — no officer even answered the telephone himself. Food was provided on such a lavish scale at the Lake View Guest House that one week of it was enough to ruin our constitution. All senior officers, guarded by double sentries, were unapproachable. I was given an American car and a very dignified driver, who had driven for the Nizam and Lord Linlithgow, the former Viceroy. We were taken round the place as if we were royalty.

Over the whole of Hyderabad State towered the personality of Gen J.N. Chaudhuri, the Military Governor and D.S. Bakhale, the Chief Civil Administrator. In the midst of rioting and looting, murder and communal trouble, these two had worked confidently and quietly to restore the situation to normal. They were an ideal team for this purpose — Chaudhuri, a generous soldier, amiable, sociable, non communal, clever diplomat and a good leader; Bakhale, a quiet, publicity shunning administrator, a student of men and affairs, extremely diligent, firm and capable. Between the two of them, there was more or less good accord and understanding and even in the worst of times, they never showed anxiety or hesitation.

The officers and other respectable men with whom I spoke said that the HPA had saved the people from the atrocities of the Razakars but plunged it straight into mismanagement and plunder by Union teams that had been sent to each district from the adjoining states. The teams tried to replace the system of governance prevailing in Hyderabad. Ala Hazrat (the Nizam) kept a firm grip on the government with the help of some of the best Englishmen belonging to the ICS and IP. His administration had been good till the fanatics seized control to keep Hyderabad out of the Union.

Soon after reaching Hyderabad, I had a spell of duty in the city under another Rustamji (Firdunji Rustamji) who was then the Commissioner of Police, as there were rumours of communal trouble. After a few weeks, I was told that I would have to take over as DIG of the newly created Western Range with headquarters at Aurangabad. Eight districts were placed under that range — Aurangabad, Adilabad, Osmanabad, Parbhani, Nander, Bir (now spelt as Beed), Gulbarga and Bidar. In the absence of an earmarked house, we were offered an old unused palace, known as Kile Arak, as a house to live in. Naju felt it could be made liveable and she did put it in fine shape. To get out of the Nagpur hole was a relief; but to come to a state where you were required and conditions were good for living and working proved a bonus.

My main task was to re-establish the culture of work in the police stations. The officers, with some fear of the conquerors, were very cooperative, sometimes more so than the officers who had come with the HPA from the bordering states. I decided to be pleasant and called regularly on the DMs, went to the houses of the SP, if called. Within two months, the police stations started functioning. I was astounded by the ignorance of the high and mighty about the condition of the constabulary. When I brought to their notice that the State had the distinction of having the poorest paid constabulary in India, they would not believe me!

Soon after taking over charge at Aurangabad, I was ordered out to Gulbarga to look into the case against Kasim Razvi, in which the SP had, without obtaining any permission, prosecuted Razvi. The case was bad. Razvi had visited Aland (Gulbarga district) before the HPA. About a fortnight later, when the HPA began, some Muslim Rohillas took out seven Hindus, who they felt might stab them in the back and shot them. One of them, who was only rendered unconscious by a bullet, escaped to Sholapur, where he recovered and came back to be the principal witness in the case. My investigation showed that the case against the Rohillas had been corroborated. But even by a feat of legal acrobatics, Kasim Razvi could not be implicated in the case. In my report I frankly said that there was no case against Razvi. There was some trouble over that. The SP persisted, tried to win support of the Advocate General who disagreed with me. Eventually Bakhale and, I think Gen Chaudhuri, held that I was right. The Rohillas, after excluding Kasim Razvi, were prosecuted and convicted.

The Shoebullah Khan[6] murder case in which Razvi was implicated was unnecessarily delayed by Bakhale and the States' Ministry.[7] Had it been prosecuted at once, he might have been convicted. Kasim Razvi was convicted by the High Court in the much weaker Bibi Nagar case.

My work in the Western Range produced satisfactory results. When I took over in March 1949, the police force was completely disorganised due to HPA. Thousands of officers and men had deserted; police stations had not been started. Gradually the police

---

[6]Shoebullah Khan was the editor of a nationalist paper, *Imroze*.

[7]The States' ministry was renamed as Ministry of Home Affairs in January 1955.

stations were reorganised, local recruitment was taken up in earnest and, contrary to expectation, we secured a class of police constables who would be an asset anywhere. Inspections and training were beefed up. Control of crime was achieved with a two-fold drive: improvement in the standard of detections and arming the police *patels* and respectable people. Personally, I think I must claim credit for only one thing — singleness of purpose. I did not deviate one inch from the plan of reorganisation I had formed in my mind and within a couple of months of my posting in the State I was able to achieve the desired results.

It was my firm belief that police work was essentially the work of locals and hence they must replace the Union officers and men. I also felt that the constabulary and other officers recruited must be from the local population, and the local language should replace Urdu at the police station level. I further found that the system of police work in the State was basically sound and all that was needed was to inject new life into it. I was of the view that we should collect the best from other states and graft it with modifications on to the Hyderabad Police. Had my views been accepted, the Hyderabad Police would have been a force with distinctiveness and character. It became instead a poor imitation of the Madras Police. Lastly, I ensured that the dignity of the service officers was restored. When I took over, the distrust of service officers was so strong that my invitation to an Additional SP of the State to dine with me caused a flutter in official circles of Aurangabad.

Gen Chaudhuri left in November 1949 in a blaze of glory. He had saved Hyderabad from ruin, from the bestial communal passions which had seized the politicians and from them crept into the army. But for him and his master Jawaharlal Nehru, the city of Hyderabad would have been laid waste like Jalna and Nander and Osmanabad and Bidar, like the little villages on the border. But shortly after he left, the political climate changed due to the East Bengal incidents and Chaudhuri was one of the first to fall a victim to it. The policy of generosity to the people of Hyderabad, which Chaudhuri had so brilliantly executed, was held to be at the bottom of all ills of the State.

On 6 March 1950, I had gone to Hyderabad to attend a conference of DIGs. When we broke for lunch, we had no idea of the storm that was to burst over the police administration of Hyderabad. The IGP, Brij Bhushan Saran Jetley was informed that the ex-Prime Minister of Hyderabad State, Laiq Ali had escaped from house arrest. After the HPA, Laiq Ali had been placed under house arrest on the orders of the government while investigation into the cases against him was carried on. As soon as permission for prosecution was received, he escaped.

He was treated generously after the HPA. But confinement in his own house, where he could remain hidden for days on end and meet several persons, have his own servants and send out his wife and children to visit his friends, was, as subsequent events proved, a very dangerous generosity.

The Laiq Ali episode made a perfect newspaper story — it contained an element of mystery, a good opportunity for vehement criticism of the police and government, and a suggestion of corruption, which was exploited to the full. The escape occurred at a time when Indo-Pakistan relations were strained owing to the happenings in East Bengal. People saw in the escape another "propaganda triumph" for Pakistan. It was certainly a heavy blow to the administration in Hyderabad. In Parliament, Sardar Patel made a spirited defence of the administration. He mentioned that two months earlier the government of Hyderabad had been told to remove the IGP as he was incapable of dealing with the communists. Ten days later, Jetley handed over charge. He was sacrificed to the blood-crazy god of public opinion.

In the summer of 1951, Naju and I had gone to the railway station to bid goodbye to the Collector of Aurangabad, who was transferred to Hyderabad. We were standing in a crowd when a lady remarked, "What a terrible smell of garlic." That seemed a signal for Naju to crumple up and slump on the sacks of garlic kept on the platform. We revived her, took her home and called the doctor, who asked, "Are you sure it is not a baby?" It was more than six years since we were married and the fact that we were not blessed with a child affected Naju more than it affected me. The child of many prayers at last arrived on a platform of garlic. When Kerman was born in a hospital in Bombay in January 1952, the doctor allowed me to watch the struggle and pain a woman undergoes while giving birth to a baby. I watched the whole birth process in the labour room and wondered whether motherly love was the result of it. The baby was pink. She had long, beautiful eyelashes. She gave us hours of the most simple delight, which I suppose is what babies are primarily meant for. Luckily she spent the first few months of her life in the haven of a palace in Aurangabad with a rose garden and a flock of geese. Whenever she was taken out into the garden in the pram, the geese used to surround her as they seemed to think it was their first duty to guard her.

❧

The elections of 1952 saw the Congress in power. It appeared that the Congress wanted to change the IGP. Due to my work in the Western Range, my reputation got enhanced. Swami Ramanand Tirth in particular was very impressed and hinted that he would like to have me as the IGP. I felt if they appointed me to that post, it would be difficult for me to work. Local opposition would bring me down. I would not be able to withstand all the intrigues in the Secretariat, the politicians, the people in Hyderabad city and the people to whom an outsider was unwelcome. Even otherwise, I knew my chances were bleak as I was merely thirty-five years of age, the youngest DIG in India. A besmirching campaign was launched against me — that I was too young, I was addicted to luxuries, I drank, I was weak and lenient to my subordinates. Hence, when the new Home Minister Digambar Rao Bindu came to Aurangabad in February 1952, I seized the opportunity to speak to him. I explained my position and finally told him, "If you will forgive a little selfishness, I feel I should get out at the top of my form, while my reputation here is still good."

Bindu listened to what I had to say before telling me frankly, "We badly need men of your calibre. We have so much reorganisation to do and we have to put the city police in order. In all this, we will need the advice of trusted men like you." A few weeks later I was informed by the Home Minister that the Government of India had turned down the State government's proposal to appoint me as the IGP on the plea that I was too junior.

❧

In June 1952, I went to Nalgonda for a meeting. There I met Bhola Nath Mullik, the Director Intelligence Bureau (IB) and he talked with me for quite some time about his plan to enforce uniformity in the composition of the armed police battalions in different states and also about the communist insurgency in the Telangana area of the State. He appeared to have been impressed with my views on both the subjects. Shortly thereafter, I got a message that I had to report to Delhi as I have been selected for deputation to the IB. The order came to me in the shape of a wireless message from the Chief Secretary of Hyderabad:

> "Your services have been placed at the disposal of GoI with immediate effect. Hand over to Krishna Menon and report to Joint Secretary, States Ministry, Mr Vishwanathan."

I had no idea what it was. At no time was I ever consulted if I was willing to go on deputation to the Government of India. However, I got an inkling that I might be selected to be the Chief Security Officer (CSO) to Pandit Nehru, provided the latter agreed to it. The turn that the events had taken had been so unexpected and so pleasant that it seemed to me that I was going to have a date with destiny. I agreed to accept the offer of deputation to the IB.

Leaving behind several good friends and well-wishers in Hyderabad, made me sad but the future beckoned me.

Prime Minister Jawaharlal Nehru trying to field a ball during the annual cricket match of Members of Parliament (MPs).

"JN bowled one over, caught one catch and made one run in partnership with (AK) Gopalan (leader of the Opposition) on 12 and 13 September 1953. Following persistent clamour from the stands, 'Nehru to bowl,' the PM put himself on for the last over of the day. He confessed later, 'Bowling for the first time in 40 years, I was afraid I might hit the (square leg) umpire.'" — (Rustamji's diaries.)

11

Six Years with Nehru

I joined the Intelligence Bureau (IB) on 7 August 1952 and was allotted a small hole of an office in a hutment attached to the Secretariat. I had to build up the job from scratch and at the same time hold a terrific responsibility. I was in a quandary for several days, as nobody seemed to know whether I had taken over Prime Minister Nehru's security or not. Even after I joined, Gopi Krishna Handoo, my predecessor continued to do the work. The arrangement suited me as it gave me time to acquaint myself with the peculiarities of New Delhi, and the strangeness of the job that had fallen to me.

A few days later, at about 7:30 p.m., I was taken before the Prime Minister by Mullik, the Director IB. The Prime Minister shook hands with me and continued his conversation with Mullik. They were talking about a visit that he was to pay to Kashmir to an aerodrome in Ladakh, supposed to be the highest in the world, which the Indian Air Force (IAF) had constructed. I felt I should say something or would be taken for a poor dumb animal, so I came out with the brilliant interjection, "Provided the weather is permitting."

I wanted to add, "Provided the weather permits" to a statement of the Prime Minister that he would like to go to see the aerodrome, but the way the words came out...after that, I decided silence was golden. I was soon asked to leave the room. The Prime Minister smiled a dazzling smile and shook hands. I went outside, sure that the interview had been a dismal failure.

"You take over duties from tomorrow," the Director IB said after coming out. Apparently the Prime Minister's approval had been obtained for my appointment and I was incharge of his security.

The strange feature of my service with Nehru was that there was no official document listing out my duties with him. Because he travelled with very little staff — he had only a Stenographer and me, plus another Security Officer and Hari, his servant — a lot of duties fell upon me, which were not part of my security duties. I even had to arrange some of his appointments and take people up to him. I had to deal with requests of all types, for lunches and dinners and social events. I had to deliver letters, which were marked confidential to the addressees. Then I had to make sure that public meetings were done in such a way that any danger could be foreseen and we were prepared for it.

It was the combined job of a Military Secretary, ADC, Security Officer and general factotum. While on tour, he would suddenly walk into my room and say, "Let me hear the news," and when I put on the radio, he would sit doodling on the table in front of me. He often woke me up, "I want to speak to so and so."

One of his first instructions to me was, "There are certain rules which must be observed. The mackintosh must go with me everywhere."

When I joined Nehru's staff he was sixty-three years of age, but he was thirty-three, if his energy level was considered; and that too a good healthy thirty-three. He was blessed with a radiant personality which made people adore him in his lifetime. He had a frugal lifestyle and his eating habits were simple. While on a tour to Calcutta, I once asked him, "What is the secret of your remarkable energy?"

"I have a very good digestion, and I don't eat much. I am never worried by insomnia. I go to bed only when I am very tired — and then I can hardly keep awake." So saying, he gulped a *rossogola* and ran upstairs. I doubted his statement about not eating much. When I used to see the quantity he ate, I wondered how he could digest so much food.

Nehru used to say, "I would like to be myself when I have my meals." He preferred not to have any company at such times. But on long journeys, he would send for me as he wanted to have someone to talk to.

Once during an election tour of Travancore-Cochin (now known as Kerala) in 1954, he addressed as many as seventeen meetings in a day. At breakfast, I remarked, "Elections are a good education." He immediately corrected me. "Democracy is a good education," he said, stressing on the word 'democracy.' He was of the firm belief that democracy was the only form of government suited to a vast country with a diverse population.

Nehru's popularity at that time was so overwhelming that my job was mainly directed to prevent stampedes or disorderly public meetings. Nehru's way of dealing with crowds sometimes puzzled me. It appeared as if he was encouraging indiscipline. If the crowd was quiet and still, he would walk through it and there would be utter confusion in a minute. If there was orderliness, he would get down to garland a child and the people would become wild with enthusiasm. I often wondered why he indulged in such pranks. Apart from the love of adulation, he probably felt uncomfortable seeing poor people with folded hands and a pitiable look on their faces staring at him with a hope that he would be able to alleviate their miserable conditions. Or probably he wanted them to get rid of their servility which centuries of subjugation by despotic rulers had reduced them to.

One obsession of Nehru that I had to deal with was his dislike of masses of uniformed men and the use of sticks and lathis to keep crowds in position. He took his anger out on me and I had to take the blame as part of my duty. It became such a regular feature that, sometimes, his anger amused me more than hurt me. I remember, once, in the early fifties, Nehru, without his cap, walked out of one gate of the Teen Murti Bhavan early in the morning and tried to enter through the other. The sentry at the gate stopped him because half the people of India could not recognise Nehru without his cap. There was a hot exchange of words between the Delhi Police Constable and the Prime Minister.

With difficulty Nehru was rescued from the situation. When I reported for duty, all his anger with the abusive constable was directed towards me. The other time some stupid young ASP in Gujarat had amassed a large contingent of uniformed men and there was no crowd of people. I can never forget, to this day, the shouting I got on that occasion.

Nehru put up a proposal to construct a small house at the rear of the Teen Murti Bhavan, facing Roberts Road, as he had been feeling guilty residing in a huge mansion. I put in my objection in writing from the security point of view. Knowing that my objection would not cut much ice with him, I took the help of Lady Mountbatten to dissuade him from going ahead with the idea. Immediately after she spoke to him, we went to attend a function where he found some policemen standing at the wrong place. This was enough for him to give vent to his pent-up anger.

The job was interesting but the price that I had to pay for it was heavy. We came to Delhi in the worst month of the year from Aurangabad, which was at its most pleasant. From a palace with a lot of servants we came to stay in two poky rooms in Constitution House along with an eight-month-old baby and just one maid to help us with odd jobs. I was away on tour for more than fifteen days in a month. Delhi was a new place for us. To add to my woes, I got steadily impoverished because the government paid me a 'princely' sum of Rs 2 – 11 annas (about Rs 2.70) as daily allowance while on tour as I was considered a state guest.

All these factors contributed to producing strains in the married life for the first time in seven years. There were times when I went berserk. There were times when I was under pressure to quit and go back to Madhya Pradesh. But I loved the job. To be in the presence of Nehru, was something magical. The large masses in India were under his spell. But to work for him, to see India with him, to judge the impact of international events in the country in his company, to suddenly find that he trusted you— depended on you — gave you the satisfaction that was worth cherishing, and yet so difficult to define or analyse. The first one year was a period of intense stress. I decided to take three months leave to sort out things on the family front. This, I suppose, is the fate of most police personnel charged with the responsibility of security of national leaders.

Apart from being Deputy Director incharge of the security desk, Mullik entrusted me with various other duties. It fell to my lot to start the 'L' Branch, which included the Central Forensic Science Laboratory (CFSL) and the Central Detective Training School (CDTS). Since writing was a pastime, I built up the *Indian Police Journal*, rewrote most of the material myself and looked after its distribution. My other pastime was compiling the statistics of crime in India. I collected them and presented them in the form of an annual report. This proved so useful that a separate organisation called the National Crime Records Bureau (NCRB) was subsequently formed to look after all-India crime statistics. I developed the work of the United Nations Correspondents Association in India and worked for putting India on the map of international crime work. I also looked after the work connected with the International Criminal Police Organisation (ICPO).[1] When the scandal over the nationalisation of 243 private insurance companies took place, consequent to the formation of the LIC of India in 1956, I was asked to enquire into the conduct of not only Haridas Mundhra, the chief accused, but also the officials involved.

My main duty in the IB was the protection of the Prime Minister and the President. In the early years there was no systematic seating arrangements at the public meetings addressed by the Prime Minister which were attended by several lakhs of people eager to have a *darshan* of their favourite leader. During a trip to Travancore-Cochin in March 1954, I had pointed out to the authorities, in the presence of Nehru, that barbed wire should not be used in public meetings and receptions as it was dangerous for children and others when they were caught in front of it while being pushed from behind, and also because it produced a wrong psychological impression that the Prime Minister had to be separated by barbed wire from the people. Till I mentioned it, Nehru had not noticed it. Then at one of the places in that state, he fulminated against

---

[1]The name of this organisation was changed to Interpol in 1956.

the wire, and on return addressed a nasty circular on the subject to all the Chief Ministers. The Chief Minister of Madhya Bharat, Dr K.N. Katju received it a couple of days before the Prime Minister's arrival at Neemuch, and as it seemed to him to be too late to make any change, he ignored it. When we reached the first meeting place, Nehru was furious. He stamped and he shouted as was his habit whenever he was very angry. He rushed into the crowd, broke down barriers and showed that he cared a damn for security. In the car he gave the Chief Minister a most undeserved dressing down.

As luck would have it, at the next meeting place, the barbed wire was more profusely used and was very prominent in front. He rushed at the first barricade, tried to surmount it, and then began to pull out one of the poles. I knew it was futile trying to dissuade Nehru when he was in such a blazing temper. I adopted my usual tactics. I too rushed into the process of taking out the poles myself and then urged him gently to leave it to me, and calmed him down to some extent. And while doing so I cut myself badly with the barbed wire and tore my trousers and my beautiful new buttoned up coat which I had worn for the first time. The cuts in my clothing incensed Nehru still further. He rushed about in a temper, walking all over the meeting, while the people clapped and children rushed for safety. This incident became headline news for days.

Thereafter, I had a series of sittings with the Director IB and a manual for Very Very Important Person (VVIP) security was drawn up with a lot of guidance from him. A method of seating in public meetings was devised which gave security without showing too much of it. The manner in which we prepared the *Blue Book*[2] in 1957 and the way in which all were trained to observe and do the job in proper way did make security much better. I would say that our system of seating in a public meeting has been copied in many countries and it has certainly stood the test of time.

Mullik was an effective ringmaster. He assigned tasks to officers who carried them out with diligence. I had never met anybody

---

[2]The manual of instructions for security of VVIPs was formalised and brought out in a book form in 1957. It got the name *Blue Book* probably because the cover initially was blue.

as hardworking as Mullik, anybody as committed to the right ideas and to convincing others about them. He assumed charge as Director IB in 1949 and continued in that post for more than fifteen years. He influenced policing in India to a large extent after Independence. He gradually built up the IB from the small unit it was in the British days to the massive organisation that could deal with both internal and external intelligence. He left his impression on a whole generation of policemen.

He was able to enlarge the IB because of his close equation with Nehru. He was assisted by a group of brilliant men: P.V. Bhaskaran, Balakrishna Shetty, Gopi Krishna Handoo, Balbir Singh, Ramji Kao, Anand Dave, A.G. Rajadhakshya and others. There was something about him that attracted confidence. He did not build up an aura of secrecy and omniscience, a pose which became the habit with many an IB man.

He would prepare long analysis in which every eventuality was spelt out. That became almost a trademark of the IB. He could never be proved wrong because he had mentioned all possibilities. He could not only probe deep into any problem but was on the spot with his closed collar coat and white felt hat to hold the hand of the police wherever the situation was difficult to handle. Every disaster, every big problem found him on the spot and he was the man to whom all good policemen could rush for refuge. He endeavoured to lead the loyalty of the entire Indian police to the Prime Minister and in turn got the support and confidence from the police.

What I recall with some pride is the unity of purpose of those days. We were floating on a wave of exhilaration that Independence had brought about and we were all pitch forked into higher positions, promoted without seniority and told to manage as best as we could. Those of us who were his Deputy Directors in Delhi: Bhaskaran, Handoo, Shetty, Waryam Singh, Balbir Singh, S.N. Hosali, Gurdial Singh and M.M.L. Hooja were a rowdy, boisterous lot. The high spirits, I think, were due to high morale, which was a reflection of the atmosphere of those times.

Mullik's famous dictum to all of us was, "Never make the police angry." There was a lot of sense in that which some of our

Rustamji, New MP's I. G. Police

Chief Ministers' Confce. Opens In City

(By Our Staff Reporter)

NAGPUR, Sunday.

The conference of the four Chief Ministers of the integrating units of new Madhya Pradesh, which opened here this morning at the residence of Chief Minister R. S. Shukla, decided to appoint K. F. Rustamji, I.P., as the Inspector General of Police for the new State.

The Government of India, it is understood, has agreed to release K. F. Rustamji, who is now Deputy Director in the Central Intelligence Bureau and often works as Prime Minister Nehru's Security Officer.

The Chief Ministers' Conference, which is being attended, besides Ravi Shankar Shukla, by Takhatmal Jain, Dr. S. D. Sharma and Shambhunath Shukla, Chief Ministers of Madhya Bharat, Bhopal and Vindhya Pradesh respectively, began at 9-30 this morning, soon after the arrival of the Madhya Bharat Chief Minister by train from Khandwa.

After an almost eight-hour non-stop meeting except for a fifty-minute lunch-break, the conference was still in an inconclusive stage when the Chief Ministers dispersed.

India's Youngest I. G. Police

(By Our Staff Reporter)

NAGPUR, Sunday.

K. F. Rustamji, I.P., who has been appointed as the Inspector General of Police for the proposed new State of Madhya Pradesh will be the youngest Police officer in the country to hold the post.

Khushroo F. Rustamji, who is just 40, was selected in the Indian Police Service at the age of 22 when he was a Lecturer in the Nagpur Science College from where he passed his M.Sc.

Son of late F. Rustamji, who was in the judicial service of Madhya Pradesh, Khushroo Rustamji studied at the St. Francis De'sales and Science College. As a student he had won trophies in the Sushilabai Elocution competition and Byramji Debating competition.

Cutting from *The Nagpur Times* newspaper dated 23 July 1956.

people do not realise today. The IB does a silent service, never defends itself, is always prepared to take the blame and has done a lot of creditable service to the nation that it does not boast about.

Yet, for all the praise that can be heaped on Mullik, there was a lot that happened in those days for which he could be blamed. His 'Forward Policy' regarding China, in which a daring mission to disputed areas was wiped out, was an instance which could be quoted against him. The case that was prosecuted against Sheikh Abdullah was another instance of a decision which was faulty.

After his departure, the role of the Director IB has been modified and in consequence, the police unity and discipline have suffered. It is a pity that we never thought of having a Chief of Police (India). Mullik functioned as one. One central authority is essential.

During my six years in the IB there were several ups and downs. On 25 July 1956, I read in the newspapers that I had been nominated by a committee of the Chief Ministers of the integrating states of the new Madhya Pradesh to be the IG of the new state. A press communiqué was issued. I was informed by the Chief Minister Ravi Shankar Shukla and the Union Home Minister G.B. Pant that I would have to move soon. Congratulatory letters and telegrams poured in from all over.

Meanwhile, the DIB sent me to Nagpur to select a site for housing the Central Police Training College (CPTC) for training of IPS officers. There I could sense the opposition to my return to the state. From Nagpur, I went to Poona where the Chief Minister of Bombay province, Morarji Desai made it quite clear to me that that he would strongly oppose my promotion as IG of the new Madhya Pradesh on the ground that I was too junior. The real reason was that he was not prepared to accept B.G. Ghate, a Madhya Pradesh cadre IP officer of the 1928 batch. (Ghate, being a Maharastrian was scheduled to join Maharastra cadre). Through the Governor (H.K. Mahatab) the "strong opposition" to my promotion was conveyed to the Prime Minister.

On 11 August 1956 I was informed that Madhya Pradesh had decided to retain Ghate, so I need not go back to the new state and I may be retained at the Centre. And so I sank to my normal level after thinking a good deal of myself for a few days at the thought of becoming the youngest IG in the country.

At that time there was a proposal that Bombay province would be divided into three states: Bombay City, Maharashtra and Gujarat. Several MPs took it into their heads that formation of linguistic states was anti-national, so a proposal for a bilingual state was made. Everyone supported it and within two days it was passed in the Lok Sabha. Disturbances broke out in Ahmedabad and other places in Gujarat.

Was this Nehru's first failure? Never before had he failed in the solution of a problem, like the one Bombay province posed. In this case it was not he, not the Congress, not the Congress Working Committee, but the MPs who found the solution. I felt sure that Nehru was unhappy about it and deep inside he was angry with Morarji Desai for forcing him to commit a mistake. I therefore felt it was not the time for me to raise my own problem of a proposal and a rejection with him.

Finally, in May 1958 I received the much awaited orders posting me as IG, Madhya Pradesh. The reason why I was sent to Madhya Pradesh as IG will remain a secret. I had an interview with the Prime Minister and B.N. Datar, the Minister of State for Home and had a peep into the corridors of power.[3]

What has been the impact of Nehru on me? I think the one facet of Nehru's character which had impressed me the most,

---

[3]These two sentences were found scribbled on a piece of paper where Rustamji had jotted down some points for writing an article. He has not elaborated on the points in his writings. One can only conjecture the reason why he was sent to Madhya Pradesh as the Chief of Police. Dr K.N. Katju was made Chief Minister of the enlarged state of Madhya Pradesh in January 1957. Katju did not have a mass base in the new state as he had his education in Uttar Pradesh, practiced law in Allahabad and his political activities were confined to that state. The political figure who had grassroot support in Madhya Pradesh was Pandit D.P. Mishra, who was not on good terms with Nehru and was in political exile during most of Nehru's period as Prime Minister. Nehru probably wanted to have a man of his confidence in Madhya Pradesh as the Chief of Police, who would keep him informed about the developments in the state. It is clear from the entries in the diaries that Rustamji used to meet Nehru often on a one-to-one basis and brief him.

and therefore had the most profound effect on me, was his faith in friendship and understanding.

On the eve of my going to Madhya Pradesh, I did not know how soon the good that I had learnt from Nehru would be interred in the wilds of the new state, and how much of the bad will live with me. But when I left his service I did so with pride, that it was given to me to be of some service to him. And with it a thankfulness to whatever gods that be that my luck held out, and I could hand over Nehru safe and sound to the Indian people.

So it was a goodbye to Nehru and to Delhi. The Parsee Anjuman, of which I was the President, gave us a memorable farewell, despite all the differences I had with them regarding opening the *aramgah* (last resting place) when friends of deceased Parsees come to pay their last respects. Thankfully, due to the stand by me then, the *aramgah* is kept open on such occasions even to this day.

PART – IV

1958–1965

The Dacoits of Madhya Pradesh

G-1 -- ROOPA 26.x.59.

G-2 -- LAKHAN

G-3 -- AMRITLAL 19.10.59.

G-4 -- GABRA 13.11.59.

G-5 -- KALLA 25.11.59.

G-6 -- LACHHI-SRIPALA 25.9.59.

G-7 -- PAHARA(Liquidated). 19.9.59.

G-8 -- BARELAL

G-9 -- PANA -Encounter 27.7.58. Pana escaped.

G-10 -- MANSINGH(Liquidated)

G-11 -- BINDUA (Liquidated)

G-12 -- TANTIA(Arrested)

G-13 --BAHADURA

G-14 -- SHANKER GUJAR Gwalior. 24.11.59.

G-15 --HOTMA KACHHI (liquidated)

July 58 G-16 -Lalsingh. 23.9.59.

Card on my table on which I have marked the end of each gang as it occurred

"Card on my table on which I have marked the end of each gang as it occurred."

Taroon Coomar Bhaduri, the Bhopal correspondent of *The Statesman* (and father of film star Jaya Bachchan) had published a book *Abhishapto Chambal*, (The Accursed Chambal), in which he made mention of Rustamji having the list of dacoits on his table and how, like the Count of Monte Cristo, he used to strike off their names with relish as and when they were eliminated. The original list was found in Rustamji's diaries. Gabbar Singh, popularly known as Gabra is shown as G-4 in the list.

12

The Bandits

Gabbar Singh and Amritlal, two notorious bandits of the Chambal region in Madhya Pradesh, gave me a 'warm reception' when I reached Bhopal to take over as the IGP .

I assumed charge on 1 June 1958 and three days later, on 4 June, when the Chief Minister, Dr K.N. Katju was touring Bhind, Gabra alias Gabbar Singh chopped off the noses of eleven people in a village of that district, to signal defiance. He had taken a vow before the goddess he worshiped that he would chop off the noses of 116 people. This was his third instalment.

Amritlal, the terror of Chambal, had kidnapped seven children of well-to-do businessmen who had gone on a picnic to a park in Shivpuri district a few weeks earlier. They were still in his captivity when I took over and he issued fresh threats that he was about to murder them one by one.

The Madhya Pradesh I had left almost ten years earlier as an SP was much smaller. It was constituted in 1861 by the British, with Nagpur as its capital. There were established practices and procedures. The Madhya Pradesh I came back to as IGP was a large state, which came into being in November 1956, as per the recommendations of the States Reorganisation Commission, by amalgamating the four Hindi-speaking states of Madhya Pradesh, Madhya Bharat, Vindhya Pradesh, Bhopal and a large number of princely States. Each of these States had their own police force, police regulations, structure, pay scales and uniforms. The vast distances from one end of the state to another compounded the problem for the police chief.

Further, I did not know many of the officers of the erstwhile States of Madhya Bharat and Vindhya Pradesh. I was apprehensive of the reception they would give me. I expected antagonism and opposition, but, to my delight, I found that the state almost took me to its heart. The police fraternity welcomed me most warmly. What took me by surprise was the media, where newspapers described me as, 'tall and handsome'. The Chief Minister, Dr Katju recalled his association with my uncle's family in his home town Jaora. His cabinet colleagues, and the Chief Secretary, H.S. Kamath, a man of outstanding ability, gave me a respected place. My advice was asked for on subjects not in my ken.

I had to struggle with the problems of four States combined into one. To assist me in the job, there was only one DIG and three Assistant Inspectors General (AIG) in the Police Headquarters (PHQ). There were five other DIGs posted in the five Range Headquarters: North, South, East, West and Central Ranges or Gwalior, Raipur, Rewa, Indore and Jabalpur respectively.

Fortunately for me, the DIG (Crime & Railways), B.M. Shukul and I were in the same university and were also posted together in Saugor. He was Deputy SP in 1938, when I joined there for my training. B.M. (or Joshi as we sometimes used to call him) was in our group of half a dozen close-knit Indian officers. With him as my second in command, it was possible for me to entrust the office work to him and devote myself to touring the length and breadth of the state — showing my face to the officers and men, building up the team, reorganising the police force, bringing about uniformity among the police of four different States, developing and expanding the force in the face of financial opposition.

Out of the three AIGs, one was incharge of Administration which included the work related to integration of the States and the SAF. K.K. Dave who was in that position started life as a lawyer under my brother Rustam in Nagpur and later when he was selected for the police he was posted under me at Akola for training. His father-in-law, Shreenath Mehta was the DC of Saugor when I was under training there. The other AIG was P.R. Rajgopal who looked after Intelligence and the third one was B. Shrivastava, incharge of the CID. A year later the government sanctioned two more posts of DIGs for SAF and Administration and another post of Additional AIG in the PHQ to assist to cope with the increased work load.

A lot of things needed attention. The standard of the police had dropped rapidly primarily because the value of the rupee had fallen so much that an average constable got less pay than a sweeper. The government was unable to afford a higher salary and in a sense, accepted all the mischief that stemmed from low pay. Along with low pay, there was absence of proper leadership, proper training, and proper organisation.

One of the first things I did on taking over was to address the senior officers. I told them at the outset that the first thing I expected of them was to tell the truth to me. I told them, "I want the truth. I can deal with any disaster, but I need to know the true facts in all cases." I further advised them not to use brutal methods but pursue the dacoit gangs relentlessly and shoot them down in genuine encounters. Some of my colleagues felt it was not possible to subdue the dacoits without torture and illegal detention of their family members. But I made it clear to them that if the police could win the trust of the people, information would come in wagonloads. I expressed my views on what constitutes the crux of policing, the importance of having reserves, practising impartiality, working towards the integration of the police units of the four States and finally looking into the general welfare of the constables and their families.

What was it like to be the chief of police of a state after spending six years in the IB?

The change from the anonymity of the IB to the IG-ship of a large state was a big one. For the first time in my career I had to face criticism in the press for police ineffectiveness. This was something which was absent in pre-Independent India. Sometimes it was the other way around. If the police took legal action against a certain individual, there were loud laments about high handedness and the police playing 'ducks and drakes' with the life and property of the citizens. For the first time in the history of the Indian people, publicity had become a powerful tool to be misused by those who had an axe to grind.

The headlines in the newspapers were mostly about the atrocities committed by the dacoit gangs and police ineffectiveness. My day began with a clutch of radio messages, mostly about dacoities by armed gangs in the northern districts of Bhind, Morena, Gwalior and Shivpuri. There were sixteen major gangs, who were referred to by the code numbers allotted to them on the basis of their ruthlessness. Rupa was given the code number (G-1) followed by Lakhan (G-2), Amritlal (G-3) and Gabra (G-4).

To understand the dacoity problem of the area, one has to go back into history. The area between the Chambal and the Narmada rivers in Central India has been the breeding ground of marauders since the beginning of history. In the twilight of the Mughal Empire, a period of transition came when weak and aspiring States tried their best to attack each other with the aid of gangs of ruffians. The rise of the *pindari*s in the beginning of the eighteenth century was mainly due to the help they got from the Maratha kingdoms between the Narmada and the Chambal in the form of *jagir* (land) and license to pillage everywhere except in their own territory. After each campaign, the Maratha Maharajas accepted with kingly grace a large share of the booty that had been collected by these bandits.

A big cavalry operation against the *pindari*s was undertaken in 1817 (known as the Pindari War). As a part of military operation, Marquess of Hastings organised two main armies of four divisions each. One in the Deccan and another in Central India (with Jabalpur as its headquarters). A total force of 81,000 foot soldiers, 10,000 regular cavalry and 23,000 irregular was placed on the periphery of Central India to strike at the *pindari*s. The *pindari*s had no heart for fighting as they were not fighting for a cause. Their main motive was to loot and plunder. When the object of people in such a group is individual gain it is not difficult to disperse them. The *pindari*s were hunted down and dispersed into small bands which were destroyed piecemeal with the help of land owners and the distraught public.

After the destruction of the *pindaris*, the thugs became prominent, though they had originated almost 500 years before they were finally exterminated in 1839. The magnitude of the problem that Col (later Maj Gen) Sleeman dealt with can be gauged from the fact that when he was appointed in 1826, the thugs were spread out in 100 gangs from Lahore to Mysore. The thugs committed murders with a degree of perfection seldom achieved in crime. Perhaps the biggest handicap that Sleeman had to encounter was that he was dealing with a band of criminals who were held together by a perversion of religion which made murder a part of worship. The moral insensibility that this perversion produced left no place for those errors committed by criminals which arise out of guilt, compassion or regret.

It was difficult getting witnesses to depose against them. Added to that was the maze of extradition treaties and the inadequacy of staff to cover such a vast area in which they operated.

However, the maximum obstruction to his work came from the British judiciary. Sleeman's dependence on statements of approvers was frowned upon by the judiciary of those days, which found it "utterly repugnant to the principles of true justice." In such judicial pronouncements, it was usually considered unnecessary to mention that as against the "oppression" of the police, the thugs belonging to the *pila rumal* (yellow scarf) gangs every year killed about 40,000 people travelling from one place to another. The successful operations conducted by the Thugee and Dacoity Department (predecessor of the IB)[1] opened up the Narmada valley and flourishing townships arose in Bhopal, Jabalpur and Saugor.

While the Narmada valley and its adjoining areas were cleared of the criminal elements in the early years of the British rule, the criminals gradually began to shift to the north. It is difficult to say why this gradual movement occurred. Two reasons could be ascribed for it: the first that the Chambal ravines which were gradually increasing in size and area owing to the denudation

[1]The Thugee and Dacoity Department was wound up in 1904 and in its place came the Central Criminal Investigation Department, which later came to be known as the IB.

of forests could offer good hiding places; secondly, the Maratha rulers of the princely States of Gwalior region adopted a policy of dispossessing local landlords, which created a disgruntled group of Rajputs antagonistic to the regime and eager to improve their fortunes by marauding. In 1869, a rebellion of Gujars of Narwar broke out against the Maratha ruler of Gwalior. The ruler's method of crushing these local revolts was primitive and severe. Whole villages were levelled and its leaders hanged in public.

Further, the formation of Madhya Bharat in May 1948 by the merger of twenty-five princely States and the subsequent abolition of *zamindari* (landlordism) system produced a vacuum which helped the legendary dacoit leader Man Singh to establish himself in an area of five districts. The chase to get Man Singh was a long one and it was with the combined efforts of Uttar Pradesh, Rajasthan and Madhya Bharat that the gang was hunted down and its leader, aged sixty-three was shot in a famous encounter in Bhind in 1955.

The end of Man Singh did not signal the end of the dacoity problem. One of the reasons for this was the easy availability of firearms and ammunition from the leftovers of World War II and these districts had a sizeable representation in the army.

Rupa and Lakhan were the lieutenants of Man Singh. Rupa, alias Rup Narain Sharma was a Brahmin and Lakhan Singh, a Tomar Rajput (Thakur). Caste was and still continues to be a predominant factor in the social life of the northern areas of the state. Man Singh, though a Gujar, was able to have a Brahmin and a Thakur as his chief lieutenants due to his personality. But as old age started catching up with him, his two lieutenants, who were with him for ten years, deserted him and formed their own gangs. They got entrenched in the area by sedulously attacking members of their opposite caste. They did not attack their own clan, and on that basis got protection and help from them.

Madhya Pradesh abounded in poverty and lack of communication. Not that the public was lethargic or cared less. In certain areas there was an awakening. There were protests at the apathy of the government. Peasants marched to the collectorate to demand food and work. The unrest caused me anxiety as a policeman but raised hope that the people would be able to improve their lot.

When I toured the countryside as an IG, the thoughts that occupied my mind were different from what I used to think when I was touring with the Prime Minister. I used to think of the constables who had not got their pay for four months, or their uniform for the year. I wondered how it would be possible to eliminate torture in police work — an area which had known no other type of official control.

In the initial months, after being with Nehru for six years, I often caught myself trying to be Nehru again and again — jokes with a small child who came forward with a garland, the quiet walk through the factory and the inquisitive questions. It amused me when some subordinate police officer trotting behind me told me in a whisper that we were getting late.

I was listening to my former chief Nehru's address from the Red Fort over the radio on the occasion of Independence Day in August 1958, when the telephone rang.

"Congratulations, sir," a journalist said.

"For what?" I asked.

"Don't you know? You have been awarded the President's Police and some sort of Fire Services Medal."

"No, I know nothing about it. This is the first time I have heard anything about it. How did you know?"

"PTI has covered it."

I went inside and told Naju that I had been awarded the President's Police Medal. She thought I was joking. When she realised I was telling the truth, she was so overcome that she started to cry in a small, happy sort of way and tears came to my eyes too. As usual, Naju and I behaved madly. When a nice tune was being played over the radio, she, in her torn nightgown and I, with shaving soap all over me, danced in the bedroom and went round and round, hugging each other.

Nehru, G.B. Pant (Home Minister) or B.N. Mullik (my boss in the IB) might have been responsible for the award of the medal, I concluded.

I did not know what to make of the honour conferred. For the previous three or four months one good thing followed another.

In that period, I had received such honours as would be sufficient for a lifetime. First there was my appointment as IGP of a large state, touching farewell given to us by the Delhi Parsee Anjuman and a sparkling article on me written by none other than Mullik himself in the *Indian Police Journal.* The most touching of all honours came from the tiny South American Republic of Ecuador. The first Penal and Penitentiary Congress conferred a diploma of honour on me, "For his valuable scientific contribution which had national and international repercussions in the penal, penitentiary and criminal subjects." The letter from its President, Roberto Pettinato pleased me more than several other distinctions that came my way.

I hoped and prayed that my luck would last for a few weeks more because we had launched in Gwalior a massive combing operation to flush out the gang of G-2 or Lakhan Singh (about twenty-five men) who had been terrorising the countryside for the previous ten years or so. 'Operation Hammer' began on 19 August 1958, when 4,000 men were pressed into service. That day it rained heavily. The men had to bear the brunt of a bad monsoon. The rains were followed by floods and what aggravated the situation was the shortage of food. The gram distributed to them by way of rations had become soggy and clung to the insides of their spare socks in which they carried it. The *gur* trailed down their clothes. As they advanced, the red pins on our maps moved up.

All through the day and night the radio messages from the area came, as we pored over our maps and moved the pins about in order to forecast what the next move of our adversary would be. The latest news we got was that Lakhan Singh was moving towards the ravines of Asan and Kunwari rivers. If that was correct, he had made a mistake. We would be able to catch him in the fork or somewhere between the rivers in a natural obstacle and *hammer* him till he remembered the hundreds of murders he had committed and the hundreds of houses he had looted. I wondered, 'Is his luck better than mine?'

For the first time, about 4,000 men and about 100 vehicles had been amassed in a dacoity operation. Hitherto, the dacoits were used to tackling about 100 or 500 men trailing them and even from them the gangs suffered heavily.

The 4,000 men were sent into an area where communications were poor, food was scarce, the population was hostile because almost all the villages had Thakurs, who were Lakhan's caste fellows and were therefore his sworn friends, or others who profited from his dacoity. Can my responsibility be ever imagined? When I thought of the poor constables in sapped uniforms, unshaven, dirty, but full of spirit although hungry, I felt a sense of pride in them. Even when they had a full meal it comprised only of chappatis and dal with a raw onion, while the dacoit gangs feasted with *puri*s (a small round deep fried bread), ghee and milk.

To add to our woes, the wireless equipment failed and the vehicles got stuck in flooded streams. We went on pursuing G-2 and his gang relentlessly. The battle was not only against Lakhan and his gang but also against the elements. On 26 August, we received information from Jora that the gang had been seen in the deserted temple of a naked sadhu residing in the ravines of Deogarh. I somehow felt depressed, concerned as I was at the safety of my men, who were out there in the wilderness, fighting a battle against a gang of twenty-five desperados.

In the evening I spoke to J.S. Kukreja, SP, Morena at Deogarh and he said that the drive although exhausting had not produced results. My spirits plummeted to zero.

'Should we carry on? Supposing the gang had already escaped? What will people say?' I was assailed by doubts. I was probably mentally tired.

On 28 August it was confirmed that Lakhan and his gang had broken the ring and escaped. Somebody had slipped up. Somebody had been negligent. I could hardly conceal my disappointment when I ordered the withdrawal of forces. All could see that I was tired and beaten. 'Operation Hammer' had failed. It was difficult for me to believe that so much hard work could produce no result at all. I decided to wait and watch and till then my critics could keep laughing.

I concentrated all my energy to the work that the amalgamation of four States produced. There was so much to do that the inner me was satisfied. I was building up a modern police force and dealing with intricate problems. Some concrete results were visible. There was happiness, hope, endeavour and hard work. There was satisfaction.

In the same month of August 1958, Naju, with the help of the wives of some officers, got busy with building up a welfare centre, where the talents and time of policemen's wives were utilised to "earn a little and learn a little" — sewing policemens' uniforms.

I kept meeting the MLAs and listening to the problems each of them raised. It gave me a more independent picture. It was another source of information of what was happening in this biggest state of India. It took me some time to get used to the honour and shame associated with the job of IGP of the state.

I soon found that a subconscious gloom was overtaking me. I should have known that the disgrace part was about to begin and I had a premonition of it. In December 1958, I took the salute at the passing out parade of Sub-Inspectors at the Police Training College at Sagar. Then I read a newspaper article in which the dacoity problem in Bhind and Morena was discussed with reference to an incident in Chattarpur district where a dacoit gang had kidnapped three constables and brutally done them to death. I was criticised for playing hockey during the Police College Week celebrations in Sagar while dacoities were being committed and policemen were being murdered.

Disgrace abounding, I was not afraid of what the government would say. But it was amazing how afraid I was of what the newspapers would say. Partly because they had no restraint and could say what they liked. Partly because they said what the people were thinking.

The law gave us no help at all and there was no protection for anyone in the hysteria of the times. If a newspaper published facts that were lies, if a man insulted your honour, if a politician called you corrupt and a murderer called you a tyrant — all that you could do was to sit in your chair and pretend that you take no notice of all that. A judgement of the Supreme Court of that time said, "Those who fill public position must not be too thin-skinned in reference to comments made upon them...(even though may be) undeserved and unjust, yet they must bear with them and submit to be misunderstood for a time...They must accept an attack as a necessary though unpleasant appendage to their office...(and) ignore such vulgar criticisms and abuses hurled against them rather than give importance to the same by prosecuting the persons responsible for the same." (Supreme Court, 1956 — Kartar Singh vs State of Punjab — Justice Bhagwati and Chandrasekar Ayyar).

Thus, according to the Supreme Court we were expected to wallow in the dirt of polemics with the wise advice that it was all in public interest. Anybody who helped the police was butchered. We could not do anything to anyone who invited a gang, funded it and guided it to a massacre. On its part, all that the government wanted was that the dacoits should be killed in action.

Added to this were the laws which did not favour the police and had become too archaic and intricate. Despite all the odds against us, thirteen of the listed gangs were liquidated within two-and-a-half years. It was all due to good teamwork, motivated officers, and above all, a new-found confidence of the people in the police. We received strong support from the Deputy Minister (Home), Narsinghrao Dixit,[2] who was himself from Bhind and who, as Home Minister of Madhya Bharat, had taken a vow on the floor of the Assembly to free the Chambal ravines of the dacoity menace. Lady Luck also favoured us.

I shall now give an account of a few of the sixteen listed gangs and how they were eliminated.

G-3, AMRITLAL: Amritlal, the incredible, killed, robbed and kidnapped for almost a quarter of a century and built up such a strong

[2]The Home portfolio was formally with the Chief Minister. The Deputy Minister was directly responsible for the day-to-day running of the department.

position in his field of operation that it was difficult to dislodge him. Call it public sympathy, timidity or national weakness, this man held the countryside of Central India, consisting of the bordering districts of Shivpuri, Guna and Morena of Madhya Pradesh and the adjoining districts of Kota and Sawai Madhopur of Rajasthan, in an iron grip of fear and extortion.

There were uncanny similarities between his life and mine. I was born in 1916; he in 1915. About the same year as I joined service in 1938, he began his criminal career. Amritlal, popularly known as Babu Dilwala, assumed leadership of his first gang in 1943, the same year that I got charge of a district. He then committed a series of crimes in Agra, Mainpuri and Etawah districts of Uttar Pradesh. During the days of British Raj, when District Collectors were a power in the land, Amritlal committed a daring burglary in the house of the Collector of Etawah.

A young British SP went after him and Amritlal was arrested in Agra in 1946. He was sentenced to eighteen years. While being tried in another case, he escaped from the judicial lockup. Amritlal took over leadership of a wild band of outlaws in 1949, about the same time I became DIG of police in Hyderabad. He went on drinking, romancing and marauding with a zest that had never perhaps been equalled in the annals of Indian crime. With a penchant for beautiful women, he had been shot at by a member of his gang, who disliked his advances towards a certain woman. After some time, Amritlal, irritated by the sauce and the superior airs of Uttar Pradesh people, concentrated on drumming support from the forest areas of Shivpuri and Guna districts, the Sheopur subdivision of Morena district and the bordering districts of Rajasthan.

In May 1953, Amritlal launched a sensational attack on the Kolaras police station of Shivpuri district with the intention of killing the SP, Chunilal, who had taken special measures for his arrest, including a little judicious harassment of his mother whom Amritlal loved deeply. (Amritlal was the son of a Punjabi forest contractor and his mistress who belonged to the Kirar caste.) The SP had a providential escape as he had left the police station a few minutes before the attack. Amritlal and his gang killed two constables and took away the arms kept in the police station.

His strategy was one of extreme cunning, and each crime was planned with deliberation and foresight, matching a military operation. He struck with surprise and ingenuity, so that people could talk about his exploits and shiver at the mere mention of his name.

Not that he lacked gestures of magnanimity which have won hearts for outlaws all through history. In the early fifties, a barber who gave him a nice haircut was gifted a note of Rs 100; a man who cycled ten miles to warn him of the presence of police received Rs 1,000.

Amritlal had become a rich man and here the similarity ended. Around that time we led an austere life in Delhi, to the extent that Naju had to go out to sell some old articles of furniture in the Jama Masjid market on Sundays, so that we could have something to live on after our European trip in 1955.

It is a striking coincidence that Amritlal's decline and fall began in the first week of June 1958, four days after I assumed charge of the Madhya Pradesh Police. I am not claiming credit for it. I am only mentioning a coincidence.

On 4 June, the police had two sharp encounters with Amritlal and he fled, leaving all his goods behind. Among them were some saris and *cholis* (blouses), a few brassieres and necklaces, gifts of the romantic bandit meant for his mistresses. Amritlal suspected, or was deliberately made to suspect, that someone from within the gang had given information to the police. His suspicion fell on Daulat Singh, a member of the gang, whom he shot dead. As a consequence, the gang broke up into three groups, and his second in command Sultan Singh got separated from him. Sultan, an ex-policeman, was the fighting core of the gang. Amritlal hated to take risks. He had no stomach for blood. Sultan was incapable of the brainy leadership that Amritlal provided and succumbed in an encounter with the police in October 1958.

Amritlal was clever, but like all clever men, he was extremely suspicious. He had no idea of how to build up support for himself, except through fear. He searched desperately for new members but could not succeed. And when he did find them, he grew suspicious of them. He killed Tula Gadaria on the suspicion that he might be a police plant.

The bandits of Madhya Pradesh are caste and status conscious. They measure their status on the basis of the reward placed on their heads by the government.[3] Amritlal, too, was proud of the reward of Rs 20,000 which the government of Madhya Pradesh had offered for him — dead or alive. This kept playing on his mind. He even informed some of the members that he was worth a bit to the government. This and his weakness for women proved to be his undoing.

Amritlal had become infatuated with a woman named Naraini, who was the wife of a gang member named Rathi Kirar. Rathi had been killed a few months earlier. I was informed that he was killed in a police encounter and we distributed rewards to the police, shook hands in congratulations and so on. But later, I had my doubts. Perhaps Amritlal had killed him but made it appear that he was killed by the police. Double-crossing in the dacoity game sometimes reaches such proportions.

The bandit's ardour for Naraini did not cool. He picked up the woman's brother, Badri, aged twenty-three years and importuned him to fetch his sister. Badri Kirar obviously resented such a demand, even if it was under a threat of extermination of the whole family. Badri decided to take revenge for making his sister a widow and the demand of bringing her so that Amritlal could satisfy his carnal desires.

Badri kept playing for time. He asked Amritlal to teach him how to shoot as he had never fired a gun before. Amritlal taught him how to load a rifle, how to put the charger in the magazine, how to apply the safety catch, how to put the rifle on the shoulder and fire. And such was the stupidity that overcame this arch villain when the end was near that he even told him about the huge reward he carried. He proudly showed Badri the proclamation issued under the signature of the DM, Shivpuri, while boasting he was an

---

[3]In 1972, Jaiprakash Narayan took the surrender of dacoits. Mohar Singh (code name E-1), who had the maximum reward of Rs 2 lakhs, told me in 1993, that he considered it beneath his dignity to sit and have meals with bandits who had rewards of a few thousands on their heads.

important man. Badri asked him innocently about the penetrating power of a rifle and how many bullets would be required to a kill a man. Amritlal, amused at Badri's ignorance, told him that one .303 bullet could go through five people in a row and kill all five.

On the night of 18 August 1959, Amritlal moved through the jungle, as he had done for twenty-five years. The gang spread out in a formation, the scouts in front, Amritlal in the middle and Motiram and the rest following behind. Early in the morning, they reached a *mahua* grove, near Gopalpura village and camped there. All of them had a bath. They had brought a goat with them, which was slaughtered. Liquor was probably consumed. The gang members played cards for high stakes while the meat was being cooked. Then after a hearty meal, they all lay down to rest at noon. Badri volunteered to be the sentry and Amritlal did not suspect the youngster. So much was his liking for Naraini that he transferred some of it to her brother also. They all slept soundly.

As soon as the dacoits were fast asleep, Badri took a .303 rifle, assumed a prone position behind Amritlal and fired one shot, the first one in his life, which went through Armitlal's chest to split up in Motiram's body. Both of them were sleeping face to face, so one shot was enough. Motiram died at once. Amritlal tried to rise up, glared at his assailant and then collapsed. It was certainly the most important shot fired in Madhya Pradesh as it killed the man most needed to be killed in India.

The other members of the gang got up when they heard the firing and tried to catch Badri. He fired at them and sent them away, running in their underpants. Badri took the two .303 rifles which were looted from the Kolaras police station in 1953 and put them across his chest before walking to his village to announce to a stupefied SAF party that he had killed Amritlal.

I was in a meeting in the PHQ when R.N. Nagu, the DIG (Administration) rushed in to break the news in an excited tone, "Sir, Amritlal is killed." I refused to believe it and said I would believe it only when I see the dead body myself. I caught the first train to Jhansi and from there motored down to Shivpuri.

The SP Shivpuri, H.K. Pahuja met me and briefed me. I found Pahuja to be a determined policeman, a man with an uprightness that gave offence, an honesty that exposed the dishonest men who were in league with Amritlal. He gnawed at the roots of the gang for months and tried to get at all the helpers and harbourers of the gang. Even when six of the witnesses were killed after giving evidence, he did not give up, though I am sure in the night he must often have feared for his three little children. The first thing we did on arrival was to go to the police station and take a look at the bloated face of the man who had lived like the 'king of bandits'.

Then, at the Circuit House, we began to piece together the story to find out what had actually happened. A suggestion was made to embroider the story and claim that Badri had been introduced as a police agent in the gang. I felt that such an attempt would be dangerous and may lead to the prosecution of Badri for murder. If such a thing happened, we would find it difficult to rescue him, particularly as the attitude of an independent judiciary could always be made flexible in devious ways. All those who were against us, including the dacoits, would be sure that the police had done it. So, for a change, why not spoil the fun for everyone by telling the truth!

In an unexpected turn of events, after a few days, the rather feeble DM of Shivpuri wrote to the SP that Amritlal's death should be registered as a case of murder and investigated. Pahuja telephoned me, "Sir, what shall I do?" I told him to inform the DM that he disagreed with him (the DM) and as per the police regulations, the SP should make a formal reference through the DM, DIG and the Commissioner to the IGP for orders. And I would issue suitable orders on the subject. At the same time I asked Pahuja to discreetly inform the DM that we had no objection to registering a case of murder but at one stage or the other the strict interpretation of the legal texts might require the prosecution to include the DM also as an accused as it was he who had sanctioned the reward, and wrongly announced it for Amritlal, 'dead or alive'. The DM backed out.

I started a systematic campaign to save Badri. I spoke to the Chief Secretary, Chief Minister and the Governor. I pleaded with the Chief Minister to sanction the reward of Rs 20,000 to Badri Kirar. The Chief Minister was of the view that it was a case of cold-blooded murder. As a sop to me, he referred the case to the Law Department for its opinion. The Law Secretary gave his opinion and like most opinions of the Law Department it was capable of any kind of interpretation. The jurist and constitutional lawyer in Dr Katju viewed it as an unethical act to sanction the reward though the government notification used the words 'dead or alive'.

Two months later, Badri Kirar finally got his 'reward' — he was shot dead by one of the surviving members of Amritlal's gang!

G-8, BARELAL: A few days after Amritlal was killed, a number of successes were achieved in the anti-dacoity operations. One after another, four gang leaders were brought down in a chain reaction of successes. And it all started because of an error on the part of H.S. Kohli, DIG, Northern Range.

The day after the Kheira murders were committed, Kohli happened to be in Bhopal. When he went out of my room, he was handed the crash message regarding the murder of eleven people in village Kheira by the gang of G-6, Sripala and Lachhi. He did not think it was necessary to inform me about it. When I went home in the evening, I saw the message and rang up the Deputy Minister (Home) to inform him about it. For reasons best known to him alone, the Deputy Minister (Home) wanted to go to Gwalior. He told the Chief Minister that it was a matter which required to be looked into by him and me. When he conveyed this to me, I was annoyed. I could not say 'no'; instead, I said we must start at once and spend the night in Morena, instead of Gwalior.

Our visit to Kheira village where the brutal crimes were committed, not only gave an incentive to the local officers, but also enabled me to obtain first-hand knowledge on the prevailing situation in Morena. That made it easier for me to guide C.S. Kadam, the SP, Morena. When the movements of the gangs came over the police wireless, I instructed the SP to concentrate on G-8 Barelal for the next fortnight as he was probably in an area where we might be able to bring him down. I sent instructions to the DIG to divert the troops from other places and encircle the gang of G-8.

On 19 September, I received a message which stated that the gang had been located in Maharajpur, near Gwalior. There was something about the message which showed that we were entering into an encounter with a powerful gang.

Kadam eliminated the gang in what was one of the finest tactical encounters we have had in the state. The informer had luckily told the SP that the gang had a lookout on a tree, so he planned the action in such a way that while he advanced with his flanks covered, he drew fire from the gang. The gang in retreating went into two carefully laid ambushes. The first encounter with the force led by the SP resulted in two members being killed. Then the gang ran straight into the Bren gun in the ambush and three more fell. Barelal, the gang leader, was the last to be killed as he had hidden himself in a *jowar* field. However, sensing that such tactics were habitually used, the SP had the place combed. Barelal fought back with a sten gun. A Head Constable was hit by a bullet in his leg. His fellow constables got worked up on seeing their leader injured. They surrounded Barelal like a pack of wild dogs and shot him to pieces.

G-16, LAL SINGH: The extermination of Barelal led us from one success to another. I cannot definitely say what it was. Perhaps it was just that indefinable quality called morale, public morale. It went up so high that information kept coming in.

Lal Singh, nicknamed 'The Terrible', was an ex-armyman who was posted as an armourer in the Babina cantonment, near Jhansi. He supplied arms and ammunition to dacoits, and ran away with a rifle from the cantonment apprehending arrest. He killed people brutally, even senselessly to create an impression and become a gang leader. His gang swelled to sixteen members and soon became a menace in Datia district. No crime was barred to him — he committed dacoity, murder, kidnapping and nose chopping with a frequency which was greater than any other gang.

In fact he committed atrocities like firing on marriage parties in order to create fear in the minds of harmless people. He was chased from pillar to post, each time losing some of his men. He fled to Rajasthan where he killed seven people in one village. In May 1959, he returned to Madhya Pradesh and committed the ghastly murder of five Meenas, whom he beheaded as a sacrifice to the deity in Kuno village of Sheopur subdivision. In the last stages, he was sick, tired and completely fed up. One of his associates even ran away with his rifle, and he was left with just two men and a couple of twelve-bore guns.

I had made an offer to him about a year earlier when he set out to become a dacoit. I wanted him out before he became a confirmed dacoit. I sent a messenger to him. He touched the feet of the messenger and thanked me for the message, but declined my offer. He said that even if the police pardoned him, the army would send him to jail; hence he preferred being a dacoit.

However, his end came suddenly. Information was received that he had taken shelter in a village. Madho Singh, the Deputy Superintendent of Police (DSP) surrounded the village and shot him down.

G-6, SRIPALA: Sripala, 'The Brute' was the dacoit who killed eleven young men in Kheira of Morena district on 11 September 1959. He lined up the boys and shot them in front of the entire village while fathers pleaded and women wept and wailed. The brutality of the crime had a profound effect on the people of the area. But, instead of frightening the people, it made them more determined to take revenge. It is a common belief in the Chambal region that a person who drinks the waters of River Chambal develops a strong sense of revenge. A father of one of the murdered boys came forward bravely and informed the police about G-6's whereabouts. We took action in the ravines. In the dark, an intrepid Gurkha constable crawled thirty yards under fire and got him.

G-1, RUPA: Encounter followed encounter. This was the finest hour for the Madhya Pradesh SAF. After Amritlal's killing on

19 August 1959, a series of actions took place in which brigands, who had operated for several years and were supposed to be invincible, were finished one after another. Barelal on 19 September, Lal Singh on 23 September and Sripala on 25 September, all in a space of one week. This resulted in boosting the morale of the people and the police. A feeling of pride ran high amongst us all.

And then on the 27 October 1959, I.J. Johar DIG of SAF, barged into my room, shouting loudly, "Congratulations, sir. Rupa has been shot dead!!"

I could not believe my ears. Rupa was the most notorious dacoit of the Chambal ravines. He was the bravest, handsomest (blue-eyed) and the most dangerous dacoit, who could shoot with a telescopic rifle with the skill of a marksman. His outstanding quality was his cool and calculated courage.

Rupa was the son of the legendary dacoit Man Singh's priest and astrologer. Rupa was himself said to be an astrologer and he led the fiercest and the largest gang of dacoits with skill and daring. He was G-1 in our list.

We waited anxiously while the message came over the wireless. It was from Terence Quinn, Commandant of the 4th Battalion SAF.

> "On behalf of all the 4th Bn officers and men, please accept my most hearty congratulations on the liquidation of Rupa, leader of G- I (.) Both Rupa and Rajaram were shot dead in an encounter with 4th Bn forces on 26th evening in Mahua ravines (.) Further search continues (.)"

The message trembled with my fingers. 'Rustamji, this is the zenith of your career as a policeman,' I said to myself. And perhaps there is a certain amount of credit for me in this, which can never be disclosed. I had turned down requests to delay the action against the gang because of its size and its marksmanship. I had insisted on an attack, whenever possible, as early as possible. I knew we would have casualties — fifteen people, perhaps twenty. But by God, I would not let the gang rest merely because it was strong.

I had raised the subject of dacoity at the Annual Commandants Conference held in October and had stressed that each encounter should be a tactically strong one — the days of rushing at the dacoits shouting, *Har Har Mahadev* were long past. I wanted movement in front with the flanks covered and support (in ambush) at the back. Ambushing was a technique that was perfected because of my insistence. Officers said it would never work — too textbookish. But it did work in the Barelal encounter, and I drove the lesson home whenever I could.

I would like to think that in making the disposition of his men for the fateful encounter, Quinn had my words at the back of his mind. He must have had some remembrance of it, because it was on his way back from Bhopal after the Commandants Conference and the Police Week that he got the news at Mahua and he organised a tactical action. Five platoons swept the ravines. Three platoons lay in ambush, guarding all the small tracks which ran out to the river. We came to know from the informer who was with the gang and a kidnapped person whom the gang held in custody, that the gang had noticed one of the ambush parties moving out. Rupa boasted, "I can escape from 10,000 such men. Who's afraid of a small party of police?"

It was his overconfidence that cost Rupa his life. The gang came upon a mound in the ravines. The small ambush party under a Head Constable opened fire. Rupa could have escaped, if he had tried. But he wanted to fight and was shot dead by a bullet that pierced his chest.

The entire night the police lay siege in the cold darkness. The next morning they discovered that they had killed the most notorious dacoit of the Chambal ravines. Fortune certainly favours the brave.

Telegrams and messages arrived. The newspapers of the state gave us kudos. 'This is the peak of your career, alright,' I said to myself.

G-4, GABBAR SINGH alias GABRA: Nehru's seventieth birthday was observed with great *éclat* on 14 November 1959. When I met him in Delhi I wondered what I, his former CSO for six long years and now the chief of Madhya Pradesh Police, could present him with.

Gabbar Singh and his gang had been killed in a bold encounter in Bhind district the previous evening, that is

13 November. I conveyed the news to him and that was the gift that the Madhya Pradesh Police presented. He appeared happy.[4]

Gabbar, the nose-chopper, had taken an oath to cut the noses of 116 persons, and had already succeeded with twenty-six. He was one of the most brutal in the ignoble gallery of the Madhya Pradesh dacoits. He was run down in an open field by R.P. Modi, a young Deputy SP who forced him tactically into an encounter and blotted him and his gang out through Bren gun fire and grenades.

There was one dramatic moment in the encounter — the gang had been mauled, four had been killed in the ambush, but there was still some life left. It was getting late in the evening. Darkness had descended. "I am going to assault," said Modi. "Volunteers," he called out. Fifteen men came forward.

They covered the distance to the gang in three short runs, firing away with their Bren guns before Modi pitched the grenades. The nose-chopper collapsed and died at Modi's feet with half his face blown off.

The encounter took place in Ghum-ka-Pura village in Gohad police station area of Bhind district. It was one of those rare encounters which was watched by hundreds of people.

After every encounter, the police prepares an 'Encounter Report'. Since the encounter and elimination of the entire gang of Gabbar Singh was due to the personal bravery shown by Modi, I felt that a report drafted by him would not have much credibility. I therefore asked him to relate the details to M.C. Trikha, the young ASP, who would prepare the report. Below are some excerpts from the report:

> Gabbar Singh, alias Gabra, was born in 1926 and belonged to village Dang in Bhind district. He was a Gujar by caste and was the son of Raghuvar Singh. He had two brothers and a sister. Raghuvar Singh had very little cultivable land

[4]Prime Minister Nehru often evinced concern about the dacoity problem. In his letters to the Chief Minister, he suggested the reclamation of the Chambal ravines to increase the land available for cultivation.

and hence his son Gabra had to take up menial jobs, like carting of stones from the quarry and working as a labourer to meet the family needs. Gabra was a well built, tough youth who was fond of wrestling and was strong-headed.

Gabra was often witness to the authoritative behaviour of dacoit gangs and the fear they instilled in the minds of the submissive villagers. The young man was influenced by the image and lifestyle of the dacoits and the power they wielded and he aspired to become one himself.

In 1955, Gabra left his village and joined the gang of Kalyan Singh Gujar. As soon as he joined the gang he was made to commit murders, dacoities and kidnappings to ensure he does not leave the gang and also that he was not planted in the gang by the police. After a few months with the gang, he broke away and formed his own gang with five or six members. During the period, October to December 1956, he committed a spate of murders and dacoities to enhance his image as a gang leader. The reign of terror that he unleashed in the surrounding villages of the districts of Bhind, Gwalior (MP); Etawah (UP) and Dholpur (Rajasthan) sealed the lips of the villagers and none came forward to give any information about his movements to the police.

Gabra, like other bandits of the region, was religious and highly superstitious. He had been told by a *tantrik* astrologer that he would not get killed by a bullet fired by the police or the people if he were to offer 116 noses to the goddess he worshipped. Thus from December 1956 to December 1957, he chopped off the noses of more than a dozen people in the villages of Machhuari, Bhakore, Chamhodi and Chirenasta, etc.

In a span of three years he had committed thirty-one murders, thirty kidnappings, thirty-two dacoities and twenty-six nose choppings. The horrifying acts committed by him made him a dreaded name in all the neighbouring villages and districts of three states. He had several encounters with the police and in most of them it was the police who suffered reverses and a few brave policemen were also killed. A couple of constables were also victims of his nose chopping. He had a narrow escape through the police cordon in one of the encounters. He suspected the informer to be from village Dinpura. He lost no time in rushing to the village to take revenge. He lined up twenty-one people and shot them at point blank range — to send a message across to all.

In 1957, the opposition parties paraded a dozen people whose noses were chopped off before the State Vidhan Sabha. The government was put to shame and it became a matter of prestige to liquidate the gang of Gabbar Singh.

The IGP, B.G. Ghate was asked to camp in Bhind to personally supervise the operation against Gabbar. He asked for volunteers and the SP, Bhind, B.B. Mane suggested that the task be assigned to the young Deputy SP, Rajendra Prasad Modi, who had taken part in the successful liquidation of the gang of the notorious one-handed, female dacoit Putli Bai earlier in the year. Modi started by making relentless efforts at building up confidence of the people in the police, hoping that one day they would lead him to Gabra.

In May 1959, Modi was at the Gohad Sector Camp with the other police personnel when he noticed a fire blazing away at a distance. On reaching the small hamlet of Ghum-ka-Pura, he noticed that the entire village was on fire. The police party immediately went about extinguishing the fire and brought it under control within an hour. A poor scheduled caste person who was there said that his son was probably still in his hut as he was not to be seen anywhere. Modi rushed inside and rescued the five-year-old boy who by then had received some burn injuries. Modi put him in his jeep and asked the father to rush him to the hospital and also gave some money to him. The person's name was Ram Charan.

After about twenty-five days, Ram Charan came to Modi to thank him for saving his son's life and in return for what Modi had done for him volunteered to give information about Gabbar. He asked Modi to accompany him and took him by foot in the night to Dang — Gabbar Singh's village. From there he took him to the highway — the Gwalior-Bhind road. After standing there for some time, he walked another 200 yards into a saucer-like depression to his village Ghum-ka-Pura. Ram Charan was particular that Modi memorise the route as his village served as the hideout of Gabbar and his gang.

Some months later, on the fateful day of 13 November 1959, Ram Charan was seen standing in Modi's house even before daybreak. Modi spoke with him through signals. He raised his eyebrows indicating whether the gang had come. Through a slight jerk of his head and movement of his eyelids, Ram Charan indicated that they were there. Modi drew him aside and asked the details. Ram Charan told him, "*Puro gang baithe ho. Sab ko maar dalo.*" (The entire gang is camping there. Finish all of them). The hideout was the same that Ram Charan had already shown Modi. Before departing Ram Charan placed one condition: "Finish off the entire gang. Not one man should escape as otherwise I and my family would be wiped out."

A force of 300 was assembled at Gohad by ten o'clock in the morning. The plan was to surround the gang from all three sides and a search party was to proceed from the fourth side. The gang was in a place which was between the Gwalior-Bhind National Highway and the narrow

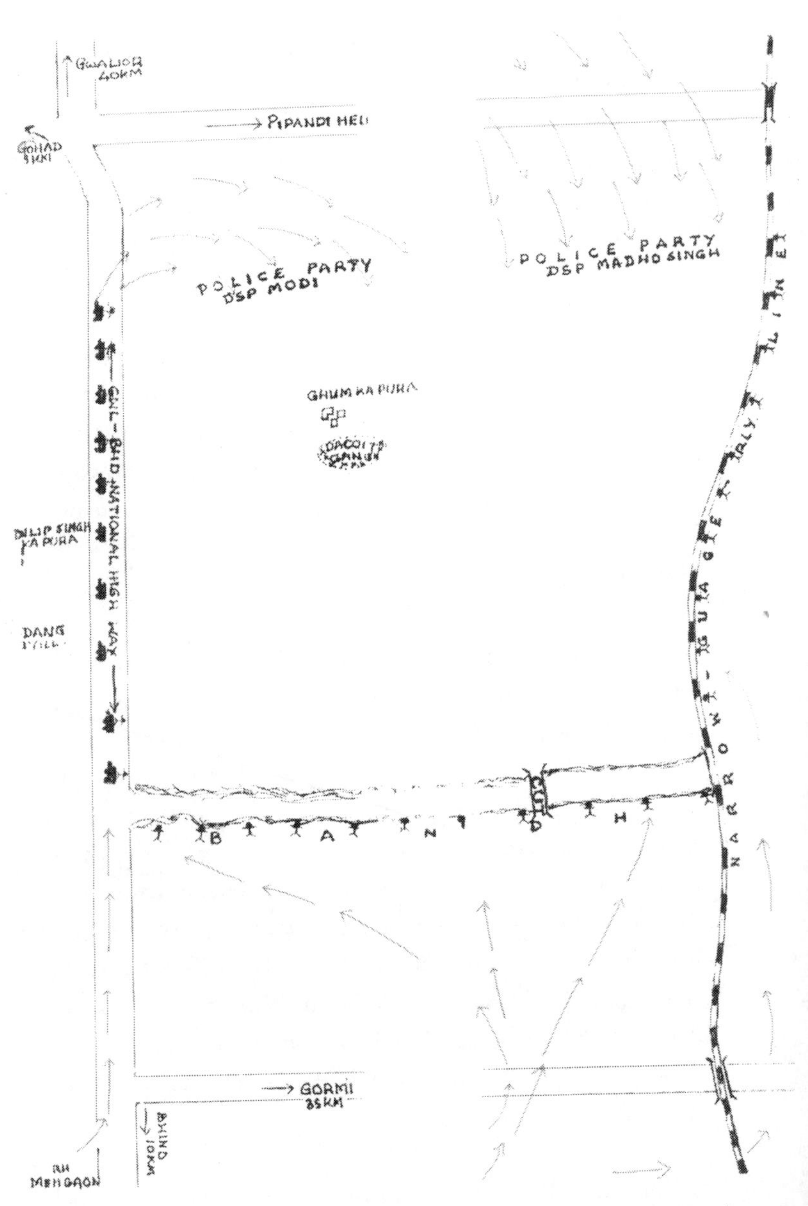

Plan drawing of the scene of the police encounter with Gabbar Singh. Trucks were placed on the Gwalior-Bhind road on the left, with armed policemen taking up position near them. Policemen also took position on the *bandh* (raised ground). The narrow gauge rail line is on the right. The encounter with the Gabbar Singh gang took place in full view of hundreds of people standing on the buses and the train.

gauge railway line running parallel to the road. The force was sent in the direction opposite to where the gang was camping so that even the policemen would not be aware where they were going. After taking a circuitous route they reached their assigned places by two o'clock in the afternoon.

Modi and the search party of thirty men went towards the spot in a vehicle. The other vehicles having one or two constables each were made to park on the National Highway at a distance of forty – fifty yards between them. Police vehicles parked on the National Highway would not raise any suspicion. The gang also was of the view that nobody would suspect it to be so close to a National Highway. By then Madho Singh, Deputy SP had also reached the spot from the other side, thus blocking the escape of the gang.

The search party had hardly advanced seventy-five yards when they noticed some black objects moving. They were the heads of the gang members who were crawling on the ground to hide from the police party. The search party kept on advancing and the gang, not finding any chance of escape, got up and started firing on the search party. The police under Modi immediately sprung into action and returned the fire.

A moment later about ten to twelve khaki clad dacoits sprang up from their hideout and opened heavy fire on the search party. They started running towards the railway line side in their bid to escape. As they approached the railway line, the policemen positioned there opened fire on the gang. Two dacoits tumbled down and the rest started running towards the National Highway. As they got closer to the highway, the constables sitting in the vehicles opened fire. Being relentlessly chased by the search party, the gang made their final attempt to cross the bund on the east. The police party covering the bund fired on the dacoits.

Notorious Nose-Chopper Slayed

GABBAR WITH 11 AIDES SHOT IN ENCOUNTER

(By Our Staff Correspondent)

BHOPAL, Nov. 13

The notorious nose chopper dacoit chief Gabbar Singh was killed today along with his associates Jagat Singh, Ram Dulare and nine others in an encounter with the Special Armed Force of the Madhya Pradesh Police near village Jagannath-Ka-Pura in Bhind district, according to an official report reaching here tonight.

The gang of Gabbar Singh was being continuously chased by the S A F since last one week and was runnig helter shelter to avoid encounter with Police.

According to just reports the encounter with Gabbar's gang took place at Jagannath-Ka-Pura in police station Gohad in Bhind district between 3 and 4 p m today.

Two kidnapped persons have also been recovered by the police after the encounter.

Further details in this connection are awaited.

The police has also recovered nine arms including one T M C fire 303 rifles and two twelve

(Continued on Page 6)

Late News

LONDON, Nov 13

The British Labour Party leader Mr Hugh Gaitskell, has sent "warmest greetings" to Prime Minister Nehru on the occasion of his 70th birthday tomorrow.

The newspaper cuttings of the killing of Gabbar Singh and his gang, and Nehru's seventieth birthday.

Finding no escape route, the remaining dacoits, took position in the shrubs almost in the middle of the operational area and concealed themselves in the bushes and went on constantly firing on the police parties.

The sun was dipping into the horizon. Apprehending chaos due to crossfiring in the darkness, and a likely escape of the remaining dacoits, Modi immediately decided to charge at the dacoits hiding in the bushes and finish the operation before it got dark. He called for volunteers. Fifteen Gurkha constables, who were with Modi in the Putli Bai encounter, readily stepped forward. Madho Singh was asked to provide covering overhead fire to the charging party. Shouting "Charge," Modi and the team of volunteers rushed towards the dacoits.

More than fifty yards was covered by the charging party when the dacoits opened heavy fire. Modi and party lay down to take cover. He signalled to the Head Constable for a grenade and threw it on the dacoits. Once it went off, he sprang and made the second lightening assault on the hidden dacoits. The dacoits kept up their fire. Modi felt the need for a second grenade to lob on the dacoits. A constable, Narvottam Singh tried to drag Modi to safety. Modi signalled to him for another grenade and after removing the safety pin with difficulty as it had got jammed due to getting rusted, Modi held it for two seconds after releasing the lever and then threw it. The grenade burst immediately on hitting the ground. With lightening speed he made the third assault on the hidden dacoits and gave swift and pointed bursts on the dacoits who were in the shrubs with his Light Machine Gun (LMG). He reached the spot where some dacoits lay dead. He kicked off the weapons which were in their hands.

Gabbar Singh, the nose-chopper, was lying there badly injured. His jaw was totally smashed and his breath was passing through his slit in the neck. There were seven or eight dacoits near him, dead or breathing their last. Any injured dacoit who moved received a LMG burst. Modi stood there with the hair of Gabbar Singh in one hand and the LMG in the other. The Company Commander of the SAF, Thapa joined him and taking the Verilight pistol from him, Modi fired in the air to signal the end of the operation. The sun had by then set completely. It seemed as if the sun was waiting for the final assault to be over before going below the horizon completely.

In all, eleven dacoits were killed including Gabbar Singh and Dulare Singh. Unfortunately two out of the four kidnapped boys were killed.

During the entire period the encounter was going on, vehicular traffic on the National Highway came to a standstill. Simultaneously, the narrow gauge Gwalior-Bhind passenger train had also stopped on its tracks. Men climbed on the roofs of the buses and train and were witnessing the whole operation. They were cheering the police party with shouts of, "*Maro! Maro! Maro, haram zadon ko.*" (Kill! Kill! Kill the bastards.) The Gabbar Singh encounter was a unique one in the sense it was carried out in full view of hundreds of people who were witness to the daring and courage that goes into encounters with dreaded dacoits.

The IGP Mr Rustamji visited Bhind and walked over the entire area of operation on foot and personally congratulated all those who took part in the encounter. An interesting dialogue took place in a meeting.

Mr. Mehta, the Commissioner, Gwalior Division said, "Modi, why did you go so close to the gang? Anything could have happened. You could have got killed."

"Sir, it was the last chance. I wanted to finish the operation before it got dark," replied Modi.
"Young man, I can only say you were mad."

Mr Rustamji interjected, "Mr Mehta, there is a fine distinction between a brave man and a mad man. Had Modi not been mad at that moment, he would not have been brave enough to make this a historic day for MP police. After all, fortune favours the brave."

The conspicuous courage displayed by the young twenty-six-year-old Deputy SP, Rajendra Prasad Modi was recognised by the award of the President's Police and Fire Services Medal for gallantry. His comrade Madho Singh, another Deputy SP was given the Indian Police Medal for gallantry.[5]

The government of Madhya Pradesh had declared a reward of Rs 20,000 on Gabbar Singh. Ram Charan was given Rs 5,000 out of this amount and the rest was distributed among the 300 policemen who took part in the encounter. Uttar Pradesh had declared a reward of another Rs 20,000 and Rajasthan Rs 10,000.

G-5, KALLA: A few months before I took over as IGP Madhya Pradesh, the police achieved signal success in the anti-dacoity operations. On 23 January 1958, a trap was laid for Lakhan Singh. The Deputy SP, R.P. Modi, who was in the raiding party, fired at a running dacoit, whom he suspected to be Lakhan. Suddenly the cap of the dacoit came off, exposing long hair. The dacoit who was hit by the bullets was not Lakhan; it was Putli Bai. The woman named by the press as the 'bandit queen of MP' was a dancing girl and was a paramour of dacoit Sultan Singh. She got trained in dacoity and was made the joint leader of a gang after Sultan Singh was liquidated. She had only one arm, but was able to fire with it. She was killed only after giving the police a stubborn fight. Kalla, the second in command of the gang managed to slip away and became the sole head of the G-5 gang.

[5] R.P. Modi told me that he presented Rustamji with a strand of hair from Gabbar Singh's beard as a memento.

After the Gabbar Singh encounter, information was received by the police in quick succession. The police acted upon it with determination and courage. On the basis of reliable information, twelve days after Gabbar was shot down, an ambush was laid for the Kalla gang in the Gohad police station area of Bhind. Kalla, who carried a reward of Rs 10,000 on his head, was the only person to be killed.

Soon after, in another encounter in Gwalior district, the only man killed was Hardayal, the leader of that gang.

G-2, LAKHAN SINGH: On 30 December 1960, I was watching a film in Bhopal with Naju and Kerman when Nagu came inside the dark hall and announced aloud, "Good news, sir, Lakhan has been shot dead." My mischievous young daughter caught on to that sentence and kept on repeating it not only in the hall, but for days afterwards.

A press conference was hurriedly called by the Deputy Minister (Home) and he elucidated on the version that we had received from Bhind:

> "An encounter occurred in Deora village of Bhind district. At a certain stage, the forces that were advancing heard a man in front saying, 'I am a police officer. Don't shoot.' Platoon Commander (PC) Ram Akhtiar Singh went forward to investigate and saw the arch criminal lying on the ground, wounded. He jumped on him and grappled with him. Lakhan shot him and he shot Lakhan. Forces advanced to find the dacoit and the police officer lying side by side, dead."

The news created a sensation. The newspapers of Bhopal splashed it in headlines as a New Year gift from the police to the state.

I refused to go to Bhind with the Deputy Minister because I felt that I did not need the kudos that would be flowing on the occasion.

A day later, I reached Bhind mainly to find out what had happened. Even after examining all the officers who played a leading role in the encounter, it was difficult to find what actually happened as I could not visit the site of action due to the rains.

In any case, there was agreement on the following points:

- The gang was being given shelter in Deora village. Lakhan had probably reached there to disgorge the fabulous wealth he had secured in the daring dacoities committed in Agra district in December.
- On receiving information, the police planned a three-pronged attack on the village.
- The gang was sighted by the group under Madho Singh, first and driven away through Bren fire. It ran towards the second party led by R.P. Modi.

After that, the version that emerged from examining the men who participated in the action was rather confusing and contradictory. It appeared that as Modi's party reached the outskirts of Deora, it came under heavy automatic fire and the advance was halted.

Meanwhile, there was firing from the right flank of the party where PC Ram Akhtiar Singh with the Bren was advancing forward. From a distance of about fifty yards, the PC and his men saw a man in khaki crawling on the ground. (It may be remembered that dacoits in Chambal wear a police uniform.) The man shouted, "I am a police officer. Don't shoot."

Firing ceased. The PC wanted to go forward and investigate but his men warned him, "There is a *badmash* (rascal) there. Don't go forward, sir." Disregarding the advice, the PC advanced forward. The distance between the party and the man lying in the mustard field was only about fifteen yards, but the dacoit was hidden from view. Lakhan suddenly lifted his gun and shot down the PC. At the same time, automatic fire burst from the dacoit's supporters who were in hiding. The police advanced with blazing guns to find that both the dacoit and the PC were lying dead, side by side.

When I heard the story I felt that the version given to me was correct, except that here and there officers and men had tried to take some credit for themselves.

I woke up the next morning with some doubts. Some journalists had asked the question, "Could the PC have been killed by his own men — as also Lakhan?"

Perhaps the doubt had matured in my mind during sleep. Things seemed to fit in. From the hairy dog-look of an officer who hated telling lies, the doubts in the statement of the Gurkha Head Constable, and the hesitation on the part of another constable, I was not able to decipher what it was or why, but a doubt persisted that there could be another possibility. The doubt was that, in the confusion, the PC might have been killed by firing from his own party. What might have happened was that when the PC went forward to investigate (there was no doubt that the advancing party was unable to decipher who was lying in front and crawling forward), he suddenly came upon the dacoit.

The PC must have certainly recognised the dacoit as Lakhan Singh, or at least as a member of his gang. The uniform worn by the dacoit could not have deceived a policeman who had taken part in several encounters. At that moment he might have shot the dacoit. (There was one shot on Lakhan which was obviously hit by a man from close range). There could have been two possibilities:

- Two or three dacoits guarding their injured leader might have fired with their automatic guns, prompting the PC to shout, "*Dhoka hua*" (I have been tricked).

or

- When the PC fired at Lakhan, the rest of the police party on hearing the shot might have countered by shooting in the direction of the firing (which made the commander shout, "*Dhoka hua*. Don't shoot.") This could have killed both the PC and the dacoit.

It was difficult to say what happened. Anyway, there was no doubt that the PC acted with great courage. And even if the PC was killed by accidental fire that did not reduce the gallantry shown by him. Besides, I owed it to him and the force to protect them from any controversy.[6]

---

[6]In the encounter, only Lakhan Singh was killed. His brother, Firangi Singh carried away the telescopic rifle. My enquiries revealed that PC Ram Akhtiar Singh was

A hundred years from now, when the history of the Indian police is written, the name of PC Ram Akhtiar Singh will be remembered as that of a man who gave his life for the sake of destroying the most dangerous criminal of Madhya Pradesh — Lakhan Singh. A hundred years from now, men will find inspiration in the exploits of this police officer, who with supreme courage led his men forward; and in doing so took the reputation and prestige of the police forward forever.

This encounter marked the culmination of teamwork at its best. If Sub-Inspector Vedram Singh had not collected the intelligence, if radio operator Narendra Singh had not used his intelligence to transmit the message, if Pahuja had not made a good operational plan and if Madho Singh and Modi, who led the encounter, delayed in any way and above all, if Ram Akhtiar Singh had not risked his life to grapple with him, Lakhan Singh would not have been killed.

G-6, LACHHI: Sripala and Lachhi formed the G-6 gang. Sripala was liquidated earlier whereas his comrade escaped.

A police party had gone out on an anti-dacoit raid in Bhind. The forces had combed the area but no dacoit came out. The young ASP, who was leading the party, sat down on a mound in the ravines and said, "What a waste of time! I wish we had a transistor set; we could have heard the Test cricket scores."

Hardly had he said it, when the gang came upon the police party. The gang had been lying low and on finding a weakness in the line, decided to break through. The officers were taken by surprise. Head Constable Ram Singh, an orderly of the ASP, suddenly turned heroic. He reached out in front, covered his officers and blazed away at the gang, hitting the leader Lachhi in the leg. The Head Constable was completely fearless.

---

probably killed in the crossfire between the dacoits and the police. It was not Lakhan Singh's bullet which killed him. Rustamji, in several articles written years later has repeatedly eulogised Ram Akhtiar's courage.

While the officers in the rear yelled at him to lie down and take cover, he stood out in the open, firing rapidly. The gang, finding its path blocked, took another course, abandoning its leader. The Head Constable ran forward and blocked their path and finished the leader Lachhi and rescued a kidnapped child of eight years of age. This marked the end of Lachhi, an ex-serviceman turned into a brutal dacoit.

Along with the elimination of dacoits, many steps had to be taken to ensure an end to the menace. One of the main causes of dacoity is land dispute. I was able to convince the government to post a Deputy Collector in the office of the DIG with the designation of Aide to DIG to coordinate with the revenue authorities regarding settlement of land disputes. A scheme was drawn up for increasing the strength of the SAF and also for the formation of Village Resistance Groups.

In my attempt to tackle the dacoity problem, I was inspired by history. I did not depart much from the basic line of action prescribed by Sher Shah Suri, (the Muslim king before Humayun), whom I have always considered to be an administrative genius — that remote areas should be opened up by roads and that new police stations and outposts be opened along these and other roads. I moved the government for constructing roads which were necessary from a strategic police point of view. Also new police stations and outposts were sanctioned.

As far back as 1863, the Commissioner of the Narmada Division, an Englishman had remarked, "We are probably not prepared to undertake the suppression of dacoity by sheer force. For this area, police might be doubled and yet be insufficient. Dacoits bold enough may probably always commit dacoity with a fair chance of eluding the police. Our object is rather to do what we can by prestige. It is prestige versus pluck, and prestige perhaps may be maintained by a certain number of small bodies of police placed where they will be most frequently visible and most easily reached, and not too far from each other, ready to receive information and clever and active at following the clues."

A factor which has often been minimised is the prestige of the government and the morale of the forces engaged in the operations. I received feedback that my visits to the dacoity-affected areas, encouraging the officers, appreciating their efforts and looking after their welfare had motivated the officers and improved their morale. "Don't keep sitting on your seat waiting for something to happen," was probably one of the lessons I learnt from my previous master, Pandit Jawaharlal Nehru. I stepped up the frequency of such visits to help make things happen.

You Said It

By LAXMAN

He broke into the house. We offered him love, mercy, forgiveness and food! He decided to stay!

The press came out strongly in support of Rustamji when he criticised Acharya Vinoba Bhave and Maj Gen Yadunath Singh's mission for making the dacoits surrender. India's most famous cartoonist, R.K. Laxman, who brings out cartoons on subjects of topical interest, brought out this cartoon in June 1960. The picture of Vinoba Bhave and the gun on the walls give the clue about the issue being referred to.

13

Vinoba Bhave's Mission

In no other country in the world would a frustrated saint and a retired Major General of the army have got together to help a group of murderers. In no other country dedicated to the rule of law, would they have made pacts with confirmed criminals that if they surrendered, they would be feted and feasted, disarmed and handed over to the police and then defended through a public fund, with the aid of voluntary lawyers; while arrangements were made for the upkeep of their families and friends and the sentence of death passed on a villain commuted to imprisonment.

But the fact is no country has produced a saint like Acharya Vinoba Bhave or a Major General like Yadunath Singh.

Vinoba Bhave was one of Gandhiji's best disciples and was given the title 'Acharya'. When Gandhiji needed a reliable man to speak against the war effort of the Allies, it was the Acharya who stood in streaming rain in a small village of Wardha district to vindicate freedom of speech. After Gandhiji's death, he had yearned for the mantle of the master, but no mantle fell on him. He trudged from village to village, asking for voluntary donation of land to distribute among the landless.

He suffered all his life because of comparison with the Mahatma. The lack of any attachment shown to him by leaders like Nehru had made him frustrated and vehement. Defeat had built up a strong ego in him and his mystical approach had ensured a following of many people who looked upon him as a saint and sought his blessing in their ventures.

Maj Gen Yadunath Singh was known in the army as the 'sadhu' General because he prayed for several hours every morning. In India, one cannot say anything derogatory about a man who has served the President of the country as his Military Secretary. During that period he sedulously cultivated relations with those who mattered in this modest republic.

"The Prime Minister wrote to me the other day... The President had given me an assurance...The Home Minister has promised all help... ." These appeared in his conversation like traffic lights on the road, for directing the flow of conversation. However, his sincerity remained unquestioned. He prayed regularly, visited ashrams, helped the poor and had all the trappings of a *sarvodaya* leader, even though he had occasionally backed the wrong man in order to get his friendship.

Anybody who claims to be a sadhu in India can never be spurned. Along with this, in Maj Gen Yadunath Singh there was the badge of service, there were the manners of a Sandhurst-trained officer, the marks of a gentleman (though the soldier faded away under the veneer of non-violence) and an ability to say "sir" to all from whom he wanted anything.

He stayed at the Circuit House, went out to meet dacoits in government vehicles, reported directly to the President his conversations with murderers; and embarked on *padyatra*s (foot march) with Vinoba Bhave. His version of the dacoity situation was invariably sympathetic to the 'harassed' dacoits when he spoke to the world at large and in whispers to Vinobaji himself.

As stated earlier, in the month of October 1959, the 4th Battalion of SAF under Quinn shot dead Rupa, code-named G-1. Differences over the choice of leadership broke out among the surviving members of the gang and in that weakened state, they were being shot down by the police wherever they appeared. The gang was in danger of extermination. At that stage, when all hopes were lost, they entered into negotiations with Maj Gen Yadunath Singh (who belonged to Bhind-Morena area and did not conceal his sympathies for dacoits) and offered to surrender. Their terms were that Tehsildar Singh, son of the legendary dacoit Man Singh, who was awaiting execution after the rejection of his appeal in the Supreme Court, should be pardoned and that they should not be sentenced to death after they surrender.

Earlier, on 26 January 1960, the gang was to surrender at Agra, but failed to turn up. Promptly the Major General accused the police for scuttling the plan. The Uttar Pradesh Police gunned down a few more members of the gang.

When it was announced that Acharya Vinoba Bhave would tour the dacoit-infested area, I felt that the visit had been correctly timed. We had been able to eliminate thirteen out of the sixteen gangs that infested the area and were confident of finishing the remaining three also. But that would not mark the end of the dacoity problem; we had to prevent formation of new gangs. And in that respect, I felt that a man like Vinoba Bhave could help.

When the Chief Minister consulted me about the visit of the mission, I offered unqualified support in my letter to him on 30 March 1960. I conveyed that the prime advantage of Vinobaji's visit to the area would be that it would have a restrictive effect on the formation of new gangs. I was convinced that if public opinion in that area was built up correctly, the dacoity situation would be solved once and for ever. Vinobaji's moral and spiritual stature would show the right path to the people of that area.

On 13 May 1960, we stood in the early hours of dawn on the banks of River Chambal at Useth Ghat to welcome the sage and the Major General to Madhya Pradesh.

Vinobaji was welcomed in chaste *sarvodaya* words. He replied in a few mumbled words, from which we could discern that he was saying something about crossing several rivers of India.

Each day Vinobaji started at four o'clock in the morning and walked about eight to ten miles till eight o'clock. He would get so exhausted that the rest of the engagements had to be cancelled till the evening.

On the first day, Vinobaji said, "I have come to the glorious land of the brave. This is the land that has produced brave dacoits.

They are noble men. The only difference between them and other men is that their train has got on to the wrong track. I think they are better men than the *daku*s (dacoits) of Delhi, because they are unsophisticated. A change of heart is easier to achieve among them than among the civilised people of the cities, who have formed a hard crust of personal self-interest over their hearts. I want them to respond to my call and surrender. The solution to dacoity lies in surrender — not in firearms. Only non-violence can enable us to solve the problem of dacoity."

This is what he said on the first day. I heard it and felt that the old man was trying to ingratiate himself with the dacoits. The reports that began to come to me began to steadily deteriorate. He did not speak much for a day or two, but as days passed and no dacoit appeared, allegations against the police increased: 'The police are responsible for making dacoits', 'Police have shot down innocent men', 'ruined families', etc.

As a tactician, few could beat the Acharya. This was the stuff to give to harbourers and supporters of dacoits who thronged his camp in large numbers. Two years earlier when the situation had got out of control with the brigands wandering about and committing murders and dacoities, Vinobaji and the Major General had not taken the trouble to visit the area and stand up against the dacoits. No saint or sadhu had offered to help at that time. It was the armed police battalions from Jabalpur, Indore, Gwalior, Chhindwara and Rewa which had to be sent. There were several Gurkhas and Garhwalis among them who braved the bullets and some even lost their lives in their effort to rid the areas of the menace.

And when the area had become comparatively safe, the Acharya makes an appearance and tells the police, "Why did you use guns? You bad men, why did you kill the dacoits? You committed murders! This problem can only be solved with love and goodwill for the dacoits. For what is a dacoit after all? An innocent man forced by circumstances to kill for a living — a policeman in reverse."

In no democratic country would the people tolerate such an attack on brave men who had saved them. But in India, in the name of non-violence anyone can be attacked. The man who stands up to death and defeatism can always be called a murderer after the crisis is over.

I met Vinobaji in his first camp and requested him not to work up an agitation against the police in order to please the dacoits. It would barely help in solving the menace. I also said that surrenders being the prime objective of the mission, failure of the mission would lead to fresh attacks against the police. He was fair; he talked about 'his police — our police' and that surrenders were only *oopar, oopar ki cheez hai* ('superficial aspects' of his work). In his prayer meeting in the evening he clarified that he had not come to solve the dacoity problem, but only to spread his message of universal love and brotherhood. Here I thought I had achieved a change of heart.

But as the days passed and no one surrendered, Vinoba's attitude towards the police hardened. He worked more, spoke more and flayed all those who came in his ken including Gen K.S. Thimayya, the Army Chief, Islam Ahmed, the DIG in Agra, the political *daku*s, the defective judicial system, etc. The most confused were the newspaper correspondents covering his visit. Yet in the midst of this confusion, Taroon Coomar Bhaduri, the correspondent of *The Statesman*, produced a brilliant despatch which summarised what everyone felt. He pointed out the dangers of denigrating the work of the police when the public depended so much on their morale.

On 16 May, the Major General went out into the ravines and got a film made on the dacoits at work and play. The next day the first surrenders of a couple of minor dacoits occurred. This imparted confidence to the gang headed by Lukka (formerly a member of Rupa's gang) and gave the signal that the psychological time for surrender had arrived. The Major General went into the ravines and Lukka's gang, consisting of fourteen men, was driven into Vinobaji's camp. From there they joined the party and became the main attraction. At the gate of the next camp, some of them saluted Quinn and shook hands with him. When it came to Lukka's turn, he withdrew his hand and scorned the brave hand that had been extended.

From camp to camp, the dacoits were feted and lionised. Wherever they appeared, the crowds deserted Vinobaji and stood gaping at the men who had lived the life of brigands and had now surrendered to wear the garlands and pay the penalty.

Why had they surrendered? The prime reason was that the gang was in danger of annihilation. Secondly, they felt that if they surrendered through Maj Gen Yadunath Singh (who had influence with the government in Delhi) and Vinobaji (who had influence with God and the people), they had a decent chance of getting off lightly. Thirdly, it provided a chance of saving Tehsildar Singh. The bait given to them was that if they surrendered, Tehsildar Singh's death sentence would be reviewed. And Tehsildar was the great Man Singh's son.

I must confess that when the news of the surrender came to me, my reaction was one of disbelief. I never expected hardened criminals to give themselves up so completely.

The conflict in my mind raged for several days. Was Vinoba Bhave's method consistent with the rule of law? Could I as the chief of the police force be a mute spectator to the glorification of dacoits and humiliation of the police?

I was aware that a part of the gang was left outside under Mewaram's leadership. It was a well thought out move to intimidate witnesses in the trial that the surrendered dacoits would have to face.

The lionisation of dacoits at Bhind was done on a scale that was massive and well planned. The dacoits appeared on the balcony, twirling their moustache like villains in a melodrama — they were adorned with flowers, worshipped by little girls doing *aarti* (a ceremony performed in adoration) and tying *rakhi*s (a sacred thread) on their wrists. They gave press interviews. At well packed meetings, they drew crowds and in fact irritated Vinobaji, when they drew away the crowd from his prayer meetings.

The conflict in my mind grew as reports came in of the glorification of dacoits in Bhind. Does this not signify the end of rule of law? They want to destroy even the social stigma against the murderers. The dacoit's repentance placed him above ordinary mortals. He can serve his terms and secure absolution. After that he could go back to his village, contest election and win with tactics of intimidation or like Valmiki sit down and write a *Ramayana*. Was this a blessing or a curse of this land?

Meanwhile, the members of the mission started creating problems for the police. It was difficult to make them agree to disarm the surrendered dacoits or hand them over to the police. Maj Gen Yadunath Singh and others in the mission believed that if the dacoits were allowed to be with them, the publicity value would be considerable and hence they did not agree to their being handed over to the police. In the process of glorifying the dacoits, the exact opposite of the effect we desired was achieved. The morale of the police dipped low. So serious was the decline that some officers refused to take action against gangs for fear of public disapproval; the other effect of the sudden 'success' of the mission was an increase in crime of a serious nature. What further aggravated the problem was the rumour that Tehsildar Singh's release would cause a sense of insecurity in the area. It was so great that even police officers, who had participated in the encounter in which his father, the legendary Man Singh was killed, some five years earlier, began to fear for the safety of their families. The surviving witnesses, who had given evidence against Tehsildar Singh, began to fear for their lives. (Tehsildar Singh's gang had killed the relatives of eleven witnesses during the trial.) The most unfortunate reaction was that even the generally reluctant help the public had started giving the police dried up and the reputation and influence of the harbourers of the dacoits and criminals living in the villages increased.

The worst feature was the demoralisation of the police and the implied assumption that if the dacoits were to be treated in this way, there was no reason to fight them and on the other hand, every reason for becoming friends with them. Further, a large number of our officers and men were suddenly carried away by the emotional thrill of the surrenders and a feeling crept in them that they had done wrong in shooting down dacoits or in causing bloodshed. Such thinking could produce disastrous results and it would have made control of the force impossible. I therefore decided to act.

Should I oppose Acharya Vinoba Bhave or not? If I attack him and his mission, it would amount to a tussle between Vinobaji, the saint versus Rustamji, the dragon. It would amount to or be construed as an attack on the highest authority in the land (President of India, Dr Rajendra Prasad) as he too had supported the mission.

If I calmly bore all that has been said, it would amount to letting down the men who had looked up to me.

I kept wondering how to resolve the conflict in my mind. One part of me said, 'Don't be a coward. Hit out and expose the thing. Your men expect it.' Another part said, 'There will be a big controversy. You will be attacked by everybody. Your work in the state will become more difficult.' But the thought that kept nagging me was that when I took over as chief of the police, I had put in a pre-condition that I shall brook no interference from any quarter in matters concerning discipline and morale of the force. They would be my exclusive responsibility. It was conceded.

I discussed the issue with Naju. I told her that in the tussle between the saint and the dragon, the dragon was bound to lose. She gave me strength; she said, "Win or lose; it's your duty to stand by your force."

On 2 June, I met the press. My hat was in the ring. But my legs felt weak. What would happen? There would be a big outcry to begin with and it might take any shape. Who could tell? I did not underestimate the seriousness of the clash that would occur. Yet I could not conceal the thrill of the conflict.

In a six-page statement I said that it was my duty to put forth a few important points for consideration and a few problems that had been created with the visit of Vinoba's mission to the area.

The first point was whether it was useful in the long run to infringe several sections of the law so that surrenders might be secured. Secondly, the provisions of the IPC regarding harbouring of dacoits have almost been negatived by the powerful mission. The law required that a police officer who sees a proclaimed offender should arrest him forthwith and place him in custody and if he intentionally fails to do so, the policeman is liable for prosecution.

Further, a part of the gang that has not surrendered has been kept out for intimidation of witnesses when the trials of the surrendered dacoits commence and would not hesitate to repeat what happened in Tehsildar's Singh's trial when dozens of witnesses or family members of witnesses who dared to testify were killed.

It was a matter of regret that the mission should have deliberately given a setback to the task of maintaining law and order in the area in order to please dacoits. Apart from the operational time lost, the mission had delivered a blow to the morale of the force by making statements against the police and insulting the courage and devotion to duty of the men who stood up to fight the dacoits. Was it right to attribute noble motives to criminals? Would it not make the situation more difficult for the state? If a single section strength of police personnel was removed from the dacoity area, there was a public outcry because the people could not do without police protection. Yet it was being stated by the mission that police presence in the areas created dacoits.

The mission had given great satisfaction to all the helpers and harbourers of dacoits, who claimed that they were helping brave and cherished men. In the minds of the general public, it had caused confusion and some amount of rancour, which may have encouraged the spirit of vendetta that had been the bane of these parts.

The situation got further complicated by the confusion of values. After all, what was an official expected to do if the law of the land was contrary to the actions of the mission? Clearly there was a conflict of views between what the law required and what the mission wanted.

I further added that Vinobaji had his own methods and we respected them. We knew that the police could not solve the problem on their own. It needed the support of everyone, particularly those who could deal with the socio-economic and criminological aspects of the problems of that region. But it was rather strange, after we had striven hard to control a menace and brought it under control, to be told that legal and authorised methods should not be followed and we had done wrong in doing what the law sanctioned and indeed imposed as a duty on the police.

I made the statement to the press. It was called 'explosive' and 'controversial' and when it went over the wires, Press Trust of India (PTI) wanted it to be repeated and okayed by me, word for word.

In the evening, I pushed off to Pachmarhi, hoping to find salvation when the sparks flew. It was however impossible to push away the subject from one's mind. Night and day it was with me.

I made the statement on 2 June and the next day, an order was passed by the President commuting Tehsildar Singh's death sentence to life imprisonment. It might have been a coincidence, but it was possible that some of the sponsors of the mission felt that if the order was not taken out at once, it would be difficult to do so later. Such strong support was given to my views by the *The Times of India*, *Hindustan Times* and *The Statesman* that it would have been embarrassing to pass an order of reprieve later.

What was disconcerting to me was that my statement, in which a hint was given that Tehsildar's Singh life would be spared, appeared along with the item about the commutation of the sentence. Most newspapers displayed them side by side. There was no need to comment.

The first reaction was entirely favourable. Most educated people said that I had only mentioned what they were thinking. In the police force there was a strong reaction in favour of me. The men felt I had shown ample courage.

Acharya Vinoba Bhave reacted with dignity. He could have torn me to bits with the help of religion, but he merely said, "One sees God according to one's own light."

The Chief Minister Dr Katju had given immediate support without even verifying the facts. The Deputy Minister (Home) supported me, but added that the statement needed examination by legal experts. He did not mention that (after I had released the statement), I read it out to him on telephone and he said, "See that the whole of it appears. They must not cut out anything."

Within the next few days, the Bhave mission and my statement were topics of heated controversy. Letters grave and gay appeared in every newspaper. R.K. Laxman produced a delightful cartoon in *The Times of India*. The most factual and impartial report on the mission was given by *Time* magazine of USA in its edition of 13 June 1960. It was a masterpiece of factual and conclusive reporting. At the height of the controversy, I said one prayer in anguish, 'God, you gave me courage, now give me the strength to endure all this.' To this day I still feel I was right. It had to be done. I have no regrets I spoke out my mind.

I met the Chief Minister on June 4 and all he said was, "On merits your case is unassailable, but you could have consulted me." He had returned from Poona after attending the All India Congress Commettee (AICC) conference. I asked him what had been the reaction of the Prime Minister. He replied, "He also feels it is a policy statement." I met the Prime Minister later and appraised him of the stand taken by me. He listened to me but did not say anything. At that point in time he was having his own differences with the President.

The Vice-President, Dr S. Radhakrishnan met the dacoits in Bhind jail. He was surprised at their uncompromising and defiant attitude. They wanted more fans and better and more food.

The Home Department of Madhya Pradesh sent a long list of questions and asked for my replies. It was clear that the questions were drafted by the clerical staff. The Ministry of Home Affairs, New Delhi wrote a long letter to the Madhya Pradesh government pointing out various provisions of the IPS (Conduct) Rules and sought my explanation for violating them. I sent the letters to the DIG, Northern Range and forwarded his replies to the Home Department and the Ministry of Home Affairs.

A stream of letters and telegrams poured in — from soldiers, sailors, lawyers, administrators and even from cranks of all types.

But the greatest boost to my morale came from the highest judiciary in the land. In an unprecedented move, the judges of the Supreme Court went in a deputation to the President of India to voice their protest against the commutation of death sentence awarded to Tehsildar Singh and confirmed by the apex court.

Among all the achievements of my service. I would put Jabalpur as the best. — and that mainly because what I did few others could have done. Perhaps I even changed the course of Indian history, [illegible]. Somehow I have the conviction that I averted an attempt to seize power. But what did I get in return. Newspaper agitations, MP's speeches, accusations of bribery and harassment of minorities, and all the impossible things in

In December 1961, in his annual review of the events of the year, Rustamji wrote: "Among all the achievements of my service, I would put Jabalpur as the best — and that mainly because what I did few others could have done. Perhaps I even changed the course of Indian history. Somehow I have the conviction that I averted an attempt to seize power. But what did I get in return. Newspaper agitations, MP's speeches, accusations of bribery and harassment of minorities…"

14

Communal Riots

In the course of my service career spanning thirty-six years, I have seen enough number of communal riots to make me a confirmed secularist. I have seen men and women in fright, in dark despair, in pain and cowardice. I can claim I have had a glimpse of hell where I saw Hindus and Muslims burning each other's house and killing each other in the name of God. It is difficult for a person who has not witnessed a serious communal disturbance to appreciate that mixture of hatred, panic, aggressiveness and fanaticism that momentarily grips the people.

During my tenure as IGP of the state, I had to deal with three horrific communal riots. The first was in Bhopal and two years later, in Jabalpur, which by far was the worst, and again three years later in Raigarh.

In 1959, we celebrated our first Holi in Bhopal. Five days after Holi, the festival of Rang Panchami is observed on a wide scale in parts of Central India. Naju, Kerman and I went about the city, dabbing our friends with colour and being smeared with it.

The DIG (Crime & Railways), B.M. Shukul[1] had been very apprehensive of communal clashes breaking out between the Hindus and Muslims, but I was certain that nothing untoward would happen. I felt that no Muslim in his senses would dare provoke the Hindus.

---

[1]The DIG (Crime & Railways) was also incharge of the three districts — Bhopal, Sehore and Raisen which comprised the erstwhile princely State of Bhopal.

So confident was I that we went about making fun of B.M. for standing by with his officers to deal with any communal trouble in Bhopal, which his intelligence officers and his own sources had forecast. I even objected to the movement of large bodies of armed police from the dacoit-infested areas. The movement did take place; but only because B.M. persisted.

It was a miscalculation or misreading of the situation on my part. Who could have expected that the Muslims would be naive enough to do something which would be totally against their interests? Who could have expected that they would be so ignorant as to feel that the situation was similar to that which persisted when Bhopal was a princely State under Muslim rulers? New men and new government had taken over Bhopal. The old social life had changed. Moreover, it was the Muslim month of Ramzan, when the average Mussalman felt more devout.

Shortly after I returned home, I was informed that a few incidents had occurred in front of a mosque. When I went to see what had happened, I went straight into a serious riot. Stones lay strewn all around. My car was hit as soon as I got down and the windscreen got smashed. An angry Hindu procession had been halted in front of a mosque. A violent group of Muslims stoned them heavily from the other side. A small party of policemen was sandwiched between the two. The SP, P.R. Khurana, the City Superintendent of Police (CSP), Hukam Singh and ten policemen had been injured due to pelting of stones. B.M. had ordered the firing of tear gas shells.

The Muslim crowd had fled, but the Hindu crowd stood transfixed — angry, excited. They clamoured for action against the stone throwers, complaining, "Every time they spoil our festivals."

We tried to reason with them but they were not prepared to listen. They wanted revenge. They were in a violent mood. If we dispersed them with force, it would have caused enormous damage, because several among them were almost hysterical. If we did not, they would inflict damage on the shops and the mosque. Slowly we began to push them back. B.M. and I formed a party along with two

Gurkha constables. The four of us moved in and out, requesting, threatening and pushing. A mistake at that point in time would have meant serious consequences.

A little while later, we jumped into a vehicle and drove through the Muslim locality of Kasaipura which had been the seat of trouble. A Hindu procession was trying to enter the Muslim locality. Tear gas was used. The excited constables threw the gas grenades so close to us that soon our eyes were burning. I rushed about like a comic figure trying to stop them from throwing the grenades indiscriminately. The Hindus dispersed; but while passing through certain areas, they attacked the shops on their way. B.M. and I, with the two Gurkha constables who stood gallantly by us, and the CSP hastily went around the area. If we had not rushed around, urging everyone to do his duty, the malaise of inaction, which was apparent in the force, would have led to rampant arson and looting. With the use of minimum force, we could control the unruly mob in a restrained and disciplined manner.

The next day, which happened to be a Friday, all was quiet till the afternoon. The Muslims had gathered in the Jama Masjid for prayers and in larger numbers than usual. We had been warned of trouble brewing. Once the prayers ended, slogans were raised, "*Allah-ho-Akbar!*" Suddenly hundreds of excited Muslims swarmed down the steps. So great was the rush that only a very few could recover their shoes from the gate in the ensuing melee. They ran in excited groups. Some waved their knives. Some took up sticks or weapons from the shops they passed. They were not able to do much damage because the police was there in strength. Later in the day, I received a call from the city *kotwali* that serious rioting had broken out in the Chowk area. As we entered the old city area, I found that the policemen were being heavily stoned in one locality. We moved through the narrow lanes towards the Chowk. An Inspector, brandishing a revolver, had narrowly escaped being killed by the men rushing out of the mosque. "Serious rioting in Chowk," he said. "All shops being attacked. Strong forces needed."

I had seen enough to feel that the police also was getting panicky. I asked the officers to be calm and vigilant. On reaching the Chowk, I found that the main trouble was over, but several hundreds were still inside the mosque and still capable of attack. B.M. was there in the Chowk police outpost known as Chowki Chowk.

There was quick consultation on the next step to be taken. If we allowed the men inside to stay on, they might rush out in groups again and attack the Hindus. If we allowed them to go, several would be attacked as they walked through the streets. A pitched battle meant sure death of thousands.

The persons inside the mosque had to be saved as early as possible. If not acted upon quickly, the night would have made things difficult.

The Jama Masjid is a high building in which the ground floor is occupied by shops and the first floor has the prayer hall.

A rotund lawyer appeared at the door of the mosque. I asked him to come out and surrender. There was a tense silence. One man came down. The rest watched intently to see what we would do with him. I made him sit down; others followed. Soon there were 800 men with us. We packed them in trucks and sent them to the jail. In the evening, all except 200 were released and escorted to their houses so that they might not be attacked.

Even after this, the forces sent to maintain calm and peace in the lanes and bylanes were stoned. Some policemen were beaten up in the side streets. My orderly's brother was nearly strangled to death; another orderly, peacefully going to duty at the bungalow, was set upon and belaboured with sticks.

As our vehicle made its way, round and round the old city, I mused, 'It shouldn't be necessary for an IGP to do all this. But supposing it helps to bring peace faster, can one refuse to do it?'

As it happens in most communal riots, the Muslims have the upper hand on the first two days. The Hindu elephant takes time to get up; it is on the third day that it tramples about madly.

As anticipated, there was retaliation from the Hindus on the morning of the third day. There was danger of the city getting out of control. On seeing a group of desperate men who were captured with petrol and acid bulbs, we clamped curfew and sent officers posted in the PHQ to the disturbed areas to put a stop to offences with a heavy hand. Even then, some of the Muslims did not realise the serious threat. In one area they again began to stone heavily and even attack the passers-by. Once again we had to use the stick.

Use of any form of force by the police is rarely appreciated for it is seldom realised that the decisions taken by the police are meant for the safety of thousands of people. A few people might suffer, but the action taken by the police is meant for the greater good of a larger number. When a policeman has to take a decision in the street of a disturbed city, he decides the fate of thousands by the look in the eyes of the potential troublemaker, the screams of a child when a man is stabbed, the flicker of nervousness in a street full of shops. The decision has to be taken promptly and correctly. There is no appeal; no review petition. On the other hand, if a judge has to pronounce judgement of death on a man, he has several days at his disposal to reach a decision besides the scores of witnesses and reams of arguments to base his decision on.

As regards police action, the pity of it all is that the man who really deserves to be beaten seldom gets it. The *goonda* (unruly element) is quick to find shelter when rioting starts. The politician too is safe behind someone when trouble brews. It is the innocent who gets beaten up.

Soon after the riots, I had to go to Ajmer to attend an interstate dacoity conference and on my way back, I took the opportunity to meet the Prime Minister at Delhi. I told him about the riots and the action that we had taken. He seemed to approve, but as always, he would not say he did. He said he had suggested that Sadiq (a Muslim General Secretary of the Congress) should go to Bhopal and try to heal the wounds caused by the riots.

'Healing the wounds' is a process peculiar to India — it has become an established custom. When a riot occurs, the politicians duck under cover but send out word that, "the authorities have a free hand;" "they must take strong measures;" "law and order must be maintained at all costs;" and so on.

But when the tumult and shouting dies down, they all emerge from their dens and take up the process of 'healing wounds' or the 'healing touch' which generally implies criticism of the police and police 'brutalities'. Each party issues a statement criticising the police; each party alleges that 'excessive force' had been used. Each one demands a judicial enquiry into the incidents; each party's aim is to stay the action taken by the police, so that the people who indulged in rioting and killing may feel grateful to them.

And when I look back on the action taken, I find that it was the police that saved the city but could not save themselves. Far from being grateful, the general public felt that we had mismanaged the situation. And in a sense we did. We did not offend the majority community. We might have definitely got less criticism in the press if we had. But the Muslims all over the state, particularly in the small villages and towns, where they were just a handful, would have had to pay the price for the aggression that their brethren committed in Bhopal. I felt we had saved the Muslims in the interiors from retaliation, but that aspect seldom strikes politicians and the press people.

Two years later, a major communal riot broke out in Jabalpur. On 3 February 1961, a college girl of Jabalpur, named Usha Bhargava received a fatal caller — a boy who molested her. She was a Hindu Brahmin and he, a Muslim. Overcome by the shame of it, she sprinkled kerosene oil over herself and committed suicide.

The story that appeared in the newspapers and as reported by the CID was that she had been raped by three Muslim boys and had, therefore, committed suicide.

Students took out a procession. Excitement ran high in the town. One community attacked the other in self-defence. A group of hoodlums ran through the town, burning and breaking all it could lay hands on.

A number of people and things were responsible for such a catastrophe to take place. I accuse them all.

I accuse the district authorities for not being vigilant and not being able to give leadership to the constable in the street.

I accuse the students and the general public for getting a whole community punished for the crime of one of them, either in revenge or economic displacement or religious fervour.

I accuse the politicians who encouraged looting in order to satisfy a mob and then turned their backs and accused the police for failing to take action against the mob.

I accuse journalists for inflammatory reporting.

I accuse the history of this land and its religious and social practises. I accuse the cowardice, avarice and spirit of destruction of its people.

Inside me there will be no forgiveness for the men I accuse. And I shall feel sorry for myself that I accuse so many people for so many things.

And with it I have seen untruth and cowardice in high quarters. I have seen officers tell lies in order to protect themselves. Those lies have brought death and destruction on hundreds of people.

After all that I saw and went through, for days on end I was choked up inside with unshed tears.

In the case of the girl, Usha Bhargava, who committed suicide, in her dying declaration, she told the doctor (as all the magistrates were away at a party) that a Muslim boy, a friend of her sister's, had attempted to take her virtue. As the body was burnt, medical opinion was indeterminate; it was an unfortunate act of a child driven to desperation.

The authorities were first complacent, then weak, then frightened, but recovered sufficiently to restore order. Students took out a procession before resorting to looting and arson. Five or seven big Muslim shops were looted and burnt; some houses were burnt. A Muslim fired a gun on a mob and killed a Hindu. (It was concealed from me that Hindus had also used firearms. This was discovered by me accidentally at a later stage). An old man, quietly waiting for his end, was stoned to death. A Muslim girl was dragged out of her house naked and raped by Hindus. They wanted to kill her but a Hindu risked his life to carry her back to her house.

I cannot describe the feelings in me when I went round the city and saw the damage that had been caused. For two days there was peace in the city. Then came the night of 7 February. At 9.20 p.m., the Hindus ran to the *kotwali* to report that they had been attacked by Muslims. Within a few minutes panic broke out. Men came out on the streets, gripped with frenzy and determined to attack anyone of the opposite community. Two columns were despatched. Firing was resorted to and some persons were killed. The commotion subsided.

When I got the telephone news in Bhopal that the Muslims had attacked, I could not believe it. I even clarified it from the DIG at the control room and he claimed that he was certain.

I flew into Jabalpur with Nagu (DIG), Terence Quinn (Commandant) and K.S. Bajpai (SP, PHQ). I was sick inside, partly owing to the plane and partly owing to the situation.

The city was engulfed in panic. We drove in our jeep around the city. I was shown Hindu houses that had been set on fire — rows upon rows of them. The situation seemed desperate.

I insisted on imposing the strictest possible curfew for thirty-six hours. In the night I held a meeting of officers at which I made two points:

- We must not panic. Everything must be done with calmness and confidence. If anybody comes and shouts at me in panic, I would say, "Lock him up or better still, get him shot."
- We must break the cycle of retaliation. If we do not stop the rot, it would engulf the state, perhaps the whole of India.

It was when we got the casualty figures from the hospital that I began to have doubts about the so-called 'organised Muslim attack.' Then, I discovered that some of the houses that were burnt were not of Hindus but of Muslims. The casualties were all on the Muslim side — almost none on the Hindu side. Jabalpur on 9 and 10 February 1961 was a stricken city. It lay paralysed.

All through the thirty-six-hour curfew, I brooded on the subject, as our jeep sped through empty streets. I felt there was something in the nature of cities like Jabalpur which was basically unstable. Incidentally it was not communalism alone that produced the disturbance in and around Jabalpur. It was a deep-seated urge of students to revolt and destroy, which was the origin of the trouble. In fact wherever the tension appeared only in the communal form it was not difficult to control. Jabalpur and Sagar were difficult because students were out on a rampage. Both these places have a large student population, who due to historical and economic reasons, have always been motley groups of easily excitable and unruly elements.

The death of Usha Bhargava, herself a student, and the circumstances in which it occurred, caused a shock to students in the first place and they proceeded to shock the city, in a manner which seemed to be a basic need of the city.

Jabalpur city is as much a psychological case as any human being who suffers from a personality disorder. It might be a different type of disorder. But there is something neurotic and hysterical in some of the cities of India (and perhaps the world) which psychologists would probably be able to unravel some day. Communalism may be one method of getting the hysterical satisfaction which the consciousness wants. But it is only a means to an end.

What does one think about in such disasters? In action — there is no worry at all. There is a sense of exhilaration at the thought of danger. 'My faith is action,' I said to myself. I was not worried when the riot was on. It was the aftermath that worried me.

My mood was not one of maudlin pity. I never said, 'My poor country.' I kept saying, 'This is a bloody country and the people need an iron hand.'

Regarding the conduct of the police, I felt proud of the way the constabulary went about their duties. There was a severe cold wave during that period and for a week they stood outside in the cold, without relief, without bedding and without regular food supplies. They were cheerful and confident. What had failed us in the beginning were not the men but the officers.

From Jabalpur, the excitement spread in eddies to surrounding districts. In Narsingpur, in a moment of crisis when the SP was not in town, a Head Constable and one constable seized leadership, fired on a crowd and saved the day. In Damoh, the frenzy was controlled in time. But in Sagar, a weak SP and his officers failed to take timely and effective action, with the result that a considerable amount of damage was done. The servants of the people had been unable to control their masters.

The above sentence of mine was included in my report which the Chief Minister forwarded to the Prime Minister. I think it was this which made Nehru fly into a temper and browbeat Dr Katju into consenting to hold a judicial inquiry.

The more I thought about the communal disturbances, the more simple the explanation to the riots became, till I reached the last, logical argument that communalism and all the small issues that trouble us, like caste and language, arise from our basic lack of character. We are fundamentally weak and dishonest. We are afraid and get panic-stricken at the time when we should be standing up and saying, "Let death come. Cowardice is worse than death."

The Prime Minister wanted to visit Jabalpur. We requested him to delay his visit till things settled down. When he did come, I had a separate one-to-one meeting with him. There were several matters that I had to discuss with him, and I prepared them carefully. I did the speaking and he did the listening. I told him that the riot was a big explosion. It was not due to local causes only. It was the beginning of an all-India build up of communalism. Describing the course of the riot, I said that if we had failed on 9 February, there would have been chaos in Jabalpur. It would be difficult to say what would have happened. I told him that the problems for us were the attitude of the students, the newspapers and the communal elements. I said it all. He listened quietly. After meeting me, Nehru met the officers. He looked a tired man. The spring had gone out of his step. He talked slowly, with a low voice. His mind seemed to lack grip and decisiveness. He spoke about intelligence failures, students and the newspapers. He said, "Beat them up if they publish exciting stuff." He stressed on dealing with communal trouble promptly and effectively.

Nehru was upset by the events in Madhya Pradesh. Apart from just an old man's alarm at finding young men discarding his ideals, he was fretful at the fact that all that he had forecasted had begun to come true, because we had not been careful to avoid communal thoughts. In several meetings and conferences he repeatedly kept on saying that the "competition in evil" must come to an end.

In March 1964, the Hindus evicted from East Pakistan started arriving in thousands to Raipur and were rehabilitated in the refugee camp at Mana. The communal fires which had been smothered by the army now shifted to Jamshedpur (Bihar), Rourkela (Orissa) and Raigarh (Madhya Pradesh).

I went to Raigarh, which was in the grip of a serious communal flare up. A hysterical woman broke away from the group of Muslims sheltering her in Undana camp and ran to me, clutching a baby in her arms. She sobbed, "My husband has been killed." A Muslim who was my Head Clerk when I was posted in Raigarh caught my feet, saying, "My only son has been killed."

After some vacillation, the government, in desperation revised its policy and ordered the police to 'shoot at sight'. The much despised police stood up to it. Screaming mobs of Muslim women and children ran to the police for protection. The public was overcome by passion and sense of revenge. The police were abused for protecting the Muslims.

At Mana Camp, I saw the sight of 35,000 refugees who had been driven out of Pakistan. We looked at each other mutely. They could tell me nothing. I could not tell them anything. I walked past the misery of a historical migration.

A few days earlier, the then US President, John F. Kennedy had said, "It is the profound tendencies of history and not the passing excitements that will shape our future." The riots appeared to be "passing excitements". I felt at that time that in the years to come, thousands would be killed in communal riots and Hindus still in Pakistan would be driven out. It appeared to be part of a tragedy which was pre-ordained, pre-planned, predestined.

The dreams we had harboured at the time of Partition lay shattered. I could not make out why the words of a song we used to sing when we were young, came to my mind repeatedly:

> I walked along the streets of sorrow,
> The boulevard of broken dreams.

Bilaspur
5/2/62.

Ashtagraha or
The Biggest Hoax in History.

The grand conjunction of eight planets occurred on the 3rd Feb: and the whole of India prepared for doom. The end of the earth, fearful calamities: earthquakes, all types of disasters (including defeat to the party of the P.M.) had been forecasted.

The best method of warding off the evil spirits was to sit in a tight group, and sing 'Bhajans' (hymns). Sadhus and sacred men performed 'pujas' and food worth lakhs of rupees was thrown into the holy fires which were lighted in the millions of villages, and in all the streets of the tightly-packed cities. "Mass feeding of the poor was also advocated by some well-meaning persons, but it does not appear to have been accepted by the Sadhus."

"Will there be a great disaster this week-end?"

"To ward off the malefic effects nearly 200 yagnas of 72 hours duration each are being held in every temple in the city." (Agra)

Meteorological experts said "nothing will happen". Nehru ridiculed the idea of disaster, refused to yield to arch-advocate of astrology Dr. Sampurnanand who asked him to be careful of himself. But the forecast of disaster spread from place to place, till even in the remotest villages, the starving beggars poured out his money to protect himself from

The astrologers' dire predictions regarding the conjunction of eight planets in February 1962 has been called a "hoax" by Rustamji, but the events that took place in that year proved they were not all that off the mark.

15

Chinese Aggression

The grand conjunction of eight planets, known as *ashtagraha* in Hindi, occurred on 3 February 1962 and according to astrologers, it signalled doom. The whole of India prepared for some disastrous events. The end of the world, fearful calamities, earthquakes, disasters (including danger to the security of the Prime Minister) were predicted.

To ward off the malefic effects, nearly 200 *yagna*s (ritual of sacrifical fire) of seventy-two hours' duration each were held in every temple in the city of Agra. Sadhus and sacred men performed pujas and food worth lakhs of rupees was thrown into the holy fires which were lighted in millions of villages and in the streets of tightly packed cities.

Nehru ridiculed the idea of disaster. He even refused to reply to arch advocate of astrology, Dr Sampuranand, the Chief Minister of Uttar Pradesh, who had asked Nehru to be careful though he might have hesitated to say, "To be careful of your position and reputation."

It so happened that a few days later, in the General Elections, the Chief Minister, Dr Katju lost from his constituency in Jaora in Ratlam district. When I met him, I could see the hurt that the defeat caused. He said, "They told me that I would win with a big majority...all those who supported me have gone. They have defeated us." I could see what he meant. He was an old soldier of the Congress and being a thorough gentleman he would not mention that it was his own comrades who had stabbed him in the back. The old man was grief-stricken that his own comrades had worked against him and made him lose. Perhaps it was the effect of the *ashtagraha*.

The *ashtagraha* effect also fell on the PHQ. I.J. Johar, the DIG incharge of SAF, had gone to Nagaland to inspect one of our battalions deployed there. The tent in which he was sleeping caught fire and he died on 6 April 1962.

It appeared as if the effect of the *ashtagraha* had fallen on the country too. In October 1962, a battle raged in NEFA (North East Frontier Agency, now Arunachal Pradesh) between Indian and Chinese troops. We had hoped and wanted friendship with China but clearly failed to suspect her intentions. We had befriended China despite warnings by some nations; we had even insisted on her being given membership of the United Nations (UN) and coined the slogan, "*Hindi-Chini bhai bhai.*" History will blame us for being such fools. We were not adequately prepared to fight the Chinese enemy. We had no idea of their strength, or of our weakness or the antiquated nature of our equipment. The foremost in the land lacked the basic knowledge of the border area and its potential for war. We had full faith in the knowledge of Krishna Menon, the then Defence Minister, and did not heed the warnings of Gen Thimayya, the Chief of Army Staff (COAS). Even after the unprecedented action of all the three service chiefs submitting their resignation as a protest against the behaviour of the Defence Minister, Nehru did not think it proper to change the portfolio of V.K. Krishna Menon.

The Chinese incursion showed the IB in poor light and subjected it and the government to a lot of adverse publicity. But, in actual fact, the primary focus of the IB during the days of the redoubtable B.N. Mullik, its Director, was on communism and China. Mullik tried to do his best but the government of the day, all along, underrated China and her intention to strike at us. The oft quoted letter that Sardar Patel wrote to Nehru when the Chinese occupied Tibet was said to have been drafted by the IB. Nehru is reported to have said, "What could we have done? March into Tibet?"[1]

---

[1] It is interesting to read the letter written by Denys Pilditch, the Director of the IB in 1942 to A.G. Scott, the IGP of Central Provinces. In a typical IB style of giving grim

Seldom has a country been as friendly to China as India. China also received Nehru most warmly when he visited that country in 1954. I had gone along with him as his CSO and was impressed with the way he was welcomed at all the places he visited — Canton, Hangchow, Peking, Anshan, Mukden, Dairen, Nanking and finally Shanghai, where there were so many people waving gladioli flowers that from the air, the colour of the airport seemed to have changed. Nehru did not fail to notice the vigour and determination that the Chinese possessed and he could foresee that the communists would stabilise the government, set up industries, improve communication and make China a powerful nation again in the not too distant future. He kept mentioning about the rapid strides being made in China in his speeches and in his talks on return. But the visit did not produce results as far as the outstanding problems between the two countries were concerned.

There are several reasons for the pendulum swinging from one extreme to the other in the course of eight years. I had accompanied Nehru to the Asia-Africa Conference in Bandung in 1955, where Nehru and the Chinese Prime Minister, Chou En-lai fell out. A few months later, Nehru went to the Soviet Union and a new chapter in Indo-Soviet relations opened up, which was, probably, not to the liking of the Chinese leadership. In April 1959, the Dalai Lama of Tibet crossed over to India to take refuge. This again was not to their liking.

During my visit to the Soviet Union in 1966, I noticed how bitter the relations between China and the Soviet Union were and

---

predictions in highly guarded language, Pilditch had forecast the Chinese incursion, twenty years before it took place. He had written, "Intelligence about Chinese affairs is very weak and some form of provision for the future seems due. The barriers whether physical or cultural, between India and China are *tending always*, however *slowly at present,* towards *a stage*, when they will be *largely broken down* and India will *perhaps be faced with a Chinese problem of embarrassing proportions much sooner than is generally thought possible.*" (Italics are mine. The full text is in Appendix I).What is significant is that the communists had not taken over China till then. What could have delayed matters by twenty years might be the unsettled conditions in China due to Mao's Long March and the Korean War, etc. Pilditch wanted the services of an IP officer of ten to twelve years seniority to be posted at Chungking. The then state government was agreeable to spare Martin Wynne IP.

[illegible]
14/11/62

Unto Us a Son is Born.

I had gone last week to see [illegible] during the confinement. Big events were happening in India. Krishna Menon was first down-graded, & then resigned. Nehru took over Defence. The Chinese intrusions did not seem to make much headway, and at the same time massive support arose from the whole [illegible] to the defence of the motherland. In the midst of all the people's firm determination, the share market of Bombay crashed. The issue of gold bonds frightened the big businessmen, who in order to [illegible], by [illegible] of their anti-national, [illegible] contributed their surplus savings to the National Defence Fund.

It was a week when all [illegible] our un-preparedness, all those of our Jawans fighting in the snow without shoes or a [illegible].

It was a week in which elderly widows made public appeals for shoes & old [illegible] — and politicians vied with one another in

Rustamji's comments on the Chinese aggression — Defence Minister Krishna Menon's resignation, crash of the Bombay stock market, unpreparedness of our jawans, etc. His son was born on 13 November 1962, the day Bomdila was captured by the Chinese.

how much they hated each other. I talked to men who were thinkers in politics in the Soviet Union and earlier with similar thinkers in China and it was difficult to find out what they differed about. It seemed to me that the differences were not really ideological, but stemmed from attitudes which had arisen because of the different ways in which communism arose and developed in the two countries. In some measure, the differences were even personal: arising out of the desire of each to be the leader. To the Chinese, the Russians appeared to be young pseudo-intellectuals, weak, ineffective, who had gone back on the faith of their fathers, dissolved international communism, forgotten even the history of their own revolution — and become decadent, peaceful and pro-individual. The Chinese with deep insight into human beings were sure that their approach of stirring up trouble was the best.

To the Russians, the Chinese communists appeared as unlettered political agitators, who did not understand either science and its ways or world politics and its ways. In consequence they had suffered defeats everywhere or indulged in costly wars and given a setback to communism in all parts of the globe. The Russians felt that the Chinese, as a people, suffered from a feeling of insecurity, which led them to think that others would invade their country and destroy it. They also felt that the Chinese were out-of-date dolts, who were self-centred, ignorant of geopolitical conditions and anxious to do all that would actually harm communism all over the world. Each considered himself the better communist.

Stalinist policies after World War II and the Chinese incursion into India in 1962 had given international communism a setback. After the war with China, I recorded in my diary that it was, "Perhaps the beginning of the decline of international communism." China had very conveniently taken us for a ride, or better still, stabbed us in the back. The Chinese aggression was the first blow to Nehru's policy of establishing friendly ties with Asian and African countries. The Chinese episode proved to be the most distressing experience of his career. Men, to whom he had extended his hand of friendship, had hit him below the belt and killed his people in return for the help and sympathy he rendered in a wide span of history — from the

Japanese invasion to the Korean War. Nehru appeared to be the first martyr to his own policy of non-alignment.

Even the CPI passed a resolution against the Chinese aggression, probably because of the display of popular enthusiasm within the country. So widespread was public anger that in Indore, a procession tried to lynch an eminent communist leader.

Massive support arose from the people in support of the motherland. In the midst of it all, the stock market of Bombay crashed. It was a week which highlighted our unpreparedness; and what was worse, our jawans had to fight the enemy in the cold snow, without being properly equipped and armed.

Meanwhile reports kept pouring in of the war in which as many as 2,500 Indian soldiers died or were reported missing. It was a war in which several forward posts were lost to China in NEFA and Ladakh. One brigade of our men was completely cut off and was never heard of again.

The Chinese forces continued to advance and captured Walong and in a flanking movement, took over Bomdila, trapping thousands of Indian troops in the Sela Pass region. In Tezpur, the evacuation of civilian population had begun.

Suddenly on 20 November 1962, the Chinese made a dramatic offer of a ceasefire.

⁂

The *ashtagraha* year turned up as an unexpected event for my family and me. Naju conceived ten years after Kerman was born. Poor lady, she suffered much from morning sickness and all the time we thought it was jaundice. Then, the moon rose and declined. We had doubts. I sent her to Bombay in May and it was confirmed that she was going to have another child. When she had her first one, the doctors said the second one might not live because of her Rh-negative factor. The child appeared to have been conceived at about the time of the *ashtagraha* as he was born nine months later, in November.

I was in the company of film stars — Sunil Dutt, Waheeda Rehman and other actors who were engaged in shooting for the film *Mujhe Jeene Do*. Some portions of the film were shot deep inside the Chambal ravines at Nagra (Morena district). Sunil pointed out that he had adapted a local Chambal ditty, *Nadi naare na jao shyam paiyyan padun*...in his film (the song became a hit). We talked about the new and old films. While I talked in despair, I knew that a treasure was being thrown at me with the careless insouciance that only God can put into his greatest gifts. Unto us a son was born.

The *late latif* refused to appear while I was in Bombay for seven days. I left Bombay on the afternoon of 13 November. I came to Bhopal and got a trunk call that Naju had gone to the hospital in the car sent very kindly by film star Nargis at 6.30 p.m. At 8.21 p.m. Naju delivered a baby boy. She said he looked like me and Kerman.

What happened in Bhopal when we got the news is difficult to record. I felt sad, I know not why! Kerman was overjoyed — she jumped about and informed all by telephone with whoops of delight. Friends came in to wish us. The Welfare Centre arranged an impromptu song and dance; telegrams and congratulations were followed by sniggers and laughs. To add to my discomfiture, Naju wrote that I was probably the only IG in creation to be 'a newborn Papa'.

Why did I feel sad? It was because of several thoughts that came to my mind — what will my son be like? Will he be like me — lonely and unable to mix? Will he be like me — an outward success but an inner failure? Will he, like me, spurn riches and not be able to foot his bills?

In fact, I returned to Bhopal in a mood of deep introspection. I was broke; I had spent a lot in the previous month or two. The bank balance had dipped. I had taken a loan from the Police Welfare Fund. How would I repay it? What a fool I was to be honest when all around me there was dishonesty? What would my son, when he grew up, think of me, my condition and of himself?

When Naju was expecting, we had planned to name a son as Cyrus, after the Persian Emperor, Cyrus the Great, who was one of my heroes in history. Naju wrote to me to finalise the name fast, otherwise she threatened to call him Satchmo[2], because of the way

[2]The famous black singer, Louis Armstrong, was popularly referred to as Satchmo. He had a bass voice and he played the trumpet.

he howled. Since he was born on the day when Bomdila fell to the Chinese, for quite some time I called him Bomdila or Bomi, a typical Parsee name.

❧

Nehru paid a visit to Bhopal, Bhilai and Raipur in March 1963. He looked old and tired; his step had lost its spring. His voice was feeble; his face showed lines of anxiety, which China and the politicians had carved on it. Yet, he held the same appeal as in the past for the common man. In fact, larger crowds came to hear him in Bhopal, Bhilai and Raipur because of their interest in the Chinese problem. He said the same things, yet people went away happy, their fears dispelled by the long, repetitive speeches and frank admission of his mistake.

I had a chat with him for ten minutes at Raipur about dacoits and Nagaland. He asked questions in whispers, but he asked questions — and his programme showed that he still had zest and energy.

Later that year, in September, Congress faced a no-confidence motion in the Parliament for the first time. Attacks on Jawaharlal Nehru of a personal and virulent type were heard for the first time and he faced the ire of the nation which was suspicious about the integrity of its leaders and apprehensive of attacks from China.

The Chief Minister of Madras province (now Tamil Nadu), K. Kamaraj came out with a plan to strengthen the Congress. He suggested that important leaders should resign from the government and devote themselves to party work in the true Indian spirit of sacrifice and renunciation. Nehru moved craftily — he succeeded in making his party men agree to the ideal solution in which he would be empowered to decide who would be the, "Pride of flock, meatiest for sacrifice." Then he accepted the resignation of all those whose opposition to him had been growing over the past few months. Morarji Desai went; so did S.K. Patil and Lal Bahadur Shastri. After all, the Prime Minister had to show that he was impartial. And several lesser lights were extinguished.

In the states, Chief Ministers who had a 'bad record', either of integrity or opposition to the High Command, also went. And among them was Bhagwantrao Mandloi, Chief Minister of Madhya Pradesh. He went with a cheerfulness which showed that he was glad to be rid of an office of responsibility.

In the spirit of the 'Kamaraj plan', elections of the leaders were ordered in those states which had sacrificed a Chief Minister. For almost a month all work was suspended, while ministers and MLAs grappled with the problem of who should succeed Mandloi.

D.P. Mishra, who hailed from the erstwhile Madhya Pradesh region, and Takhatmal Jain from the erstwhile Madhya Bharat region, fought it out for two days. There was intense excitement in the MLA's Hostel near our house.

Naju and I, as was our practice, sat on the culvert near the MLA's Hostel where the battle was being fought. Some MLAs triumphantly declared that their side had won; those who had lost were not visible. Torn bits of leaflets lay scattered on the road — these were the reputations that had been torn into shreds. As they went flying aimlessly in the wind, my thoughts revolved around them, making me wonder what changes lay in the offing! Finally D.P. Mishra, who had been in exile for twelve years, returned to power with a majority.

Newspaper cutting of 8 January 1964 showing Prime Minister Nehru being lifted by his security personnel at the AICC session at Bhubaneswar with Indira Gandhi standing by.

Being from Cuttack, my good friend Dr R.N. Das, who was studying in the local Medical College, and I (editor) did not want to miss the opportunity to go to Bhubaneswar to see Nehru. I could not make it for some reason. He told me on return, "Pandit Nehru was sitting in the back row. The others had left the stage. I kept staring at him. I found he was trying to get up but was unable to do so. He assumed a crawling position. Without a second thought, I rushed up on the dais and facing him, asked if I could help. When he said 'yes', I put my hands beneath his shoulders and pulled him up. He put the entire weight of his body on me. Just then, Indira Gandhi walked in and asked, 'What are you doing?' When I said, 'He is paralysed,' she shrieked, 'Leave him alone.' I put him down. Nehru, with pain in his voice said, 'I think I won't be able to walk again.' Panditji turned to me and said, 'Bless you, son.' The security men came and elbowed me away. There was no stretcher. As he was being carried away, Nehru kept looking at me till he was put in the ambulance."

Even now, Dr R.N. Das says, "That pathetic look on Nehru's face haunts me to this day."

16

Nehru's Death

Friends, I owe more tears to this
dead man than you shall see me pay.

– Shakespeare

I had gone down to Piparia from Pachmarhi to bring my family. When we came back I was informed that a message had come from Bhopal that the Prime Minister was seriously ill. In the afternoon, when I was sleeping, a *chaprasi* (peon) shouted, "The Prime Minister is dead!"

I returned to Bhopal from Pachmarhi with Ron Noronha, Chief Secretary, and all the time I wondered why I did not feel any grief at his death. Perhaps the whole nation was prepared for it. We wanted it to come quickly, painlessly, to relieve the man who had done so much, to free him from the burden of a difficult time in our history when Kashmir threatened to engulf the whole subcontinent in strife. After the first stroke at Bhubaneswar, the Prime Minister had made good recovery. In his last press conference, on 25 May 1964, two days prior to his death, he had said, "My life is not ending so soon."

Till the end, his mind was quite firm. No doubt, there was some effect of the medication he was taking. Once or twice he had fallen asleep in meetings; pouches had appeared under his eyes; he had begun to walk with a slight stoop, prostate troubled him and returning from the last helicopter ride from Dehradun he had left behind a message of Robert Frost on his table regarding, "I have miles to go before I sleep," signifying the work of a man who was totally devoted to the people of India, his country. Pain at six o'clock on 27 May, and by 2:30 p.m., he was dead.

It had been the type of death that Nehru would have liked. He wanted to die on duty. He hated to retire. And he had died in Delhi, at such a time that a state funeral could be arranged.

I suspect that he wanted to die. He met his death bravely, without becoming decrepit, and a drag on the nation. The heart that had done so much had at last been stilled.

He died in all his glory — as Prime Minister — before the people who adored him, realised that he was a sick man, and that he would never be able to lead them in the same way again.

I was right not to grieve. I would have grieved if he had been insulted and discredited. I would have been sorry if he had found it difficult to go, when he ought to have done so. Now I could feel relief that he had left with tears in the eyes of millions, in this land and elsewhere.

As long as he was alive, new leaders could not arise. In the last one year, he had been slipping badly. His grip over affairs had slackened. Here was a leader, who languished in sickness, unable to lead, and yet unable to make anybody else lead.

The man whom I had known as Prime Minister, the man who rode hard, worked hard, got easily irritated, who was exacting and irrepressible in all matters — that man had died a year or so ago. In his place there was a man who tried hard to be the Prime Minister but never quite came up to it, and who, after the Bhubaneswar Congress lingered on while his enemies abused him, and friends felt that he ought to go. Now he was gone. And that was the last triumph of Nehru — gone out at the right time; gone with distinction and honour. Gone so that he will be remembered as a noble man, and a good Prime Minister.

I had known Nehru too well to write a tribute to him on his death. And our lives had got so entwined that it is difficult for me to be objective about him. He and I had undertaken many journeys, travelled millions of miles, shared the same experiences, and for hours he was either with thousands of people or alone with me.

Nehru had come to Raipur in 1960 to attend a public meeting, after which he went to the palace of Rajkumar Ragho Raj Singh (Divisional Commissioner) who had also invited me for dinner. I found it was a small party where only Ragho Raj Singh, his family and Pandit Nehru were present. Ragho Raj Singh said to Nehru, "Sir, you may remember Rustamji, who was with you some time ago."

Nehru said, "I know Rustamji very well." I could not understand the import of the sentence. Then he laughed and after a pause, added, "And Rustamji knows *me* very well."

About this man whom I had known so well, I decided to set down my thoughts in my diary sitting beside the radio and listening to the running commentary broadcast by AIR of his last journey.[1]

AIR commentary: *The body is about to emerge from the Prime Minister's House in New Delhi.*

I still feel no grief. Neither am I moved at the thought that his mortal remains would be making the journey to their last resting place. Since I am not moved by intense emotion, I want to ponder upon the man Nehru, calmly, dispassionately, without love or malice.

I do not want to remember the Nehru who is dead. I want to remember the Nehru that lived, the man whom I had met in Kashmir in 1952 — youthful, fair — who always ran up the steps; handsome, striking, who rode horses harder than any of us, who could walk like a young man, swim like a champion, work sixteen hours a day, regularly day after day. I want to remember the man who had a spurt of uncontrollable boyish laughter at Hospet when a photographer's

---

[1]Rustamji wrote fifty-five pages on Nehru on the day of the funeral. I have used several extracts from this write-up for *I Was Nehru's Shadow*. Interestingly, the last article written by Rustamji three weeks before his death was on Nehru.

flashbulb exploded behind an older gentleman reading an address, and frightened him. I want to think of the man who stood up in the car, throwing garlands to women, murmuring something to himself — bits of Urdu poetry, bits of English poetry, or humming a song in a cracked voice.

The chants and hymns can be heard in the background. The body is being brought out from the foyer into the portico.

Yes, that is the place where I left him always. "Goodbye Rustamji," he used to say with a handshake and a bit of a smile that sent you away happy. He had the knack of getting people to like him. He could divine people's thoughts and say the right thing. He could disarm his enemies with his words.

The AIR commentator read out the epitaph that Nehru had written: "I do not mind in the least what happens to my reputation after I am gone. But if any people should think of me, I should like them to say that this man with all his mind and heart, loved India and the Indian people and they were indulgent to him and gave him all their love most abundantly and extravagantly."

The Jamun *trees in Teen Murti House are breaking one by one...a sea of faces...masses of people in silent grief (the uproar of slogans and shouting can be heard in the background).*

Painfully the AIR commentators are trying to manufacture grief, while all that I feel is: Nehru would have loved this type of funeral. Crowds...stampedes...in the morning, in his house. Women climbing the railing of the gate, and when the police check them, stones and shoes are hurled at them. Four people killed in the stampede and several hundred injured.

The darling of the masses. How he exulted with the crowds, how he teased them, how he loved their adulation what strength he found in that!

The crowds break the barriers! Once again it is a sea of faces. Cascade of humanity.

He liked you to exaggerate the numbers present in the crowds and because you exaggerated, he always asked you the question in front of others, and you deceived everybody willingly because it was such an innocuous deception, and yet it pleased him so much. "Three lakhs, sir," you said with confidence and to avoid any newspaper coming out with a lesser figure, you often gave the official or expert estimate to the press.

He would never get to know how many came to the funeral... but perhaps, in the hours when he knew the end was coming, he must have guessed. In the morning he had felt a pain in the back and had asked his servant to massage him. The servant rang up the doctors. They came. He was conscious till 8:30 a.m. before drifting into a coma while outside a storm gathered in Delhi. Even an earthquake occurred while the funeral procession was on its way.

The procession is reaching Rajpath, where he had his Republic Day celebrations.

There was something of a good soldier in Nehru. He was completely unafraid of death as no man I have known.

I recall the day when I went up to him and told him that the port engine of the aircraft we were in was on fire and we may need to make an emergency landing. He looked up from the book he was reading, asked where we were, and went back to reading, while I sat opposite him, composing the last message to Naju which I still have.

Again and again our aircraft gave trouble, particularly on long journeys to Indonesia, China, NEFA but he always sat stoically, prepared for the end, unmoved, or deliberately not showing any fear. If a man lost his nerve, he invariably derided him. Like a soldier, he prized courage above all. His constant statement was, "Gandhiji taught us to be unafraid."

We are now at the top of India Gate from where we can see a sea of women in fluttering white. Lord Home, Lord Mountbatten, Dean

Rusk, Mrs Bandaranaike, ministers from Russia, UAR, Yugoslavia all are here from so many countries. The muffled band, Gandhiji's favourite hymns can be heard!

Perhaps, I muse, it will be the diplomatic world that would feel his absence the most. No other man could get receptions in Moscow and Washington (and even Peking at one time); no other man could talk to Kennedy and Khruschev as a personal friend.

Perhaps he would be remembered in the UN for being the architect of Asian unity and champion of the downtrodden. And they may realise that the unity of undeveloped nations can be easily shattered by fear, religion and prejudice.

After the liberation of Goa, I sent him a New Year card: "To the Prime Minister who sacrificed his reputation in the West for the sake of his country and Goa." He scowled at me weakly when we met next, but it was the truth.

He had an immense personal correspondence — friends in Europe and all over, relations, politicians and diplomats — and with it his attention to small matters, which always surprised me. "The Ajanta caves have been neglected," he complained. I remember how he shouted at the Chief Minister of Assam for not paying sufficient attention to the growing hyacinth problem. When the Chief Minister expressed his difficulty to control it, he shouted, "privatise, privatise" and went on explaining how to hand over the water bodies to private persons and get rid of the problem. In one of his public meetings, he laid down his ideas for the education of children. He said, it should start with lessons for two years in character building and not for learning alphabets. Or, "Why was that cultural artist denied foreign exchange?" and so on, through the nights, night after night, while the millions of his land, all accustomed to lazy ways, worked as little as possible, and often less than what they were paid for.

One of the typical features of his personality was the desire to travel, to see things first-hand or to meet people. He had a childlike curiosity, which kept him acquainted with and interested in India, as also countries abroad. About India he was always the best informed man in the country. His travels, his readings, his contacts, his private correspondence — kept him in touch not only with India but with several countries in the world.

And if there was a disaster, Nehru was the first to reach there. "We will fly tomorrow to Orissa to see the floods." Rayalseema famine — "We must go there soon," was his usual refrain. And when he got there, his intention was not to show pity to the weak and the crushed. He did not believe in individual charity. What he wanted to find out personally was how we were progressing with relief work — whether we were slow and bureaucratic. How he hated the word 'bureaucratic' and all that it signified.

The AIR kept repeating the same thing about multitudes and seas and oceans of people. Why can they not prepare little anecdotes about him — little bits of nonsense — which would have shown the human being and not just the Prime Minister.

The funeral has reached Rajghat, and there is much confusion, much dust, much hysteria.

Why am I still not moved? I ask myself, again and again. True his life has been rewarding, the end has come in time when it has spared him much. Is that the reason? Or am I made callous? Or am I by nature ungrateful, cold, fretful of my respect, my devotion, my love for him when he is not alive? Or is it because I have reached the age of scoundrelism — forty-eight — the age of scepticism, lacking in enthusiasm for the enthusiasm of anybody?

Mammoth crowds, women weeping, the union of hearts between a Prime Minister and his people. Indira Gandhi squats on the ground tired and spent.

She had given her life to him to work as a team, and that team was now broken. What would she be now? The reluctant person on whom a glowing people might thrust all power, or would she go to Allahabad and live among the squabbles of the Congress or stay in England, where she may be able to live her life away from public glare.

Mrs Indira Gandhi places pieces of sandalwood on the pyre...Sanjay, her son, lights the pyre. And amid the grief of millions, the remains of Pandit Jawaharlal Nehru are consigned to the flames.

In the winter of 1964, I went to Jhabua and Dhar on an inspection tour. Jhabua held a special place in my heart as my father had begun his career there. Later he got married and my parents lived there for some years with my sisters.

The Bhils of Jhabua and Dhar, as a rule, are pleasant, docile and contented men and women; happy in their own song and dance and you-leave-me-alone way. But the Rathia Bhils of Alirajpur are tribals, who are primitive in the real sense of the word — naked, except for an embroidered cloth which hangs in front to symbolise their sex; liquor, drums, music, dance is accompanied with savage outbursts of temper; and a strange, ever-present desire to kill or die. All brutality is veneered with a blend of innocence and tempered with a strong sense of logic, which is far beyond the comprehension of an educated mind.

That is the Bhil — small, wiry and arrogant. He lives in a small hut in the middle of his stony field. The mango and the *mahua* trees help him to survive. When even the fruits are withheld by Nature, the Bhil begins to survive on toddy. He takes long drinks, which kill his hunger and enable him to live in a world of desire and hatred. Even his hatred is primitive. He does not hate the moneylender who never gives him an account and is always willing to lend. He does not hate the clerk who swindles him. He does not hate the policeman, who comes to investigate the theft of a cock and in the process devours his best goat. He hates in a small, spiteful sort of way, his brother, who, on a full moon night when they are dull with liquor, refuses to give him a *beedi* to chew; or when another Bhil caresses his wife with his eyes or visits the market to sell a cow, which he so much wanted to possess but did not have the means to buy. An overpowering hatred arises like foul vapour from the half-starved body and the alcohol- dazed mind.

During an evening walk, I met a Bhil who had come out of jail. I asked him why he had been sent to jail and he replied, "I sent my wife to collect *mahua* and we made some liquor. It was too weak, but we drank a lot of it. People came in from other homes, with their own liquor. We drank."

"Did you dance?" I asked.

"No, we only drank. It is no fun dancing when there is less liquor."

"Makes sense," I said, "Then what did you do?"

"We quarrelled," he said weakly.

"And then?"

"*Arrey* Sahib, there wasn't enough liquor for a good row. Just a small quarrel, *bol chaal*. "Ah yes," he added, as an afterthought. "There was no food. So we went to Balu's house where we beat up his wife because she refused to give us food but we cleansed her pot; not a thing was left," he bragged. "There was no need to clean it; we had cleaned it so much."

He was arrested and released after six months.

This little drama is the problem of the barren land of the Bhils. Bare, rocky hills, shorn of vegetation by man in order to live, are the cause of his decline.

Crime is rampant in the tribals' land where the wretchedness of the land, the abject poverty and the breakdown of tribal culture contribute their bit. How could the police, with codified laws laid down by the British, apply them to the tribal society? Should the bare bodied Bhils be allowed to commit crime on their own bare bodied brothers and face their own people in the tribal panchayat? Or should the cases be registered under the provisions of the IPC? Suddenly, in one year there was a steep increase in the number of cases registered. In this I had my own views, while my officers had theirs. Government was alarmed and wanted the officers to be shifted, but I resisted the pressure.

❧

I made a couple of visits to Bastar. Apart from the hills, the forests and the scenery, the other attraction was the sight of bare breasted women. The tribal woman has a shapely figure and firm breasts.

Whenever such women were seen along the road, the liaison officer accompanying me would, invariably, try to distract my attention by engaging me in some silly talk. It was irritating to see the blighter trying to assume the role of my mother!

In February 1965, I flew to Bastar to see Bailadilla, the project which till then was yet a name known only to a few. It was evening in the hills; the nip in the air that had possibly arisen from the green valleys swept over the veranda of the *dak* bungalow. I watched a tribal dance, led by a girl of stunning beauty. At first I thought she was the daughter of one of the European or Anglo-Indian staff members. Later I was told that, "Scattered in the tribal hills are a lot of fair children, who bear unmistakable resemblance to the British administrators who had left their mark in the district."

The girl twisted her hips, turned and laughed at me with beckoning eyes before twirling away. First the General Manager was captured and he had to don the Bison-horn Maria headdress to dance to the rhythm of big drums. Then he had to join the girls. Next came my turn. The girls linked their arms and one tribal shoulder came softly into my grip, while the fair one put her arms round my other shoulder, pulling me along in the dance steps. She was lovely and slightly tipsy. I broke away to look at her — her shining crown of brass twinkled in the lights as her hips swayed and her eyes sparkled. She was fair and different — the product of an Empire builder's union with a simple tribal girl.

❧

Then back to Bhopal. Soon I got my transfer orders to Delhi to head a non-existent Border Force. After being the chief of Madhya Pradesh Police for seven long years, several invitations for bidding farewell awaited me. The farewell to Naju by the Welfare Centre was memorable. We refused to make it a sentimental one — no tears and no dinners, yet the thought of leaving the picturesque Bhopal and the apprehensions about Delhi plagued our minds.

The Chief Minister D.P. Mishra wrote an affectionate letter in which, among other things, he stated, "I would like to place on record my deep appreciation of your services to Madhya Pradesh and to assure you that we will not forget them...Under you, the police force has improved its efficiency and discipline...At all times you maintained an exemplary standard of devotion to duty and absolute integrity; even in the midst of stormiest debates in the Madhya Pradesh Vidhan Sabha, no one has at any time questioned your efficiency and honesty of purpose."

The Hindu, in a lengthy write-up under the heading 'Tough Man for Tough Job', on 22 July 1965, said about me:

> "He is a policeman, gentleman and a Good Samaritan, all rolled into one. In doing good, his left hand did not know what the right was doing. He has helped many a lame dog over the stile.
>
> "The police in Madhya Pradesh have many things to thank him for — he worked hard to get a Police Commission under the chairmanship of Mr C.M. Trivedi, ICS (Retd). The Commission's recommendations, even with partial acceptance and implementation by government, will go a long way to give the policemen a fairer deal."

Our railway compartment was decorated with flowers and the band played *Ham Bharat ke jawan*. Two-and-a-half-year old Cyrus did his last bit of conducting. Kerman cried a little as we pulled away from the place where Naju and I had worked with a degree of satisfaction that was rare in those times.

As the train steamed out of the Bhopal railway station the lines of Dora Sigerson came to my mind as I knew that I would never again be posted to Madhya Pradesh, my home state.

> I have left you behind
> In the path of the past,
> With the white breath of flowers,
> With the best of God's hours,
> I have left you at last.

PART — V

1965–1976

Tough Man for Tough Job

By Our Bhopal Correspondent

To the fine feathers flourishing in the cap of Mr. Khusro Framroz Rustamji, Inspector-General of Police of Madhya Pradesh, has just been added a new one. He has been appointed Director-General of the Border Security Force. It is a challenging task that will frighten away many but it fascinates this man who is equal to the task.

A friend tried to dissuade Mr. Rustamji from taking up this enormous job because it was a crown of thorns. Mr. Rustamji refused to be dissuaded. It shall not be said of him that he declined to do a difficult job, he said.

Another friend when he heard of this appointment commented: "Yes, Rustamji has twisted the tail of the dacoits in Madhya Pradesh. He is now wanted to twist the tail of the trans-border dacoits". Dacoities in Madhya Pradesh have indeed not been ended. But under Mr. Rustamji's dynamic leadership the ending of dacoities has been brought many miles nearer.

The drive against the dacoits is a purple patch in Mr. Rustamji's official career which has been fascinating. When he joined service in 1938 after passing the competitive examination (he was born in 1916 and educated at Nagpur), the official bosses said: "This young man will go far". And go far he did.

For ten years he held the posts of Assistant Superintendent of Police Sub-Divisional Officer and District Superintendent of Police in the various parts of the old C.P. and Berar and Madhya Pradesh. For some time he was Principal of the Police Training College at Sagar. He was also D.I.G. of Police in Aurangabad, Hyderabad. Rapidly rising, he went on deputation to the Government of India and was the personal security officer of the late Prime Minister Nehru. He returned to Madhya Pradesh (the new one) in 1958 as the Inspector-General of Police.

He has a shining record of service. Official recognition came in the form of the award of the Indian Police Medal in 1943 and the President's Police and Fire Service Medal for distinguished service in 1958. In whatever field of activity he found himself—and he has been in many fields—he gave a good account of himself.

The Police in Madhya Pradesh have many things to thank him for. The ordinary jawan and the constable feel that there is somebody who is looking after their welfare and always fighting for their cause. He worked hard to get a Police Commission appointed. And the Commission under the chairmanship of Mr. C. M. Trivedi, former member of the Planning Commission has concluded taking evidence. The recommendations of the Commission even with partial acceptance and implementation by Government, will go a long way to give the policemen a fairer deal.

The people of Madhya Pradesh are deeply beholden to Mr. Rustamji for the many improvements he brought about in the Police administration. The performance of the Police during the communal riots of which this State had a generous share is commendable.

Mr. Rustamji is a great believer in public relations for the Police and he himself is the best public relations man for them. Not long ago, he invited this correspondent to talk to his senior officers on public relations of the police and how to improve them.

He is a policeman, gentleman and a Good Samaritan all rolled into one. In doing good his left hand does not know what the right is doing. He has helped many a lame dog over the stile.

Mr. Rustamji is widely read and extensively travelled. He belongs to the brand of the few that have kept up the reading habit. He keeps himself abreast of events and thought currents in the contemporary world. He has travelled far and wide. True to the spirit of the proverb, "he who would bring home the wealth of the Indies must carry with him the wealth of the Indies", Mr. Rustamji carried knowledge with him and brought knowledge home. He has gone round the world with Mr. Nehru many times. Recently he went on his own to Japan and the Far East.

With his wife and two children, a girl and a boy, Mr. Rustamji has a happy family.

A write-up in *The Hindu* dated 22 July 1965 about Rustamji on his posting as DG of the BSF.

17

Start of the BSF

In early May 1965, at a high level conference in Delhi, I was the lone voice from the police side to oppose the formation of the BSF. A few days later I was called to Delhi and asked to take over the responsibility of raising that Force. I raised it and nurtured it for nine long years. To this day, I love the Force and my attachment for it is deep.

To trace the reasons for raising the BSF, one has to go back in history to 1947 when Pakistan was formed. Since Independence, that country was determined to see that India did not progress. She worked with single-minded determination to build up hate. Hate divided the subcontinent, and that hate remains undivided even to this day. Hate is the only factor which has kept Pakistan together. She longed and worked for the day when she could humiliate us. And when China and India fell out, Ayub Khan, the President of Pakistan decided to be friends with China. Initially Washington was cold about it, but with Ayub assuring lifelong loyalty to USA, relations between the two warmed up. Pakistan thought that she could, with the help of China, make a quick campaign and take Kashmir. Pakistanis would cheer, and the world might not feel very concerned. USA was then occupied with fighting in Vietnam. Ayub felt his position would become secure in his own country and with China. He was bent on shaking the new government of Prime Minister Lal Bahadur Shastri to its foundations. He probably felt that politically our country had become weak after the death of

Jawaharlal Nehru and therefore any dissatisfaction would lead to an internal collapse.

It all began with intrusions across the ceasefire line in Kashmir. It was not so easy because the army was readily available to repel the infiltration and UN observers were quick to point out that Pakistan was the aggressor. Therefore, from January 1965, there were intermittent skirmishes in the Rann of Kutch. On 9 April 1965, when Hindus were celebrating Ramnavami (birthday of Lord Ram), the Pakistan Army attacked the Sardar post held by the Central Reserve Police (CRP, now called Central Reserve Police Force, CRPF) in Kanjarkot area of the Rann of Kutch. The police units warded the attacks but were overwhelmed. Soon the whole border of Kutch became active and several 'retaliatory' attacks from both sides were launched.

The Government of India set up a committee to examine and recommend the most effective way of manning the entire Indo-Pak border. The committee formed a study group headed by Lt Gen Kumaramangalam, the Vice Chief of Army Staff. It submitted its report in April 1965. The Home Secretary, L.P. Singh and the COAS, Gen J.N. Chaudhuri examined the report and prepared a scheme for the creation of a central force on the border. The question then arose as to who should head the new force. Gen Chaudhuri was of the view that a police officer should head the police force, whose task would be mostly concerned with police duties.[1]

A meeting of the Home Ministers and the chiefs of police from all the states was called by the Union Home Minister in the first week of May 1965. There was an address by Prime Minister Lal Bahadur Shastri, who dwelt on the Pakistani troop movement on the

---

[1]Two articles appeared in the newspaper *The Statesman* written by "Our Military Correspondent" on the 22 April 1965 and 8 July 1965. Much later, it was divulged that the author of the articles was none other than the serving COAS, Gen J.N. Chaudhuri. In his articles, Gen Chaudhuri spelt out clearly the objectives of the new Border Force and also stated that it should be headed by a policeman and not an army man. He wrote, "This may cause a bit of disappointment in army circles, as obviously some covetous eyes have been cast on the post, but as a decision it is correct. The head of a police force must be an able policeman."

Gujarat border. The Indo-Pak border in those days was looked after by the respective state police units. With Pakistan attacking the police posts in the Rann of Kutch, the Prime Minister wanted the international border to be guarded, as per the constitutional requirements, by a separate Border Force under the aegis of the Central Government. When I raised my objection citing economic reasons, the Prime Minister suddenly got up and said, "Gentlemen, I am glad you all agree. We will go ahead and raise a new Central Border Force."[2]

A few days later, the Chief Minister, Pandit D.P. Mishra telephoned me and said, "They want you urgently in Delhi. Take my plane and go tomorrow morning."

"What is it for?"

"They will tell you in Delhi," he said.

I wondered what had happened. I remembered I had shot down a proposal at the earlier meeting in Delhi that we should spot dacoits from the air and then shoot them down. There was an exchange of hot words about police inefficiency. I thought it was something to do with that or it could be for sending me to another state, most probably, Assam as IGP.

L.P. Singh, ICS, the efficient Home Secretary, whom I met the next morning, was also evasive and this made me still more uncomfortable. L.P. took me to the Home Minister, Gulzarilal Nanda, who was seated on a bed as he was unwell. He looked at me carefully,

---

[2]I was told by Vidya Charan Shukla, a former Union Minister that he was present in the room of the Chief Minister D.P. Mishra in the Madhya Pradesh Bhavan in New Delhi when Rustamji was called in and told by the Chief Minister to oppose the formation of the new force. Shukla further added that since Rustamji was attending the conference in his capacity as a representative of the Madhya Pradesh government, he had no other alternative but to comply with the orders of the Chief Minister. Madhya Pradesh has no international border. The possible reason for D.P. Mishra's instruction to the IGP could be that after Prime Minister Nehru's death, the Chief Ministers of some states wanted to exert their independence and resist the Central Government's attempts to encroach on the powers of the states. Further, a section of the senior Congress leaders was not reconciled to Shastri becoming the Prime Minister. Shastri appears to have sensed the reason for two or three states opposing the move and hence brought the discussions to an abrupt close.

which increased my discomfiture. Then he said, "We want you to raise our new Border Force."

I was taken by surprise. "But why me? I am quite happy in my state."

"Your post would be upgraded. You would be given an extra star in your badges of rank and an increase of Rs 250 in pay."

"But, there are so many senior to me. Can't I continue in my present rank?" I pleaded.[3]

"We have considered all that. In your equation with the army, this rank is required."

Whenever in doubt and conflict as to what I should do, I let my heart decide — because the heart has its reasons. And the heart is never wrong. I decided to take up the post. At the back of my mind was the thought that I still had nine years of service left. I had already put in seven years as IGP, Madhya Pradesh. Some of the officers serving under me were older than me. They would have no chances of promotion if I continued there. Further, I was always a great believer in leaving at the correct time, that is before people start feeling what a nuisance I am.

When we came out of the Home Minister's room, I pleaded with LP that we must put an 'S' in between Border and Force, otherwise we would be called BFs. He had a hearty laugh and agreed. That was my first achievement for the BSF. LP asked me if I had any other conditions. I said, "None, except that I would need 'massive support'." He assured me of all support.

---

[3]Golok Majumdar, former IG, BSF (Eastern Frontier) told me that he once asked L.P. Singh how the choice of the first DG, BSF fell on Rustamji, who was then comparatively junior. L.P. Singh told him that raising a new force was a Herculean task and he wanted someone who had fire in his belly to be the first DG. He found that Rustamji had that fire and he was made the DG over the heads of twenty-five officers senior to him. (See Appendix II). I asked Majumdar whether there were any protests from the officers who were overlooked. He said that, to begin with, it was an ex-cadre post and when Rustamji was made DG of a non-existent force, the seniors, who were well established in the key posts they were holding, probably felt relieved that they were not consigned to an innocuous assignment. Gen Chaudhuri, the COAS, probably also had a say in the matter. Rustamji had served under him in Hyderabad.

A week later, the Home Secretary had a discussion with the COAS and the Defence Secretary regarding the role and organisation of the BSF. The Home Secretary recorded the ideas that emerged from the discussion in a note on 17 May 1965. The plan had been drafted with such precision and in such a lucid way that the Force, to this day, functions as per the broad conclusions reached by the three wise men.

After handing over charge as IGP Madhya Pradesh, I reached Delhi and wrote in my joining report on 21 July 1965, "I have taken over charge of the BSF." I became the head of a one-man organisation. I was the sole Borderman; nobody below me, nobody above me.

I was back in Delhi after a gap of seven years and sat in too cold an air-conditioned room, wanting to build a headquarter for the BSF and not having the chance to do so. Delhi always lacked direction. When I took over, it seemed to be pulling in several directions. The problem with Delhi has always been that there is nobody who everyone accepts. So my time was spent in a most unprofitable manner — fighting for telephones, getting rude about a garage, brazening it out with a borrowed staff car, going round looking at all sorts of houses and offices and not being able to get the place that I needed to start the control room. In Delhi, Pakistan and the borders seemed too far away. We kept on fighting amongst ourselves, rather than those who needed to be fought against.

In those difficult days, I kept on telling myself, 'All this will pass. There will be space found. We will get all that we want, but it will come in only after we have been attacked once or twice as in Kutch and made to feel small.'

After the Indo-Pak War, I went about the task of collecting the men who would assist me in raising the new Force. I handpicked each one of them and got the best of men from the police, the army, air force, the navy and the academic world. By a coincidence almost all the names of the men around me began with an 'R' — Ranjit Singh, Rajgopal (P.R.), Ramamurti (K), Rosha (P.A.), Rajdeo Singh and Ran Singh (Brig). And then there was Rathore (R.S.) from the Indian Revenue Service (IRS), whom I had known from my days in Bhopal.

The team at the top with Ashwini Kumar in Jullunder, Ram Gopal in Srinagar and P.K. Basu and later Golok Majumdar in Calcutta was full of ideas and the key word was innovation. I have always held that if you want to move fast, you need good brakes; and the brake for me was the Deputy Director (Intelligence) P.R. Rajgopal, an old friend from Madhya Pradesh who had the right to criticise me in any meeting. He was my "no" man. He did not take it amiss if I did not listen to him.

Thus, the BSF formally came into existence on 1 December 1965.

Many of the battalions belonging to the states manning the international border with Pakistan were taken over by us. The twenty-five battalions formed the core of the BSF initially. Gradually we built up the strength by sending teams of officers to rural areas all over India to select the sturdy types and raised another twelve battalions. Fifteen more battalions deployed in Jammu and Kashmir were taken over in 1966 and within a year we had fifty-two battalions. The battalions belonging to the different states had their own strength and composition. Since they became part of one organisation, it was necessary to bring about uniformity in their strength and composition by readjusting them. The process of reorganising and readjusting increased the number of battalions to sixty.

In determining the strength, one BSF battalion was earmarked as reserve from about ten battalions. The reserves were meant not only for situations which required temporary strength, like some law and order problem, but also for rotation to enable training, rest and recreation.

One of the things that any force requires is facility for training its various levels of officers. During my tenure as IGP, Madhya Pradesh, I knew that the state had a large number of palaces belonging to the erstwhile rulers of the princely States which were hardly used by them.

I met the Rajmata of Gwalior, Vijaya Raje Scindia and asked her if we could acquire the Jal Mahal, some miles away from Gwalior in a village named Tekanpur. She agreed. The BSF paid a token amount of Rs 6.41 lakhs for the palace and the huge area all around. The palace was in such a dilapidated condition that on my first visit I was going down the steps to the boat deck, I slipped and went sprawling down all the way to the bank of the lake. The palace had become the haunt of dacoits and in the initial days we had to exercise caution about an attack on our arms and ammunition.

The Academy was fortunate to have Brig B.C. Pande as its first Commandant. When Gen Kumaramangalam offered him to me, he said, "Take him, take him Khusro. He is a powerhouse of energy and unorthodox in his methods and that is what you need."

Kay (Gen Kumaramangalam) was one person everyone trusted. Anyone who loves horses, as he did, has something of that noble animal in him. So, on his recommendation, we took Brig B.C. Pande for the post of Commandant of the Academy. B.C., as I called him, gave a vigorous start to the Academy. A whole generation of BSF officers and men remember Brig B.C. Pande with affection and pride. Young in mind always, he was there all the time to lead, to guide, to motivate and to cheer on and fire his men with idealism that was beyond professional competence.

Due to the reorganisation of the battalions, a need was felt for a large number of officers. In 1966, about sixty-six officers of the rank of Assistant Commandant were recruited. I had a fairly good idea of the type of officers I wanted. It is difficult to find out in a short interview the qualities of a man; but I suppose years of selecting men instinctively made me choose the right type. The qualities I looked for were: courage that is not affected by rumours or setbacks, strength of mind to judge and not be stricken by panic at any important moment, health, mental ability and educational background and finally, the ability to be a leader of men.

The essential prerequisite for any battalion is good officering. Officers were not forthcoming from the states and when I placed the problem before the Home Secretary in 1967, he said that the army would be releasing some of their Emergency Commissioned Officers (ECO) and I could select from them. I also felt that these men would be a good addition to the BSF and would make it an efficient and dependable Force. Many of them had fought in the Indo-Pak War of 1965. They literally came from hearth and mansion to serve the country when Emergency was declared after the Chinese incident. Some of them were killed in the Pakistan fighting; and the rest were screened and tested by boards and from among them some were retained in the army for permanent commissions. The experience that these boys had acquired in the army was invaluable. But apart from it, several of them were highly educated before joining the army, and it seemed to me that due credit had not been given to them for their educational attainments. Perhaps the army needed only one type, the younger type, but for us these men were suitable for filling up the vacancies.

I went to Srinagar in March 1968 to select the ECOs for the BSF. Out of the 1,200 officers who were being released, 1,000 opted for service in the BSF/CRP/Indo-Tibetan Border Police (ITBP). We selected about 300 from them in the first lot.[4]

I went to T.T. Krishnamachari, the Finance Minister to present the first BSF budget. I was fortified with facts and statistics and reams and reams of notes. He looked at the papers before him and said, "Next item." The Finance Minister approved our first BSF budget proposals without a question. This was soon after the Indo-Pak War and it was an indication of how much the government valued the Force. But he made it clear that foreign exchange was not possible for weapons or for radios.

The denial of foreign exchange proved to be a blessing in disguise. We had a genius at improvisation on the communications side in C.P. Joshi and some highly efficient technicians in P.N. Chopra,

[4]In all, 548 ECOs were taken into the BSF as Assistant Commandants. The simultaneous recruitment of ECOs and Assistant Commandants from the open market (Direct Entrants, DEs as they were referred to) resulted in bunching. It led to clogging the avenues of promotion for both categories of officers. The problem was compounded by the fact that the ECOs, who were screened out by the army, were allowed to count their army service for fixing their seniority upon joining the BSF. They were initially taken in as Class II officers but through the efforts of Rustamji, they were made Class I officers. Though the experienced ECOs initially proved useful in filling up vacancies in the fast expanding organisation, yet the moves taken at that time disturbed the command structure in the BSF for several years, besides causing heart burning between the ECOs and the DEs.

S.P. Gorowara and others. C.P. Joshi revolutionised the concepts in radio with the help of Chopra at Jullunder and workshops all over. At the annual exhibitions, the ingenuity of our men made me marvel at the capacity of the middle rank technicians for improvisation.

Under the leadership of G.P. Bhatnagar, Col Prem Sharma, Naresh Mehra and others, we developed workshops which helped us overcome the shortage of weapons. We raised a factory to make spare parts and repair weapons. We even made 3 inch mortars at Ranchi and used them.

A small group worked under G.P. Bhatnagar at Tekanpur in rocketry. They began with rockets of the range of 200, 300 and 400 yards. Then they developed rockets to the range of twenty kilometres with the help of Vikram Sarabhai and A.P.J. Abdul Kalam.[5] These rockets were used at the instance of the BSF for the first time in the Bangladesh conflict. Research continued and at the Pokhran range, the BSF threw a rocket ninety kilometres from the base.

We were trying to get the tear smoke unit, but there was a lot of opposition from the Defence side. Eventually, the then Defence Minister agreed to give it to us provided we could produce tear smoke in six months' time. The unit was able to do it before the prescribed time limit.

In the initial stages, the disbursement of salaries and fixation of pay to the officers and men drawn from several states through their State Treasuries posed a lot of problems. We wanted to create a Pay and Accounts Division but were not able to get the clearance from the Comptroller and Auditor General of India (CAG) despite all efforts. In the course of a conversation, Rathore humorously remarked that accounts people have one weakness — they get highly flattered with salutes. That was a cue enough for me to decide to go to the CAG along with two officers in police uniform and two in army uniform (in 1967 the army officers in the BSF were still wearing their olive green uniform). All five of us went over to his office and saluted him in unison. Things worked like a miracle after that. He was very receptive and despite his deputy raising objections, our

---

[5] He became the President of India in 2002.

proposal was agreed to. This small step resulted in having a separate Pay and Accounts Division which was a big boon for the men posted in distant corners of the country.

In my view one of the biggest welfare measures for any force is not only payment of salaries to the men in time but also letting them know all details of their pay, allowances and leave due to them. I was discussing this with L.P. Singh and he suggested, back in 1968, that the only solution to the problem was to go in for computerisation. He promised to give funds for the purpose. Two young IPS officers, S.K. Sharma and T.A. Chari were selected to undergo training in Australia and take up the project. From the beginning we attached much importance to computerised management of the office and the two young officers, along with Rathore, lived up to the trust I reposed in them. By 1969, even a man posted in the remote area got a computerised pay slip along with his salary. In the course of my round-the-world trip sponsored by the Ford Foundation, I also underwent a capsule course in computers in New York.

While the top brass at the headquarters was busy organising the Directorate, I paid a good deal of attention to selecting every single man required for the Force. I also went throughout the length and breadth of the country, showing my face to the men and acquainting myself with the problems in the field. While in the office, I kept open doors which resulted in quick disposal of other peoples' work with me, but it resulted in making me work for longer hours. I tried to go at a fast pace to get things off the ground and when procedural obstacles presented themselves, my impatience grew at every step.

I found that the only problem before me were the sudden gusts of temper. Their frequency increased and it became more difficult for me because I did not want to explode. There were some officers who made my gorge rise. They would regularly upset me. I felt I should think of some device to counter them. Be philosophical? Try to help them? Understand them? Give them less to do? I was aware it was affecting my health. I realised that I had started feeling a bit uneasy climbing stairs.

Things came to a head at the Training Conference in Indore in November 1969. The conference was tiring, and more than that, the parties were endless. By God, what a terrible price I had to pay for being unable to say — 'no' to work — 'no' to entertainment — 'no' to the dinner parties that fell to my lot on tours.

On 4 November, to be exact, I had a showdown. A local Commandant asked all the orderlies to deposit Rs 80 as advance for mess food which they did not eat. I asked for details and when Ranjit (Singh), the Deputy Director incharge, tried to give a weak explanation, I blew my top.

The Central Health Service doctor examined me, said it was "heartburn." On 6 November, I went to Nagu's house in Bhopal. He called Dr N.P. Mishra, who examined me the next day, declared that I must rest for at least two weeks, hinting that it could be a heart problem. From 9 November, I took rest and even gave up alcohol and cigars to cleanse my system.

Gradually the uneasiness disappeared. I went with the COAS to Tekanpur. Naju, Cyrus and I went to Jammu for the BSF Raising Day. Then I went to Mhow with the COAS again for the Army Rifle Association (now known as Army Marksman's Unit) Championship. I kept saying to myself while I was under the threat: "It's not life that matters, but the courage you bring to it."[6]

Yet, at times, in the evening, or in the street, a dread, a fear used to attack me. Will it all end suddenly? I dreaded getting admitted to a hospital for I consider it is the worst place one could be in.

I was to go on a tour to Indore and Bhopal. I developed a slight pain in my chest, in the sternum region. I walked up to the plane in Delhi, despite the pain. 'Will I suddenly fall dead in the plane and my dead body be dragged out at Indore?', I thought. Seated next to me was a beautiful American girl in the skimpiest of skirts. We read newspapers. Our arms rubbed against each other. And curiously enough, the damn pain disappeared for the entire duration of the flight. I discovered that the trouble about heart problem is that it affects the head more than the heart. Every now and then, you begin to imagine all kinds of pain which often is illusory. Finally, Dr Padmavati, the cardiologist at All India Institute of Medical Sciences (AIIMS) cleared me; there was nothing wrong at all.

[6]The quoted lines are from Hugh Walpole's novel *Fortitude*.

During the first three years as DG BSF, I had the chance of coming close to the army — a chance which in India is hardly ever possible. In the early years, the army found it difficult to accept the BSF. The first major complaint of the army against the BSF was, 'The BSF keeps on expanding.' Secondly, the army officers claimed that that they were not clear what the role of the BSF was. Every time it was mentioned, they seemed to forget it quickly. Thirdly, there was a tinge of jealousy that the BSF seemed to get everything it wanted. Fourthly, they felt that the Home Ministry was raising a parallel army and we must do our little bit to see that the BSF officers do not 'become too big for their boots.' And lastly, that the BSF was commanded by a policeman and not by an army officer, which would have resulted in one more post of a Lieutenant General, apart from several other ranks.

This was not the view of the COAS or the seniormost officers of the army. On my part, I had excellent working arrangement with Kay right from the time he was Vice-COAS. Anybody in a position of responsibility realised that the BSF was there to help. It was the lower level of officers who viewed the BSF with suspicion. In fact Gen Kumaramangalam stated in his letter to me after his retirement as COAS in 1969:

> "I hope I have left in the army a certain respect for the BSF. It was difficult initially to get people over their prejudice for the police...That you have in this short period brought the BSF upto this standard is a big tribute to you, without me having to pay you any more compliments....You have put back my faith in the policeman and it is thanks to your honesty and sincerity of purpose that we have (had) such understanding between the BSF and the army. This has (made) my work in getting the army to shed their prejudice much easier."

The enormous strength that can be derived from the paramilitary forces has never been accepted by military leaders. In the first place it does not fit into their plans for expansion if they are told that the job can be done by the paramilitary forces. Secondly, it hurts their pride that there can be anybody who equals them in training and elan.

In raising the BSF, the conditions proved fortuitous. It came at a time when the country needed such an organisation. Pakistan's incursions into the Rann of Kutch helped to give birth to the BSF. The Indo-Pak War of 1965 produced a patriotic zeal which helped it to grow fast. Every ministry and every officer, even at the lowest level, was eager to help it to develop and expand rapidly. Even the MPs were sympathetic and we could get the BSF Bill passed without any criticism of the Force or me. We got it on the ground very fast. The Home Secretary, L.P. Singh, and the Home Minister, Y.B. Chavan helped me considerably during the formative period of the BSF.

New Delhi
1/9/65.

To

Naju, Kerman & Cyrus.

Darlings,

I am going to Srinagar again tomorrow morning. Our country is now at war. We have to do our bit.

If anything should happen to me, you must remember me as your own, for ever.

Yours

Khusro

"To, Naju, Kerman & Cyrus, Darlings, I am going to Srinagar again tomorrow morning. Our country is now at war. We have to do our bit. If anything should happen to me, you must remember me as your own, for ever. Yours Khusro."

(Rustamji's diary entry at the start of the Indo-Pak War of 1965)

18

Indo-Pak War

In the first week of August 1965, the Home Secretary, L.P. Singh called me and said, "There seems to be something suspicious going on in Kashmir. Can you go across and see what is happening?" Since it was just over a fortnight when I had taken over as DG BSF, I did not want to protest or ask him, "What am I supposed to do there?"

There were reports that large groups of Pakistani soldiers and *mujahids* (raiders) had infiltrated across the ceasefire line and converged on Srinagar, cutting off the lines of communication. The initial reaction in Delhi was one of disbelief and scepticism. The Home Ministry felt it was a major threat.

I reached Srinagar on 10 August 1965. An earlier attempt to reach there the previous day had failed. We had to return from Banihal (mountain range) due to the inclement weather.

The Home Secretary wrote to the Chief Minister of Jammu and Kashmir, G.M. Sadiq that I, along with B.A. Sharma, DIG from Madhya Pradesh, were being sent to Srinagar to help in dealing with the law and order problem and to ensure that the most effective use was made of the armed police battalions and that their morale was kept high. It was probably for that reason the Home Minister of Jammu and Kashmir, D.P. Dhar took me along with him wherever he went.

In Srinagar, there were moments of anxiety and spells of jubiliation: long drives across the valley, with sudden meetings, with lot of whisky and midnight dinners with Dhar at the Oberoi Hotel.

All the time there was fear that we did not know what Pakistan would do next. Why the lull? Why the collection at odd places? Are the guerillas tired or short of food and ammunition?

I returned to Delhi with the report that we needed to strengthen the defences of Srinagar. LP and Gen J.N. Chaudhuri, worked together. The army could not reduce forces on the Jammu and Kashmir border or even elsewhere, though some units were quickly moved to Srinagar. As for the police, LP had already moved about fourteen armed police battalions from the states and asked me to go back to Srinagar to look after them.

The infiltration into Kashmir, which was the start of Pakistan's 'Operation Gibraltar', was a clever and daring plan. Evading the hard crust of the army on the border, the infiltrators slipped into the valley. It was a helpful prelude for me because it gave me an idea of the type of units we needed on the border and the type of equipment and support that was required.

It was the tourist season in Kashmir. Far away on the green golf course in Gulmarg, one of the finest in the world, there was a slow waddle of men and women playing golf. The houseboats were full and their owners were happy with the profits they were making from foreign tourists.

One local who had gone up into the mountains to graze his cattle saw a strange sight. A group of about 300 heavily armed men was camping in the hills. They spoke a different dialect and their activities looked suspicious. He came back and told someone. A rumour spread in Gulmarg, "The *kabaeli*s (marauders) have come." It was 3 August 1965.

A patrol was sent out by the army. Contact was established on 6 August, and the first round began with an artillery salvo in which a large number of infiltrators were buried in the soil of India.

Meanwhile, from 5 – 9 August, the other guerilla groups worked their way inland from the ceasefire line. On the night of 9 August, a crucial day in the history of India, the Pakistani raiders numbering about 3,000 reached Srinagar. Most had come on foot. The surprise part had already worn out. In fact the same evening at nine o'clock the army had been put incharge of the defence of Srinagar.

Maj Gen S.S. Kalhan, who like most army officers, was not very fond of police units, had to defend the city with disorganised police units and a few army companies.

The raiders came up to a transit camp and shot a sentry and then began to probe the defences. They fired a few shots. The hastily thrown in police units, who had not had the time even to dig defences or to know the positions of other units began firing at the army and at each other in a battle that will be remembered as the most comic in the history of warfare. Nevertheless, it was this that saved the city. The enemy ran away with the impression that the city was extremely well defended by a solid mass of men who could put up as much prophylactic fire as ten battalions of the army.

Gen Kalhan had saved the city in a manner which no military General would like to tell the world. He repeatedly stressed there was no danger at all, while his young assistant in the control room, Capt Arvind Malhotra discreetly asked for a "little more police" because there were no rescuers at all and the situation was "rather difficult." The estimates of the situation and the number of raiders varied from man to man. Even those who had the responsibility of careful evaluation did not seem to have carried out their responsibilities carefully.

Intelligence reports indicated that Pakistan had been training guerillas in four places in Pakistan occupied Kashmir (PoK). There had been wild threats of 'other methods' hurled by Zulfiqar Ali Bhutto, the Foreign Minister. Even while a ceasefire in the Rann of Kutch was being talked about, the rulers of Pakistan were implementing their plans to take over Kashmir.

Then, in a day of good fortune, two or three events occurred which confirmed what we suspected. One of the weak ones in the guerilla group decided that he cared a damn whether Kashmir belonged to India or Pakistan, so he strayed out of the group, surrendered and gave a full account of the infiltrators and their designs.

The second event was of a stray dog, named Kallu, which used to hang around the police post on the ceasefire line and feed on the leftovers. He sniffed out a Pakistani *Havaldar*, who was captured by the post. He had come harmlessly with a sten and six magazines to blow up the post and cheerfully gave a full account of the extent of the infiltration. Their aim was to seize the vital installations and make an announcement over the radio station that Kashmir had been taken over.

D.P. Dhar reacted at once. L.P. Singh in the Home Ministry also acted quickly and on the crucial day, which was a holiday, we three ceaselessly begged the states for more men. Punjab, Uttar Pradesh and Madhya Pradesh responded. The air force lifted them to Srinagar. Soon the policemen, many in summer clothing, were rushed to the city to man the defences of the area.

There was no doubt, however, that the raiders were getting a beating wherever they attacked the police. Wherever they met the army, they suffered even more heavily. Food became a problem; some were running out of ammunition; quarrels were arising. Their officers had to be replaced by wireless instructions. Within a fortnight the great guerilla force had begun the retreat.

The miscalculations of the Pakistani General, who planned the operation, were numerous. He miscalculated the strength of India. But his worst miscalculation was regarding the attitude of the Kashmiris. The Pakistanis never expected it. They thought they were brothers in Islam. The Kashmiris, they felt, would rise as one man and support the fight for liberation. They had come to divide Hindus and Muslims, but Kashmir stood firm in the days of crisis — gloomy but unable to run away from the sound of guns and apprehensive about the clash of armies in their beautiful land. And all over India, people marvelled at these men who foiled an invader by non-cooperation.

In the next phase the guerillas began to concentrate in certain pockets near the ceasefire line. They were obviously waiting for the D-Day.

On 1 September 1965, Pakistan made heavy attacks across the Akhnoor sector. The Punjab Armed Police (PAP) in the front fought alongside the forward posts of the army. The Pakistani forces advanced rapidly. We brought in air support and within the first few days shot down ten aircraft. Despite the magnificent performance of the IAF, the Pakistani advance continued. Jaurian was blasted, mosques and homes tumbled down in flames due to the air attack. Pakistan had probably committed the best part of their armoured division in the attack with the objective of capturing the Akhnoor bridge and cutting off our line of communication to Rajouri, Poonch and the Hajipir area where Gen Kalhan had been halted in his drive to connect Uri with Poonch.

On the morning of 6 September, I was at Udhampur. I woke up to the sounds of a cannonade and the words uttered loudly by someone outside — "Amritsar." I wondered if Amritsar had been attacked. At about ten o'clock, news came that we had advanced on Lahore. Two columns, we were told, had moved quickly — one from Wagah (Amritsar) and the other from Ferozepur and we were within a few miles of Lahore. Meanwhile, the Pakistani tanks that were being pulled out from the Akhnoor-Chhamb sector were blasted. In middle age, one does not know whether to be overjoyed on such occasions or be mournful and prophetic. Whatever one was, history was being made and I was glad to be standing on the sidelines and hearing the guns roar.

A third front had been opened up towards Sialkot. By 9 September, fighting had intensified and we had opened another front at Barmer. Air attack by the Pakistan Air Force (PAF) intensified.

13 September was a busy day. We went to Pathankot and heard of a Pakistan paradrop which was the most slipshod drop ever attempted. Several paramen from a Baluch regiment were dropped five miles outside Pathankot. The plan was probably prepared by some paper saboteur. According to the plan, after destroying the Indian planes, the same aircraft that had dropped them was to land at Pathankot and take them back to Peshawar. Many were rounded up and some were killed.

In the Indian Army, there was no fanaticism, no great enmity; it was: "We have to fight the buggers and by God we will lick them." But in the rear, the countryside in Punjab was aflame. A Pakistani fighter plane had plunged deep down a field and had almost completely disintegrated. The pilot had parachuted out and when he landed, he raised his hands up. Ashwini Kumar and I raced to take him, but before we could reach him, a Nihang struck him a blow with an axe while another villager pierced his heart with a spear. An incredible sadness seized me. The sadness was not so much for him as it was about his country and mine; it was for his family and mine.

The next night we had a thrilling journey from Pathankot to Jammu. The road was dark. Blackout had been enforced. Our jeep driver weaved his way in and out with great skill to get ahead of the slow-moving army trucks loaded with tanks and ammunition. We reached Jammu at 9:30 p.m. and heard of an air raid in which eleven men had been killed. I found in the war we had lost so much due to panic and inexperience of warfare that I almost felt my experience had been worth it.

On 15 September, Terence Quinn (Commandant of Madhya Pradesh's SAF battalion) and I set out from Jammu for Amritsar at about one o'clock in the afternoon. We reached a place fourteen miles away when a Pakistani aircraft dived down and the ack-ack guns opened up. I jerked the jeep to the side. We jumped down and stood behind a small mango tree. The Sabres (four of them) kept diving down on the road before swooping up to dodge the guns. We had a comfortable position near the guns, so we could see the whole show dispassionately. Soon the Sabre came lower and rocketed the road. Now how to get out of the road? I rolled under a truck. I felt the truck was what they were after. We ran to a *peepal* tree. Its trunk was so thick that no rocket could have penetrated it. On the ground, hugging the roots, we saw the Sabre come again. Head down, I wondered if they would get us! They left gracefully doing a roll while our ack-ack followed ineffectively. For once, I felt like worshipping the *peepal* tree, like a devout Hindu.

I wanted to rush out of the area quickly. Quinn said, "Don't go to the bridge now, sir." But I overruled him. And when we were at the other end of the bridge, where the road was closed by a tanker, the jet swooped down again. We jumped to the side of the bridge. Quinn shouted, "They have dropped a bomb."

I tried to fit myself into the stone edge, waiting head down breathlessly, no explosion! "Another dud," I shouted and we ran to the side which had the tall elephant grass. Again the jets came rocketing. I hit the ground. Got up and ran again. There was a nice trench under a tree. I got into that, covering my head; and thinking that if they got me in that position, I would really look like an ostrich. Still alive! Again we ran inside the big grass. Again the planes came so low this time that we could see every detail. "What the hell!" I shouted to the Andhra boys, "Get the bloody Bren going. Fire with your rifles."

One jeep was on fire. 'That's the end of my war journal,' I said to myself.[1] But, fortunately, the one that carried our baggage was still intact. We trudged the river-bed taking cover under the concrete of the bridge. We walked back to the village, before racing back to Jammu. I suddenly noticed my knee was infested with thorns, my arms were bruised. I must have jumped into some thorns but I could not recall having done so. 'What a wonderful experience!' I said to myself.

I do not understand the tactics and effects of aerial warfare, but I felt that the PAF was doing the job in an amateurish sort of way. Their targets were wrongly selected. Their maps were probably outdated or their intelligence briefing was faulty. They spent hours in hitting or missing the main targets and giving senseless poundings to places of no strategic consequence. Were we worth half an hour of flying time?

The PAF dropped bombs on the airport at Jammu and missed the radar. The bomb fell in the compound of a retired Colonel's house. I came across a hysterical woman sobbing with the severed leg of her daughter in her hand. The young girl lay calm and serene, nodding to me as we rushed up to help. I wanted to tie a tourniquet but there was no place. Her hip and leg had been cut away. She looked sadly at me — how young, how composed. She never said a word and

[1]Rustamji wrote his journal on a day-to-day basis during the entire duration of the conflict. His detailed entries have been condensed to form this chapter.

signalled to her mother, "Be calm. Help has arrived." Jawans rushed with an ambulance. The bleeding bodies were lifted in.

> Take her up tenderly,
> Lift her with care;
> Fashion'd slenderly,
> Young, and so fair!
>
> – Thomas Hood

An old man was left behind, forgotten and wanting to be forgotten, bleeding to death with a patient agony so difficult to describe.

As we drove away, for the first time, I found it difficult to hide my tears at the thought of that brave girl — and all my life I felt I shall remember her, as I remember the boy who was injured in Kanergaon during the HPA. I will remember them as our sacrifice to the god of hatred.

I have seen scenes which have made me proud of India. I have seen the courage of the soldiers and the tenderness of the public for the casualties in the hospital. I pay tribute to the anonymous donor who used to send a truckload of fruits to the hospital each day; I have seen the sisters and nurses moving quietly, as usual, while the seriously injured screamed.

On a cracked and plastered transistor set of a *Tehsildar*, we heard on the night of 20 September, right in the heart of the mountains, the resolution of the Security Council; "Ceasefire within forty-eight hours and go back to the August 5 positions." Will that mean giving up Hajipir and the Uri-Poonch road?

A ceasefire had been agreed to by both sides which would come into force from 22 September.

On 23 September, Dhar and I spent an interesting afternoon with Gen Kalhan and his officers at Baramula. We sat under the willows near the mess. Below, the river meandered peacefully and a man rowed across a small boat.

Kalhan said there were so many tales of heroism that he did not know which ones to tell. He related the one of a Sikh Bren gunner who got a shell hit that separated his legs from the body during an engagement. "My legs feel rather light," he said and went on attacking the enemy. Suddenly the gun stopped; he had collapsed and died.

These were the men about whom a captured Pakistani officer remarked, "We were told you people never get out of your pickets even to ease yourself. How is it you have suddenly acquired the courage to invade Pakistan?"

Kalhan went on to explain his tactics. "For mountain warfare," he said, with the terseness of an old soldier, "I don't want your tanks and armoured cars. I want to master the night. Anybody who can master the night can master anything. All my attacks that succeeded were at night. We approached the enemy silently. We got right up to them, threw grenades, got them by surprise and ejected them by hand-to-hand fighting."

His men had the distinction of making a Pakistani Brigadier run in his pyjamas, leaving behind all his top secret documents in a hurry. Among the documents left behind was his final advice which was a real master stroke of tactics: "Troops may operate in uniform."

In the mess we met a quiet Sikh, (probably Ranjit Singh was his name[2]) the hero of Hajipir. He was strangely quiet, almost shy and at the same time dark with a suntan and with a quiet confidence which comes to men who go through the valley of death and come out victorious. He said, "At one time we were extremely hungry and so were the prisoners we had captured. I went to the village and asked for three goats. I told them we had no money but I would pay them later. One goat we gave to the prisoners so that they could halal it. The captured officers ate with us, in fact from my plate. We shared some rum that we had." I wondered, 'What were our achievements from the war?' He went on to say, "Not territory, except a bit. Not equipment, except very little. We have gained confidence in democracy, in our army, in a fine and secular state. We have gained faith in ourselves."

---

[2]Lt Gen R.S. Dyal.

We went to the Sialkot front, impelled by an insatiable curiosity to see what had happened. It was a long dusty journey. All along the road could be seen rotting bodies of dogs and cattle and bomb craters. One of the biggest achievements of the 1st Corps was to take tanks over a roadless area — through streams and waterlogged areas. It was done silently and at night.

We could get the smell of burning houses and rotting flesh from a distance. A skeleton — its teeth white in a black skull; a woman's broken arm; a *Quran* left in a hurry. It was picked up by a Sikh carefully. He said, "It's for a Muslim officer, who is a friend of mine."

After the war, the talk in the mess was something like this: "One bastard, when we cornered him shouted, 'My religion forbids me to surrender to a *kafir*.' I gave him a grenade for the sake of his religion and mine."

Said another, "Never saw anything funnier than one of the chaps having a bath when a shell landed in his bucket, going clean through. It was a dud. He came out of the bathroom, all bathed and clean and naked and asking everybody, 'Am I alive or dead'?"
"They shelled at regular intervals. We called it breakfast, lunch, dinner and snacks in between."

They talked about the artillery fire of the enemy and said, "Their air force troubled us quite a bit," and "if only we had more forces."

And then the final and last tribute, "I must say the buggers fought well; fuckin' bastards gave us hell that night." Somehow I felt that on both sides of the border, the fighting soldiers must have uttered similar sentences.

Throughout the war, the good lookers among the women were never seen in Jammu and Srinagar. And with the announcement of a ceasefire they appeared like the first flowers of peace — colourful and happy — the symbols of birth and a new vitality.

At the end of September, I spent some time with Gen J.S. Dhillon of the XI Corps. This group that went into Pakistan with the intention of attacking Lahore, captured some territory up to the Ichhogill canal and held on to it, while facing the onslaught of the 1st Armoured Division at Khemkaran. Both sides, equal perhaps in numbers, with Pakistan superior in tanks and artillery, failed to achieve their objective. The story of this front, even when it is told in detail, will be one of the most controversial chapters of Indian military history.

The world watched the drama, at first with amused interest, then with some concern and later with alarm. Fortunately we were not much interested in world reactions. It must be said, the world respects the stronger in the final analysis.

After the ceasefire, Soviet Union took upon herself to broker a lasting peace between India and Pakistan. The Indian Prime Minister accompanied by a team of officials and ministers went to Tashkent. But he did not come back alive.

"It's a good agreement that we arrived at." These were the last words of Prime Minister Lal Bahadur Shastri. He was saying goodbye to President Ayub Khan at Tashkent.

"*Khuda hafiz*," the President said.

The Prime Minister replied, "*Khuda hafiz*."

Shastri retired to his room and little after one in the night he died of heart failure. The little man, who had held the office of Prime Minister through eighteen difficult months, had retired forever.

When he became Prime Minister, he was unsure and humble. He had a heart attack within days of taking over charge but he valiantly fought out of it, and guided the country with courage and determination through the difficult period of its conflict with Pakistan. There was something about the man which was friendly, sincere and dependable. He did not try to act big but a combination of circumstances and basic goodness, made him, in the words of Lyndon Johnson, President of USA, "The head of the largest democracy in the world."

A senior army officer remarked, "It was good we had Shastri rather than Nehru at the time of the trouble with Pakistan."

Perhaps he was right. Shastri was a man who depended on the reasoning of his subordinates and, in his wisdom, did his best to make them see reason. Nobody was afraid of giving his viewpoint to him. Nobody was overawed or silenced by the great personality.

He was a symbol of the democratic spirit of India — an average man doing a big job with determination.

During the hostilities he was calm and unruffled. The biggest decision of his (perhaps) was to launch the Lahore front to which his attitude was, "If the army considers this necessary, it will have to be done."

By the time the ceasefire came into effect the little man was a national hero. His receptions at Calcutta (and Calcutta receptions always seem to be an index of popularity) were enormous. The last one was as big as any Nehru had received.

Then came the Tashkent conference. The talks began optimistically. Feverish attempts were made by the Soviet Prime Minister Kosygin to bring about an agreement. In the end a declaration was signed by both India and Pakistan, in which the withdrawal of forces was accepted with the promise of maintaining good relations in future.

Ayub appeared to have accepted it because he wanted a withdrawal of forces from Dograi and Barki. As long as we were there we had our hands around the throat of Pakistan. They would not have moved an inch to threaten us without being strangulated. So what did it matter if promises of good behaviour were to be made? What did it matter if they had to promise to be friendly with India, when all knew that such promises meant nothing? I was inclined to be cynical whether the declaration would stand the test of general ignorance and fanaticism of the people of both the countries.

Had Shastri come back alive, the unconditional withdrawal which was what Pakistan wanted would have been severely opposed. But with his death, people of India accepted the agreement.

As we waited for the plane to arrive from Tashkent with the mortal remains of Lal Bahadur Shastri, memories of the days with Nehru more than seven years earlier came back to mind. How I remember Shastri being at the side of Nehru whenever he was wanted. The ridiculously small man would slip through the crowd of people and get to the place where his presence was required. The last time we met Shastriji was at an investiture at Rashtrapati Bhavan. He spoke to Naju and me and asked us to meet him, but I could not penetrate through the thicket of his personal assistants and staff to meet him.

The well-known columnist of *New York Times*, Walter Lippmann summed up Shastri's life and death in the following beautiful words.

> "Death came to Mr Shastri at a high moment in his life; and grief, which is worldwide, is therefore lighted with the poetic grandeur of circumstances. He did his best day's work and died in the evening when he had completed it. The world is better for what was done in Tashkent. For mankind has needed badly to be shown that it is still possible to get on top of the intractable violence of human affairs."

On 24 January 1966, Indira Gandhi was sworn in as the Prime Minister. What would the new Prime Minister be like? Reading an obituary in *Times* newspaper on Somerset Maugham, I found he had said of himself: "There are few people who know anything about me. And even they do not know as much as they imagine."

This was true of Indira Gandhi also. The world knew her as Jawaharlal Nehru's daughter. She was the hostess, the servitor and the friend of the great. They knew nothing of her politics, her political acumen or her administrative capacity. Yet, such is the Nehru luck that she assumed office at a time when there was confidence and goodwill all around us, not comparable with the enthusiasm amidst which her father became Prime Minister, but certainly more favourable than the circumstances when Lal Bahadur Shastri became the Prime Minister. We came out of the Pakistan War with a sense of confidence. The reputation of the army, which had taken a beating three years earlier, after the Chinese debacle, was restored. The only fear that loomed over the country was of a large-scale famine.

After the declaration of amity between India and Pakistan at Tashkent and the sudden death of Shastri, a wave of emotion swept over the land. Indira Gandhi assumed charge in a calm sea, with a well-behaved crew and a destination which lay on course and which appeared to be straight.

A few days before she was elected Prime Minister, I met her as well as her friend Padmaja Naidu. She did not seem to expect or want election and her friend said, "Her health would not be able to stand it." I knew she suffered from kidney stones and despite the excruciating pain that the ailment causes, she carried on with her duties as President of the Congress party in 1959. The frail little girl certainly had inner reserves of strength which I did not know during the days we toured together with Nehru from 1952 onwards. One thing I certainly would not have been able to forecast during that period was that she would be the Prime Minister of India. I do not suppose she could have thought of it either. Ever often, I used to see her tripping behind her father [3]— she had lovely feet — calling out "Papu" in that voice which I remember so well.

When I met her again, a few weeks after she had become Prime Minister of India, I found that the frailness of her health seemed to have gone. She had put on weight and the white splash in her hair had increased.

I had gone to meet her to tell her that I was not keen to go on a visit to the Soviet Union. We were asked to go to the Soviet Union in March 1966, because at Tashkent, Premier Kosygin had said, "Why are you afraid of infiltrators? If you like, we will show you how to lock up a border." I had earlier expressed my disinclination to go to the Home Secretary who insisted on my going. The Prime Minister listened to me gravely, the mirage of her father, and gave some non-committal evasive reply when I asked her whether she would issue any orders. In those initial days of Prime Ministership, she appeared to be either incapable of handling the responsibility of the post or was afraid of being herself.

Deep inside me something wanted me to decline. Was it the fear of the freezing temperatures on the Siberian border? Being watched and spied upon? Was it the disinclination to leaving Delhi when the BSF was taking over the border?

---

[3] I was told by an officer who had served in the Prime Minister's security that they have instructions to keep an eye on the footwear and ground ahead of the VVIPs so as to ensure they did not trip and fall. Hence the observation of Rustamji, who had served for six years as CSO to Prime Minister Nehru.

During our visit, the Soviet officers showed us how they had built up a Border Force, which was the biggest and perhaps the best in the world and had successfully stopped infiltration. Their Generals spoke to us with disarming candour. They showed us their equipment with ingenious restraint. We were perhaps the only people outside the Soviet bloc with whom representatives of the Soviet Union talked with friendly understanding. They knew our politics. They knew about our finances and our dependence on USA and yet there was a certain faith in India, which one felt happy about.

In the Soviet Union, I found one is divided from the people not only by the language barrier but also by the terminological barriers which communism has produced. The generation we talked to found some difficulty in conveying its ideas, unless we could understand their terms and expressions. I also found that the young ones in the Soviet Union wanted to sing, laze, loaf and criticise. They appeared to be the prophets of that freedom, which eventually comes after an expanding economy has been able to provide all the material goods. I found that the yearning for the 'western' way of youth, the desire to care more for the individual and a to-hell-with-the-state mentality appeared to be the 'revolutionary ideas' which were influencing the children of even diehard Marxists. Since the basic tenets of Marxism — improvement in the conditions of the working class — had already been accepted as a doctrine in the developed and so-called capitalist countries of the world under the name of socialism, the appeal of communism had got reduced. This was borne out even more forcefully in communist Czechoslovakia which we also visited. They did not want equality; they did not want planned development or the military protection of the Soviet Union. What they wanted was what their cousin who emigrated to USA or a friend who migrated to UK had. They wanted all that 'free enterprise' could give — because they had taken for granted all that a communist economy had given them.[4]

---

[4]Rustamji's comments on communism are based on what he wrote in his diary in 1966 after his visit to the Soviet Union and some East European countries. A mass upsurge took place in Czechoslovakia in 1968.

New Delhi
16/6/68.

Sheikh Abdullah

Has Sheikh Abdullah offended Pakistan by checking the communal tension in Srinagar organised by Pakistan agents? I am sure there must be doubts in Pakistan about his Islamic background.

A serious communal outburst appears to have occurred in Maharashtra – first Aurangabad, and then Nagpur.

In Srinagar, two groups of Muslim and non-Muslim students decided to fight it out, and in the process a completely innocent Muslim boy received a bad injury, probably with an iron bar, and died. Agents ran to Hazratbal — "thousands of Muslim boys are being butchered." Thousands began to run towards the Engineering College. Sh. Abdullah also reached there, stood with a stick in his hand, and pushed back the crowd.

The Sheikh's stock has risen considerably. Today the C.M. spoke in glowing terms of Abdullah's non-communal background. D.P. was full of praise. After all, the Sheikh has never been small in his thinking.

The third paragraph reads, "In Srinagar, two groups of Muslim and non-Muslim students decided to fight it out…Thousands began to run towards the Engineering College. Sk. Abdullah also reached there, stood with a stick in hand, and pushed back the crowd."

19

Internal Security Duties

In the initial years of the BSF, the battalions were rushed to places all over the country, whether it be the communal riots in Ahmedabad, the strike by policemen or the bandhs in Calcutta or demonstrations in Kashmir. Very often I was asked to rush to the spot.

In the later part of 1966, Sant Fateh Singh in Punjab and Jagadguru Shankaracharya of Puri in Orissa decided to put an end to themselves if the government did not concede to their demands.

The Sikh saint, who had threatened to immolate himself at the time when India was threatened by Pakistan, gave up his attempt in the nick of time. In return for his cooperation, the Government of India carved out a Punjabi Suba, which every single Indian felt was wrong and which every simple Punjabi felt had broken up a beautiful Punjab into the smaller states of Punjab and Haryana and gifted away Simla, the summer capital of the English and the beautiful hill districts to Himachal.

He again expressed the desire to end himself unless Chandigarh and control of Bhakra were transferred exclusively to Punjab.

Seated in the *Akal Takth* of the Golden Temple of Amritsar, Sant Fateh Singh went on a hunger strike and set the date for self-immolation. Concrete cisterns had been built in the Golden Temple. Petrol and kerosene was collected and stored in jerry cans. About 1,500 men and women, locked themselves in the temple and spears were handed around, so that in the event of police attempting to interfere with the suicides, suitable resistance would be offered.

Peacemakers rushed to and fro between Prime Minister Indira Gandhi and the two saints, "We shall not yield to coercion," she declared proudly, partly because she could find no way to yield without offending the Hindus all over, resulting in more agitations and 'bloodshed' (a term which became a popular word in 1966).

Sant Fateh Singh and five or seven others were to immolate themselves at four o'clock in the evening on 26 December 1966. All of us — mere officials — waited, wondering what it felt like to get burnt alive. Guesses were made regarding the time it would take, the degree of agony and the extent of screams. The politicians, however, were all hopeful; they perhaps knew better. At the designated hour while the chosen victims sat in white robes awaiting sainthood, an announcement was made over the mike that the immolations had been postponed for an hour.

Sardar Hukam Singh, the Speaker of the Lok Sabha, along with some Akali Dal MPs, came out and announced that there would be no immolations. The sudden disappointment led to a free fight among the Sikhs assembled. Order was restored and it was decided that the issues under dispute would be referred to the Prime Minister for arbitration.

The fast was broken with orange juice and honey. Suitable photographs of the event were taken. Curfew was lifted. The police was sent back to its barracks. The army was told to stand down.

At the other end of India, another saint — a Hindu had reached the thirty-fifth day of his fast in an effort to force a ban on cow slaughter. The Jagadguru was not content with the partial ban that existed in most states. He wanted a complete and total ban so that 'our mothers' might not be sold to butchers in their old age.

The Punjab episode was hardly over when a message came over the PTI teleprinter that the Jagadguru had no bowel movement for the last ten days. Government was apprehensive of a violent Hindu reaction in case the Jagadguru died. Fortunately he gave up the fast after seventy-one days when everyone implored him to do so.

Two years later, another Sikh, Darshan Singh Pheruman went on a fast making similar demands. The BSF was asked to keep a close watch as the leader was determined to commit suicide. After forty-one days of fast, he died. The Sikhs were determined to take his dead body around Punjab and whip up feelings against the Centre. His body was escorted by the BSF and taken immediately to his native village where he was cremated.[1]

On 14 April 1967, I was summoned by the Home Secretary, L.P. Singh at lunch time to discuss matters relating to Delhi Police. While I was in the Home Secretary's room, the IGP of Delhi was on the telephone at the other end. He said that a procession had been taken out by policemen against prohibitory orders and he feared violence which might lead to firing. The Home Secretary suddenly asked me if I could go and assist the IGP. Like a fool, I agreed. Skipping lunch and feeling cross about it, I reached the IGP's office with a small escort and some of my officers.

In the IGP's control room came conflicting news about the procession. We went out with a small force to see for ourselves what was happening. We drove all over but there was no trace of a procession. Finally, on our way to Rashtrapati Bhavan, we were told that 5,000 policemen were raising slogans and that the CRP men, who had been placed inside the North Avenue security lines, had joined the demonstrations.

I felt that merely closing them up in the lines would be the first step. As we were advancing by platoons to close up the entrance of the lines in North Avenue, a running procession emerged. We tried to block them, but they pushed through and ran towards the Rashtrapati Bhavan. The move by the policemen was so sudden and audacious that we were overwhelmed. If we had foolishly used tear smoke or firearms, we would have endangered the entire locality. We followed the procession which had moved into South Avenue

[1]The government was apparently pleased with the role played by the BSF in preventing a flare up after Pheruman's death. Taking advantage of that, according to some old BSF officers, Rustamji pressed a case for having an air wing for the BSF which got sanctioned.

and was going up Teen Murti Marg. Hastily we threw a cordon and fired tear smoke shells. The strikers ran in different directions. They gradually swelled up into a crowd of about 1,500. The senior officers of Delhi Police were inside the Home Minister's house, engaged in forecasting agonising deaths for themselves and their families.

Late at night a senior officer rang me up to say that the situation outside the Home Minister's house had gone out of control and asked me if I would agree to hand it over to the army. I was caught in a dilemma. I had no authority in Delhi, except to advise. I went to the Home Minister Y.B. Chavan's house. The Home Secretary, was also there and the discussions went on till four o'clock in the morning on the lawns of the Home Minister's residence. A decision was made to arrest the whole group outside the Home Minister's residence the next morning.

The striking policemen made a funny picture. They lay on the ground, sleeping peacefully after the vociferous shouting and breathless running they had indulged in.

In the morning, we postponed our action reasoning that the reinforcements we were expecting had not arrived. While the excuse was a good one, the fact was that we were reluctant to act. I was not sure what would happen. The BSF was new and comprised of policemen themselves.

At noon there was a meeting in the Home Secretary's room. I said clearly that if the Home Minister wanted us to act, he would have to hand over the situation to us and allow us to deal with it in the way we considered proper. He agreed. He wanted us to act as early as possible. The time for the operation was fixed for 3:30 p.m.

In that meeting a positive contribution was made by Ashwini Kumar (IG, BSF, Western Frontier). His was the voice of confidence, "Of course we can do the job. I can depend on my men." In the midst of defeatism, the Punjabi is always an asset.

At 3:30 p.m., I reached the roundabout near the Delhi Gymkhana Club. Our forces were assembled in platoons on Teen Murti Marg under Col Brijpal Singh.

Then I gave the signal and the platoons began to move up to the strong body of policemen who were demonstrating on the road. They must have been about a thousand or so. They jumped up excitedly, clapping their hands above their heads, behaving in a manner which was repulsive.

I was still not sure how our force would react. The stout-hearted Rajasthan boys were the first to reach. They formed the first cordon round them. Then platoon after platoon went round to cordon them. The striking policemen were sure we would not arrest them. Our boys neatly cordoned off the whole lot of excited policemen. Then from Akbar Road, the BSF Punjab (Ashwini's men) marched up, section upon section — a whole battalion which had fixed bayonets to their rifles. That broke the morale of the policemen completely. They now rushed out to be put in the vans. Some tried to run away and were chased, caught and pushed into the vehicles.

Within twenty-one minutes the unprecedented operation of arresting 800 policemen, mostly from the armed units of the Delhi Police, was completed.

I felt elated that the BSF had it in them to do a dirty job, which nobody else would touch. And I felt grateful to the jawan and his trust in us. I felt grateful to Col Brijpal, the retired army officer and Ashwini, who had planned and carried out their roles quietly and efficiently.

We got involved in some speeches because Ashwini felt we must drive home the moral value of the incident. The arrest of 800 men marked the turning point in the agitation. It boosted the morale of the BSF boys while the striking policemen realised that there was a force stronger than theirs.

The Delhi policemen could never have accounted for the fact that the DG, BSF would, like a fool, enter into a battle in which he had no authority and lead his men under doubtful command merely because the Home Minister and Home Secretary depended on the BSF and had asked him to do it.

There was yet another agitation by policemen which the BSF was asked to handle and this time it was the Uttar Pradesh Provincial Armed Constabulary (PAC) in 1973. I was called to the Home Ministry and told that an Uttar Pradesh PAC unit had set fire to the university in Lucknow and had behaved in a most indisciplined manner. As a result the ferment had spread to all the units because the members of the force had been downgraded in wages. I was told that the BSF should send two battalions and disarm the indisciplined units by the following week. To my mind it was a most alarming picture. I spoke rather bluntly that first I would like to see the situation for myself and then formulate plans and that I would need to collect at least twenty battalions from the border and be assured of backing from five army units. I made it clear that disarming would be resisted by the men as an act of unjust humiliation. The same afternoon, a full dress meeting was called by the Home Minister and while we were there, the news came that the army had agreed to do the job. I heaved a sigh of relief.

My reluctance to act was because I have had the experience of working with the PAC right from 1949 when I was DIG in Hyderabad State. I considered it as the best armed police in the country. There was elan and energy in the unit and dependability of high order. My friend and neighbour in Delhi, Shanti Prasad, an officer of outstanding ability and charm commanded the PAC for a number of years, expanding on the plans prepared for the armed police during the British Raj by Lt Col Bryand, Mohammad Kassim Raza and G.A. Pearce.

The army entered Uttar Pradesh and newspapers carried reports of a serious conflict between the army and the PAC units at various places. The police suffered serious casualties, though the army too lost some men. On the third morning I received a call from the Home Secretary, Govind Narain that the Prime Minister wanted to go to Lucknow immediately because the situation had taken a turn for the worse and the conflict between the army and the PAC had to be stopped.

On arrival in Lucknow, we had a meeting with Commander Govind Narain, who managed the situation with great firmness and tact. He insisted that instructions must be issued to all army units to stop firing. The situation cooled down gradually. Most units settled down to work. One unit was surrounded by the BSF and the men of the PAC handed over their weapons. Lt Col R.P. Bassi of the BSF did the job with a totally friendly approach to the men.

The government appointed a committee under me to go into the causes of the entire episode. An unstable situation was found in several units caused by downgrading of pay of the policemen and inefficient officers, lowering the morale of a fine force to breaking point. We made a number of recommendations, which were accepted.

❧

The year 1967 saw a gradual weakening of the Congress. No political party appeared to have made any solid gains throughout India. In one place it was the Jan Sangh. In the south, it was the Dravida Munnetra Kazhagam (DMK), with its strong antipathy to Hindi and Brahmanism. All over India, politics appeared to have entered a new phase. There was a search for new leadership and affiliation. The political breakdown in Bengal led to the formation of the United Front. In eastern India, the CPI appeared to be gaining ground. The gradual ascendancy of *goondaism* in politics and criminal intimidation enabled weak parties to secure a political hold far bigger than their political strength would justify. The West Bengal experiment was repeated in several states in India — notably Uttar Pradesh, Bihar, Madhya Pradesh and at the Centre.

It appeared to me that in the future, the Congress would have to come to a patchwork compromise with some Leftist or Rightist parties. Then the same contrary rules would begin — pressures from party followers who have put the party to power merely to get the most from disorder.

In November 1967, Haryana produced the best type of turncoat politicians who changed sides with utter glee. So the Governor intervened and President's rule was imposed.

The process was most striking in West Bengal, though it was complicated by the efforts of the Government of India to oust the United Front government — a mixture of all shades of political thought united due to their opposition to the Congress and the efforts of the CPI to retain control through threats of bandhs and strikes. The Ajoy Mukherjee government lost its majority but the Chief Minister refused to convene the Assembly immediately. The Governor intervened and swore in a defecting minister as the Chief Minister.

The political instability in West Bengal led to unprecedented incidents in Calcutta in 1969. Policemen raided the Legislative Assembly and beat up some persons. They did all that they had seen groups and parties do on a rampage. The Speaker was helped out through a window, and in the process two Congressmen were beaten up. The occasion that gave rise to the rampage was the death of a policeman in one of the inter-party riots that plagued West Bengal.

The police in West Bengal had steadily become weaker, because the state administrators had become politicians, wanting support from this or that party to exist in the wild rumpus of an overpopulated state.

Way back in 1969, I had noted in my journal that the revolt of the West Bengal Police will be remembered as a sign of approaching anarchy. West Bengal and perhaps Bihar are set for a breakdown of law and order in the not too distant future. It is a common saying, "What Bengal does today, the rest of India will do tomorrow."

The law and order situation in Calcutta gave an indication that the city was gradually sliding into chaos. In 1970, the BSF was sent to Calcutta when violence lurked in every street. Charu Mazumdar and the Naxalite extremists singled out their enemies — policemen and landlords. As many as 23 police officers were murdered and 400 injured. The process of extermination continued unabated. The Naxalite activities thrived on exploiting the weaknesses prevalent in society and in the administration — our inability to work together.

Charu and his men, notably Sushital Raichaudhary, Kanu Sanyal and Asim Chatterjee also known as Kaka, were arrested and the police came down heavily to nip the menace in Calcutta city.

It was a gloomy puja in 1970. There was a forced, desperate sort of gaiety. I felt sad. I asked, 'What is happening to you, my dear Calcutta?' My love for Calcutta is like the love that a man has for his beloved. There is something about the city that grows on you.

The populace of Calcutta is like a sick man trying out every doctor and every remedy that seems to promise a cure. Every ten or twenty years a deep ferment arises in the minds of the youth in Bengal. While it lasts, it is a period of trial for everyone, most of all the women of Bengal. The violence subsides, but the thinking behind it is taken up by the rest of India. The very violence of their thoughts seems to force acceptance in the social and political life of the country. Bengalis are still the trendsetters.

In 1969, Leftism had become a fashionable political doctrine. Indira Gandhi nationalised banks and declared she was all for the poor and that nationalising banks would help the poor. She probably did it on the advice of some of her Left leaning group of Kashmiri advisors who belonged to the Krishna Menon group. Krishna Menon had led a procession to the office of *The Statesman* because the newspaper criticised the manner in which bank nationalisation was done and bravely burnt a copy of the paper. In a bold move she threw out Morarji Desai, her principal opponent, calling him a Rightist.

The so-called Leftists in India belong to the category of Right. Most of them had or have a sound financial background. In my opinion, the 'Left' in India is the left out — the tribal with his 15 paise-per-day wages, the village shoemaker and barber, the peasant with a pocket-size plot. The beggars in the cities — these are the real Left. I noted in my journal dated 16 September 1969: "It is the Left tribal that will be the real problem for this country."

The grip that Left wing extremists have over remote tribal areas in the present day has proved my worst fears.

Within the Left itself there were numerous parties — the two factions of the CPI were unable to see eye to eye, like communists all over the world. Likewise, the Jan Sangh was divided between those who wanted to give it a modern touch so that they did not have to depend on communal rioting for an image, and those who felt that only a revival of fierce anti-Muslim and anti-Pakistan stand would enable it to win the polls.

The real cause of the division among the parties is that there is so much to be done that anyone can give priority to anything.

I was asked to go to Srinagar by the Home Ministry every time there was a problem there. I made umpteen number of visits to Jammu and Kashmir during the nine years I was DG BSF. In June 1967, there had been demonstrations in the city. The All Saints Church was burnt down by hooligans. The beautiful church with its unique garden, where as honeymooners Naju and I had lingered for hours, was burning. However, the century old stone structure still stood up. The woodwork of the roof was destroyed and lay on the ground — a heap of burnt-out junk. A copy of the *Bible* lay torn and burnt. I picked up a hymn book which opened on *Abide with me*.

Another church was also burnt down; foreigners were manhandled and women molested. A diplomat from Bulgaria was robbed and his car set on fire. The UN headquarter was attacked and the flag pulled down. Tourists molested, a retired officer spat on and everyone asked to put black flags on vehicles. Why? All because Israel had attacked an Arab land.

Some days later, there was an agitation by the Pandits in Srinagar because a Muslim boy had eloped with a Pandit girl. It took a communal turn. The agitation subsided on the intervention of the Home Minister, but the tense situation was seized upon by Pakistan. One riot followed another.

Weak politically and administratively, the state of Jammu and Kashmir was peaceful for years because of the tradition of communal amity.

In the last week of September 1969, communal riots broke out in Ahmedabad as the city was preparing to celebrate the birth centenary of Mahatma Gandhi. Khan Abdul Gaffar Khan, the Frontier Gandhi as he was called, was to reach Sabarmati.

The BSF and the army were asked to rush there. The peaceful IGP of Gujarat wanted the BSF to be disarmed — carry no weapons when they went out to deal with the rioters. The DIG, BSF, who accompanied the battalions and who could never look beyond the rules said, "Sir, then please give three of your men and we will put three of our men and you must promise that your own men will not open fire."

The BSF was given the task of manning the area inside the walled city and the army took over the outskirts and the areas in which communal frenzy had spread like a raging fire. Within a few hours, people realised that the BSF meant business.

The whole of Gujarat meanwhile was on fire — Baroda, Palanpur, Rajkot and other places. Just when the towns were coming under control, trains were attacked and families murdered in the name of God. Hysterical crowds ran through the streets to attack members of the opposite community.

The hand of Pakistan was glaringly evident in the Ahmedabad riots.

The Muslim summit was due at Rabat. The riots were timed by the Pakistani agents to show the Muslim world that India was practising genocide. Their attempts were rewarded a hundred times over. If a few hundred men, women and children died, they, according to Pakistan, died for their country. They added to the two nation theory.

The Commissioner of Police of Ahmedabad and IGP of the state were both Parsees but they were not on speaking terms. The Chief Minister, a true Gandhian, wanted a semi-violent approach on the part of the police, "The people of my state are by nature peaceful. We must not hurt them." It seemed that the rank and file of the police were totally committed to the homicide theory of disturbances, 'Let them perish. They asked for it.'

Deep down in the Indian character, along with pity, there is compassion. There is almost a feminine desire not to hurt anybody. Killing is not natural to us. It is resorted to because it is unusual and creates a hysterical impact. We, as a race, do not kill in anger. The Indian hates killing and that explains his inability to stop a riot or a rampage with force.

The BSF was called out again and again to deal with communal riots in several parts of the country and I had to rush to those places often. The BSF displayed impartiality and initiative of a high order. The tribute we treasure was that of an old infirm Muslim in Uttar Pradesh, who said, "*Jab borderwale aaye toh hum saans lene lage.*"(When the Bordermen came, we began to breathe again).

In February 1974, I was sent to Gujarat, which was in the grip of a severe law and order problem spearheaded by the youth. Morarji Desai had undertaken a fast unto death demanding the dismissal of the Chimanbhai Patel government. Since I had known Morarji from the days I was with Nehru, I met him. On my return to Delhi, P.R. Rajgopal received me at the airport and took me to the residence of Jamila and B.G. Verghese, the editor of *Hindustan Times*. We discussed Morarji's fast and the situation in Gujarat.

On returning home, I was that told the Prime Minister wanted to see me urgently. When I went to meet her, I found her in a meeting with senior officers. She screamed at me, "How many times have I to tell you to keep me informed about your whereabouts." I briefed her on the Gujarat situation and said in no uncertain terms, that there was no alternative to conceding to Morarji Desai's demands. I also spelt out the dire consequences if he were to die. She said, "You seem to be the only one suggesting such a course of action," and immediately concluded the meeting.

However, two days later the Chimanbhai Patel government was dismissed and President's rule imposed.

❧

During the nine years that I was DG BSF, there were several attempts to ease me out, probably because I was selected for the post during Prime Minister Shastri's tenure. The first was in 1967 when my name came up again in the panel for the post of Director IB. It was rumoured that Prime Minister Indira Gandhi was in my favour. Once again I spoke to L.P. Singh and told him that I was not cut out for that job. The previous year also I had mentioned to him that I was not interested in the job and L.P. Singh agreed to my dropping out.

Again the day before I left for Kashmir on a month's holiday (taken after nine years) in June 1970, I was sounded as to whether I would take over the job that dealt with economic and revenue intelligence. I was told merrily by one of the men who was high up in the Indira Gandhi set up that BSF had been developed, and that the new job had some importance because there were a lot of connections between smugglers and politicians. It was clear they wanted me out of the BSF.

While on a holiday in Kashmir with the family, came the news of a cabinet reshuffle, principally designed, I think, to lower Y.B. Chavan. Against his will, Chavan was sent from Home to Finance and in the process, the Home Ministry was broken up and the services along with the CBI were transferred to the Cabinet Secretariat. The Prime Minister took over the Home portfolio, Jagjivan Ram went to Defence and Swaran Singh to External Affairs. The Prime Minister assumed supreme command.

The few doubts that I had about the change of my job, that it was being considered soon disappeared. It seemed to me to be clear that they did not want to keep me as head of the BSF and the fact that the Home Secretary (L.P. Singh) and the Home Minister (Y.B. Chavan) had praised my work must have been the last straw.

A few months later, in December 1970, L.P. Singh was shifted from the Home Ministry, where he had spent a better part of thirteen years. All changes that had been made by Indira Gandhi were designed as a personal protection, though the reason, as she remarked to me once, was that her cabinet colleagues were finding it inconvenient working with bureaucrats who had been entrenched in their posts for long years.

New Delhi
15/7/70.

HI-JACKING AN INDIAN AIRLINES PLANE

ASI Intelligence has literally shaken us all in our comfortable New Delhi seats.

A high officer of the ASI infiltrated an agent into an amateurish group that wants to 'liberate' Kashmir by sabotage. A few years ago they came into Kashmir, and got arrested or shot up, and one was sentenced to imprisonment for life but escaped. Then this more amateurishly walked into J&K area again, and outpaid a tonga-wallah so much that they were arrested.

The ASI agent was training in guerilla activities and then taught how to hi-jack a Fokker plane with a hand grenade. He came back, told us all about the scheme, and said that we must act quickly or something terrible would happen.

We acted in our own New Delhi way, and found to our consternation that the Fokker pilot on the Jammu run was the PM's son.

So far no hi-jacking has occurred. The agent seems to be telling the truth. He seems to have saved a crore of rupees, if human lives and national disgrace are excluded.

Diary entry of 15 July 1970 — Hijacking an Indian Airlines plane.

20

Attempt to Hijack Rajiv Gandhi's Plane

In July 1970, the BSF intelligence literally shook us in our comfortable New Delhi seats.

A bright officer of the BSF intelligence infiltrated an agent into an amateurish group that wanted to 'liberate' Kashmir by sabotage. The BSF agent was trained in guerilla activities by Pakistan and taught how to hijack a Fokker plane with a hand grenade. He came back, told us all about the scheme and said we must act quickly or something terrible would happen.

We acted in our own New Delhi way and found to our consternation that the Fokker pilot on the Jammu run was the Prime Minister's son, Rajiv Gandhi, who was then a pilot with the Indian Airlines.

Till July 1970 no hijacking had occurred. The agent seemed to be telling the truth. He seemed to have saved a crore of rupees, if human lives and national disgrace were excluded.

The day after I got the above report, I had an interaction with the Prime Minister. After she took over charge of the Home Ministry in the big reshuffle, she paid a visit to our control room. In the evening I was asked to see her.

When she began talking, I felt that she wanted to unsettle me. She talked about the army's impression that the BSF would need army leadership in war. She asked how my relations were with the army. I said a certain amount of tension between the forces at lower levels was inevitable, but apart from that I did not see anything else which would indicate trouble.

I did most of the talking — Kashmir, Bengal, communal trouble, intelligence — and gradually I felt more and more at ease. When I got up after half an hour, she looked up from the doodling and said she had to meet the DG CRP.[1]

On 30 January 1971, two young men, Hashim Qureshi and his cousin Ashraf Qureshi hijacked the Indian Airlines plane *Ganga* on a flight from Srinagar to Jammu. It was taken to Lahore. There were twenty-six passengers and four crew members on board. There was wild jubilation in Lahore and a large number of people came to the airport to see the hijacked aircraft. The two hijackers were treated as national heroes. The Pakistan Foreign Minister, Zulfiqar Ali Bhutto came the next day and embraced the hijackers as true champions of the Pakistani cause. The passengers and crew members were allowed to leave for India on 1 February 1971. The hijackers held a press conference on the same day wherein they claimed they were members of the Jammu Kashmir Liberation Front and demanded the release of thirty-six people detained in Indian jails. India demanded the return of the aircraft on 2 February, but the same evening the plane was set afire. Some say it was done by the hijackers but the hijackers themselves denied doing it. India responded by cancelling all overflights by Pakistan military aircraft on the same day. On 4 February 1971, India extended the ban to commercial flights also. Both the hijackers were feted for a few days. When the overflights were banned, Pakistan came down hard on the hijackers and charged them as Indian agents and sent them to jail. The court sentenced them to nineteen years' imprisonment.[2]

---

[1]Rustamji carried a small chit with him on which he had written down points for briefing. The chit was filed in his journal. It mentions the words 'Intelligence' and 'Rajgopal'. It appears he must have briefed the Prime Minister about the hijacking plan though he has not mentioned it in his diary entry of the next day.

[2]Hashim Qureshi and Ashraf Qureshi were exonerated by the Pakistan Supreme Court in 1984. Hashim Qureshi went to the Netherlands and in 2001, came back to

The Government of India instituted a Commission of Inquiry, headed by P.N. Haksar, on the circumstances leading to the hijacking. I explained all the facts, taking the blame on myself. I pointed out that the BSF was handicapped by the fact that we did not have the wherewithal for a break of this type. I told the Commission that we promised Hashim Qureshi a job and even that had to be at a subordinate level. He accepted it and asked for a meeting with me. P.R. Rajgopal brought him to see me in Delhi and we had a short talk about how we would utilise his services initially at Bangalore where he would be inducted as a BSF officer. He seemed quite happy and said he would be glad to serve. When he went back to Srinagar, there was, I felt, pressure from his agency in Pakistan to hijack a plane or his relatives would be killed. He could not withstand that pressure and unknown to us he hijacked a plane which was destroyed in Lahore. For a short time, Hashim Qureshi was hailed as a hero in Pakistan, but the period spent with us was what probably went against him and when India retaliated by stopping the air traffic between East and West Pakistan, the suspicion appeared that the hijacking of the Indian Airlines plane was done at the instance of India. The Inquiry Commission probably concluded that this was a lapse on the part of intelligence service. The Commission conceded, however, that saving Rajiv Gandhi was a job well done.[3]

Kashmir and is presently the Chairman of the Jammu and Kashmir Liberation Party.

[3] Siddharth Varadarajan, the then Deputy Chief of Bureau, *The Times of India*, New Delhi had written to Rustamji in May 2001, inviting his attention to a mention in the book, *Samba Spy Case* (Vikas, 1981) by B.M. Sinha about Rustamji meeting Qureshi, appealing to his sentiments and persuading him to work for India. Varadarajan asked Rustamji if there was any truth in the allegation. Extracts of Rustamji's reply to Varadarajan are reproduced in the above paragraph.

The number of websites on the liberation war of Bangladesh seems to be growing by the day. The above is a photograph that is displayed on several sites under the heading "Ethnic Cleansing." Immediately after the military crackdown in East Pakistan on the night of 25 March 1971, there was a massacre of the students of Dacca University, Awami League workers and Hindus.

21

Liberation of Bangladesh[1]

A statement that is strongly resented by the leaders and people of Bangladesh is that we liberated them. Their resentment is justified because our part was relatively small when we consider the whole spectrum of events that formed their freedom struggle.

It began in the first year of Pakistan when Jinnah paid a visit to East Pakistan and was hooted and jeered in the university when he declared that Urdu would be the language of both East and West Pakistan. The Bengalis resented the imposition of Urdu and ban on poet Rabindranath Tagore. Pakistanis felt insulted when fathers of Bengali girls were prepared to give their daughters in marriage to Indian Muslims but not to West Pakistani Muslims. There were also many strange doctrines, one of them from Gen Akbar Khan which stated that the Bengalis could only be kept in check by harsh punishment and an even more crude theory that West Pakistani blood should be inducted into the Bengalis.

[1]As mentioned in the Introduction, Rustamji's diaries for the period January 1971 to May 1974 could not be located. This chapter is therefore based mostly on some points jotted down by him in 1971, which were found in his personal papers, a note prepared by him around March 1972 and partly on the articles on Bangladesh operations written many years after retirement from service. There were several gaps in the narrative. These have been filled by inputs from Golok Majumdar and Brig B.C. Pande, two senior officers who served in the BSF.

After the Indo-Pak conflict of 1965, President Ayub Khan started losing ground and Sheikh Mujibur Rahman, the leader of the mass-based East Pakistani political party, the Awami League shot into prominence with the announcement in 1966 of his party's six-point programme for greater autonomy. The rising popularity of Mujib made Ayub to resort to implicating him in the Agartala conspiracy case of 1968 and arresting him along with several others, including some from the armed forces. Large-scale unrest erupted all over the eastern wing. It became clear that the people of East Pakistan were determined to overthrow their West Pakistan rulers at the earliest opportunity. The case against Mujib was withdrawn. Field Marshal Ayub Khan had to step down after students in West Pakistan took to the streets agitating for restoration of democratic institutions. Gen Yahya Khan, who took over, prepared grounds for elections based, for the first time ever, on universal adult franchise. In November 1970, a devastating cyclone hit East Pakistan and the tepid relief provided added to the dissatisfaction of the people against the Central Government.

Due to all these reasons, when the elections to the National and Provincial Assemblies were held in December 1970, the Awami League swept the polls to the National Assembly, winning 167 out of the 169 seats allotted to East Pakistan. As the leader of the single largest party in Pakistan, Sheikh Mujibur Rahman became the rightful claimant for heading the national government. His party had more seats than that of Zulfiqar Ali Bhutto's party which had won the majority of the seats in West Pakistan, but far less than that of the Awami League. The military junta and Bhutto refused to hand over the reins of the government to Mujib.

From 2 March 1971 onwards the Awami League had started a non-cooperation movement. It set up parallel rule to the martial law administration. Government employees had also joined in a big way, to the extent that the Chief Justice refused to swear in the new Governor, Lt Gen Tikka Khan. On 7 March 1971, Mujib addressed a mammoth gathering at the Race Course Ground in Dacca in which he asked the people of East Pakistan to be prepared for the supreme sacrifice and, for the first time, raised the slogan of Independence.

Gen Yahya Khan flew to Dacca on 15 March and was later joined by Bhutto. Protracted parleys were held with Mujib, the real intention behind which was to buy time to unload shiploads of arms and ammunition and personnel in East Pakistan.

When the deadlock in the Dacca talks seemed imminent, Golok Majumdar was sent from the BSF headquarters, where he was Deputy Director incharge of Administration and asked to take over as IG of the Eastern Sector of the BSF at Calcutta. He was given terse instructions (a) do whatever is necessary in national interest, (b) follow your own methods, and (c) set your limits. No written orders were issued. He immediately revived his intelligence sources developed over the years in his various assignments in West Bengal and Tripura police.[2]

At exactly the same time, India was in the midst of parliamentary elections and hence clear directions were not forthcoming when the question arose as to how to meet the situation and what help, if any, could be given to the movement that was developing in East Pakistan. India was acutely aware of the fact that Pakistan had all along been using the Chittagong Hill Tracts area in East Pakistan to train insurgents in Nagaland right from the fifties and later on, the Mizo insurgents who rose in revolt in 1966.

We had a large number of discussions at the seniormost level of the government in New Delhi from 10 March onwards. The general reading was that the dominant sentiment among the East Pakistanis appeared to be one of autonomy rather than separation.[3] But we had no concrete plan regarding what we were to do. Three possibilities were spelt out by me but the meetings produced no tangible results on how we should act, though all recognised that the hour had struck. The argument I put forward was, "Please authorise us to act. We will

---

[2] Input from Golok Majumdar.

[3] My enquiries from the officers who were in touch with the Bangladesh leaders revealed that Sheikh Mujibur Rahman never initially thought in terms of Independence. After sweeping the elections, he had dreams of becoming the Prime Minister of Pakistan. It was only when he found Bhutto and the army would never concede to his becoming the Prime Minister, that he changed his line and pressed for Independence for East Pakistan.

find out what has to be done. In such cases no advance planning can be made. The situation has to be studied first." I found that there was a general mood of hesitancy, which was compounded by the fact that the general elections were on and Naxalite activity was at its peak in West Bengal. It was apprehended that the Naxalites would make it difficult for the elections to be held in that state and therefore the government's attention was focused more on the deployment of large contingents of the army, CRP and BSF in the sensitive areas to ensure peaceful polls.

Reports kept on coming of a heavy movement of army personnel to East Pakistan. There were altogether eight battalions of the East Bengal Regiment (EBR). All of them were commanded by West Pakistan officers, though the men were Bengalis. Three battalions were stationed in West Pakistan. The military junta had made a comprehensive, phase-wise plan to crush any armed uprising in the EBR.[4] Pakistan's plan was to disarm these units. The senior officers of the army made a near successful bid to disarm EBR battalions at Chittagong, Jessore, Brahmanbaria and Joydebpur. Some of the Bengali officers could discern the impending danger and took precautions against the sinister designs of the West Pakistan officers.[5]

Chittagong, the port city, was the centre of great activity as shiploads of armed personnel and ammunition came from West Pakistan. The civilian labourers and port workers refused to unload shipments of arms and ammunition to be used against their brethren. The Awami League, whose main supporters consisted of students and the youth, took up this issue and instigated the workers against unloading the ships on 23 March 1971. The West Pakistani troops resorted to indiscriminate firing to force the civilian labour to unload the military stores.[6]

---

[4]Pakistan had made detailed plans in February to launch 'Operation Searchlight' to deal with the situation in East Pakistan. According to the plan, all EBR and East Pakistan Rifles (EPR) battalions were to be disarmed, Bengali officers sent on leave and Awami League workers arrested. 'Operation Searchlight' was to be completed in one month. So confident was the military junta of the success of their operation that they did not prepare an alternative plan in case of its failure.

[5]Input from Brig B.C. Pande.

[6]Ibid.

In order to study the situation, Gen Hamid Khan, the Chief of the Pakistan Army and his Quartermaster General, Maj Gen A. O. Mitha, went to Chittagong from Dacca on 24 March. They had a hurried lunch, a hush-hush discussion with the local West Pakistan officers, went round the area in a helicopter and brought back with them Brig G.W. Majumdar, the lone Bengali Brigadier stationed in East Pakistan, who never returned.[7] A rumour spread through the city that Majumdar had been taken away and shot dead. Violent demonstrations occurred.

On the afternoon of 25 March 1971, some men of the 8 EBR were sent to the Chittagong jetty for unloading arms and ammunition brought in by the ship *MV Swat*. The men refused to unload the ship and were placed under arrest. A clash took place. The Baluch regiment opened fire and thirteen Bengali soldiers were killed while the rest were disarmed and arrested. When the news of this killing reached the city, serious rioting broke out.

The Commanding Officer of the 8 EBR, Lt Col Janjua, a West Pakistan officer thought of an ingenious plan to disarm the rest of the battalion. He ordered his second in command, Maj Ziaur Rahman to go to the jetty to control the situation. A naval guard consisting of West Pakistan officials came to take him. As he was about to board the vehicle, a junior officer signalled danger. The young Major got the clue that there was something fishy. While proceeding to the jetty, he dodged the naval guard en route and came back. He hastily called all the Bengali officers and related what had transpired. The men and officers of the 8 EBR got enraged and rushed to the office of the Commanding Officer and killed him on the spot. Two more officers were also killed in the unit area. The entire 8 EBR unit thus had no other option except to join the revolution.[8]

Then the men drew their weapons and marched out. Zia, Shaukat Ali and the other officers collected the men and

---

[7]There were four brigades in East Pakistan. All of them were headed by West Pakistani officers. Brig Majumdar was the only Bengali Brigadier posted as the incharge of the Chittagong area.

[8]Input from Brig B.C. Pande.

followed by the people, they went towards the bridge on the Karnaphuli River. They made forays into the city and fought the Pakistan forces when the latter tried to advance towards the bridge and the radio station.

The Baluchis and the naval commandos went into the EBR lines advancing under cover of some big drains in the training centre and slaughtered the unarmed and innocent recruits.[9] Lt Col Chowdhury, the second in command of the training centre who was held in high regard by the men, went out to see what was happening. He was met with a burst of fire in his chest and died on the spot, in front of his wife.

The revolt of the 4 EBR commanded by Lt Col Khizr Hayat Khan had several unusual features. Located in Brahmanbaria, it seemed the Commandant was waiting for an opportunity to disarm the companies. Maj Shafat Jamil, on his own, decided to act because intercepts on the wireless had shown that preparations were going on to disarm the unit. At ten o'clock in the morning the next day, Maj Shafat marched up to his Commanding Officer and placed him under arrest. The crowds at Brahmanbaria soon came to know and tried to attack Khizr Hayat. He was carried from place to place. Nobody would shelter him and even the police refused to keep him in a police lock up. Eventually, they took him to the border and handed him over to the BSF to look after. The whole battalion joined the liberation forces.

The unit that suffered heavily was 3 EBR at Rangpur. It was attacked by Pakistani tanks and heavy weapons. 200 men of the EBR were killed. It was left to Capt Akram, a young officer, to regroup, to reorganise and lead them out.

Pakistan's military authorities intensified operations against the freedom fighters with all their military might and ruthlessness. The 24 Frontier Force Regiment located at Comilla was ordered to move to Chittagong by road on 25 March, brushing aside any opposition en route. The civilians also joined the revolutionary forces in hunting

---

[9] About 2,000 recruits were present in the camp. Pakistan was to raise one or two more battalions of the EBR.

down the West Pakistan forces. The Pakistan Army suffered heavy casualties.[10]

On 25 March, the talks failed. Yahya Khan made his blustering speech in which he threatened East Pakistan with the bayonet and immediately left for West Pakistan. A commando raid was launched on the Dhanmondi residence of Mujib at midnight and he was arrested. The same night the Governor, Lt Gen Tikka Khan, imposed martial law and ordered a crackdown, unleashing a reign of terror and destruction on the masses through a most ruthless, inhuman and heinous military action. Several thousands of students and staff of Dacca University were brutally massacred, girls raped and several arrested because they had played a decisive part in the agitation. Significantly, the first hostel to be attacked was the Jagannath Hall, which was a Hindu hostel where about 600 to 700 students were brutally murdered. West Pakistan troops swooped on the Hindu areas in Dacca killing several thousands. The Bengali troops of the East Pakistan Rifles, (the force meant for guarding the border), at Pilkhana (Dacca) were killed in the most wanton and dastardly manner. Lt Gen Tikka Khan ordered the arrest of all Awami League leaders. Fighting erupted in the military cantonments of Dacca, Chittagong, Comilla and other places. The Bengali populace joined the freedom fighters and the popular resistance gathered strength. It was now a war between the West Pakistani Muslims versus the East Pakistani Muslims.

On the night of 25/26 March, Awami League workers and Hindus were chased like rats all over East Pakistan and the West Pakistan troops vied with one another in taking credit for the highest number they could kill. Foreign correspondents who were eyewitnesses to these ghastly scenes were maltreated and packed off.[11]

In New Delhi we took stock of the fast changing situation, but people concerned were hesitant to act. I was then told on Saturday, 27 March, to wait till Monday.

---

[10] Input from Brig B.C. Pande.
[11] Ibid

Later in the day Maj Ziaur Rahman made the historic announcement of the formation of a sovereign democratic republic of Bangladesh from the Chittagong radio station. He announced that he had taken over as the Commander of the liberation forces. He asked all able-bodied Bengalis to join the war for liberation of the motherland. He also asked the men of the EBR and EPR to report at Chittagong for overthrowing the colonial regime of West Pakistan. He appealed to the neighbouring countries to come to the aid of the teeming millions of Bangladesh who were locked in a life-and-death struggle for their freedom.

We met in the house of the Home Secretary on Sunday, 28 March. The newspaper reports were gone through. We heard the briefing from Kao.[12] There were alarming reports of the crackdown. I felt depressed and disgusted with our inaction. I could see a great human tragedy was being enacted and all that we were doing was to stand on the wings of the theatre and say, "This is an internal affair of the dramatic company." I recommended some firm steps. Kao was diffident. He advised caution — the watchword in Civil Service. It required some convincing and finally he accepted. I was asked about the battalions that I had and was told to move the spare units we had to the border and put the senior officers and staff of the training institutions incharge, after dividing the border into sectors. We moved fast with our arrangements and lost no time in positioning them at the most strategic places on the border — Brig B.C. Pande at Agartala, Col Rampal Singh at Cooch Behar, Brig M.S. Chatterjee at Balurghat, Col Megh Singh at Bongaon. They were charged with protecting our borders and dealing with the Pakistan Army operating against the civilians and freedom fighters and providing rations, allowances and clothing to them.

On 29 March, the COAS issued orders providing limited assistance. What was of concern to the army was the reaction of China in case Pakistan appealed to her for putting pressure on the Sino-Indian border.

---

[12]R.N. Kao, the chief of the Research and Analysis Wing (RAW), the organisation looking after external intelligence.

Finally, on 30 March, the decks were cleared for action. What helped was the assurance of constant help from the COAS following the agreement of the leaders of the Opposition to support the Resolution of Parliament on 31 March 1971. Tracing the incidents leading to the disturbances, the Resolution, moved by the Prime Minister, ended with the words, "This House records its profound conviction that the historic upsurge of the 75 million people of East Bengal will triumph. The House wishes to assure them that their struggle will receive the wholehearted sympathy and support of the people of India."

I was given a laconic directive by the Prime Minister, "Do what you like, but don't get caught." Nothing more was spelt out as nothing could be foreseen of the rapid developments that would follow. The direction gave me the liberty to take steps which ultimately produced results. Thus the BSF entered the scene in the midst of a surcharged atmosphere and rising expectations. The Force consisted of a few officers and about 100 men well versed in commando raids, demolition, etc. The Force was organised to carry out tasks in support of the freedom struggle by the people of East Pakistan. The aim was to provide aid to the freedom fighters to carry out their assignment successfully.

Within three days of the crackdown, Golok received information from his contacts in East Pakistan that some senior Awami League leaders, including possibly Mujib himself, were heading for Khustia in the guise of poor peasants.[13]

On 30 March, one of the EPR officers sent a note, which was probably the first note that we received from them, asking us for assistance. Golok went to Krishnanagar along with Col Chakraverty of the 76 Battalion. At the Banpur-Gede border they met Taufiq, the Sub-Divisional Officer and Mahboob, the Sub-Divisional Police Officer of Meherpur. The East Pakistan officers said they had been in touch with the leaders because the telephone system was still intact. When asked what type of assistance was needed and what we could

[13]Input from Golok Majumdar.

do, they pleaded for all kinds of help, including petrol, oil, kerosene, finances and ammunition.[14]

Golok asked them if he could meet some of the accredited leaders of the movement. After a short while, Tajuddin Ahmad, who had been designated by Mujibur Rahman as his successor, came out of the dark and met him along with Amirul Islam, the chief whip of the Awami League in the National Assembly. Both were barefooted, haggard and dishevelled and were wearing a lungi and a singlet. They had walked across from Dacca.

"Do you recognise me? I am Golok Majumdar."

"Of course, I can," Tajuddin said. "Our leader, Mujib Bhai has told us to disperse and take charge of the resistance movement in different areas. Mujib himself could not escape. He has repeatedly warned us not to do anything which would embarrass India, provoke China or assail India's position in international forums."

Golok asked him, "What is it you want; and what is it that we can do for you? Can you come with me to Calcutta?"

Tajuddin refused. He said he would have to stay behind with his people. Golok told him he would be shot dead because the Pakistani Army was fanning out and they would seek him out. He went back to consult his people and after a short while said that he was willing to come.

Golok informed me of the development and I flew to Calcutta. When I landed just after twelve o'clock in the night between 30/31 March, Golok was there with his usual smile, welcoming me to his Calcutta. He took me aside and said that the number two man of the movement had come to us. "Would you like to meet him?" he asked.

"Of course, I would. Immediately."

We walked over to the jeep where he was sitting, flanked by two men for protection. We took him and Amirul Islam with us to the Assam House. I gave them my kurta and pyjama to change into after having a bath. Golok made an omelette for them. Rajgopal, our Deputy Director incharge of Intelligence, confirmed

[14]Ibid.

that he was the number two in the movement and was of great significance to us.

The next two days we spent in obtaining the whole story from Tajuddin of the negotiations that they had with the West Pakistan leaders. Tajuddin blamed Bhutto entirely for the breakdown. Yahya was inclined to agree but was intimidated by the military junta and Bhutto. Yahya therefore broke up the negotiations and went back on his assurances, perhaps against his better judgement. I asked him what the intention of the leaders of Awami League was. He was clear. They wanted Independence. He explained all the plans that they had made to fight the Pakistani rulers. He was convinced that the entire Bengali population of East Pakistan would rise against the Pakistan Army.

Tajuddin was anxious to visit the border. On 1 April, accompanied by Rajgopal and Golok, he went to a Border Out Post (BOP) near Krishnanagar. By a previous arrangement Maj Osman,[15] who was incharge of the Jessore sector met Tajuddin and stated that if he did not get weapons and plenty of ammunition, he and his men would not be able to hold up the advancing Pakistan Army. Tajuddin looked at our officers and his eyes seemed to say that our bona fides were on test by our refusing or relenting to the request of Maj Osman. The two senior officers decided to give Maj Osman some weapons and the required quantity of ammunition. As Osman and his men left, Tajuddin was heard saying, "There they go. They carry with them our hopes and aspirations."

It was decided to take Tajuddin and the other leaders to New Delhi and arrange a meeting with Prime Minister Indira Gandhi. Golok was to go with them. Golok and I went to New Market and brought all the clothing (including undergarments) and other accessories, like suitcases and toiletries required for them. Golok remarked, "Sir, we are equipping them as if we were sending our daughter to her husband's house."

I quipped, "Golok, people in New Delhi have not seen freedom fighters in the last twenty-three years. The present generation

---

[15] Maj Abu Osman Chowdhury, the Commander of the freedom fighters in the Khustia-Jessore sector.

of leaders there does not think highly of a person who is not dressed properly."

Golok took Tajuddin Ahmad and Amirul Islam on the night of 1 April, to New Delhi where they were kept in the charge of S. Chattopadhyaya, the Assistant Director, BSF. Golok hurried back to Calcutta in order to get other leaders.[16]

Tajuddin and Amirul Islam met the Prime Minister on the evening of 4 April. They had a series of meetings with not only the Indian leaders but also with some top ranking officers and their own East Bengal intellectuals who happened to be in New Delhi, including M.R. Siddiqui, Prof Yusuf Ali, Sirajul Haq, Shubban[17] and also some selected pressmen. After spending about a week in New Delhi, they came back to Calcutta on 9 April, fortified in their determination and in their efforts. We set up a whole hotel to look after the East Pakistan leaders and it began to expand steadily till at one time we had fifty guests.

At one of the high level meetings in Delhi, on a half torn map of East Pakistan, we speculated how best we could support the resistance movement and give a fillip to the Mukti Fauj[18] which held the key to the situation. (Ever since Independence, all the attention of the Indian Army was turned towards West Pakistan. East Pakistan was so remote that we could not even muster a map of the area when orders came to me to organise help to the Bengali resistance.) It was clear from the map that there was a bridge over River Fenny at Shobapur. Since India had cut off all air links between East and West Pakistan, reinforcements and supplies could only be sent by sea to Chittagong and then moved up by road to reach Dacca and beyond. "Cut the bridge" was the advice of an ICS strategist in the government. He felt if the bridge was cut, the efforts to supply the additional forces and stores to Gen Amir Abdullah Khan Niazi in East Pakistan would be seriously impaired.

[16] Input from Golok Majumdar.

[17] I checked up but could not identify Shubban. I presume Rustamji's reference is to Rehman Shobhan, the well-known economist.

[18] Rustamji and Brig Pande, in their writings, have used the words 'Mukti Fauj' in the initial stages. Later it was changed to 'Mukti Bahini' because 'Bahini' is the Bengali translation for the Urdu word 'fauj' meaning a force or army.

Meanwhile, Rajgopal had studied the situation and presented an excellent analysis. According to him the freedom fighters had, thus far, received little by way of material help from foreign countries and they had a lot of expectation from us. Their expectations were of an all embracing nature and if we did, in fact, respond to them, it had to be without any expectation on our part of their loyalty or good behaviour in the years to come. We had to be very clear in our minds that they had turned to us not because of any inherent love for us, not even on the implied assurance of feeling obliged to us, but merely because of the exigencies of the situation which had one and only one overpowering compulsion — the hatred for their rulers in West Pakistan.

We analysed the strengths and weaknesses of the Pakistan Army and came to the conclusion that its strength lay in its field trained and well equipped units with all the paraphernalia required for a modern war. It could and had unleashed terror on a helpless population on a scale which had no parallel in recent history. The Pakistan Government could succeed in playing upon the religious sentiments of the population and whipping up communal passions which might prejudice the cause that the people had taken up against it. The propaganda machine of Pakistan was no mean instrument and it could turn the tide in its favour.

As for the weaknesses, poor road communication, which would get worse with the onset of monsoon and secondly, the logistics problem were the main ones. With the refusal of re-fuelling facilities to the Pakistani planes by Ceylon, reinforcements from West Pakistan would have to come by ships. Maintaining a continuous supply of oil would worry the army considerably. The non-cooperation of the population coupled with the subversive activities of the hardcore in the resistance movement would mean a limitless drain on the manpower and other resources of the army. Further, the army had control only over the urban areas, leaving vast tracts in the countryside with no semblance of authority except through an occasional visitation. In short, the cost of ruling a large population which was bitter and which utterly hated its rulers could only be reckoned in terms which were imponderable.

The main strength of the resistance was the inexorable motivation and the widespread desire to free itself from the ruthless Pakistani domination. The freedom fighters had a band of young and dedicated army officers whose courage and ability to live through privations and agony of a tortured population were as astounding as they were infectious. As regards the weaknesses of the movement they lacked everything for carrying on the fight except the will and the courage to fight. Emotions, we felt, could swing a movement into action; but evanescent as emotions were, what would sustain a movement was the timely availability of adequate material. They had no accredited leader commanding the loyalty of a large cross-section of the people. As regards the leaders who were still over ground, there were already signs of petty jealousy raising its ugly head and there was no coordination among them regarding the course of action to be adopted.

We came to the conclusion that the officers and people fighting the Pakistani forces were having negative feelings of being rebels against the existing government. The economic hardships of the people were many and it was apprehended that they would multiply in the face of Pakistan's attempts to break the morale of the people by destroying large quantities of grain. In the absence of an authority in the government and in the absence of leaders whose words and guidance could command obedience among the populace, a state of anarchy would arise which would be further fuelled by Pakistan. It was therefore felt that a recognised and provisional government would provide the much needed rallying point for the populace and the freedom fighters.

During my discussions with Tajuddin in New Delhi on 6 and 7 April, he seemed anxious to ensure that a formal government-in-exile was constituted which should start functioning as soon as possible. He asked for our help to secure the presence of some of the elected representatives from inside East Pakistan. A government comprising of the recently elected representatives, he felt, would give greater legitimacy to the government-in-exile. The help was duly extended.

We contacted several other leaders and requested them to come over. These included Syed Nazrul Islam (Mymensingh), Col M.A.G. Osmany (Sylhet), Capt Mansoor Ali (Pabna), Khandkar

Mushtaq (Comilla) and Kamruzaman (Noakhali). Later Maulana Bhasani also joined from his boathouse near Dhubri.

A brief constitution for a Presidential form of government with a Prime Minister and Cabinet was drafted by Col N.S. Bains, the Chief Law Officer of the BSF and duly vetted by Subrata Roy Choudhury, a barrister of Calcutta. It was shown to Tajuddin and his colleagues who after some discussions approved it with minor changes.

At the outset, the question came up what should be the name of East Pakistan after liberation. Some suggested 'East Bengal', some suggested 'Banga Bhumi', some only 'Banga' and some 'Swadhin Bangla'. East Bengal was rejected because it could be confused with West Bengal and doubts about its being an independent country might arise. 'Banga Bhumi' was not considered appropriate as it might be difficult for foreigners to recall easily. 'Banga' (pronounced in Bengali as *Bongo*) was rejected as it was felt that people might distort it. 'Swadhin Bangla' (Independent Bangla) was rejected as it was felt that the word *Swadhin* would lose its relevance with passage of time. Tajuddin suggested 'Bangla Desh'[19] because the name had once occurred to Mujib. It was suggestive of a linguistic state — the language for which some youth had courted martyrdom on 21 February 1952.[20] All the leaders agreed at once.[21]

To design the national flag of Bangla Desh, the leaders sat in a conference, first among themselves and then Golok and I joined them. After many modifications, the final shape emerged. A rough design was drawn in which the lush green East Bengal was symbolised by the green background and the dawn of freedom by the red sun. After a lot of discussion amongst themselves, it was agreed that the map of East Bengal be sketched in a red circle so as to distinguish it from the flag of Japan and also to dispel any misunderstandings or anomalies.[22]

---

[19] Bangla Desh stands for land of Bangaal. The area comprising East Pakistan was referred to as Bangaal from the ancient times though in the present times it is used more as a pejorative term. Initially Bangla Desh were two words as can be seen from the stamps issued in July 1971. Later it was changed into one word — Bangladesh.

[20] 21 February is remembered every year as "Ekuishe." In 1999, the UNESCO adopted the day as the International Mother Language Day.

[21] Input from Golok Majumdar.

[22] Input from Golok Majumdar. Soon after the liberation of Bangladesh, the design

In the same meeting, the country's national anthem was selected. Two poems were considered. One was Dwijendra Lal Roy's *Dhano dhannye pushpe bhora* (Full of wealth, grain and flowers) and the other was Rabindranath Tagore's *Amaar sonar bangla* because the words *Sonar Bangla* evoked the images of golden jute and paddy crops, the mainstay of Bangla economy. The first one was a strong contender for the national anthem but after a lot of discussion the leaders unanimously decided that since the latter poem was a favourite of Mujib Bhai, it should be chosen as the national anthem of the new nation.[23]

Tajuddin was keen that I should personally take charge of the arrangements for the swearing-in ceremony. I impressed upon him the imperative need for the swearing-in ceremony taking place on the soil of Bangla Desh under the full gaze of the world press and TV cameramen despite the risk involved.

I had in mind two areas on the soil of his country as the possible venue for the function — one near Rajshahi and the other near Chuadanga. Since events were moving fast and the Pakistanis had started bombing and strafing the civilian areas including those close to important towns, it was decided not to have the function around Rajshahi.

As the function was to be witnessed by the world press, I was anxious that the site should be so situated as to attract the largest number of people of that country to witness the ceremony. In selecting the spot we had also to provide for the contingency of possible strafing by the Pakistani planes which did this job ruthlessly all over East Pakistan. Accordingly, a triangular piece of land jutting into India with a beautiful mango grove was selected in a village, the original name of which was Baidyanath Tala. (Its name was soon changed to Mujib Nagar). The first process of the government of a newly born nation was to commence not in a man-made, gaily decorated and illuminated building of carpeted

---

of the flag was changed and the map of the country was removed. This happened in January 1972. The stamp issued in July 1971 shows the map.

[23]Input from Golok Majumdar.

floor and chandelier decorated ceiling, but in a place which had for its canopy the sky, and for its decoration the trees. Decades or centuries hence when the citizens of Bangla Desh would look back on the birth of their country and the tragic circumstances attending it, they could legitimately be proud, among other things, of the fact that their first government sworn to democracy, secularism and socialism came in an area where Nature had bestowed her gifts in profusion and in the wake of ceremonies which were not only immaculate but also daring in their conception and courageous in their execution.

Our Public Relations Officer, S.C. Basu took a calculated risk in informing the world press, which had gathered in Calcutta to cover the developments inside East Pakistan, late on the evening of 16 April for the function scheduled for early next morning so as to ensure that the news did not reach the Pakistani authorities. The venue was not disclosed to foreign journalists. Basu brought them himself.

The Bangla Desh leaders and the BSF officers left Calcutta before four o'clock in the morning to avoid the Naxalites in the city, as their activities were at a peak and people on the roads did not feel assured of their personal safety. The motorcade was lined up and just before giving the signal to start, I trembled for a fleeting second — the only time during the entire crisis when I seemed to be a little unsure of myself. This may well have been the tremble when one faces the moment of truth — the truth of the birth of a nation. The tremble may well have been out of excitement of the opportunity given to me for associating myself with an event which eventually would have a far-reaching effect on international affairs in general, and on the history of nations of the subcontinent in particular.

I went round and saw the arrangements with Rajgopal and Golok to satisfy myself. There was a dais for seating the Prime Minister and the cabinet. Provision was made for singing the Bangla Desh national anthem. BSF was able to locate some good singers in Krishnanagar and prepared them for the swearing-in. A guard of honour with the Mukti Fauj was provided, though not in the best of uniforms but still quite presentable. The Mukti Fauj had taken positions all round the area of the venue to intercept any likely rush by the Pakistan Army personnel.

The actual function was to start at ten o'clock in the morning by which time it was expected that the world press and TV cameramen would be in position. I decided to leave the place, leaving behind Rajgopal and Golok. I left the spot at 8:30 a.m. and returned to Calcutta. There I waited with bated breath for news of the ceremony. I learnt that a party of about eighty-two Indian and foreign journalists, photographers and TV cameramen had trooped into the area by eleven o'clock in eighteen jeeps, cars and two buses and the crowd at the venue swelled up to 15,000.

The flag of Bangla Desh was unfurled and the national anthem of the new nation was sung for the first time and according to Golok, it electrified the entire gathering and scarcely an eye was dry. The ceremony was followed by a press conference. The leaders returned to Calcutta by 6:30 in the evening.

To me the successful termination of the proceedings connected with the swearing-in ceremony was the culmination of a week long anxious effort, the ultimate shape of which I was at no stage able to foresee or forecast with any degree of precision because of the large number of imponderables involved. I would have attracted on myself, and justifiably too, the most vituperative attacks from the world over and not least from the people of Bangla Desh themselves who would never have forgiven me for making available to the Pakistan Army and Air Force the entire team of front ranking politicians in exile. These were the people who were expected to give the necessary drive and direction to the Independence movement of Bangla Desh from Indian soil. Instead of what was to be achieved in terms of the actual ushering in of the government of a free Bangla Desh on Bangla Desh soil under the glare of the teams of press and TV, we would have well ended up in disaster if only the Pakistanis had their ears to the ground. Once it became an accomplished fact, we can only say, in all humility and in utter gratitude that Providence stood by and gave a helping hand to the efforts of man.[24]

---

[24]The Pakistan Army tried its best to locate Mujib Nagar and award exemplary

Even while the formation of the government-in-exile was being finalised, I felt that Pakistan would receive a bigger blow if its Deputy High Commissioner in Calcutta defected in favour of Bangla Desh. Golok and I went out for a walk, came back and decided that we would do it. Golok established preliminary contact with Hussain Ali, the Deputy High Commissioner, who wanted Tajuddin's assurances. They were provided. A meeting was also arranged with Tajuddin. We then went round in a house-to-house survey in the vicinity where Col Megh Singh's ruffians stood by while the meeting was going on. In the jazzy Gaylord Restaurant, two meetings were held with our officers. On 18 April, the Pakistan flag flew off in a storm and Bangla Desh's flag went up. The Deputy High Commissioner defected in a quiet and unobtrusive manner. This encouraged the Bengali diplomats in other countries to change their allegiance and strengthen the liberation struggle.

While I was in Canada in 1997, I read some reviews of a book by one senior Indian Army officer who took part in the Bangladesh operation. It was full of distortions concerning me. I wondered how a senior officer, a friend, could make up such stories. How could an author cheat so brazenly claiming that the defection of the Deputy High Commissioner and the proclamation at Mujib Nagar were organised by him.

❧

The defection of the Deputy High Commissioner, in the words of Golok Majumdar, is as follows:[25]

> "While the plans for having the swearing-in of the cabinet were going on, the DG BSF told me that something had to be done on the diplomatic front and Calcutta was the best place to begin. Mr Rustamji could ring up the Prime

---

punishment to the people of that village, but they received no cooperation from the people to identify it till the end.

[25] Based on my four interviews with Golok Majumdar. I showed him the transcript and he went through it and made corrections wherever it was necessary.

Minister at any time. In fact he was almost in daily touch with her during that period. When he rang her up, she was furious and said in a loud voice, which I could hear, 'Don't try to do any such thing. If there is even the slightest mistake, it would be difficult for me to handle the fallout.'

"Mr Rustamji had a peculiar habit of going out on long walks even when the sun blazed overhead. He used to joke that only Englishmen and mad dogs did such things. He took me out for a walk in the Calcutta Maidan at mid-day in the uncomfortably hot April sun and began the conversation, saying, 'Now that Pakistan has fallen on its face, it is time for us to deal it blow after blow, and throw it into a ditch with a final kick.' (Evidently, the case of hijacking of the Fokker plane and its destruction in Lahore in the presence of a jubilant Bhutto was rankling in his mind. He passed through a period of deep stress when the enquiry was on.) He said, in a conspiratorial tone, 'The PM's objection is because she feels that there could be a mistake. Supposing we do not make a mistake and do a clean job, the gains would be immense and she will be happy.' He asked me if I could do a clean job and if he could depend on me for it. I told him he could depend on me for anything.

"I put my officers on the job. They had a couple of meetings with Hussain Ali. We went on playing upon his mind. He wanted a meeting with Tajuddin and this was arranged in the Gaylord Restaurant on the river front. We had to be careful that the Pak intelligence did not get wind of it. We assured him and his family of strong commando support. All his difficulties and doubts were set at rest. We got a flag of Bangla Desh prepared and kept ready. We also made a signboard which read 'Gana Prajatantri Bangla Desh'.

"The date was fixed for Sunday, 18 April 1971. I sat on a stool outside the Deputy High Commissioner's office at

Circus Avenue wearing a kurta and pyjama in front of a roadside cobbler under the pretext of getting my shoe repaired. The DG BSF, Rajgopal and Maj Gen Narinder Singh passed by that way thrice but could not spot me. The DG, I was told, was fretting and fuming that I was not on the spot as planned. A man came to me and said that I should speak to him at once. I asked him to go back and tell him that I had seen him and the others pass by that way thrice and that they could not notice me.

"Meanwhile, my officers came back and told me that the Deputy High Commissioner was feeling very nervous and was wavering. After all the arrangements we had made and the assurances given by us and Tajuddin, it would have been disastrous if he backed out at the last moment. I asked my officers to convey to him that if there was any further delay, the consequences could be disastrous. Every passing second increases the risk of the agents of the ISI or the US consulate getting wind of it.

"Fortunately, at about ten o'clock in the morning, on that Sunday morning there was a rainstorm. The streets became deserted. The Pakistan flag-pole fell down and immediately afterwards somebody from the Deputy High Commissioner's office hoisted the Bangla Desh flag. Our boys who were ready with the sign board removed the Pakistan Deputy High Commissioner's board and hammered in the board which read 'Office of the Deputy High Commissioner, Gana Prajatantric Bangla Desh'. In no time huge crowds collected and there was wild cheering. The press people came in droves. Our journalist friends splashed the news boldly and whipped up a sensation. The Prime Minister was informed and she was surprised that we had done it — there was a 'stiff' happiness on her part.

"This heralded desertions from Pakistan chanceries all over the world and gave the provisional government a status and a tacit recognition. Diplomats and officials streaming into Calcutta put the Bangla Desh government on sound secretarial footing.

"Tajuddin was not allowed to open a bank account in the State Bank of India (SBI) as he was not an Indian national. I went to New Delhi and met Ardhenu Bakshi, Secretary, Banking in the Ministry of Finance and all the difficulties were ironed out after brief discussions with the Governor of the Reserve Bank of India. Three crores of rupees, which were in the account of the Deputy High Commissioner in an American bank in Calcutta were withdrawn on Saturday, 17 April 1971, that is, a day prior to the defection. The American agent had left the bank early as it was a Saturday. The money was deposited in the SBI after an account was opened in the Chowringhee branch of the SBI in the name of the Deputy High Commissioner, Bangla Desh a couple of days later. The money brought from the treasuries and sub-treasuries of Bangla Desh by the freedom fighters was deposited in the account. Bengalis from Sylhet, Chittagong, Noakhali and other districts who had settled aboard and done well for themselves were keen to send money in aid of the freedom struggle. Opening of the bank accounts facilitated diverting their remittances into the bank."

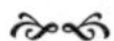

I went round the semi circle of East Pakistan on 22 April 1971 with Golok by road and en route we saw the reactions of the people of West Bengal. We observed a large number of trucks carrying people shouting "*Joy Bangla.*" The liberation struggle in Bangla Desh had infected the people of West Bengal who began to feel emotionally involved with the people of Bangla Desh. The press was also in a euphoric, supportive mood. But the reaction in the West Bengal unit of the Communist Party was subdued. Probably, they did not want to invite the displeasure of China by seeming to sympathise with the forces against Pakistan. Taking up the issue of refugees, who began pouring in after 15 April, the CPI (M) increased its tirade against the Central Government.

Across the border, the motivation of the freedom fighters was something which had to be seen to be believed. They knew they had no hope against the ruthless and well equipped Pakistan Army, but the whole area was fired with the hope of liberation and freedom from the humiliation that had been heaped on them by the rulers of Pakistan. Something seemed to tell all of them that they would triumph ultimately.

Our first halt was at Bongaon. A journalist by the name of Haq, who was editing a paper in Jessore, met me. He suffered terrible domestic calamities consequent to the army crackdown. He was moved to tears by intense emotion. "What is India doing? Why is she not coming to our help? We are being killed mercilessly by the army men. India, on whom we had pinned our hopes for our freedom struggle, stands by and takes no notice of the bloodshed. Please act. Please act. Ask your government to help us. Save us. This is the hour of our destiny. Do not let us down." And with that he began to shake with an emotion that was so intense that I had to put my arms around his shoulders and console him that we were trying to do our best.

We found that the Pakistani forces had cracked down on the Bengali troops in all the cantonments. A large number of them were killed, but an even larger number of Bengalis revolted, killed their officers, and began to harass the Pakistani forces. At all places, staff and students of all age groups played a decisive part.

We left Bagdogra and arrived at Tura en route to Silchar. At Tura, we had our first encounter with Pathans of the Pakistan Army who had rushed to the BSF posts for protection against the wrath of the Bengalis. They were given the necessary protection by the BSF and fed well. They were produced before me blindfolded as is the practice with captured soldiers. I got the folds removed and told my officers to look after them. I told the Pathans they would be allowed to go back to their country in due course. They seemed too overwhelmed to speak, but the gratitude was visible in their eyes.

We arrived at Agartala. Brig Pande, in the short time he was there, appeared to have taken full charge of the area and the activities around it. It was difficult for me to contain the exuberance of the young officers and men of the BSF who for the first time since they joined service, had come across a cause for which they could vindicate all that is best in human values.

My first meeting with the Bengali officers was in the BSF mess at Agartala. Col Osmany, the newly appointed Commander-in-Chief was also there. He was a roommate of Brig Pande during their training period at the Indian Military Academy in Dehradun, prior to India's Independence. Col Osmany, who had retired four years earlier, was Deputy Director (Operations) in the Pakistan Army Headquarters for ten years before his retirement. He told me that during the Indo-Pak War of 1965, if India had continued for a few days more, Pakistan would have been prostrate as they were running out of ammunition.

A tent was put up as an improvised mess and on the ground sprawled a group of officers who had revolted, studying a tattered map with the help of two hurricane lanterns. There was Osmany, Zia, Shaffiullah, Khaled Musharraf, Shaukat and Zaman.[26]

"We will put up Mukti Bahini camps here, here and here. All the men will be volunteers, a mixed lot — army, EPR and motivated young men. Will you look after them?" Osmany asked.

"We will support them and we will look after them as our own boys," Brig Pande replied.

"I am sure of that," Osmany said, holding out his hand to Pande, "Then we will hit the bastards here — Comilla, Jessore, Sylhet — can you back us?"

The discussions ended. Drinks were served. "Bangla Desh" was a toast proposed by Pande and we all gulped them with fervour.

According to the plan, all over the border, the BSF and Mukti Bahini established a compact which made history. What impressed me was the identity of interest, the manner in which a perfect understanding was achieved between us.

[26]Though the full names have not been given in Rustamji's article, the reference is probably to Col M.A.G. Osmany, Maj Ziaur Rahman, Maj K.M. Shaffiullah, Maj Khaled Musharraf, Maj Mir Shaukat Ali and Maj Kazi Nuruzzaman.

The contribution of Brig Pande in organising the freedom fighters is unforgettable. In the initial stages of the movement, there was mistrust between the leaders of the Awami League and the Mukti Fauj. Most of the Bengali officers had no contact with the Awami League leaders before 25 March 1971. Due to a spell of military rule for thirteen years, the Bengali army men had developed contempt for civilians and the political leaders and the civilians had developed similar feelings for the army men. That was the main cause for the state of unpreparedness on the part of the liberation forces. Consequently any direction or advice from politicians and civilian administrators was accepted with reservation. The average Bengali army officer thought that the politicians were opportunists and would try to exploit the situation to their own advantage after the agitation was over. The army officers felt that while they themselves had reached a point of no return and had no option but to fight for their existence, the politician would, if opportunity arose, let them down in any future bargaining.[27]

Orders issued by the Bangla Desh Army Headquarters were not respected or in some cases completely ignored by the Mukti Fauj commanders, who considered themselves as warlords of their areas. The Commander-in-Chief, Col Osmany, who was stickler for rules, regulations and correct accounting procedures, proved to be a liability in such abnormal circumstances. Brig Pande wrote to me saying that, "The Mukti Fauj officers came to my office and requested that I arrange a meeting with the political leaders. Maj Khaled Musharraf was their spokesman and Col Osmany was from the Awami League side. Khaled narrated all the problems faced by them in conducting the operations and wanted the politicians to take immediate steps to remove them. This created a furore in the meeting and all the political leaders started condemning the officers loudly. Col Osmany became excited and said that the army officers were power hungry and since they had no confidence in the Awami League, he would resign as Defence Minister. I took Osmany out and explained to him not to create a crisis at the start of the movement. Col Osmany talked to me many times in private about the young majors. According to him one

[27]Based on inputs from Brig Pande.

of them was a Pakistani plant, the other belonged to the China lobby and there was whispered talk regarding the integrity of the others."[28]

Most of the freedom fighters thought that the Indian Army would move into East Pakistan within a week of the declaration of Independence — on 27 March 1971. Consequently they had put in their best within the first fortnight of the hostilities. And when India did not march in, they started showing signs of frustration and disappointment. They were unable to understand the attitude of India, which was the biggest and only enemy of Pakistan. Most of them felt that unless India attacked, there would be no respite for them. They were not prepared for a long drawn out struggle. By May 1971, it appeared that the Mukti Fauj would not be able to stand up to five divisions of the Pakistan Army with modern weapons and supported by their air force and navy. The freedom fighters, both civilian and army, had hopes of a quick success. When they found that the situation would be a long drawn out affair involving human lives and national property, their enthusiasm gave way to apathy, particularly in areas where the Pakistan Army had full control. The senior officers of the Mukti Fauj generally avoided moving into the operational areas and gave out to the press the highly exaggerated accounts of the operations, given to them by the junior and non commissioned officers as their achievements.[29]

As the Pakistan Army fanned out, the Awami League Members of the National Assembly (MNA) and the members of the Provincial Assembly moved with their families into the interiors or to the border areas for refuge and shelter. Thus a political vacuum was created which was taken advantage of by the martial law administrators who started projecting the unrest as communal trouble created by Hindus and supported by India. As the liberation movement was associated with the Awami League, the Muslim League leaders openly supported the Pakistan military establishment. The Muslim League leaders and

[28]Ibid.
[29]Ibid.

other vested interests addressed congregations after the Friday prayers and spoke against the Awami League and Hindu domination.[30]

~

Due to the pressure of the refugees and the public opinion in India clamouring for action, the Prime Minister wanted the army to go into action in the month of May but the COAS refused to oblige as the army was not prepared. The chief was clear in his mind that he would go into battle only when he was sure of victory and was also confident of having enough men and material on the Sino-Indian border to guard against a thrust from that side.[31]

Apart from the army's refusal to go into action was its refusal to give us a few big guns that we needed and which would have changed the situation in our favour. The supply of ammunition was also cut off. Would it have been difficult to shoot down the eighteen planes that were in existence in Dacca? Those eighteen planes day after day attacked the Mukti Fauj viciously and drove them from one corner to another, strafing their positions and rocketing their strongholds. It was the students and the Mukti Fauj that bore the brunt of the attacks. Nearly 9,000 men had to suffer for what might have been accomplished by 1,000 casualties at that time. I was depressed with our army staying so completely out of it. Why this belief in neutrality? The Indian Army probably had its own reasons. I felt I was fighting a one-man battle with the Pakistan Army.

Gen Sam Manekshaw, the COAS was not happy with me and the part being played by the BSF. He kept on asking me, "Khusro, do you realise how dangerous the action taken by the BSF can be? You are creating a situation where we could easily drift into something big in the next few days. And it will not be in an area which would suit us."

I could see what his anxieties were about. The eastern side was totally unsuitable for operations. In fact, in the 1965 War, when we had a chance to penetrate, we had given it up because we felt

---

[30] Ibid.

[31] Input from Golok Majumdar.

it would damage our credibility with the Bengalis. There were no big cantonments, no transport, no roads to take military traffic, and only one shaky railway line which could be held up by insurgents at various places. What the army apprehended was that if they let down their guard in the west and diverted their attention to the east, it would be easy for Pakistan to dismember Kashmir; and they had tried that repeatedly ever since the birth of the nation.

By April 1971, the Pakistani troops entered the cantonments. The additional troops that arrived from West Pakistan were moved towards the border and occupied some border posts replacing the EPR.

The BSF had limited capabilities and resources to meet the Pakistan Army. The Indian Army therefore stepped in and on 30 April 1971, the operations along the West Bengal border were taken over by the army. Sixteen days later they took over the Assam and Tripura side of the border. The BSF came under the operational control of the army. 'Operation Jackpot' was launched.

The army continued to lean on the BSF for information, coordination with Mukti Fauj and local knowledge. The COAS instructed us to be 'audacious' and 'aggressive' in our actions. The BSF boys started assisting the Mukti Fauj in causing subversion and sabotage deep inside East Pakistan and even in district headquarter towns, where cash and weapons were looted and made over to the Government of Bangla Desh. Panic and confusion spread in the countryside. Soldiers were too scared to come out of their posts. The Pakistan Army launched a systematic drive to flush out the rebels from East Pakistan. Muslim Leaguers, Bihari Muslims, Al Badr and Al Shams, the followers of the Jamaat-e-Islami joined hands with the Pakistan Army to perpetrate unimaginable savagery which assumed the shape of a genocide.[32] Doctors, professors, teachers were their

---

[32]According to estimates available on scores of Bangladeshi websites, the total number of people killed is estimated between 2,00,000 to 30,00,000. According to the Hamood-ur-Rehman Commission — the Judicial Enquiry Commission set up by Pakistan to enquire into the causes of its defeat in East Pakistan — the number killed was admitted by the army sources to be 26,000. Sheikh Mujibur Rahman repeatedly said it was three million.

special targets. They were called out at night, taken to a secluded spot and shot dead. The corpses lay rotting for days and weeks. No one escaped their barbarity. The entire world recoiled in amazed revulsion when accounts of their ruthless brutality got around. The locked gates of an exodus were flung open.[33]

The wanton killing of innocent men, women and children reached such a stage that the killers themselves appeared to have become sick of it. In the beginning of May 1971, news started coming in of differences between the Punjabi and Pathan troops. Some of the Pathan troops objected to the killing of unarmed and innocent women and children on the ground that it was against the tenets of Islam. A clash took place over this issue between the two groups of Pakistani troops near Bijaipur in which six Punjabi soldiers and four Pathans were killed.[34]

The ruthless killers in the Pakistan Army who had scant regard for human lives, appeared to be cowards themselves. They were afraid of stirring out of their cantonments. It was impressed upon the Mukti Fauj that the fear of the unknown should therefore be increased in the hearts of the army men. Unfortunately their fear made them even more ruthless. The army men adopted a novel method. They instructed the civilian population to keep vigil over bridges and culverts in their villages. When the Mukti Fauj demolished them, the villagers were subjected to severe and drastic collective punishments. The Mukti Fauj thus came across stiff resistance from the civilian population. The villagers would not allow the Mukti Fauj to operate near their villages due to fear of extreme reprisals by the Pakistan Army. The civilian population also stopped cooperating with the resistance movement when air activity increased. Wherever bridges or culverts were demolished the villages were strafed. This increased the opposition of the locals to the actions of the Mukti Fauj and consequently demoralised the freedom fighters.[35]

The atrocities committed by the Pakistan Army roused the conscience of all right-thinking people. Many famous names in the

---

[33]Input from Golok Majumdar.
[34]Input from Brig Pande.
[35]Ibid.

arts and in music, many on the streets of London and Paris, came out to shout against the atrocities of the Government of Pakistan. Andre Malraux, the foremost French intellectual, the hero of the Spanish Civil War and the resistance movement during World War II, offered to take a military command in Bangla Desh against the Pakistan military regime. He clarified Bangla Desh was not defending a political system; it was defending its life. Singer Joan Baez rendered a moving song.

The BSF also took upon itself the responsibility of briefing and helping the international journalists, including Peter Hazelhurst, Clara Holingworth, Sydney H Schanberg, James Cameron and many others. They publicised the happenings inside the country. The attitude of the BSF is best reflected in James Cameron's book, *An Indian Summer.*[36] C.L. Sulzberger writing for *The New York Times*, in June 1971 said:

> "When the ancient Greeks said 'multiple death is not death' they meant that death's qualitative agony could be drowned in quantitative shock…Classical times could never comprehend the ultimate meaning of multiple death. Yet in recent times, dying is not acutely understood when its scope transcends certain limits. …The fish-eating, Bengali-speaking, rice-growing, over-populated area that became East Pakistan represented in fact the westernmost stretch of Southeast Asia. It had nothing but religion in common with meat-eating, Urdu-speaking, wheat-growing, under-populated area, a thousand miles away, that became West Pakistan and represented the fringe of the Middle East…The world's heart is already almost paralysed by the multiple death that has stricken Bengal; the world's mind may soon be even more hopelessly bewildered by the problems spewed up by this hecatomb."

At the height of the unrest in East Pakistan, the intelligence agencies of USA and the Soviet Union tried to infiltrate the ranks of

[36] Input Golok Majumdar.

the freedom fighters. The Soviet agency naturally took the help of the local communist party and there were serious attempts to reach out to the leaders who were all in Calcutta and free to move about. The US intelligence agency men were in regular touch with some of the Awami League leaders and more so with Khondakar Mushtaq Ahmed. Maulana Bhasani was not to be seen for some time. He had his contacts with the pro-Chinese agents. Later, another group of freedom fighters, named the Mujib Bahini was formed with the help of the Left oriented Indian leaders and funded by an intelligence agency. D.P. Dhar, a Leftist at heart, felt that it was necessary to form this force as it was not prudent to keep "all our eggs in one basket". Col Osmany was agitated about the activities of this better equipped and better paid volunteers and decided to withdraw. Golok brought it to my notice, but I expressed my inability to intercede. He approached the COAS, who went down to Calcutta and persuaded Col Osmany to change his decision and agree to continue to lead the freedom fighters.[37]

The situation in Bangla Desh was fast deteriorating. The service chiefs knew that they would have to be ready for action. They were not aware of what the Prime Minister had in mind and when she would give the green signal. The Prime Minister went to the Corps Headquarters in Siliguri on 31 August 1971. Golok Majumdar had also gone there. The Governor of West Bengal A.L. Diaz and his Advisor, Siddhartha Shankar Ray, were with her. From Siliguri she was to fly to Cooch Behar the next day to see the refugee camps. Golok and Brig Oberoi rushed in their jeep at night in pouring rain as she had expressed the desire to visit the Mukti Fauj training camp in Tapurhat. There Golok had an interesting conversation with her. He informed me of the dialogue. I asked him to convey it to the Home Secretary, Govind Narain. He did that and the Home Secretary said, "Catch the next flight and come to New Delhi."[38]

All of us, the Home Secretary, the three service chiefs, the Defence Secretary, the Director IB and the chief of RAW and myself

---

[37]Ibid.
[38]Ibid.

were there to hear him. He began from the beginning. He said that the Mukti Fauj camp was situated on the other side of a *nullah* (big drain). He felt it would be difficult for the Prime Minister to cross it. He tried to make an excuse that it was raining. Pointing to the raincoat she was wearing, she said, "I have my rain coat and umbrella. Let's go." He asked his men to stand in the *nullah* with thick bamboo poles on their shoulders. With an umbrella in one hand, the Prime Minister nimbly sailed over the poles like an expert trapeze artist and reached the other side. She spoke to the Mukti Fauj people undergoing training and gave them some assurances.

When she came back to the small *shamiana* (tent) Brig Oberoi asked her with great diffidence, "Ma'am, would you care for a cup of tea?"

"That's just the thing I want," she said. Turning to the Advisor, she said, "Siddhartha, you look after the Governor while I have a word with Mr Majumdar." She poured a cup for Golok and took him aside and referring to the on going struggle in East Pakistan, asked, "At this rate when do you expect to be in Dacca?"

He said, "Never — without our army moving in."

"Why? I have been told that the BSF alone can do it."

"The BSF cannot. We would be up against the armour, artillery and air force of Pakistan. Our army and air force would have to be involved."

"I also thought so." After a pause, she said, "I was only thinking of the West."

Golok presumed she was referring to the Western public opinion and said that it would be necessary to take care of it.

"No, no. I have already taken care of that. I was thinking about our ability to hold the thrust from the western border."

"For that the ground should be tankable," Golok remarked, "We should have cover for our tanks. The ground should be dry. The sugar cane would have to come up."

"Yes," she admitted.

"In that case, when can we expect the green signal?" he asked.

"Say in the third week of November," she said.

The Home Secretary asked Golok the obvious question, "How is it that the Prime Minister tells you things that she does not tell us?"

"Sir, that's a question you have to ask the Prime Minister," Golok said with an innocent expression on his face.[39]

This was the bit of information the army was waiting for. Gen Manekshaw got up and gave Golok his typical bear hug and said, "Golok, from now on you and I will share information and work together."

"But I would have to keep my DG in the picture."

"Oh! You don't have to tell Khusro. In the army we work on a 'need to know' basis," he said with a smile.[40]

In the BSF we started discussing what would be its role in the event of war flaring up. I thought the BSF would get some respite. Golok was of the view that the BSF, with the help of the Mukti Fauj, would have to act as the pathfinder for the advancing army. The prisoners taken would become the charge of the BSF and we would have to ensure that the lines of communications were kept open. Above all, we would also have to gear up our intelligence about the Naxalites and ensure that, at the instance of China, they did not indulge in acts of sabotage on both sides of the border.[41]

❧

In the beginning of November 1971, Air Chief Marshal P.C. Lal went to Calcutta and met the IG BSF, Golok Majumdar in his office to discuss the help that the BSF could give in keeping track of Pakistan air infiltration. We devised a system. The air force gave us photographs of all types of planes with a nom de plume for each. Our own BOPs were given different nom de plumes. If any incursion

---

[39] Prime Minister Indira Gandhi believed in getting information from various sources. She felt the senior officers in New Delhi gave her information or advice she wanted to hear. She knew Golok Majumdar from 1957 and felt he was an officer who did not hesitate to tell her the true and unpalatable facts.

[40] Ibid.

[41] Ibid.

took place, all that the BOP had to do was to declare its nom de plume and that of the plane. Like for instance if Tungi BOP saw a sabre jet, it would cry out "COFFEE–TOOFAN", "COFFEE–TOOFAN". 'Coffee' and 'Toofan' being the nom de plumes of Tungi BOP and the sabre jet respectively. The air force radar would catch the wireless information of the incursion and pass it on to the pilots on the "Ops Readiness" pads. The pilots would immediately scramble into the air, gain height and head for the spot. The intruders flying low (to avoid radar detection) would be easy prey for the fighters which were higher up. (In aerial dog-fights, a plane which is higher up always has the advantage as it can swoop down on the plane below.)

On 22 November 1971, a tea party was going on in IG BSF's house. The Chief Secretary, West Bengal, the IG police, the Divisional Commissioner and I were present. The IG BSF got a telephone call informing him that two Pakistan sabre jets had been shot down at Boyra in Bongaon subdivision. Two Pakistani pilots, aged about twenty-one and twenty-two, who had bailed out were taken to his office. They were treated very well. They said that the Pakistan propaganda machinery had instilled in their minds the fear that if they bailed out and fell into Hindu hands, their bodies would be cut into pieces and offered to Hindu deities as sacrifice and eaten by the Hindus. The boys were pleasantly surprised at the treatment meted out and readily divulged their mission plans.[42]

These boys were on a recce mission for their tank regiment to dash down the Bongaon–Krishnanagar–Plassey Road to prevent the planned military tie up between our forces on the south of Farrakka barrage and those in the north of the barrage. That would have hindered the battle plans of our Eastern Command Army. Two or three days later some thirteen US made Chaffe tanks of the Pakistan Army which had concentrated in a grove north of River Kapo-taksi were detected. There was a fierce battle and the tanks were destroyed.[43]

---

[42]Input from Golok Majumdar. The two Pakistani pilots were Flight Lieutenant Parvej Mehdi Qureshi and Flying Officer Khalil Ahmed. In 1996, Qureshi became the Chief of Air Staff of the PAF.

[43]Ibid.

On 3 December 1971, the PAF made pre-emptive air attacks on some of our air bases. The Prime Minister was then in Calcutta. I rang up Golok and asked him to immediately inform her. She was addressing a huge public meeting. Golok felt he would not be able to reach her through the vast spillover of the crowd. He rang up the Raj Bhavan and informed G.C. Dutt, the CSO to the Prime Minister, to pass on the information to her.[44]

Just before the war broke out, we had received instructions from the army regarding the general plan of action. We were asked to make the Pakistani forces come out of the cantonments and have them scattered in penny packets. The raids conducted by the men of the Mukti Fauj assisted by the BSF achieved that. We had skirmishes all along the border and kept nibbling at it so as to draw the Pakistan Army out and get them to spread out thinly all over East Pakistan. We were asked to leave the cantonment areas alone. The Pakistan Army got stretched out and the officers leading the forces became confused and less effective. Hence when our columns moved in, there was no concentrated opposition.[45]

Lt Gen Sagat Singh's forces skirted the cantonments and headed straight for Dacca. The strategy of Gen Manekshaw helped as the advance to Dacca from all directions became relatively easy. As the BSF marched into Bangla Desh side by side with the army from all directions, the Bengali officers gave us intelligence which was carefully processed by Rajgopal and passed on to the army.

One battalion went to Jessore and Khulna with Maj Gen Dalbir Singh. Two battalions accompanied Maj Gen L.S. Sehal's division from the north and two battalions went from the south. As the army occupied enemy territory, the BSF was charged with the responsibility of restoring civil administration, guarding arsenals, securing lines of communications and looking after the public relations work and liaison.[46]

BSF brought up its rocket team to the front and fired with deadly accuracy on Jessore destroying a few buildings and causing

---

[44]Ibid.
[45]Ibid.
[46]Ibid.

panic everywhere. After the fall of Jessore we could see for ourselves the deadly accuracy of the rockets even when fired from a distance of twenty kilometres.

❧

The Indo-Pak War of 1971 which resulted in the creation of Bangla Desh was a short one. It was a total victory for us: an abject surrender by Pakistan, of 90,000 prisoners, a peace accord signed at Simla. The main cause of success in the war was the patience and persistence with which Prime Minister Indira Gandhi pursued her goal to help the Bengalis achieve freedom. How discreetly and carefully she organised support for them in the world when leaders like President Nixon were bent upon opposing Indian intervention. She could stand up to the Western powers and tell them, "The Allies claimed that World War II was fought to save democracy. But when democracy is being so flagrantly destroyed, we do not hear much. Could there be greater and clearer suppression of democracy than what we have witnessed in Bangla Desh, under a military regime?"

After the victory, she said in Parliament, "It is a victory but a victory not only of arms, but also of ideals. The Mukti Bahini could not have fought so daringly but for its passionate urge for freedom and the establishment of a special identity for Bangla Desh. Our own forces could not have been so fearless and relentless had they not been convinced of their cause."

Pakistan's plans were certainly defective. In the first place, starting the war with an air attack was a blunder. That gave us an excuse to advance into East Pakistan. Secondly, if the Pakistan Army had withdrawn to the river line and built up defences, the bold bid by Gen Sagat Singh to skirt the defences and head for Dacca would not have succeeded in such a short time. It might have become a prolonged war which would have given opportunities for intervention by world powers.

I would also say that had the BSF not linked up with the Bengali officers who had revolted, the liberation of Bangla Desh might not have come as fast as it did. Many of the Bengalis laid down their lives for the Independence of the country they valued and some BSF men also lost their lives.

I do not think the number of Bengalis killed in those nine months can ever be counted. The Hamood-ur-Rehman Commission instituted by Bhutto has given details of the atrocities committed by the Pakistan Army. The most pathetic was the brutal murder of a large number of intellectuals and other leading men just before the surrender on 16 December 1971. We discovered a large number of mass graves when we went in.

When the history of our times is written, I am sure the part played by the Bengali officers and their units would be remembered with gratitude. For us it was the starting point of a collaboration which would have bound India and Bangla Desh together, but we had not counted on the pinpricks of the Indian Army — the Indian flag on staff cars, a high officer's loose remark, "Why should Bangla Desh have an army?" and the attempt to take away captured weapons to India. A great friendship was wrecked by small men on both sides.

After the surrender of the Pakistani forces on 16 December 1971, the Bangla Desh leaders, who were with us since April 1971, left for their country on 22 December 1971. I must say that they were the most considerate guests that one could ever imagine. They never complained, they never asked for anything, they never once said that they had not been looked after as well as they should have been. Our contact with them was all along through Golok Majumdar, who was the best diplomat we could have produced.[47] They all knew his heart was in Bangla Desh. The day Golok and I saw off Tajuddin and the other leaders at Dum Dum airport, I said to Tajuddin, "I hope our countries will be friends forever."

"Yes, certainly," he replied, "As equals." That statement brought out the feeling that has existed from the beginning.

---

[47] Golok Majumdar was awarded a Param Vishisht Sewa Medal (PVSM). He is the only civilian, thus far, to have been awarded this second highest military decoration.

Maulana Bhasani and others left in a separate plane. They were all in a jovial mood as they were going back to their independent country and were cracking jokes. Just before leaving the Maulana made a light-hearted remark to Golok, "*Majumdar Saheb, apni ki korleyn. Amadeyr otho jotno korey raakhleyn. Amadeyr bhalo korey khawaleyn. Otho dekha suna korleyn. Kintu bhooley geyleyn ki amra moshalmaan. Amra namak haraam. Prothom chhoteyi apnake kaamraabo.* (Mr Mazumdar, what have you done? You took so many pains to host us. You have fed us so well. You have looked after us so well. But you have forgotten we are Muslims. We are ungrateful. At the first opportunity we will bite you.")

Golok told him, "*Apni amar songhe tomasa korbeyn na.*" ("Please don't joke with me.")

He then changed the subject and pointing towards the leaders who were leaving made another jovial remark that, that excepting Tajuddin, the rest were all *chhagol* (goats). Then he went to complain that the *sala* Punjabis had taken away his third wife. [48]

❧

Mujibur Rahman was given a rousing reception in Calcutta when he was released from captivity in January 1972. The mammoth public meeting he addressed was attended by the largest ever crowd witnessed in Calcutta. Very moved with the reception he said, "*Rikta ami, nishwai ami, debar kichchu nai, achhe shudu bhalo bhasa, deye geyleyn taai.*"(I am a pauper. I have lost all. I have nothing to give you. I have only love, and I am leaving my love for you.)

---

[48] Maulana Bhasani of the National Awami Party had pro-Chinese leanings. He was known for taking an anti-India stance on several issues. Soon after reaching Dacca, he started his anti-India tirade, calling for the withdrawal of Indian troops from Bangladeshi soil. His remarks, while leaving, were probably meant to forewarn Golok Majumdar in a humorous way. Golok Majumdar told me that Maulana Bhasani wanted to see the statue of Deshbandhu Chittaranjan Das situated in front of the AIR building, near Eden Gardens in Calcutta. When he was taken there, Bhasani stood there and cried like a child, much to the embarrassment of the escorting officer. Maulana Bhasani and Netaji Subhas Chandra Bose were protégés of C.R. Das in the early twenties.

Mujib was generous in his public compliments to us. When I met him in Dacca, he said, "So, you are Mr Rustamji about whom I have heard so much."

It was a sad day for me when Tajuddin was murdered in Dacca in November 1975 along with Nazrul Islam, Capt Mansur Ali and Kamruzzaman. It can be said without any fear of contradiction that had Tajuddin not been the head of the government-in-exile when the liberation war was on, it would not have been possible for the resistance movement to work so successfully. It would have taken a long time for the country to free herself from the yoke of Pakistan. Tajuddin remained a sad man. It appears that after Mujib took over the reins of the government, he never once asked Tajuddin how he had conducted the affairs for the crucial ten months when he (Mujib) was imprisoned by Pakistan.[49]

I remember a discussion with Tajuddin about the future of our two countries. He stressed on the need for dependence on each other, the friendship which was bound to last and he had so much faith and trust on the BSF that he said, "We will consider a common border force."

Some years after the liberation, I spent a long evening with Gen Ziaur Rahman in Chittagong in the very room he was later assassinated. We talked about the old times. The team that we had assembled on the border proved to be a winning team. The story can never be fully told. But to me Bangladesh shall always remain a precious country as I was there and have witnessed the excessive pain and unprecedented bloodshed that accompanied its birth.

---

[49] Input from Golok Majumdar.

What tribute does he pay to the 135 men who died, the 392 that suffered serious injuries. He makes no mention of the 423 who were given gallantry medals. What were they for? Is this the way in which gallantry in operations should be treated by the man who pretends he was directing everything. He does not mention the courage of the BSF company led by Col. O'Connor that captured a military post, or the gallantry of those who fought and dispersed many army posts, including that of Raja Mohattam on the Western front led by Ramkrishna Wadwa who died in the battle, and was awarded the second-highest military decoration for gallantry,

Extract of an article written by Rustamji in which he debunked the claims made by a senior army officer in his book about his achievements preceding and during the Indo-Pak War of 1971.

22

War on the Western Front

In the war that broke out, the BSF played a notable part in standing up to the Pakistan Army even on the western front, a long, live and fiery border, with stupendous activity.[1] The BSF held the advance of the Pakistan Army at several places — took a terrible pounding from their guns and bombings from their aircraft, and courageously advanced into Punjab to capture pickets held by the regular Pakistan Army. Conspicuous acts of courage were displayed by the men and officers on the western front. Ramkrishna Wadhwa, our Assistant Commandant died in battle trying to take over the Raja Mohattam post. He was awarded the second highest military decoration during a war for gallantry — the Maha Vir Chakra — though I thought he deserved the highest.

Proportionately, on the eastern and western fronts the BSF casualties were as many as those of the army. In the Sindh and Rajasthan sector, BSF on its own, made sizeable captures of territory which stood us in good stead at the peace table.

---

[1]Rustamji was more pre-occupied with the happenings on the eastern front and did not visit the western front so often. He had left it to Ashwini Kumar, the IG of the BSF (Western Frontier) looking after the entire Indo-Pak border on the western front (Punjab, Rajasthan and Kutch). There is therefore not much mention of the role of the BSF on that front in Rustamji's notes and articles. This chapter is based on inputs from Ashwini Kumar.

In the middle of 1971, due to the disturbed conditions in Punjab, the Government of India decided to bring the state under President's rule. A number of officers, particularly police officers in Punjab and their family members were murdered by Naxalites, who created mayhem in the state. Ashwini Kumar was asked to take over as IGP, Punjab. When Ashwini expressed reluctance to leave the BSF, the Prime Minister called him and asked him to take over as IGP, Punjab, in addition to being IG BSF. Soon the Punjab Police was able to cleanse the state of the unruly elements by strategic strikes on the various hideouts of the local saboteurs and by September, had maimed their menacing movement.

Heavy skirmishing had started by then between India and Pakistan on the East Pakistan border. Adequate precaution had to be taken on the western front also in the event of a real 'scrap' with Pakistan. Close liaison with the army was established and intelligence spruced up regarding anti-Indian activities both within and across the borders. Officers at the border were put through special rigorous training in building up quality intelligence about the Pakistan 'backyard'. Soon our border forces and civilian police became extremely adept in collecting intelligence about the movement of enemy elements and their armed forces. There was information galore about Pakistanis masquerading as Indian citizens in our border districts, and developing 'spy nests'.

In the second half of November 1971, a Pakistan national in the garb of a Hindu sadhu, who situated himself on the border in Ganganagar district of Rajasthan, was apprehended. On questioning him closely, it transpired that he was a Pakistani spy passing on information about the IAF. He was won over and fed with wrong information and from him we came to know the plan of Pakistan to launch a pre-emptive strike on 3 December 1971. Soon after, this information was corroborated by a reliable contact of Ashwini in Pakistan.[2]

Since the other officers were not available, he rang up the Prime Minister and informed her. He also informed Air Marshal

---

[2] Ashwini Kumar hailed from Lahore, where his father was a reputed doctor. He also had his education in Lahore and had many friends in Pakistan.

M.M. Engineer. At first the information was not believed. But Air Marshal Engineer who was the officer incharge of Indian Air Force, Northern Command, acted on it and removed his planes to the smaller air force stations in North India. In their place some 'dummy' planes were kept. From the air these looked like real fighter planes.

War between the two countries broke out at six o'clock in the evening on 3 December 1971 and PAF struck at forward Indian air bases in Adampur, Halwara, Delhi and Agra as was predicted, and the 'dummy' targets were destroyed. The PAF returned to their bases, thinking erroneously that they had destroyed our border air sentinels. Instead they themselves became 'sitting ducks' for our planes which followed them and destroyed them in the ensuing counter-attack. The enemy lost a large number of their fleet in the counter-attack, and was forced to retreat with a considerable part of the rump to a neighbouring country where they were given refuge, but in the process got 'marginalised', and could no longer fly back to Pakistan to take part in hostilities.

On the basis of information supplied also by the BSF (Western Frontier), Karachi and the entire Kutch coast were 'disciplined' by our navy, which played havoc not only with their naval craft but also Pak morale. Karachi lost its importance as a fighting base and limped back to life only after the ceasefire.

In Rajasthan, a Pakistan Armoured Unit from Mirpur (near Bahawalpur in Pakistan) which was nearing towards Jaisalmer was neutralised and destroyed by our Jaisalmer air unit on timely information given by the BSF outpost at Longewala in Jaisalmer district. Longewala force had been strengthened by an army battalion, and later reports recounted to give a wrong impression of the fighting that the army had thrown back the armoured assault. Though the BSF and the Indian Army units fought bravely, the situation was completely retrieved by the IAF which destroyed and decimated the entire Pakistan armoured unit of over thirty tanks. This was a great victory for our Force — the BSF and the army units withstood an enemy armoured tank assault for over sixteen hours, in a barren treeless desert, till the IAF delivered, most elegantly and pungently, the coup de grace. The Pakistan tank commander stupidly came deep into the Indian borders without any air cover, and paid a heavy price. The BSF's timely information had again scored a bull's eye.

The BSF also captured strategic places in Kutch from Pakistan. The entire area of Thar and Nagar Parkar deep in the Sind desert, was independently seized and captured by the BSF. The role of the BSF in Sindh was an expanding one and though the original duties given meant protecting the flanks of the Indian Army which had closed on Rahim-Yar-Khan and Naya Chor, it got into top gear on entering deep into enemy territory.

On the Punjab border many gallant offensive actions were fought against the regular troops of Pakistan in Raja Mohattam, Ranian and Burj. In Fazilka it held out against all odds and the nation owes it to them for not having lost it, despite the main defence line's abandonment plans by the army.

The BSF covered itself with glory in Gurdaspur by facilitating an easy crossing for our army of the Ravi River, opposite Dinanagar, and capturing a large area of Sialkot district and taking some important prisoners.

In her letter at the end of the hostilities, Prime Minister Indira Gandhi, praised the BSF during 1971 operations:

> "As the first line of our defence, the Border Security Force had to bear the immediate brunt of the enemy onslaught. The manner in which they faced the fire and the support they gave to the army played a crucial role in our ultimate success."

The intelligence provided was recognised by the government with the award of Padma Bhushan to Ashwini Kumar in January 1972 and the citation mentioned it in no uncertain terms:

> "Shri Ashwini Kumar (51), holding the dual charge of Inspector General of Police, Punjab and Inspector General, Border Security Force during the last few months, brought his wonted zeal, energy and enthusiasm to bear on organising defences, arranging proper protection for vital installations and in general getting the Punjab state ready to face the impending Pak attack from across the border. The credit for

> the tough front put up by the Border Security Force on the Punjab border goes to Shri Ashwini Kumar, whose liaison with the top echelons of the Army, under whose operational control the Border Security Force worked, was close and effective. Besides constantly visiting the borders and infusing confidence and fighting spirit into his men, *Shri Ashwini Kumar provided a fund of information on the intelligence side and a considerable share of the credit for the failure of the pre-emptive strike of the Pak Air Force on Indian bases on 3rd December 1971 should go to the intelligence conveyed by him.*"[3]

The Defence Secretary, K.B. Lall, in his letter to the Home Secretary also praised the role of the BSF in the Indo-Pak War of 1971. The letter might seem a little effusive but it had an indication of government's estimate of the work of the BSF. He said:

> "A special word of thanks to the Director General of the Border Security Force and to the men and officers under his command, is overdue. *It is their initial initiatives, their boldness, courage and, if I may say so, imagination, which provided eventually an opportunity to the Defence Services to do their part.* The nature and pattern of cooperation which was evolved between the BSF and the army provided a substantial accretion of strength to the nation. *The performance of the BSF Units in Sindh, in J&K, on the borders of West Punjab and in Bangladesh was creditworthy.* The Chief of Army Staff found their assistance to be invaluable."[4]

I was to retire from service in May 1974 but was given a two year extension as Special Secretary in the Ministry of Home Affairs. The last day in service was indeed an eventful one. First, I was delayed for the Home Secretary's farewell party because I got

---

[3]As published in *The Gazette of India (Extraordinary)* dated Saturday, 22 January 1972. The italics are mine.
[4]The italics are mine.

a telephone call from a friend's wife that she was going to commit suicide by throwing herself in front of a moving bus in Connaught Place. I was thankfully able to avert the tragedy.

I rushed back to office and apologised profusely for the delay. Then after the party I went to say goodbye to P.N. Dhar, the Secretary to the Prime Minister. While I was leaving he said, "Oh! I forgot to tell you. The Prime Minister wants to know whether you can go to Mizoram as Governor." The first thought that came to my mind was that my son Cyrus's education would be disturbed. The second was that I had been offered the job as Special Secretary in the Home Ministry, which would mean a continued stay in New Delhi. I declined and came back to my office in the South Block.

Then occured a comic incident on the last day of my service in the BSF. My confidential records almirah suddenly started to totter and fall. It almost came down on Harish Soneja, my faithful secretary for nine years, and me. With a massive effort we managed to get it straight again and I ran for help to the peons in the corridor. What a glorious obituary the incident would have made, "On the last day of his service, the DG BSF was buried under his own confidential records."

Since my successor was not named, I continued to look after the work of the BSF even as Special Secretary. The Prime Minister had also asked me to monitor the All India Railwaymen's strike. With the help of C.V. Narasimhan, the Joint Secretary in the Home Ministry, we kept monitoring the biggest railway strike organised by George Fernandes and company in May 1974. BSF officers and battalions were deployed at several places to ensure movement of the trains.

I finally handed over the charge of BSF to Ashwini Kumar on 30 September 1974. He was my natural successor. We both had joined the BSF at its inception. A formal farewell was organised for me at the BSF Academy at Tekanpur. At the end of the party, when they threw me up in the air, I felt they had sent me to the stars. On 21 July 1965, I was the lone man in the BSF. When I left it after nine years, there were 60,000 men. Over the years, the BSF has acquitted itself very well because the Force has developed character and resilience and above all, because it has acquired the confidence of the nation.

My successor and long time colleague, Ashwini Kumar was gracious enough to say that I became a legend in my lifetime. In my reply, I bid farewell citing the lines of Rabindranath Tagore from his Nobel prize winning work, *Gitanjali*, "I bow to you all and take my departure."[5]

I left the BSF with one regret — a regret which remained with me even in my old age. The sacrifices made by the men and officers of the police organisations could not be recognised by the nation in a visible manner. On 26 January 1972, the *Amar Jawan Jyoti* (the flame of the immortal warrior) was lit by Prime Minister Indira Gandhi at India Gate in New Delhi to honour all the soldiers of the army, navy and air force who had laid down their lives in the Indo-Pak War of the previous month. The BSF and other Central Para-Military Forces (CPMFs) had also lost several jawans and officers in the conflict. I tried hard to get their names included. There was opposition from the Services side till the last minute. I could not understand their logic. Our boys fought side by side in the same war, against the same enemy and when it came to honouring them, why treat the police martyrs as being unfit to be mentioned under the same cenotaph?[6]

Later, I followed up the matter with the Prime Minister and she stated we could have a separate memorial for the police. She was also magnanimous to state that she would give Rs 2,00,000 from her personal account for the memorial as and when it comes up. But the matter, which was being dealt with by the Bureau of Police Research and Development, (BPR&D) got held up at some stage.[7]

I was happy to note that after the attack on Parliament in December 2001, the government of Prime Minister Atal Behari Vajpayee had sanctioned a police memorial in Delhi.[8]

---

[5] The Bengali rendering is as follows, "*Peychi chhutti, Bidhai deho bhai, Shobarey ami pronam korey jaee.*" The English translation was done by Tagore himself.

[6] Based on my interview with Cyrus Rustamji and another person who wished to remain unnamed.

[7] Based on my interview with Gautam Kaul, retd DG ITBP, who was dealing with the file when he was in the BPR&D. Rustamji, he said, had recorded a note in that file in which he mentioned the above details.

[8] The work on this memorial was progressing fast when some parties obtained an injunction from the court.

PART-VI

1976–2003

No. 1022 /D/96-HMP

गृह मंत्री
भारत
नई दिल्ली-११०००१
HOME MINISTER
INDIA
NEW DELHI-110001

October 7, 1996

Dear Shri Rustamji,

I have read with interest your "open letter to the Home Minister" titled **"Clown's rumours, cleric's sermons"** in the Hindustan Times, New Delhi dated the 9th September, 1996. I thank you for not only sharing some of your valuable thoughts on the present system of functioning of the police in India but also for your suggestions regarding certain remedial measures.

2. Like you and many other enlightened citizens of this country, I too am deeply concerned about the present state of affairs relating to the criminal justice administration. You may be happy to know perhaps that soon after assuming charge as the Union Home Minister, I have started an exercise in all seriousness to bring about some basic police reforms in the light of the recommendations of the National Police Commission (1977-81). Much, however, will naturally depend on the cooperation and commitment on the part of the State Governments and others including the judiciary, the media and, above all, the police officers and men of all ranks.

3. I will look forward to having your views, suggestions and cooperation in due course in achieving the above tasks.

With regards,

Yours sincerely,

(INDRAJIT GUPTA)

Shri K.F. Rustamji, IPS(Retd),
"Ness Baug",
Annexe No.1,
Nanak Chowk,
BOMBAY - 400 007.

Former Union Home Minister Indrajit Gupta's reply to the open letter, which Rustamji wrote to him and which was published in a newspaper in 1996.

23

National Police Commission

The police structure and role that one sees today is a consequence of the report of the Police Commission set up by the British rulers in 1860. The recommendations were incorporated in the Police Act of 1861. The organisational structure has remained the same except for an increase in the strength of the police. Barely forty years after the first commission, when the government started receiving complaints of corruption, inefficiency and high-handedness, the police came under scrutiny again by another commission appointed in 1902 by Lord Curzon, the Viceroy.

It was urged before this commission that the police should be made to function as servants of the law and not the executive authority. This demand was rejected. However, the commission made other useful recommendations, like the introduction of formal training for police officers and men. It also recommended the creation of a separate department for criminal investigation. Thus the CID, was introduced. These important steps injected some degree of professionalism and cohesion into the police force of the country.

In the early years after Independence, the conference of the chiefs of police repeatedly asked for another commission on the ground that the normal method of police reform was to form a police commission which would study the problem in detail and then implement those recommendations that seemed desirable. The suggestion of the chiefs was turned down on the plea that police was a state subject.

Hardly any government at the Centre or in the states has been able to remove the taint which centuries of feudalism stamped on us. We still want a rule which is only meant for the benefit of the ruler and his robber barons. That is the essence of feudalism — the relationship between the ruler and his vassals. Politicians do not want to change that.

In 1977, when the Janata government came to power, it marked a fortuitous turn. I happened to be in Bombay with Rajdeo Singh, head of the CBI, to look into some smuggling problems on behalf of the Home Ministry. Rajdeo suggested that we meet Jaiprakash Narayan (popularly known as JP), who was convalescing in Express Towers of Ramnath Goenka. I was not sure whether I should meet him because we had been on opposite sides in the Vinoba Bhave mission controversy of 1960. Still I went to see him with Rajdeo and was totally charmed by the man. We drifted into a discussion on police problems. I said that the main problem for the police is created by verbal orders of political leaders, often contrary to the law or the intentions of the government. Rajdeo and I then mentioned other problems and said that there were so many of them that only a police commission could solve them. JP wrote a letter to Choudhary Charan Singh, the Union Home Minister, about the need to examine the subject, and within a few days I was informed by the Home Secretary, T.C.A. Srinivasavardan that the Government of India had decided to set up a NPC.

The commission set up in 1977 had a good team at the top consisting of Dharma Vira, ICS (Retired) as the Chairman, Justice N.K. Reddy, N.S. Saxena, IP (Retired), M.S. Gore, the social scientist, C.V. Narasimhan, IPS as the Member Secretary and me. In addition it had a very well-informed group of police and other service officers to assist it.

We in the NPC proposed a method of reducing, if not eliminating, the grip of the party in power on the police, which was exercised by the unabashed use of the party's power of transfers, promotions or protection of those who helped it in corruption, and transfer to oblivion posts of those who showed an inclination to be subservient to the law and not towards the party in power. We proposed the setting up of a State Security Commission presided over by the state minister incharge of police with one member from the government and one from the opposition, and four others unconnected with politics. This Commision should give the directions for police performance and discipline. The NPC felt that such a body was essential in any democratic society to ensure that political direction as required in a democracy was present and the political forces do not attempt to use the police for their personal and party ends, as they had been doing.

There were many other safeguards for the protection of the public in the eight reports which were drafted by C.V. Narasimhan almost single-handedly such as, a mandatory judicial enquiry in cases of alleged rape or death in custody, or deaths of two or more persons in police firing. We had also suggested a method of redressal of grievances of the policemen.

The NPC also touched upon the training aspect and stated that though the training programme for the officers and the men had been recast from time to time mostly due to the efforts of some thinking police officers, but it still was confined to the inculcation and promotion of skills and unable to break into innovative areas for the propagation of values and attitudes. The real inputs needed for the police to be converted into a service organisation was attitudinal change, and for this to become possible, the whole organisation from the top to the constable on the beat, would have to imbibe a set of new values and faiths based on the principles of strict adherence to law and abiding respect for the dignity of the individual.

When the report came out in 1981, Indira Gandhi had taken over again as the Prime Minister. When I met her, she asked me to see the Home Minister, Giani Zail Singh, and apprise him of the recommendations. The Home Minister kept postponing the meeting and I finally gave up. Instead, he issued a statement that the recommendations of the NPC were undemocratic. I said to the press, in an unguarded moment, that the Home Minister had not read the report, and even if he had or if he does so, he would not understand it. This came out prominently on the first page of newspapers, and in the next column it was mentioned that Giani Zail Singh had been nominated to be the President. So much for tact and diplomacy on my part, but he never held it against me.

For sixteen years the report of the NPC was kept in cold storage by the Home Ministry. Again and again a revival was said to be under consideration, but nothing happened. Then came a man of integrity and purpose as Home Minister — Indrajit Gupta. I wrote an open letter to him, which was published in the *Hindustan Times* urging him to look into police reforms. He sent a letter to the states in 1997 in which he said that no serious attempt to implement many of the basic and salutary recommendations of the NPC to bring about the required changes in police performance and behaviour pattern had been made. He stressed that proper implementation of the recommendations of the NPC will amount to not only curbing many of the existing powers of misuse by the police but also by the controllers of the police — the political executives and the bureaucracy. I had not expected the report to be accepted at once, even though the Home Minister had recommended it.

While we in India ignored the recommendations of the NPC, Pakistan picked up some of the recommendations and implemented them. K.S. Dhillon, the former DG police of Punjab, in his excellent survey of police reforms in Pakistan, stated:

> "Pakistan has now clearly stolen a march over India by introducing major reforms in the organisation, structure and working of its police, with a view to fully depoliticising it. Ironically, most of the reforms are based on the recommendations of our own NPC. While we have only allowed the eight excellent reports submitted by the NPC to gather dust, Pakistan has quietly gone ahead and freed their police from political control by enacting the Pakistan Police Ordinance 2001."

When successive governments at the Centre and the states did not implement the recommendations of the NPC, Prakash Singh, former DG BSF filed a PIL in 1996 in the Supreme Court for the implementation of the Police Commission report.[1] In the meantime, the government appointed three committees to go into police reforms, including the Justice V.S. Malimath Commission for expediting the trial of criminal cases. I took an active interest in the work of this Commission as the subject has always been of concern to me.

It was the aim of the NPC to raise the status of the police in such a way that the common cause was served in good measure by an impartial performance. It is a strange feature of the government that it wants to push down the police, but keeps on asking and expecting more and more from them in performance.

I feel that events would eventually compel the states to insulate the police from political and other pressures and take other measures to improve its performance.

---

[1]On 22 September 2006 the Supreme Court delivered the judgement in the PIL instructing Central and state governments to comply with a set of seven directions laying down practical mechanisms to kickstart police reforms. It ordered the establishment of three institutions at the state level to insulate police from extraneous influences, according functional autonomy and ensuring accountability. Ten states have wholly or almost wholly complied with the directions of the Supreme Court. Nine states have passed laws or ordinances to circumvent implementation. Three states have taken the stand that the Court's directions are inconsistent with the statutory provisions in existence.

CASES OF PATNA

7. I detail below some typical cases. They may have incomplete data, even wrong facts, but we should look into them because the effect of it on crime and law and order can be appreciable. I must emphasise again that each case has to be checked from the court record, which I have not seen. I have gone only by the jail record and conversations with jail and police officials at Patna and Muzaffarpur and the District Magistrate joined us at Muzaffarpur:

(i) Hussainara Khatoon: Seven years ago she ran away with her family from Dacca after the crackdown by Yahya's forces, and was arrested and sent to "protective custody". She carries about with her the tattered paper - the distintegrating jail ticket - all that protects her from total rejection by the system and permanent incarceration. She has spent four years in jail although instructions have been issued that all those who were arrested under the Foreigners Act coming from Bangladesh should be released on a bond. She looks neat, clean, well-adjusted to the jail, and one wonders why she wants to go back when she is held only in protective custody. But you have to ask her.

... 6

A page from Rustamji's tour note number fifteen of December 1978, in which Hussainara Khatoon's case is mentioned. She was made the main plaintiff in the first PIL case. See footnote on facing page.

24

I Started the PIL[1]

I am sure it will come as a surprise to many, especially the anti-police types, that PIL which started the phenomenon of judicial activism in this country, came into existence due to the efforts of a policeman.

It all began in Bihar in December 1978 when, as a member of the NPC, I went to study problems in that state, where, apart from caste, there was everything in human beings to make you feel joyous.

I took time off while my colleagues were busy with police work to see what was happening in the jails of Patna and Muzaffarpur. Before going to Bihar I had seen how callously the system had treated undertrials in Karnataka and Maharashtra, two well run states. The visit to the jails of Bihar made me froth with indignation at what man could do to man, woman and child.

---

[1]This chapter has excerpts from Rustamji's tour note number fifteen of December 1978 and an article written by him in March 1994 under the heading, 'Undertrials for How Long? – The Inhumanity of What Man can do to His Fellowmen.' In law journals, the case is reported in Hussainara Khatoon and others vs State of Bihar (AIR 1979 SC 1360). The judgement delivered by Justice P.N. Bhagwati, R.S. Pathak and A.D. Koshal does not refer to Rustamji by name though reference is given to the two articles published by him in *The Indian Express* of 8 and 9 January 1979. However some websites and books have given credit to him for the first PIL. In my first interview I asked Rustamji what his main achievements were. He mentioned the PIL, his role in the Quit India Movement and raising the BSF (in that order).

One by one I called out those who had been longest in the jails as undertrials. The DM, the SP and the jail staff, all cooperated because I was dealing with a problem of human misery that all could see. They all felt that something needed to be done, but none could say what should be done. I myself was astonished to see the magnitude and barbarity of the problem. There were thousands of people caught in a cruel system, not knowing what to do, how to get out of the clutches of the law. I fell back on my usual method of dealing with such situations. The same method I adopted at the time of the Vinoba Bhave mission to the Chambal region in 1960. I felt the best course would be to expose what was happening, build up media support, and finally the genius of Indian people would do the rest.

I came to the conclusion that the majority of people in our jails ought not to be there and the majority who ought to be there are outside living as free men. After the visit to the jails, I dipped my pen in venom and sketched out the stories of some of the worst cases to show how oppressive and defenceless our criminal justice system had become for the poor, and how much the blame lay with policemen, administrators, judicial officers and politicians who tolerated such cruelties. I reproduced a few of them:

Hussainara Khatoon: In 1971 she ran away with her family from Dacca after the crackdown by Gen Yahya Khan's forces and was arrested and sent to 'protective custody'. She carried with her the tattered paper — the disintegrating jail ticket — all that protected her from total rejection by the system and permanent incarceration. She had spent four years in jail although instructions had been issued that all those who were arrested under the Foreigners' Act coming from Bangladesh should be released on a bond. She looked neat, clean, well adjusted to the jail and one wondered why she wanted to go back since she was only held in protective custody. But you had to ask her.

Itwaria Ahir: The woman was completely vague about what had happened to her. She behaved as if some big object had struck her and she did not know what to do and why it occurred. Even the jail authorities did not know what the charges against her were. The police could offer a vague explanation. She had apparently been sent to prison under Section 171 of Criminal Procedure Code (CrPC) because she refused to give an undertaking, or could not give a bond to appear as a witness in a case. Five years for that. She had a child aged four, a girl born in jail, innocent and beautiful. What had the little girl done to deserve the treatment we had given her?

Bhola Mahto: His jail ticket showed that he was arrested under Section 363, 368 of the IPC. He did not remember how long he had been in prison — probably nine years, perhaps thirteen. He had lost count of the years. For the previous six years it had not been possible to find out which criminal case he was wanted in. His file was untraceable. In the meantime he had lost his wife and son. In a peculiar sort of a way he got adjusted to jail. He said to me, "Whatever happens, will happen. Man struggles vainly in the web of destiny."[2]

Devkali: A Pasi (scheduled caste) girl who was arrested in a case of dacoity five years ago. Whether this poor, bashful creature, still tearful at the mention of her connection with the case, could ever have committed a dacoity was a matter of conjecture and evidence. Was it possible that caste operated against her too, and the people who were against her father or her brothers had put her in jail? Whatever be the case, I shall never forget the sight of that shy, frightened girl, said to be a dacoit, unable to tell why she was in jail, unable to comprehend the ways of his majesty called law. Her eyes have haunted me ever since I saw her. "Forgive me," I said sadly to her as she walked away crestfallen, "I can do nothing for you."

Reena Kumari of Burdwan: She did not know what the charge against her was, but presumably it was soliciting. She was arrested in 1976 and sent to a protection home, which was closed down. She then went to an aftercare home and from there she was sent to jail, because she was a lost person who had no home. Here was a little girl, almost a child, lost, defenceless, fighting against a blind system,

---

[2]In its judgement, the Supreme Court gave direction to the local High Court to ensure quick trial in this sessions case. With respect to other cases, the court pulled up the police and enjoined them to complete their investigations in three months.

without knowing how to fight and with nobody to help her. Her jail ticket showed 24/11, 4/12, 8/12. She was taken to court on these days. Each time the court had no time to see her.

Lalji Pande: He had been in jail for ten years. The girl whom he was alleged to have kidnapped was in the same jail. He wanted to marry her. I was told he was courting her secretly, carrying food for her and a few words of love for a minute or two in the gloom of prison. She was believed to be agreeable. But how would one manage a situation of this type under the law? You needed a Hindi filmmaker to give ideas.

Jhagrimusma Kori: The old woman had been in jail for nine years for a case of attempt to murder. For seven years her little son lived with her but he died at the age of thirteen. When I looked at her, I wondered why the state should condemn a woman of that age to such degradation. Why should a person have to wait for nine years under hard conditions to get her case heard by the court? What big outbreak of crime did the police expect if an old woman like her was sent out on personal bond?

Janki Devi: A young scheduled caste girl who had been in jail for seven years as an undertrial. She looked like a dark beauty; frightened, shy, despairing. She had been prosecuted for infanticide of her newborn child, who she maintained was stillborn and the villagers conspired to give evidence against her. There was a son with her, who had spent his entire life in jail. He did not seem to have seen the outside world. He was an ill-starred citizen of this land. How can one reconstruct the tragedy of this mother and son? How could one look back and find out what happened? Perhaps she was raped and did not want the child of the man who had humiliated her. Perhaps she was desired by someone else and since she would not agree, he had sent her to jail in revenge. Perhaps it was her caste — she was a Chamar — and therefore unqualified for police protection. Seven years was a long time of pain and agony for a woman accused of killing her own child. What damage would occur to society if she were sent out, with or without a bond: just to live?

The day the account of the undertrials appeared in *The Indian Express* I got a telephone call:
"I am Kapila Hingorani. I read your account of the undertrials of Bihar and it brought tears to my eyes. Several lawyers and judges feel that this is a case for an independent petition. The Chief Justice of India is prepared to take up the case if you are willing to give an affidavit regarding the facts."

I signed the two articles and sent it to her; the rest, as they say, is history. A compassionate judge (Justice P.N. Bhagwati) took up the matter, passed comprehensive orders and in consequence 40,000 undertrials were released all over India. A new hope in litigation appeared.

In times of yore, whenever a subject felt aggrieved, he could ring the bell hung at the gate of the palace or fort of the king and he was given an audience and his grievance heard. A new and unique method of ringing the bell of justice has been tried in the shape of the PIL and found worthy. Its only defect seems to be that there are too many cases, some frivolous perhaps, resulting in some abuse of the system.

The surfeit of PIL cases has in turn given rise to the phenomenon of judicial activism, which has resulted in the feeling that the judiciary is extending its wings over matters which are purely functions of the executive or the legislature. But I feel the judiciary in this country knows its limits. As the former Chief Justice of India, Justice A.M. Ahmedi has put it very succinctly, "...By virtue of the fact that the present situation is a corrective measure, the phenomenon of judicial activism in its aggressive role will have to be a temporary one. Fears of judicial tyranny are really quite unfounded, because judges themselves are aware of the fact that the non-elected judiciary is neither meant nor equipped to act as a policymaking body."

5.2.91

I wish I had not got the Padma Vibhushan. What have I done to deserve it? Everyone talks of belated recognition.

"I wish had not got the Padma Vibhushan. What have I done do deserve it? Everyone talks of belated recognition."

An entry in Rustamji's diary of 5 February 1991.

The BSF and Rustamji played a major part in the Indo-Pak War of 1971, more particularly, the liberation of Bangladesh. While the three service chiefs were awarded the Padma Vibhushan, Rustamji was given the Padma Bhushan. According to some officers, Rustamji made no secret of his unhappiness. His words 'belated recognition' probably refer to this aspect. It is common knowledge that a lot of lobbying goes into getting national level honours or denying such honours to others. Though the Prime Minister and the Defence Secretary appreciated his role and that of the BSF, I learnt that pressures from other quarters denied him the Padma Vibhushan.

25

Honours and Old Age

The decision to leave New Delhi and move to Bombay in 1989 did not upset me as much as I thought it would. Naju's parents had a flat on Grant Road which was given to them on a nominal rent by the Parsee Panchayat and after their death it was transferred in Naju's name. The flat was redesigned and made comfortable. It was overcrowded with furniture. I had a room for myself, where I could work in peace.

Thanks to Nusli Wadia of Bombay Dyeing, I got a job as Advisor in his company at the age of seventy-three, with some pay and perks. I had an office to go to and a good room to work in and all the time in the world to write as there was hardly any work.

I was accepted very well by the police officers of Bombay. It was a nice gesture on their part to keep inviting me to their functions and to give me the respect due to a retired senior officer, though I did not belong to their cadre. I had, of course, served for some years in places which are now part of Maharashtra.

Early next year, *The Post* carried a news item that I was tipped for Governorship of Jammu and Kashmir. The item seemed to have emanated from the Ministry of Home Affairs. On 12 February 1990, I got a call from the Prime Minister's Secretary: "Would you agree to being shortlisted for Governorship?"

"Where?" I asked.

"There are four vacancies," he said. "Tamil Nadu, Karnataka, Goa and Gujarat."

"Yes," I said.

And at once I was seized with deep anxiety. Am I doing the right thing? Naju seemed upset because, like every Bombayite, she was happy to be back in Bombay, her hometown. After a year's stay in Bombay, she said, "These have been the happiest days of my life." I waited for some written orders from the government but none came.

I felt old age has no takers. My disappointments started increasing. Around the same time a doctor had given me an appointment, but when I went to him, he said, "I have no time today." I was not used to being treated like that. The incident rankled so much in my mind that I didn't sleep that night. There were some other such incidents when people far junior to me kept casting remarks which hurt. A feeling of being unwanted started creeping in, but I took it all with equanimity.

In the midst of such feelings, I was truly amazed when, suddenly in January 1991, a friend from Delhi informed me that my name was on the list of awardees on the occasion of the Republic Day. What had I done to deserve it? Then when an income tax officer came to the house to conduct the routine checks which precede such awards, the news was confirmed. I said to Naju, "There is some mistake. They have not realised that I have already got the Padma Bhushan."

"Can they give you something less?" Naju asked.

"They could," I said, "though they have never done it in the past. They could give me a Padma Shri on the ground that my present work in journalism qualified me for it. A Padma Shri is given to sportsmen, artistes, men of letters and others who have distinguished themselves in their professions." In my heart of hearts I felt joyous that my writing had been recognised.

In the evening, when Naju turned on the TV, I found that I had been awarded the Padma Vibhushan. 'For what?' I kept asking myself. For years when I strove for recognition, nothing came my way. Now when I had turned my back to it, it came in abundant measure. For several weeks I kept thinking, 'I wish I had not got the Padma Vibhushan. What have I done to deserve it? Everyone talks of belated recognition.'[1]

---

[1]Rustamji was awarded the Padma Vibhushan for his work related to social causes.

Accompanied by Naju and Kerman, I went to the investiture ceremony at Rashtrapati Bhavan on 23 March 1991. It was preceded by a rehearsal. In a glittering and well organised ceremony, the first name to be called out was I.G. Patel, former Governor of the Reserve Bank of India. Then my name came. President Venkataraman said a few kind words and I thanked him. After the investiture, there was tea where we met Prime Minister Chandrashekar and others. Kerman and Naju spoke at length with Sonia Gandhi. I must confess I have never seen a Western woman tie a sari as gracefully as she does. Rajiv seemed a bit silent. The Vice-President, Dr Shankar Dayal Sharma whom we knew from Bhopal was very friendly and communicative.

The Prime Minister wanted me to take over as a member of the Minorities Commission and later, after a year, to become the Chairman. This was probably a result of all that I was writing for the protection of the minorities, particularly, the Sikhs and the Muslims.

I received several accolades in the course of my long retired life. I was invited very often to deliver lectures at prestigious institutions and flattering words were said about me. But a few regrets remained. Among them the greatest was that none of my plays had been performed on stage. I had written novels and short stories but they were not accepted for publication. These small things depressed me in my old age. I had all the advantages — a good job, a good wife, a place to live and work but small disappointments appeared to make me a total wreck. I presume my ego was to blame.

There were a series of deaths in the family. First, it was my brother Rustam, who passed away in February 1991. We were all at his bedside when the end came — it was peaceful. He wanted a cremation, so the ceremonies were done in the house and all participated. As I drove with the body in the hearse, memories came flooding back to me. He loved public speaking and was a brilliant orator. He trained us all. He loved beauty in all its forms. As a collector of artefacts, he built up an unique collection. What marked his life was his complete devotion to his family. Nothing else mattered.

And then in February 1999, Cyrus rang up to inform us about the death of Minoo, the husband of Naju's sister, Coomi in Toronto.

I broke down completely when I heard the news of the death of the man whom I loved and respected, who had helped us a thousand times, always encouraged me to write, who was intellectually compatible and a firm friend. I cried as I had never cried for anyone else. What a friend! What a man! Minoo and Coomi, thou are the salt of the earth!

In 2001, the death of Naju's cousin, Behram Contractor (known as Busybee) affected both of us. He was editor of *The Afternoon Courier*, a delightful company, full of anecdotes and full of life. He and his wife Farzana were a source of great support to us. My column kept appearing in their daily.

What I looked forward to in my old age was my annual visit to Toronto. It was a great joy to be with Cyrus and his wife Namrita in their beautiful house girdled with pine trees. It was a pleasure exploring Toronto in the company of Minoo and Coomi.

At the age of eighty-two, when I was leading a peaceful retired life and when I had reasons to believe I had no enemies in the world, there was an attack on me at Worli.

On 4 June 1998, Naju and I went for a walk on the Worli Sea Face Road in the evening. We walked a bit and then sat down on a bench in front of the *dargah* (Muslim shrine). I walked across to a hawker selling coconuts and bought one. Suddenly from behind a man hit me on the shoulder with a lathi. We saw him distinctly. He was a short, stumpy man, wearing a beach cap and something wrapped round his waist and carrying a big lathi with which he hit me. He ran towards the hawker, who tried to grapple with him, threatened another man who stood in his path and ran away nimbly. He hit nobody else except me. I felt it was a trifling incident and we came home joking about it.

In the night when I went to bed, I felt he was not a mad man — he had some grouse. Who could single me — an old man — out of the hundreds who frequent that place for a lathi blow? Was there someone trying to send a message? Then it suddenly struck me that an article of mine had appeared in *The Mid Day* four days earlier in which I had severely criticised the ISI, the intelligence outfit of Pakistan. Could it have something to do with that?

I mentioned the matter to my friend, Arvind Inamdar, the DG Police of Maharashtra and to Ronnie Mendonca, the Commissioner of Police. They sent an Inspector to look into the incident. My police instincts seemed to tell me that the assailant was not a lunatic. Or was it a case of my thinking and instincts going wrong because I was the victim?

N.D.
12/1

The Imperishable Me.

One station before Pathankot, I stood at the door of my compartment, chafing at the delay that had occurred en route.

The train started. Then the attendant of the air conditioned coach — seemed to go off his head. He jumped and shouted

'Guard — station master — stop the train. Stop or there will be an accident

He then jumped up to my compartment and pulled the alarm chain, and as I had never done that before, I too gave him a hand.

The train stopped. The guard came to me frowning angrily. Then he changed — Apparently the brake of the compartment ahead of me had separated from its ~~coupl~~ coupling and fallen on the wheel, and if we had gone fast the carriage might have got derailed.

At Pathankot a railway officer came and congratulated me.

"The Imperishable Me" Rustamji escaped death several times. He wrote detailed accounts of his escapes in his diaries.

26

The Imperishable Me

Like the proverbial cat I have had nine lives — maybe even more. Some of the escapes were providential. Probably I was destined to live longer.

The first escape was in the winter of 1938, when I was under training in Saugor. I got a horse to ride which was earlier used for racing. Whenever he came into an open field, it was difficult to hold him. One day he ran away with me and in taking a *nullah*, both of us came down and I passed out for the first time in my life. Luckily the Police Lines was close by. I was carried there and the doctor said that though there did not appear to be any damage, he advised rest as my back was aching very much.

I had earlier planned to go with the DC, Jaya Rao and the District Judge, Bose (a cousin of Netaji Subhas Chandra Bose) to Jubbulpore for the weekend. Both of them came to see me in the hospital and felt sorry that I would not be able to accompany them. On their way to Jubbulpore, they met with an accident and both were killed.

A horse had saved me.

❧

I have described earlier how I was fired upon by an English officer of the Mahar Regiment with a Tommy gun in a grain godown during the Civil Disobedience Movement in 1942 in Nagpur. It is difficult to forget the experience of bullets whizzing past you. I can still remember how I shouted with fear. Three shots were fired. They missed me narrowly.

It was nine o'clock in the morning on 21 July 1956. All was quiet in the peaceful countryside of Cutch. Suddenly the earth shook, the walls crashed, and houses collapsed. The severe earthquake in Anjar and surrounding areas had caused a lot of damage.

Prime Minister Nehru visited Anjar and from there went to Adipur, where the Sindhi refugees had put up a beautiful township. After lunch we left for Kandla port. As usual we got delayed because the organisers had squeezed in too much into the programme and Nehru was not prepared to cut it down because it would have been an aspersion on his age and physical fitness.

From Ratnal village we changed on to a jeep as the next village, which had suffered the earthquake damage, was twenty miles in the interior. The Chief Commissioner of Cutch (Ghatge) took it upon himself to drive the jeep. Lal Bahadur Shastri sat next to him, and Nehru occupied the end seat in the front row. I sat behind Nehru and next to me was Bhimji Khemji, MP.

We were already an hour behind time, and Ghatge tried to make up a part of it. We sped along rapidly in the jeep, across grassy hilly plains. Partridges went darting across the road. Nehru was in a talkative mood. He asked me, "Rustamji, what do you call a *chaha* in English?" I said, "Bustard." (Later on, I checked up, I was wrong.)[1]

Nehru was saying, "You need good eyes to see where the road is," when suddenly the jeep took a turn in the sandy road, skidded, hit a mound and slowly turned over on its side. As we went over both Nehru and I said,"*Theek hai, Theek hai.*" (It's okay, it's okay).

The jeep crashed on the side on which the Prime Minister and I were seated. We lay on the ground side by side. I wondered how much more the jeep would fall. Would it go completely over and crush us beneath it? Shastri fell on Nehru and nimbly went

[1] A *chaha* is a snipe, which belongs to the family of partridges.

over him. The MP fell over me with a heavy thud, accompanied by two large jars of water, the pillows and tools in the jeep and an assorted number of raincoats.

We lay on the ground quite comfortably for some time. I drew a sigh of relief that nobody seemed hurt.

The men of the escort car came running, and I shouted at them. "Hold the jeep, hold the jeep." I was afraid that the vehicle would tilt over. Nehru said, "Don't shout! I am perfectly alright. I am not hurt at all."

First they pulled the Prime Minister out from under the vehicle and then Khemji and the water jars followed. Lastly, I was pulled out.

Panditji stood on the ledge of the road (even in a moment of crisis he had selected a high piece of ground to stand on), shakily lighting a cigarette, but laughing heartily. "It was very lucky that the small weight of Lal Bahadur fell on me," he said. And then, "I came to Cutch to see an earthquake, and had a minor one of my own."

We could have left the jeep where it was but Nehru insisted that we set it right before going. So, all of us lifted the jeep out, and put it on its wheels again.

Nehru had received a small bruise on his hand, which was attended to by the doctor in the next village. We started again in another jeep. I told the Prime Minister, "Sir, your luck is still holding out. If the jeep had turned over, we would've been finished."

Even though all of us laughed and joked about it, each one of us knew that it had been a providential escape.

⁂

Early morning of 26 February 1957, Prime Minister Nehru took off from Mangalore for Raipur in Madhya Pradesh in an Ilyushin aircraft, *Meghdoot*, which was presented to him by the Prime Minister of the Soviet Union, N. Bulganin.

At nine, I woke up. Suddenly, I heard a dull thud and the drone of the engine changed. I looked out. Smoke and flames were coming out of the port engine. I jumped out of my seat and rushed to the cockpit.

The flight engineer (Warrant Officer Paddington) was standing near the captain of the aircraft, R.A. Rufus. "Rufus," I shouted above the din of the aircraft, "Your engine is on fire."

Sq Ldr Rufus looked back at me. His face was strained. "Yes sir, we have received the warning and applied the extinguisher." Paddington explained that the fire had been put out, and the port engine was out of commission. Rufus added that we would have to land at Hyderabad.

I went back. While I was away, my companions had seen the flames grow bigger and bigger and literally eat up the metal of the cowling. They looked at me with anxious faces. "We had a fire which has been put out," I told them.

I realised that we were in a difficult situation. If this was a sabotage, I reasoned, the second engine too would fail, and then it would be death for all of us. The Prime Minister must be warned.

I went to him and said in as normal voice as I could muster, with a bit of a smile, to hide the fright in me, "I am afraid we are having some trouble with one engine. A fire or something. The fire has been put out, but that means we have only one engine. This will upset your tour, as we don't know whether another aircraft would be available immediately, but I don't want to bother the crew about this just now."

The Prime Minister smiled a wee bit, "Where are we now?"

"Somewhere in Hyderabad State, I think," I said, forgetting that there was no longer a Hyderabad State in existence.

He continued to read his book. He was completely unperturbed. I went back to the skipper and asked him exactly where we were. Jaya, the navigator who was standing near him said that we were about twenty miles from Raichur.

"Why not land at Raichur?" I said. "Wouldn't it be best to get down as quickly as possible?"

Jaya said that Raichur was marked in his register of landing strips, but he was not sure whether it was in good condition. Rufus said it would be unsafe to come down, as going up again in case the strip was unsuitable, with a single engine, would pose problems. Eventually he decided that he would have a look at the strip from the air, and see if it was in a good condition. If so, he would land.

Soon after the captain sent word that he would land at Raichur. We should strap up our safety belts and not move about.

What were the thoughts in those minutes when death seemed near us? I felt that the chances of our getting out of this alive were fifty-fifty. We were quite excited. Even the Prime Minister who tried his best to appear calm, showed it. But there was not the slightest sign of panic or helplessness. In fact, one's sensibilities were alert, very alert. It was a time for alertness. 'If this is a sabotage,' I kept on saying to myself, 'the other engine will also pack up. You must think out what you must do in case the aircraft begins to hurtle downwards. If the fire has not been completely extinguished, it may reach the fuel tank and then the plane will explode. We wouldn't even feel it. But what about those we leave behind?'

In those minutes, when I stood at the bar of eternity, waiting to hear the verdict of life or death, my thoughts were all with Naju and Kerman. What will happen to them? Poor Naju, I know she would miss me terribly. I wondered if Kerman would remember me when she grew up. What would Mummy and all the folks in Nagpur think? To all of them, even to my best friends, it would not be a serious loss, but for Naju, it would be difficult to bear.

We were circling over the airstrip at Raichur. Down below someone was driving the cattle away. The aircraft banked; we held our breaths.

'What is Nehru thinking about?' I wondered. He was happily chatting with B.R. Vats, the correspondent of the PTI, giving him an account of another plane mishap in which the tyre of the plane had burst on landing and the plane circled round and round before coming to a stop.

We were now coming in to land. But still the undercarriage was not released. Had Rufus forgotten?

Then just before we came down on the ground, there was a shudder. The aircraft tilted to one side. We clutched our seats desperately. The undercarriage came out and we could see the ground flying rapidly past the window.

"We are safe," I announced loudly and immediately the tension was released and everyone started laughing.

A court of enquiry was held into the cause of the accident. But, I felt, what no court can find is what saved us! Was it God, destiny, our luck, or chance? Whatever it was, I felt, the whole episode we passed through must teach me humility and fearlessness.

B.N. Mullik, Director IB, attached a great deal of importance to the performance of one's duty and the *Gita*, which was the mainspring of his thinking, was often quoted to us. A sense of duty probably saved us on many occasions.

In 1957, when I was CSO to the Prime Minister, I returned home in the evening from a tour very tired. I was also feeling feverish. At about ten o'clock in the night, the telephone rang and the Director IB said that an attempt had been made to derail a Very Important Person (VIP) special on the Baroda-Bombay railway line and would I go over and look into it immediately? My wife with her lip and hand movement signalled me to say, 'I have just come back. I am not well. I will go tomorrow.'

Mullik's voice and instructions were so firm that I could not muster the courage to suggest it. In a mood of depression I took the last flight to Bombay. Had I temporised with duty, it would have meant death. The flight I would have caught early next morning crashed while landing, killing all the passengers on board.

During the Indo-Pak War of 1965, four Sabre jets of the PAF came down and rocketed the road from Jammu to Amritsar. Terence Quinn and I had a narrow escape. This incident has been described earlier.

In the first week of February 1966, after a meeting regarding withdrawal of armed forces from the borders, I went from Jammu to Srinagar, to keep in touch with the events in the valley and also to find out how the boys were standing up to the cold and snow.

The Hajipir Pass, which was captured by Indian troops and which had spelt death in many an Indian home, was to be handed over to Pakistan as per the Tashkent agreement. Gen Kalhan was very keen that I should see Hajipir before my return to New Delhi. "You can still do it, only go a day later to Delhi," he said.

I told him that I could not change my plan for returning to Delhi on Sunday as I had an "important appointment" the next day, 7 February 1966.

On the 7th, the Fokker took off from Srinagar at 11:20 a.m. and eighteen minutes later was reported missing with thirty-three passengers and a crew of four. One of the control room boys came and gave me the teleprinter slip that the Fokker from Srinagar was missing. I got a queer feeling of having become loose all over. What a close shave! I wondered what must it be like when the end comes? What does one do if one is not given to praying like me? I suppose one takes the names of those who matter, and in a moment all is over. Unless the plane begins to drop and there are screams and panic and then oblivion.

I told Mrs Indira Gandhi in my first meeting with her after she became Prime Minister about the incident and that I had hurried back in order to keep the appointment with her. She looked up at me with her large beautiful eyes and with a smile said, "I've saved your life, then?"

"It seems like it," I said.

❧

In January 1967, one station before Pathankot, I stood at the door of my compartment, distressed at the delay that had occurred en route.

The train started. Then the attendant of the air-conditioned coach seemed to go off his head. He jumped and shouted "Guard! Station Master! Stop the train! Stop or there will be an accident!"

He then jumped up to my compartment and pulled the alarm chain and I too gave him a hand.

The train stopped. The guard came to us, frowning testily. Then he changed. Apparently the brake of the compartment ahead of us had separated from its coupling and fallen. If we had gone fast, the carriage might have got derailed.

At Pathankot a railway officer came and congratulated me.

In May 1968, I boarded a flight to Calcutta. There were only three of us in the *Dakota* aircraft — an elderly couple and I. It all began with one or two small bumps. Then the plane was thrown about like a toy. Dark clouds through which we were passing made it dark in the aircraft.

The old woman had been strapped to the seat with her legs up. She looked like a nice tidy packet for the next world. The old man moaned in broken English as the plane bumped and appeared to be determined to die like a true Bengali — complaining till the last against the government.

We came down low and were rocked so badly that we went higher. Then we tilted to the side and we all leaned over to the other side, hopeful that our little support to the captain would help him balance the *Dakota* and keep the plane on even keel.

We were close to Dum Dum. Again we soared up at a tilt. Lightning flashes had left out nothing to make the final act really dramatic.

'It would be the end any moment'. 'Nice short casualty list,' I said to myself. The two poor oldies would hardly get a mention. A lot of people will say what a good chap I was.

The only persons who would really lament would be one's own family. Poor Naju would become a beautiful widow. The children would miss me. Their mother would hang up a picture of mine in the drawing room and a garland would be placed over the frame and God's good wishes invoked. The real worry to me was — would Naju be able to manage our financial affairs? In dying, I only wished that my wife and kids would look after themselves properly.

Regarding my mother, brother and other members of the family, I decided to only think of them when the final crash came.

It didn't. Suddenly we emerged though the clouds and safely landed on a wet and windy Dum Dum airstrip.

ক্ষ

In conclusion, I would like to relate an amusing conversation. In 1999 I had gone to Bhopal and was staying in the Police Officers' Mess. The beautiful building, which was known as Abgina Bungalow, is situated on the bank of the Lower Lake. There were two tennis courts in its large compound and was purchased for less than two and half lakhs of rupees from the proprietor of the erstwhile Bhopal Cotton Mills in 1963 when I was IG Police of the state.

In the evening, Naju and I went for a walk on the road along the lake. We saw a group of constables and started talking to them. I asked them if they knew Nagu Sahib. One of them said, "*Haan Sahib, bahut achche officer the. Woh gujar gaye.*" (Yes Sir, he was a very good officer. He passed away.) Then I said, "*Ek Rustamji the, unka kya hua*?" (There was one Rustamji, what's happened to him?) The man said, "*Haan, woh bahut purane the, kabke chal basey honge.*" (Yes, he was there much earlier. He must have died long back.)

Naju was livid. I patted her, "Darling, calm down. Nobody is remembered forever."

Police force mourns Rustomji's demise

EXPRESS NEWS SERVICE
MARCH 3

**Khusroo F Rustamji
1917-2003**

IN THE last 24 hours, policemen from every nook and corner of India have been calling up the Rustamjis with choked voices and restrained emotions. Such was the love and respect they had for the founder director general of the Border Security Force, Khusroo F Rustamji, who died of a heart attack on Sunday.

He was 86 and his funeral at Chandanwadi crematorium was conducted with full police honours — 28 years after he retired from service.

"My father was indeed a father figure to the entire force. Police officers have been ringing up to say that they feel like they have lost their own father," says the ex-IGP's daughter, Kerman Rustamji.

A strapping 6 feet, 2 inches tall, Rustamji was fit and athletic even in his 80s. Having served as the IG of Madhya Pradesh during the height of the dreaded *daaku raj* between 1958-65, Rustamji was also the founder director general of the Border Security Force from 1965-74.

"Even after retirement, he kept writing articles in newspapers on social reforms. For example, he highlighted the plight of 5,000 undertrials in Tihar jail, some of whom were waiting for a basic court hearing for as long as 20 years," Kerman points out.

For his social and humanitarian causes, Rustamji was honoured with a Padma Vibhushan in 1991. Earlier in 1971, he received a Padma Bhushan for the exemplary work done in forming the new Border Security Force for the country.

Rustamji had joined the IPS in 1938. During his distinguished tenure in the police, he was also in charge of Pandit Jawaharlal Nehru's personal security. He was also a member of the Justice V S Malimath Commission that delved upon police reforms.

Cutting from *The Indian Express* of 4 March 2003.

Epilogue[1]

My father suffered for fourteen days before he died on 2 March 2003. My mother was gravely ill for fourteen years before she united with him on 22 September 2005.

In the middle of February 2003, my father developed a severe backache after he tried to lift my mother who had fallen down. In the last week of February I was asked to come down to Mumbai immediately as Dad's condition had taken a turn for the worse. He was taken to the hospital and tests were done. The MRI scan revealed that a nerve had got pinched between the vertebrae, causing him acute pain. He was advised complete bed rest as the doctor feared that, due to his age, he might not be able to walk again. He was not even permitted to sit down.

The one place he detested to be in was the hospital. All his life he had enjoyed good health and was never admitted in a hospital. He refused to stay confined to his bed in the hospital and got angrier and angrier, day by day. He kept shouting at everybody. On 1 March, he told me he was sick of having hospital food and wanted to have 'roti', 'dal', 'fried fish', and 'palak bhaji'. He was always a frugal eater, but he enjoyed the meal prepared at home.

In the evening he watched the entire World Cup cricket match between India and Pakistan in South Africa, which ended late at night.

---

[1]This epilogue is written by Kerman, Rustamji's daughter.

He was happy that India beat Pakistan and his favourite batsman Virendra Sehwag played well. When going to bed he expressed regrets repeatedly that Sachin Tendulkar had missed his century.

An hour after midnight, he called for the bedpan and then went to sleep again. At about four o'clock in the morning, I got a call from the hospital asking me to come immediately. I thought he was again creating problems for the hospital staff wanting to go home. When I reached the hospital at 4:30 a.m. the doctor on duty said, "He's gone."

"Gone where?" I asked, thinking he must have walked away from the hospital.

The doctor repeated, "He's gone."

I rang up my cousins and we brought the body home at 8:30 a.m. in a police van.

News of the death spread fast. A large number of senior officers of Mumbai came over to the house to pay their respects. The house was full of relatives and friends, but what surprised all of us was the huge collection of servants, sweepers, constables and other workers near our flat. They were all weeping and relating how my father had helped them.

As per my father's wishes, his body was taken for cremation. He was against the Parsee way of disposal of the dead, which he felt was anachronistic. He was taken to the Chandanwadi crematorium where he was cremated with full police honours. His favourite force, the BSF which he had raised, sent wreaths to be placed on the body. Cyrus was on his way to India and he had halted at Brussels, where he was informed about father's death. As it would have taken him several hours to reach Mumbai, we went ahead with the cremation.

Parsees have a function on the fourth day, called 'chautha'. The ceremony starts at four o'clock in the morning with prayers. There was heavy thunder and lightning at that time, although March is not a usually month when it rains in Mumbai. When I woke up on the morning of the next day, I saw a white dove sitting on the window sill. White doves are a rare sight in Mumbai. The priest told us that it was a message that the soul had left the earth. My father never went to a temple or agiary, but it was his wish that Hindu rites be followed in his death. We took the ashes and went by boat and immersed them in the sea.

As days passed, my mother started feeling the loss of her husband. In another five days time they would have celebrated their fifty-eigth marriage anniversary though my mother would have called it the fifty-ninth. As my mother once wrote to my father, "We got married on 7 March 1945. But from the moment I met you for the first time on 2 May 1944 I gave my heart to you and for a woman that means marriage."

My mother suffered from diabetes and due to the failure of her kidneys, she had to undergo dialysis twice a week. She had undergone heart surgery a few years earlier. In his last years my father was more concerned about her health than his own. The two-and-a-half years' period after his death was a difficult one for her. I went to Mumbai from Hyderabad frequently to be with her as she was unable to bear the loneliness. She developed a stomach ulcer which burst. She was rushed to Jaslok Hospital and due to her frail health, she did not survive. She was also cremated and her remains were immersed in the sea. I am sure, even in death, my mother and father are united. They were a devoted couple.

In 1954, my father had gone to China with Pandit Nehru. He had put on a new suit, which he got stitched in Delhi, for the dinner hosted by Chairman Mao Zedong. When he put his hand in his pocket, he found a piece of paper. The message written on it read, "Wherever you are, my dear, always remember there is someone waiting for you with love and faith. – Naju."

Appendix I

INTELLIGENCE BUREAU (HOME DEPARTMENT)
Government of India
New Delhi, dated 8 July 1942

My dear Scott,

A suggestion has recently been put up to me that the present time provides good opportunities for attaching an I.P. officer to the British Embassy at Chungking as an observer. The grounds for this suggestion – and I am in full agreement with them – are briefly that our present position in regard to intelligence about Chinese affairs is weak and some form of provision for the future seems due. The barriers, whether physical or cultural, between India and China are tending always, however slowly at present, towards a stage when they will be largely broken down; and India will perhaps be faced with a Chinese problem of embarrassing proportions much sooner than is generally thought possible. A Police Attache or Observer at Chungking would help to build up the foundations of a store of knowledge about China on general and specific lines such as we do not at present possess and so in some measure help us to take stock of the first big impact.

I realise that the present is a bad time for asking you to spare an officer for this appointment but am risking a refusal as I feel you will agree that the subject is of sufficient importance to deserve serious attention.

It is proposed that if a suitable officer can be made available to go to Chungking, he should make as thorough a study as may be possible within a comparatively short period of Chinese affairs, customs, national characteristics, and so on, and qualify in some measure to be regarded as one on whom we could rely for advice on matters relating to the Chinese on return to India. Another, and we understand an important part of his functions, would be to make friendly contacts among the Chinese; the latter make a great ritual of friendship and will do a surprising amount to help a friend. But this naturally implies that the officer on his side must be prepared to live up to the obligations of friendship as understood by the Chinese.

The appointment will probably be for a period of not less than six months in the first instance, but more than that I cannot say as the proposal is as yet no more than a proposal and is likely to be pursued if there appears to be a chance of finding a suitable man. As regards the seniority of any possible nominee, I suggest ten to twelve years service.

Yours sincerely,

To: A.G. Scott, Esq., I.P.,

D. Pilditch

Appendix II

List of IP officers as per Civil List of 1965

1.	B.N. Mullik	Director IB
2.	D.P. Kohli	Director CBI
3.	S.P. Verma	Director IB from 1965
4.	A.R. Jayawant	
5.	Gurdial Singh	
6.	K.J. Nanavatty	
7.	Shanti Prasad	
8.	S.C. Misra	
9.	J.D.A. Pollock	
10.	B.B. Banerjee	
11.	S.M. Dutt	
12.	Upananda Mukherji	
13.	V.G. Kanetkar	
14.	S. N. Akhoury	
15.	S.M. Ghosh	
16.	A.K.K. Nambiar	
17.	M.A.H. Masood	
18.	D.G. Bhattacharya	
19.	Kunwar Shamsher Singh	
20.	Islam Ahmed	
21.	R.A.P. Sinha	
22.	T.N. Ghosh	
23.	P.K. Sen	
24.	Jia Ram	
25.	Baldev Singh	
26.	J.C. Ghosh	
27.	S.N. Hosali	
28.	J.D. Nagarwala	
29.	K.F. Rustamji	

Index

Abdullah, Sheikh 151, 272
Abraham 76
Adampur 333
Adi (Naju's nephew) 115
Adilabad 122, 136
Adipur 360
Afghanistan 58
Agartala 292, 298, 313, 314
Agra 168, 189, 197, 199, 219, 333
Agra University 4
Ahir, Itwaria 348
Ahluwalia, Shekhu 14
Ahmad, Tajuddin/Tajuddin xxxvi, 300 – 302, 304 – 306, 309 – 312, 327 – 329
Ahmed, Islam 199, 375
Ahmed, Khalil 324
Ahmed, Khondakar Mushtaq xxxvi, 321
Ahmedabad 152, 273, 282, 283
Ahmedi, A.M. (Justice) 351
Ahmednagar Fort Jail 95
Ajanta caves 234
Ajmer 211
Akhnoor 260, 261
Akhnoor-Chhamb sector 261
Akhoury, S.N. 375
Akola 121 – 127, 133, 158
Aland 137
Ali brothers 11
Ali, Hussain 309, 310
Ali, Mansoor (Capt) 304
Ali, Mir Laiq/Laiq Ali 123, 139
Ali, Mir Shaukat (Maj)/Shaukat 295, 314
Ali, Yusuf (Prof) 302
Alirajpur 236
Allahabad 152, 235
All India Radio/AIR 119, 231 – 233, 235, 236, 328
Amraoti 70, 73, 88, 89, 115, 116, 122
Amritlal/Babu Dilwala 157, 160, 167 – 173, 175
Amritsar 261 – 262, 273, 364,
Andaman Islands 13
Anjar 360
Arabian Sea 124
Armstrong, Louis 225
Arunachal Pradesh 220
Asia xvii, 221
Assam 77, 234, 245, 318
Atal, Jai Kumar 23, 25, 27, 28
Attlee, Clement 91, 98
Aurangabad xxiii, 29, 49, 122, 136 – 140, 146
Aurangzeb 109
Aurobindo, Sri xix
Australia 252
Awami League 290, 292, 294, 297, 299, 300, 301, 315 – 317, 321
Ayyar, Chandrasekar 167
Azad, Maulana 95

Babina cantonment 174
Bachchan, Jaya 156
Badri/Kirar, Badri 170 – 173
Baez, Joan 320
Bagdogra 313
Bagri, Maganlal 65, 70, 72
Bahawalpur 333
Bai, Putli 180, 185, 187
Baidyanath Tala 306
Bains, N.S. (Col) 305
Bajpai, K.S. 214
Bakhale, D.S. 136, 137
Bakshi, Ardhenu 312
Balurghat 298
Banda 35
Banerjee, B.B. 375
Bangalore 134, 289
Bangla Desh/Bangladesh xiv, xviii, 103, 251, 290, 291, 293, 298, 305 – 312, 314, 315, 318, 320, 321, 325 – 329, 335, 348, 352

Banihal 257
Banpur 299
Baramula 264
Barelal 173, 174, 176, 177
Barki 268
Barmer 261
Baroda 283, 364
Baroda (village) 65, 72
Basim/Washim 122, 125, 127, 129 – 132
Bassi, R.P. (Lt Col) 278
Bastar 237, 238
Basu, P.K. 248
Basu, S.C./Basu 307
Bay of Bengal 124
Benton, G.W. 64
Berar 18, 31, 122, 130, 132
Besant, Annie (Dr) 17
Bhaduri, Taroon Coomar 156, 199
Bhagwati, P.N. (Justice) 167, 347, 351
Bhakore 179
Bhakra 273
Bhasani, Maulana 305, 321, 328
Bhaskaran, P.V. 149
Bhatnagar, G.P. 251
Bhattacharya, D.G 375
Bhave, Acharya Vinoba 194 – 197, 200, 201, 204, 342, 348
Bhilai 23, 226
Bhind 157, 160, 162, 166, 167, 177 – 182, 186, 188, 191, 196, 200, 205
Bhopal xxiii, 41, 122, 156, 157, 161, 173, 177, 188, 207, 208, 211, 212, 214, 225, 226, 229, 238, 239, 247, 253, 355, 367
Bhubaneswar 228 – 230
Bhutto, Zulfiqar Ali/Bhutto 259, 288, 292, 293, 301, 310, 327
Bibi Nagar 137
Bihar xv, 217, 279, 280, 347, 351
Bijaipur 319
Bikaner State 4
Bilaspur 59
Bindu, Digambar Rao/Bindu 140
Bir/Beed 136,
Bombay/Mumbai xxi, 4, 5, 25, 28, 61, 80 – 85, 88, 94, 106, 120 – 122, 134, 140, 151, 152, 224, 225, 342, 353, 354, 364, 369 – 371
Bomdila 222, 224, 226
Bongaon 298, 313, 324
Border Security Force/BSF xiv, xvii, xviii, 76, 242, 243, 246 – 251, 253 – 255, 257, 270, 273 – 278, 280, 282 – 285, 287, 289, 291, 293, 294, 296, 299, 302, 305, 307, 309, 311, 313, 314, 317, 318, 320, 322 - 327, 329, 331 – 337, 345, 347, 352, 370
Bormaunt, S.M. 16
Bose, Netaji Subhas Chandra 328, 359
Boyra 324
Brahmanbaria 294, 296
Brig Oberoi 321, 322
Britain xvii, 12, 45, 56, 91, 94, 98, 101, 106 – 108, 111
Brussels 370
Buldana 125
Bulganin, N. 361
Bulgaria 282
Burdwan 349
Burj 334
Burma 78, 103
Burmaan 50, 51
Burrell, R.H.A. xxix, 24

Calcutta/Kolkata 15, 96, 144, 248, 268, 273, 280, 293, 300, 302, 305, 307 – 310, 312, 321, 323, 325, 328, 366
Cameron, James 320
Canada 309
Captain Cox 16
Caroe, Olaf 96
Cawashaw 4
Central Bureau of Investigation/CBI 285, 342, 375
Central Criminal Investigation Department 161
Central Forensic Science Laboratory/CFSL 147
Central Provinces 4, 18, 23, 31, 39, 53, 56, 69, 74, 94, 115 – 117, 122, 125, 131, 132, 134, 220
Central Reserve Police/CRP 244, 250, 275, 288, 294
Ceylon/Sri Lanka 103, 134, 303
Chambal 156, 157, 160, 161, 167, 175 – 178, 189, 197, 225, 348

Chamhodi 179
Chanda/Chandrapur 86 – 88, 122
Chandanwadi 370
Chandigarh 273
Chandrashekar 355
Charan, Ram 181, 187
Chari, T.A. 252
Chathankar, Vinayakrao 125
Chattarpur 166
Chattopadhyaya, S. 302
Chatterjee, Asim 280
Chatterjee, M.S. (Brig) 298
Chaudhuri, Benoy Kumar 23
Chaudhuri, J.N.(Gen) 133, 136 – 138, 244, 246, 258
Chauri Chaura 103
Chavan, Y.B. 255, 276, 285
Chelam, Daddy 76
Chevalier, Maurice 54
Chhattisgarh xiv, 121
Chhindwara 59, 198
China 101, 151, 220, 221, 223, 224, 226, 233, 243, 298, 300, 312, 316, 323, 371, 373
Chirenasta 179
Chitham, Charles C. (Sir) 29
Chittagong 293 – 298, 302, 312, 329
Chopra, P.N. 250, 251
Choudhury, Subrata Roy 305
Chowdhury, Abu Osman (Major) 301
Chowki Chowk 210
Chowringhee 312
Chuadanga 306
Chungking 221, 373
Chunilal 168
Churchill 91, 98
Civil Disobedience Movement/Civil Disobedience xvi, 9, 13, 14, 69, 93, 103 – 105, 359
Clive 88
Col Chakraverty 299
Col Sleeman/Sleeman 43, 161
Collins, T.M. 64, 66
Colombo 134
Comilla 296, 297, 305, 314
Communist Party of India/CPI 106, 224, 279, 281, 313
CPI (M) 313
Congress xvi, xvii, 14, 39, 40, 52, 56, 57, 59, 61, 65, 66, 67, 69, 73, 91, 93 – 98, 106, 108, 140, 152, 205, 211, 219, 226, 230, 235, 245, 270, 279
Connaught Place 336
Conservatives 91, 98
Constitution House 146
Contractor, Behram 356
Cooch Behar 298, 321
Coomi 115, 134, 355, 356
Cooper, Gary 47
Cotton, Sydney 126
Count of Monte Cristo 156
Coventry, J.P.C 48
Criminal Investigation Department/CID 66, 73, 118, 159, 161, 212, 341
Cripps, Stafford (Sir) 94
Crusoe, Robinson 84
Cursetji, Jal (Admiral) 59
Cuttack 228
Cyrus the Great 225
Czechoslovakia 271

Dacca 290, 292, 293, 295, 297, 300, 302, 317, 322, 325, 326, 328, 329, 348
Dacca University 290, 297
Damoh 31, 45, 48, 122, 215
Damrulal 33
Dang 178, 181
Danzing 44
Das, Deshbandhu Chittaranjan 328
Das, R.N. (Dr) 228
Date, Antarchand 125
Datia 174
Dave 37, 38, 87
Dave, Anand 149
Dave, K.K. 158
Deccan 133, 160
Deccan College 15
Dehradun 230, 314
Delhi/New Delhi 13, 94, 141, 143, 145, 146, 149, 153, 169, 177, 198, 200, 205, 211, 230, 231, 233, 238, 243, 245, 247, 253, 257, 258, 270, 275 – 278, 284, 287, 289, 293, 297, 301, 302, 304, 312, 321, 323, 333, 336, 337, 353, 354, 365, 371, 373

Deogarh 165
Deora 188, 189
Dera Ghazi Khan 94
Dera Ismail Khan 94
Desai, Bhulabhai 18
Desai, Morarji 151, 152, 226, 281, 284
Devi, Janki 350
Devkali 349
Dhanmondi 297
Dhar 236
Dhar, D.P./Dhar 257, 260, 264, 321
Dhar, P.N. 336
Dhillon, J.S. (Gen) 266
Dhillon, K.S. 344
Dholpur 179
Dhubri 305
Diaz, A.L. 321
Dinanagar 334
Dinpura 180
Dixit, Narsinghrao 167
Dograi 268
Dolat 120
Doongaji, Nawal 14, 15
Dravid Munetra Kazhagam/DMK 279
Dr Cheema 15
Dr Krishnamurti 15
Dr Padmavati 253
Dr Sampuranand 219
Drucker, Peter 31
Dum Dum 327, 366, 367
Dunkirk 68
Dutt, G.C. 325
Dutt, S.M. 375
Dutt, Sunil 224, 225
Dyal, R.S. (Lt Gen) 265

East Bengal 95, 138, 139, 294, 299, 302, 305
East Pakistan 217, 290 – 295, 297, 299, 301, 302, 304 – 307, 312, 316, 318, 320, 322, 325, 326, 332
Eden Gardens 328
Edroos, El (Gen) 133
Ellichpur 70, 122
Ellis, D 45
Emergency 250
Engineer, M.M. (Air Marshal) 333
England 13, 18, 111, 235
Etawah 168, 179
Europe 42, 52, 56, 234

Faramurz 4
Farrakka barrage 324
Farzana 356
Fazilka 334
Fernandes, George 336
Ferozepur 261
Ford Foundation 252
Frost, Robert 230

Gandhi, Indira 228, 235, 236, 269, 274, 281, 284, 285, 301, 323, 326, 334, 337, 343, 365,
Gandhi, Mahatama Mr Gandhi/Gandhi/ Gandhiji xvi, 8, 12, 13, 14, 16, 17, 39, 40, 69, 81, 92, 95, 96, 99, 103 – 105, 114, 118 – 120, 195, 233, 234, 282
Gandhi, Rajiv/Rajiv 287, 289, 355
Gandhi, Sonia 355
Ganganagar 332
Garbo, Greta 8
Garhakota xxi, 22, 31, 32, 34 – 37, 41, 122
Gede 299
George 14
George V 13
George VI 66
Germany 44, 45
Ghate, B.G./Ghate 130 – 132, 134, 151, 180
Ghatge 360
Ghosh, J.C. 375
Ghosh, S.M. 375
Ghosh, T.N. 375
Ghum-ka-Pura 178, 180, 181
Ghuraya, Ajit Singh/Ajit/Col Ajit 127, 128, 131, 132
Goa 122, 127, 234, 353
Godse, Nathuram 119
Goenka, Ramnath 342
Gohad 178, 180, 181, 188
Golden Temple 273
Goldsmith, Oliver 13
Gooly/Goolcheher 3, 81, 82

Gopal, Ram 248
Gopalpura 171
Gore, M.S. 342
Gorowara, S.P. 251
Gotegaon 56
Gotetoria 58
Gujar, Kalyan Singh 179
Gujarat 146, 152, 245, 282 – 284, 353
Gulbarga 122, 136, 137
Gulmarg 258
Guna 168
Gupta, Indrajit 340, 344
Gurdaspur 334
Gwalior 158, 160, 162, 164, 173, 174, 179, 181, 182, 186, 188, 198, 248

Hajipir 261, 264, 265, 365
Hajipir Pass 365
Hakewill, C.T.L. 23, 25, 28
Haksar, P.N. 289
Halwara 333
Handoo, Gopi Krishna/Handoo 143, 149
Haq 313
Haq, Sirajul 302
Hardayal 188
Hari 144
Harsud 85
Haryana 273, 279
Hastings, Warren/Hastings 88, 111
Hazelhurst, Peter 320
Hazrat, Ala 136
Himachal 273
Hindustan Red Army/HRA/Hindustani Lal Sena 65, 72
Hingoli 122, 128, 130
Hingorani, Kapila 351
Hitler 45
Holingworth, Clara 320
Homai 82
Hooja, M.M.L. 149
Hosali, S.N. 149, 375
Hoshang xxi, 14
Hospet 231
Humayun 192
Hussain, Vilayat 59
Hutchins, Francis G. 69
Hyderabad 55, 76, 122 – 133, 135, 136, 138 – 141, 168, 246, 278, 362, 371
Hyderabad Police Action/HPA xiv, 127, 133, 136, 137, 139, 264
Hyderabad State Congress/HSC 123 – 126, 130

Ichhogill 266
Inamdar, Arvind 357
Independence (India) 8, 14, 23, 35, 51, 68, 73, 77, 89, 91, 93, 95, 98, 102, 103, 105, 106, 107, 108, 111, 115, 118, 119, 123, 135, 149, 163, 243, 341
Independence (Bangladesh) 292, 293, 301, 302, 308, 314, 316, 327
India xi, xiii – xvii, 8, 9, 13 – 15, 18, 19, 23, 27, 29, 35, 36, 38, 40, 41, 44, 50, 51, 56-59, 61, 68, 69, 77 – 80, 88, 90, 95, 97 – 111, 115, 118 – 121, 123 – 125, 129, 137, 140, 141,145 – 147, 149, 151, 159, 160, 166, 168, 171, 194, 196 – 198, 201, 205, 207, 211, 214 – 216, 219, 221, 223, 230, 232 – 235, 243, 244, 248, 251, 254, 258 – 260, 264, 267 – 271, 273, 274, 279 – 281, 283, 288, 289, 293, 299, 300, 302, 306, 313, 314, 316, 317, 327, 328, 332, 333, 342, 344, 351, 369, 370, 373, 374
India Gate 233, 337
Indonesia 233
Indo-Pak War (1965) 247, 249, 250, 255, 256, 314, 364
Indo-Pak War (1971) xiv, xvii, 326, 330, 335, 337, 352
Indore 4, 158, 198, 224, 252, 253
Indo-Tibetan Border Police /ITBP 250, 337
Intelligence Bureau/IB xi, 69, 141, 143, 144, 147-149, 151, 159, 161, 163, 220, 284, 321, 364, 373, 375
International Criminal Police Organization/ICPO/Interpol 147
Iqbal, Mohammed 76
Ishwardas 87
Islam, Amirul 300, 302
Islam, Syed Nazrul 304, 329
Israel 282

Jagadguru Shankaracharya/Jagadguru 273, 274
Jain, Takhatmal 227
Jaisalmer 333
Jallianwala Bagh 97, 104
Jallianwala Bagh massacre 65, 104
Jalna 138
Jal Mahal 248
Jama Masjid market, Delhi 169
Jama Masjid, Bhopal 209, 210
Jamil, Shafat (Maj) 296
Jamila 284
Jammu 253, 262, 263, 266, 287, 288, 364
Jammu and Kashmir 248, 257, 258, 282, 353
Jamshed 4
Jamshedpur 217
Jaora 4, 158, 219
Japan 56, 59, 80, 98, 305
Jaurian 261
Jashpur 115
Jaya 362
Jayawant, A.R. 375
Jenkins 96
Jessore 294, 301, 313, 314, 325, 326
Jetley, Brij Bhushan Saran 139
Jhabua 4, 236
Jhansi 4, 171, 174
Jinnah, Mohammed Ali/Jinnah 18, 94 – 96, 98, 106, 129, 291
Johar, I.J. 176, 220
Johnson, Lyndon 267
Jora 165
Joshi, C.P. 250, 251
Joydebpur 294
Jubbulpore/Jabalpur 11, 31, 48, 49, 54, 55, 59, 122, 158, 160, 161, 198, 206, 207, 212, 214 – 216, 359
Juhu 82
Jullunder 248, 251
Jumma Talao 61
Justice Radcliffe xvii

Kabul 38
Kadam/Kadam, C.S. 173, 174
Kalam, A.P.J. Abdul 251
Kalhan, S.S. (Maj Gen)/Gen Kalhan 259, 261, 264, 265, 365
Kalla 187, 188
Kamath, H.S. 158
Kamptee 3
Kamruzaman 305
Kandla 360
Kandy 134
Kanergaon 127 – 132, 264
Kanetkar, V.G. 375
Kanjarkot 244
Kao, Ramji 149
Kao, R.N. 298
Kapur 87
Karachi 333
Karnaphuli River 296
Karnataka 347, 353
Kasaipura 209
Kashmir 59, 124, 126, 143, 229, 231, 243, 244, 257 – 260, 273, 284, 285, 287, 288, 289, 318
Kasim, Muhammed bin 40
Katju, K.N./Dr Katju 148, 152, 157, 158, 173, 204, 216, 219
Kazi 11
Kedar 63, 72
Kennedy, John F. 217, 234
Khamgaon 70
Khan, Abdul Gaffar Khan/Frontier Gandhi 282
Khan, Akbar (Gen) 291
Khan, Ayub 243, 267, 268, 292
Khan, Bahadur Fazle Karim Khan 76, 81
Khan, Hamid (Gen) 295
Khan, Shoebullah 137
Khan, Tikka (Lt Gen) 292, 297
Khan, Yahya (Gen) 292, 293, 297, 301, 348
Khandwa 75, 76, 80, 81, 85 – 87, 101, 122, 133
Khapa 65
Khatoon, Hussainara 346 – 348
Kheira 173, 175
Khemji, Bhimji 360, 361
Khemkaran 267
Khilafat Movement 11, 58
Khruschev 234

Khulna 325
Khurana, P.R. 208
Khursheed 3, 120
Khustia-Jessore 299, 301
Khyber Pass 58
Kirar, Rathi 170
Kohli, D.P. 375
Kohli, H.S. 173
Kolaras 168, 171
Korean War 221, 224
Kori, Jhagrimusma 350
Koshal, A.D. 347
Kosygin 268, 270
Kota 168
Kotwali 133
Kriplani, J.B. 95
Krishnamachari, T.T. 250
Krishnanagar 299, 301, 307, 324
Kuckreja, Kesar Singh 62
Kukreja, J.S. 165
Kumar, Ashwini 248, 262, 276, 331, 332, 334 – 337
Kumari, Reena 349
Kuno 175
Kunwari River 164

Labour party 91, 107
Lachhi 173, 191, 192
Ladakh 143, 224
Lady Mountbatten 146
Lahore 161, 261, 266, 268, 288, 289, 310, 332
Lalkaka, Rusi xx
Lal, P.C. 323
Lall, K.B./Kishan 23, 65, 71
Lall, K.B. (Defence Secretary) 335
Landi Kotal 58
Laxman, R.K. 194, 204
Liaqat 96
Libya 56
Lippmann, Walter 269
London 27, 98, 320
Long March 221
Longewala 333
Loni 125
Lord Curzon 341
Lord Home 223
Lord Linlithgow 135
Lord Pethick-Lawrence 94
Lord Wavell 94
Lt Col Bryand 278
Lt Col Chowdhury 296
Lt Curtis 61, 63
Lt Gen Kumaramangalam/Gen Kumaramangalam /Kay 244, 249, 254
Lucknow 278
Lukka 199

Madanlal 118
Madhya Bharat 148, 157, 158, 162, 167, 227
Madhya Pradesh 4, 18, 23, 65, 134, 146, 151 – 153, 157, 162, 168 – 171, 175, 177, 178, 187, 191, 197, 205, 216, 217, 227, 238, 239, 245 – 248, 257, 260, 262, 279, 361
Madras 115, 116, 226
Maharajpur 174
Maharashtra 13, 18, 152, 347, 353, 357
Mahatab, H.K. 151
Mahboob 299
Mahto, Bhola 349
Mahua 176, 177
Mainpuri 168
Major Katrakji 128
Majumdar, Golok/Golok 246, 248, 291, 293, 299 – 302, 303, 305 – 309, 312, 317, 319 – 325, 327 – 329
Majumdar, G.W.(Brig) 295
Malaya 56, 68
Malhivra 130, 132
Malhotra, Arvind (Capt) 259
Malimath, V.S. (Justice) 345
Malraux, Andre 320
Mana 217
Mandhata 101
Mandloi/Mandloi, Bhagwantrao 227
Mane, B.B. 180
Manekshaw, Sam (Gen) 317, 323, 325
Mangalore 361
Mannin, Ethel 76
Maqbul 76
Marhatal 11
Marquess of Hastings 160

Masood, M.A.H. 375
Maudha 64, 65
Maugham, Somerset 269
Maynard 66
Mazumdar, Charu 280, 328
Mckeevar, R.F. 54
Meghnagar 4
Meherpur 299
Mehra, Naresh 251
Mehta, Shreenath 23, 158
Mello, Melville de 119
Mendonca, Ronnie 357
Menon, Krishna 141
Menon, V.K. Krishna (Defence Minister) 220, 222
Mewaram 200
Mhow 253
Milne, A.A. 26
Minoo 134, 355, 356
Mirpani 41
Mirpur 333
Misra, S.C. 375
Mishra, Bhawani 117
Mishra, D.P. 134, 152, 227, 238, 245
Mishra, N.P. (Dr) 253
Mishra, Ramadhir 116 – 118
Mitha, A.O. (Maj Gen) 295
Mizoram 336
Modi, Rajendra Prasad/R.P./Modi 178, 180, 181, 183, 185 – 187, 189, 191
Morena 160, 165, 166, 168, 173, 175, 196, 225
Moscow 234
Motiram 171
Mountbatten/Mountbatten, Louis (Lord) 92, 98, 234
Mrs Bandaranaike 234
Muhammad, Noor 9, 81
Mujib Bahini 321
Mujib Nagar 306, 308, 309
Mukherji, Upananda 375
Mukherjee, Ajoy 279
Mukherjee, Torun 18
Mukti Bahini 302, 314, 326
Mukti Fauj 302, 307, 315 – 319, 321 – 323, 325
Mullik/Mullik, Bhola Nath 141, 143, 147 – 149, 151, 163, 164, 220, 364, 375
Mundhra, Haridas 147
Musharraf, (Maj) Khaled/Khaled 314, 315
Mushtaq, Khandkar 305, 321
Muslim League/League 56, 92 – 96, 98, 108, 129, 172, 316
Mutiny of 1857 104
Muzaffarpur 347
Mymensingh 304

Nagaland 220, 226, 293
Nagar Parkar 334
Nagarwala, J.D. 375
Nagpur 3, 7, 12 – 18, 29, 52, 59, 61, 64 – 67, 72, 73, 77, 116, 120 – 122, 130, 132, 134 – 136, 151, 157, 158, 359, 363
Nagpur University 8
Nagra 225
Nagu, R.N./Nagu 171, 188, 214, 253, 367
Naidu, Padmaja 270
Naidu, Sarojini 119
Naik, Riaz 76
Naju xx, 83 – 89, 115, 116, 119 – 121, 133 – 136, 139, 140, 163, 166, 169, 188, 202, 207, 224, 225, 227, 233, 238, 239, 253, 256, 268, 282, 353 – 356, 363, 366, 367, 371
Nalgonda 122, 141
Nambiar, A.K.K. 375
Namrita 356
Nanavatty, K.J. 375
Nanda, Gulzarilal 245
Nander/Nanded 122, 126, 136, 138
Naoroji, Dadabhai 8
Narain, Govind 278, 321
Naraini 170-171
Narasimhan, C.V. 336, 342, 343
Nargis 3
Nargis (Nargis Dutt) 225
Narayan, Jaiprakash/J.P. 170, 342
Narsingpur 31, 45, 47 – 49, 51, 52, 54, 58, 61, 215
Narwar 162
National Awami Party 328

National Crime Records Bureau/NCRB 147
National Police Academy/NPA (Hyderabad) xv
National Police Commission/NPC xiv, 341 – 345, 347
Naval mutiny of 1946 106
Naya Chor 334
Neemuch 148
Nehru, Jawaharlal/Nehru/Pandit Nehru xiv, xvi, 17, 40, 95, 97, 119, 138, 141, 142 – 149, 152, 153, 163, 177, 178, 184, 193, 195, 216, 219 – 221, 223, 224, 226, 228, 230 – 233, 235, 236, 244, 245, 267 – 270, 284, 360, 361, 363, 371
Netherlands 288
New York 252
Niazi, Amir Abdullah Khan (Gen) 302
Nixon 326
Noakhali 92, 305, 312
Noronha, C.V.P Ronald/Ron Noronha 23, 65, 229
North Borneo 56
North East Frontier Agency/NEFA 220, 224, 233
North West Frontier Province/NWFP/ North West Frontier 58, 92, 96, 108
Nuruzzaman, Kazi (Maj)/Zaman 314

'Operation Gibraltar' 258
'Opration Hammer' 164, 165
'Operation Jackpot' 318
'Operation Polo' 127, 133
'Operation Searchlight' 294
Orissa 115, 217, 235, 273
Osmanabad 122, 133, 136, 138
Osmania University 135
Osmany, M.A.G. (Col)/Osmany 304, 314, 315, 321
Owen, Morris (Prof) 19
Oxford University/Oxford 8, 27

Pabna 304
Pachauri, B.P. 52
Pachmarhi 204, 229
Pachpaoli 63
Pacific 56
Paddington 362
Pahuja, H.K. 172, 191
Pakistan 58, 59, 77, 93 – 99, 103, 105, 106, 109, 119, 120, 125 – 127, 139, 217, 243 – 245, 247, 248, 250, 255, 258 – 261, 265 – 269, 273, 281 – 283, 287 – 299, 301 – 314, 316 – 320, 322 – 327, 329, 331 – 334, 344, 356, 365, 369, 370
Pakistan Occupied Kashmir/POK 259
Palanpur 283
Pande, B.C. (Brig) 249, 291, 294, 295, 297, 298
Pande, Lalji 350
Pant, G.B. 151, 163
Parakh, Boman 14, 15
Parakh, Ratru 14
Paranjpe 71, 72
Parbhani 122, 133, 136
Parin w/o Rustam 121
Paris 320
Parsonia 44
Partition 92, 94 – 99, 105, 115, 120, 217
Patel, Jal 59, 61
Patel, I.G. 355
Patel, Sardar Vallabhai/Patel 95, 116, 119, 126, 139, 220
Patell, Adi 11
Pathak, R.S. 347
Pathankot 261, 262, 365, 366
Patna 347
Patil, S.K. 226
Pearl Harbour 56
Pearce, G.A. 278
Peking 221, 234
Peshawar 261
Pettinato, Roberto 164
Pheruman, Darshan Singh 274, 275
Pilditch, Denys 220, 374
Pilkhana 297
Pindari War 160
Piparia 229
Plassey 324
Pokhran 251
Polish Corridor 44
Polish Ukraine 45
Pollock, J.D.A. 375
Poona 15, 122, 126, 151, 205

Poonch 261, 264
Pope, Alexander 117
Portugal 126
Posamma 9
Prasad, Rajendra (Dr) 201
Prasad, Shanti 278, 375
Press Trust of India/PTI 163, 203, 274, 363
Prof Moghe 18
Prof Vaidya 16
Punjab 13, 76, 92, 94, 96, 115, 167, 260, 261, 273, 274, 275, 277, 331, 332, 334, 335, 344
Puri 273

Quinn, Terence/Quinn 176, 177, 196, 199, 214, 262, 364
Quinn-Young, F.C.S. 43, 44, 49, 110
Quit India Movement xvi, 105, 106, 347
Qureshi, Ashraf 288
Qureshi, Hashim 288, 289
Qureshi, Parvej Mehdi 324

Rabat 283
Radhakrishnan, S. (Dr) 18, 205
Rahim-Yar-Khan 334
Rahman, Sheikh Mujibur/Mujib 292, 293, 297, 299, 300, 305, 306, 318, 328, 329, 334
Rahman, Ziaur (Maj)/Zia 295, 298, 314, 329
Raichaudhary, Sushital 280
Raichur 362, 363
Raigarh 115, 116, 118 – 122, 207, 217
Raipur 118, 121, 122, 158, 217, 226, 231, 361
Raisen 207
Rajadhakshya, A.G. 149
Raja Mohattam 331, 334
Rajaram 176
Rajasthan 4, 162, 168, 175, 179, 187, 277, 331 – 333
Rajgaon 125
Rajghat 119, 235
Rajgopal, P.R./Rajgopal 159, 247, 248, 284, 288, 289, 300, 301, 303, 307, 308, 311, 325
Rajgopal, P.V xix
Rajouri 261
Rajpath 233
Rajkot 283
Rajshahi 306
Raj Bhavan 325
Ram, Jagjivan 285
Ram, Jia 375
Raman, C.V. (Dr) 18
Ramamurti, K. 247
Ramdas 14
Ramlal 32, 33
Ramtek 65, 66
Ranchi 251
Rangpur 296
Ranian 334
Ratnal 360
Rao, Balwant 15
Rao, Jaya 359
Rashtrapati Bhavan 268, 275, 355
Rathore, R.S. 247, 251, 252
Ratlam 219
Rann of Kutch/Kutch 244, 245, 247, 255, 259, 331, 333, 334
Ravi River 334
Ray, Siddhartha Shankar 321, 322
Rayalseema 235
Raza, Mohammad Kasim 278
Razvi, Kasim/Razvi 123, 124, 137
Red Fort 124, 163
Reddy, N.K. 342
Rehaman, Hamood-ur 318, 327
Rehman, Waheeda 224
Research and Analysis Wing (RAW) 298, 321
Reserve Bank of India 312, 355
Rewa 158, 198
Risod 125
River Chambal 175, 197
River Fenny 302
River Kelo 120
River Kanhan 64
River Kapo-taksi 324
River Nerbudda/Narmada 50
Rooney, Mickey 83
Rosha, P.A. 247
Roshan 3

Rourkela 217
Roy, Dwijendra Lal 306
Rufus, R.A 362, 363
Rusk, Dean 234
Russia 234
Rustamji, Cyrus K./Cyrus xx, 90, 225, 239, 253, 256, 336, 337, 355, 356, 370
Rustam 3, 8, 9, 14, 15, 66, 70, 121, 158, 355
Rustamji, Firdunji 136
Rustamji, Kerman/Kerman xx, 140, 188, 207, 224, 225, 239, 355, 256, 363, 369
Rustamji, Khusro Farmurz/Rustamji v, xi, xiii – xviii, xx, xxiii, 10, 22, 30, 35, 46, 57, 58, 60, 65, 66, 72, 73, 76, 86, 90, 100, 111, 134, 142, 152, 156, 176, 186, 187, 191, 194, 201, 206, 218, 222, 231, 232, 242, 245, 246, 250, 256, 263, 270, 271, 275, 288, 289, 291, 302, 309, 310, 314, 329 – 331, 337, 340, 346, 347, 352, 354, 358, 360, 367, 369, 375
Rustamji, Manchershaw/Awari/General 14

Sabarmati 282
Sadiq 211
Sadiq, G.M. 257
Sagar/Saugor xxi, 23 – 32, 35, 43 – 45, 61, 88, 122, 158, 159, 161, 166, 215, 359
Sahib, Tatia 72
Sakti 115, 122
Sanauda 30, 31
Sanjay (Gandhi) 236
Sanyal, Kanu 280
Sarabhai, Vikram 251
Sarangarh 115, 116, 122
Sastri, V.S. Srinivasa 18
Satyagraha 52, 59, 103, 123
Sawai Madhopur 168
Saxena, P.C. 130, 134
Saxena, N.S. 342
Sayed 87
Schanberg, Sydney H. 320
Science College 5
Scindia, Vijaya Raje 248
Scott, A.G 52, 64, 72, 220, 373, 374
Secunderabad 122, 127, 133
Sehal, L.S. (Maj Gen) 325
Sehore 207
Sehwag, Virendra 370
Sela Pass 224
Sen, P.K. 375
Seoni 45
Shakespeare 229
Shaffiullah, K.M.(Maj)/Shaffiullah 314
Sharma, B.A. 257
Sharma, Prem (Col) 251
Sharma, Dr Shankar Dayal 355
Sharma, Rup Narain/Rupa 160, 162, 175 – 177, 196, 199
Sharma, S.K. 252
Shastri, Lal Bahadur/Shastri 226, 243 – 245, 267 – 269, 284, 360
Shaw, George Bernard 48
Sheopur 168, 175
Sherwani 125
Shetty, Balakrishna/Shetty 149
Shivpuri 157, 160, 168, 170 – 172
Shobapur 302
Sholapur 137
Shrivastava, B. 159
Shukul, B.M./B.M./Joshi 66, 158, 207 – 210
Shukul, Shankar Dayal 116, 134
Shukla, Ravi Shankar 118, 151
Shukla, Vidya Charan 245
Sialkot 261, 266, 334
Siddiqui, M.R. 302
Sigerson, Dora 239
Silchar 313
Siliguri 321
Simon Commission 89
Sind/Sindh 40, 94, 331, 334, 335
Singh, Baldev 375
Singh, Balbir 149
Singh, Banta 5
Singh, Brijpal (Col)/Col Brijpal 276, 277
Singh, Choudhary Charan 342
Singh, Dalbir (Maj Gen) 325
Singh, Daulat 169
Singh, Dulare 186
Singh, Sant Fateh 273, 274
Singh, Firangi 190
Singh, Gabbar/Gabra/Gabbar 156, 157, 160, 177 – 182, 184 – 188,

Singh, Giani Zail 343, 344
Singh, Gurdial 149, 375
Singh, Hukam 208
Singh, Jaswant 32, 37, 38
Singh, Kartar 167
Singh, Kunwar Shamsher 375
Singh, Lakhan/Lakhan 160, 162, 164, 165, 187 – 191
Singh, Lal 174, 176
Singh, L.P./L.P. 244 – 246, 252, 255, 257, 260, 275, 284, 285
Singh, Madho 175, 183, 185, 187, 189, 191
Singh, Man 162, 176, 197, 200, 201
Singh, Megh (Col) 298, 309
Singh, Narendra 191
Singh, Narinder (Maj Gen) 311
Singh, Narvottam 185
Singh, Prakash 345
Singh, Raghuvar 178
Singh, Rajdeo 247, 342
Singh, Rajendra 126
Singh, Rajkumar Ragho Raj 231
Singh, Ram 191
Singh, Rampal (Col) 298
Singh, Ram Akhtiar 188 – 191
Singh, Ran (Brig) 247
Singh, Ranjit 247
Singh, Ranjit 253
Singh, Ranjit 265
Singh, Sagat (Lt Gen) 325, 326
Singh, Sardar Hukam 274
Singh, Sultan 169, 187
Singh, Swaran 285
Singh, Tehsildar 197, 200, 201, 204, 205
Singh, Vedram 191
Singh, Waryam 149
Singh, Yadunath (Maj Gen) 194 – 196, 200, 201
Sinha, B.M. 289
Sinha, R.A.P 375
Sitabuldi 67
Sly, Frank (Sir) 13
Soneja, Harish 336
South Africa 369
South American Republic of Ecuador 164
Southeast Asia 320
Soviet Union 44, 45, 106, 109, 221, 223, 267, 270, 271, 320, 361
Spanish Civil War 320
Special Armed Force/SAF 125, 130 – 132, 158, 159, 171, 175, 176, 186, 192, 196, 220, 262
Srinagar 248, 250, 256 – 258, 260, 266, 272, 282, 288, 289, 364, 365
Srinivasavardhan, T.C.A 342
Sripala 173, 175, 176, 191
State Bank of India/SBI 312
States Reorganisation Commission 157
State Security Commission 343
Suatala 55
Sulzberger, C.L. 320
Sukhraini 33
Sullivan, Michael/Sullivan 62 – 64
Suri, Sher Shah 192
Sylhet 304, 312, 314

Tagore, Rabindranath 291, 306, 337
Taj Mahal Hotel 83
Tambe, V.S./Tambe 127, 128, 130
Tamil Nadu 226, 353
Tandon, Prakash xxii
Tapurhat 321
Tasdiq 76
Tashkent 267 – 270, 365
Taufiq 299
Taylor, B. C. 49, 53, 55
Teen Murti Bhavan 145, 146
Teen Murti House 232
Tekanpur 248, 251, 253, 336
Tendukheda 52
Tendulkar, D.G. 69
Tendulkar, Sachin 370
Tezpur 224
Thapa 186
Thar 334
Thimayya, K.S. (Gen) 199, 220
Timi 48, 49, 71
Tirth, Swami Ramanand 126, 140
Toronto 90, 355, 356
Tottenham, George (Sir) 69
Travancore-Cochin/Kerala 145, 147
Treganza, E.L 61, 62, 67, 68
Trikha, M.C. 178

Tripura 293, 318
Trivedi, C.M. 239
Tura 313
Tuticorin 134

UAR 234
Udaipur 115, 122
Udhampur 261
UK 271
Umar 65
United Nations/UN 220, 234, 244, 282
UNESCO 305
USA/America 204, 243, 267, 271, 320
Uri 261, 264
Useth Ghat 197
Uttar Pradesh 4, 94, 152, 162, 168, 187, 197, 219, 260, 277 – 279, 283

Vajpayee, Atal Behari 337
Valmiki 200
Vandemataram Movement 125
Varadarajan, Siddharth 289
Vats, B.R 363
Venkataraman 355
Verma, S.P. 375
Vevaina, Rusi 80, 82
Vietnam 243
Vindhya Pradesh 135, 157, 158
Vira, Dharama 342

Wadhwa, Ramkrishna 331
Wagah 261
Wahab 11
Wahab 32
Walcott 134
Walong 224
Warangal 122
Wardha 17, 195
Wadia, Nusli 353
Washington 234, 243
Watson, D.G. 55
Weekes 134
West Bengal/Bengal 13, 73, 77, 78, 138, 139, 279 – 281, 288, 293, 294, 305, 312, 318, 320, 321, 324

West, Mae 51
West Pakistan 289, 291, 292, 294, 295, 297, 298, 301 – 303, 318, 320
Worrell 134
World War II 46, 73, 107, 162, 223, 320, 326
Worli 356
Wright, F.C.G. 67, 68
Wyad 125, 130
Wynne, Martin 88, 221

Yeotmal 125
Yugoslavia 234

Zarina 3
Zedong, Mao/Mao 221, 371